THE
BEST
OF
Gourmet

THE
BEST
OF
Gourmet
1989 EDITION

ALL OF THE BEAUTIFULLY
ILLUSTRATED MENUS FROM 1988
PLUS OVER 500 SELECTED RECIPES

FROM THE EDITORS OF GOURMET

CONDÉ NAST BOOKS
RANDOM HOUSE
NEW YORK

LIBRARY OF CONGRESS CATALOGING-IN-PUBLICATION DATA
(Revised for vol. 4)

Main entry under title:
The Best of Gourmet.
    Includes Indexes
    1. Cookery, International. I. Gourmet.
TX725.A1B4827 1986   641.5   87-640167
ISBN 0-394-55258-X (v.1)
ISBN 0-394-56039-6 (v.2)
ISBN 0-394-56955-5 (v.3)
ISBN 0-394-57529-6 (v.4)
Most of the recipes and menus in this work were previously published in *Gourmet* Magazine.

Manufactured in the United States of America

98765432   24689753   23456789

First Edition

Grateful acknowledgment is made to the following for permission to reprint recipes previously published in *Gourmet* Magazine.

Jean Anderson: ''Gingered Corn Chowder with Coriander'' (page 116); ''Ginger and Bourbon Shrimp on Snow Peas'' (page 134); ''Ginger Pound Cake'' (page 232); ''Crystallized Ginger'' (page 232); ''Walnut Ginger Tart'' (page 251). Copyright © 1988 by Jean Anderson. Reprinted by permission of the author.

Georgia Chan Downard: ''Marinated Seafood and Blood Orange Salad'' (page 204); ''Blood Orange Sorbet'' (page 259); ''Blood Orange Cordial'' (page 268). Copyright © 1988 by Georgia Chan Downard. Reprinted by permission of the author.

Faye Levy: ''Rotelle with Avocado Pesto'' (page 197); ''Avocado and Chicken Salad Mediterranean-Style'' (page 202); ''Avocado Aioli'' (page 223). Copyright © 1988 by Faye Levy. Reprinted by permission of the author.

Richard Sax: ''Prune and Pecan Caramel Sticky Buns'' (page 102); ''Prune Purée'' (page 102). ''Prune Batter Pudding'' (page 256). Copyright © 1988 by Richard Sax. Reprinted by permission of the author.

Miki Wheeler: ''Chocolate Walnut Sponge Cake'' (page 240); ''Orange Walnut Torte'' (page 241). Copyright © 1988 by Miki Wheeler. Reprinted by permission of the author.

PROJECT STAFF

For Condé Nast Books

Jill Cohen, Director
Jonathan E. Newhouse, Special Consultant
Ellen Bruzelius, Manager
Kristine Smith, Assistant Manager
Margarita Smith, Assistant
Mary Ellen Kelly, Fulfillment Manager
Diane Pesce, Composition Production Manager
Serafino J. Cambareri, Quality Control Manager

For *Gourmet* Magazine

Jane Montant, Editor-in-Chief
Evie Righter, Senior Editor, Gourmet Books
Elizabeth Heilman Brooke, Editor
Romulo Yanes, Staff Photographer
Irwin Glusker, Design Consultant

Produced in association with
Media Projects, Incorporated

Carter Smith, Executive Editor
Jeanette Mall, Managing Editor
Judith Tropea, Project Editor
Martina D'Alton, Associate Project Editor
Wm. J. Richardson Associates, Inc., Indexer
Michael Shroyer, Art/Production Director

The editors would like to thank the following people for valuable services rendered for *The Best of Gourmet—1989:* Georgia Chan Downard for her helpful and creative assistance in once again compiling ''A Gourmet Addendum,'' and Blair Brown Hoyt.

The text of this book was set in Times Roman by the Composition Department of Condé Nast Publications, Inc. The four-color separations were done by The Color Company, Seiple Lithographers, and Kordet Graphics. The book was printed and bound by Arcata Graphics Company. Text paper is 80-pound Mountie Gloss. Papermill: Northwest. Paper merchant: Allan and Gray.

Front Jacket: ''Lemon- and Garlic-Marinated Shrimp with Green Beans and Endive'' (page 206).

Back Jacket: ''Ginger Pound Cake'' (page 232).

Frontispiece: ''Nectarine Sorbet with Strawberry Nectarine Sauce'' (page 259).

CONTENTS

INTRODUCTION

any of you have been our loyal friends for close to fifty years. Some of you have been introduced to us more recently. Whether old friend or new, you have, no doubt, noticed our subtle evolution. As "the magazine of good living," we attempt to appeal to you by presenting suggestions for fine living that are creative and contemporary, tasteful and discriminating. A number of you have faithfully followed the pages of *Gourmet* and valued our presentations enough to begin your own *Gourmet* magazine libraries. For the past three years, we have been continuing our tradition of *Gourmet* service by producing annual volumes of "the best of *Gourmet* magazine." Once again, we present *The Best of Gourmet*, a lasting, hardbound resource for today as well as for tomorrow.

For the fourth volume in our series—the unique 1989 edition—we have both maintained the format of volumes past and also developed our Gourmet Addendum section to give you some additional original ideas and recipes. The book has been divided into three parts: The Menu Collection, A Recipe Compendium, and A Gourmet Addendum. In an exquisite album of over seventy color photographs, The Menu Collection brings together all of the menus from the past year's *Gourmet's* Menus and Cuisine Courante columns. After your eyes have feasted on such gracious entertaining possibilities as A Country Luncheon featuring lemon and herb marinated Cornish hens or Cocktails in the City recommending smoked salmon, avocado, and horseradish spirals, you will find in Part Two, A Recipe Compendium, including all of the recipes in Part One as well as recipes from *Gourmet's* seasonal feature articles and the monthly columns: Gastronomie sans Argent, In Short Order, and The Last Touch. Basic recipes and procedures have been cross-referenced throughout Part Two. This year's Part Three, A Gourmet Addendum, celebrates the merits of healthy, flavorful vegetables. Eight new menus offer various classic and inventive vegetable combinations, and each menu can be prepared within an hour.

Time is a rare commodity for many of us these days, but no matter how delicate our personal balancing acts may be, our love for fine food and drink endures. Enjoying the company of friends, sipping a Sauvignon Blanc, tucking into an aromatic Provençal vegetable gratin—these are moments for which we will always find the time. In this volume, you will see that, as the editors of *Gourmet*, we are well aware that for many of us having the opportunity to make a frozen hazelnut meringue cake, as on page 232, is a special treat.

Parties and holidays, where friends and family are gathered, need not be formal and demanding occasions. This year, we suggest A Spring Skiing Weekend, featuring cozy, comforting onion- and sage-stuffed pork chops with *kielbasa* and sauerkraut, lemon sweet potato purée, and a glorious Granny Smith apple pie with honey spice whipped cream. A lovely sun-dapped Cocktail Party Alfresco suggests another opportunity for easy-but-oh-so-pleasurable entertaining. As the sparkling Summer Breezes are passed around, guests can nibble on marinated shrimp with yellow bell pepper and red onion or carrot and herbed goat cheese spirals. Many of the menu's recipes can be prepared well in advance of the cocktail hour, so you, the host or hostess, can casually mingle and enjoy the sunset. At Christmas time, many of us feel in a more dignified festive mood. A Formal Christmas Dinner of roast prime ribs of beef, Yorkshire pudding, potato caraway croquettes, cauliflower and broccoli timbales, and a pineapple orange meringue torte is a delicious cause for celebration.

The Best of Gourmet, Volume Four is more than a compilation, more than an average cookbook. With page after page of colorful ideas for entertaining and enjoying "good living," this edition will, hopefully, continue in the *Gourmet* tradition to be an invaluable resource for the present as well as for the future.

Jane Montant
Editor-in-Chief

PART ONE

THE MENU COLLECTION

he Menu Collection is a visual feast, seventy pages of color photographs designed to inspire and intrigue. This album of illustrations from the past twelve months of *Gourmet* magazine's Menus and Cuisine Courante columns should compel you to flip forward to review and try the recipes in Part Two, A Recipe Compendium.

Many of this year's menus have a wonderfully warm, casually gracious feel to them. Inviting friends in to watch the Rose Bowl over venison stew and buttered spätzle with scallions is cozy and intimate, and is elegant as well. Balloon bursts of color and a peanut butter train cake with milk chocolate frosting and vanilla ice cream will delight the six-and-under set at a merry birthday celebration, but adults also can toast the addition of another year with Mumm Cordon Vert and filets mignons with orange béarnaise sauce. Some menus are creatively simple, others challenge, but, in general, this year, the menus seem to say, "Come in, enjoy, we've put together something special for you." You'll find a platter of shrimp and *jalapeño* brochettes being offered at Cocktails in the City. At A Brunch for Six, the morning begins with minted citrus juice, coffee, and lemon walnut scones.

Glancing at Gourmet's Menus will inevitably bring back memories of successful parties past, and, we hope, will encourage you to host your own Country Luncheon for six or Mediterranean Dinner for ten. Or, invite both family and friends over for A Smorgasbord, fill baskets with crackers, arrange platters with Finnish dilled crayfish, casseroles with Swedish meatballs, and trays with smørrebrød, decorated with *cornichons*, springs of dill, and slices of scallion.

The Cuisine Courante menus have been designed for occasions when time is of the essence. A Meatless Lasagne Dinner featuring roasted broccoli and zucchini lasagne, *radicchio* and romaine salad with sunflower seeds and mustard vinaigrette, and chocolate chip bourbon angel pie is hearty, filled with sweet and piquant flavors, and can be partially prepared ahead of time. It is perfect for an early dinner, after a day on the ski slopes. Cuisine Courante menus and recipes are favorites with people who love to cook but cannot always find the time. These contemporary menus offer recipes that can often be assembled in advance.

Gourmet's holiday menus once again aim to be annual highlights. As you contemplate these showstopper menus, let your festive mood be your guide. Columbus Day doesn't stir the entertainer in you? Perhaps the Ides of March or a totally uneventful Tuesday is your idea of a cause for celebration. Holidays need not be determined by the ever-predictable calendar. Mix your mood with a *Gourmet* holiday menu. Ring in a new week or a new year with Tequila Sunrises, Mexicali Marias, and *huevos rancheros* with shredded tortilla chips: A New Year's Day Brunch is spirited and spicy. As glittering rockets of light dazzle the skies above, savor a Fourth of July Dinner of grilled salmon, fireworks salad, and peach almond torte. A bountiful buffet of roast turkey with chestnut and apple corn bread stuffing, potato and turnip purée, glazed carrots and parsnips, sweet potato cloverleaf rolls, pumpkin spice cake roll, cranberry walnut tart, and cinnamon ice cream is bound to make a memorable country Thanksgiving feast.

Gerald Asher, *Gourmet*'s wine editor, provides complementary cocktail, apéritif, and wine suggestions. For instance, Aquavit traditionally accompanies Scandinavian specialties. A lovely Easter Luncheon is an event worthy of a Château Lalandes-Borie Saint-Julien '83. Each menu has also been annotated with page references to easily guide you to the recipes in Part Two.

Color photographs bring the menus and recipes of *The Best of Gourmet, Volume Four* to life. In The Menu Collection you will see imaginative table settings, novel ideas for food preparation, hors d'oeuvres, entrées, and desserts that, we hope, will pique your curiosity and serve as inspiration for your own cocktail parties, dinners, breakfasts, lunches, and brunches.

Bittersweet Chocolate and White Chocolate Pecan Mousse Swirl

ROSE BOWL OPEN HOUSE

Oysters with Pickled Carrot and Daikon, p. 92

Bonny Doon Vineyard
Grahm Crew
California Red '85

Venison Stew with Root Vegetables, p. 152

Buttered Spätzle with Scallions, p. 178

Red Cabbage and Celery Slaw, p. 212

Chewy Rye Caraway Breadsticks, p. 100

Bittersweet Chocolate and
White Chocolate Pecan Mousse Swirl, p. 255

Oysters with Pickled Carrot and Daikon,
Venison Stew with Root Vegetables,
Buttered Spätzle with Scallions,
Red Cabbage and Celery Slaw,
Chewy Rye Caraway Breadsticks

Tequila Sunrises

NEW YEAR'S DAY BRUNCH

Tequila Sunrises, p. 269   *Mexicali Marias*, p. 269

Huevos Rancheros, p. 166

Shredded Tortilla Crisps, p. 166

Avocado Salad with Red Onion and Coriander, p. 211

Broiled Ambrosia with Toasted Coconut, p. 260

Huevos Rancheros, Shredded Tortilla Crisps, Avocado Salad
with Red Onion and Coriander

Frozen Hazelnut Praline Meringue Cake

TWO BIRTHDAY PARTIES

For the Adults

Balgownie
South Australian
Pinot Noir '84

Marinated Artichokes in Green Peppercorn Pimiento Vinaigrette, p. 86

Filets Mignons with Orange Béarnaise Sauce, p. 138

Roasted Green Beans, p. 183

Roasted Scallions, p. 197

Fried Potato Thins, p. 193

Mumm Cordon Vert
Champagne

Frozen Hazelnut Praline Meringue Cake, p. 232

For the Children

Milk

Peanut Butter Train Cake with Milk Chocolate Frosting, p. 234

Vanilla Ice Cream

Filet Mignons with Orange Béarnaise Sauce, Roasted Green Beans, Roasted Scallions, Fried Potato Thins

Peanut Butter Train Cake with Milk Chocolate Frosting

Almond Lemon Torte

MEATLESS LASAGNE DINNERS

Shrimp, Scallop, and Monkfish Lasagne, p. 173

Keenan Napa Valley
Chardonnay '83

Watercress and Bibb Salad
with Parsley Dressing, p. 210

Almond Lemon Torte, p. 240

❧

Roasted Broccoli and Zucchini Lasagne, p. 172

The Gainey Vineyard
Santa Barbara County
Sauvignon Blanc '85

Radicchio and Romaine Salad
with Sunflower Seeds and Mustard Vinaigrette, p. 209

Chocolate Chip Bourbon Angel Pie, p. 248

❧

Shrimp, Scallop, and Monkfish Lasagne,
Watercress and Bibb Salad with Parsley Dressing

Granny Smith Apple Pie with Honey Spice Whipped Cream

A SPRING SKIING WEEKEND

Friday Night Supper

Wente Brothers
Arroyo Seco
Gewürztraminer '85

Cheese Fondue, p. 163

Romaine and Red-Leaf Lettuce Salad
with Scallion Vinaigrette, p. 210

Assorted Fruit

❧

Saturday Night Dinner

Charles F. Shaw
Napa Valley
Gamay Beaujolais '87

Onion- and Sage-Stuffed Pork Chops with Kielbasa and Sauerkraut, p. 144

Lemon Sweet Potato Purée, p. 196

Granny Smith Apple Pie with Honey Spice Whipped Cream, p. 246

❧

Sunday Breakfast

Orange Pecan Waffles with Orange Maple Syrup, p. 168

Breakfast Sausage Links, p. 168

Orange Juice   *Coffee*

❧

Onion- and Sage-Stuffed Pork Chops with Kielbasa and Sauerkraut,
Lemon Sweet Potato Purée

Orange Pecan Waffles with Orange Maple Syrup,
Breakfast Sausage Links

Treacle Cake with Cinnamon Applesauce

CUISINE COURANTE

AN IRISH SUNDAY DINNER

Mussel and Parsley Soup, p. 119

Parducci Mendocino County
Chardonnay '86

Lemon-Baked Chicken Breasts, p. 154

Creamed Leeks, p. 188

Irish Whiskey Carrots, p. 185

Watercress, Mushroom, and Radish Salad, p. 212

Treacle Cake with Cinnamon Applesauce, p. 234

Lemon-Baked Chicken Breasts, Creamed Leeks,
Irish Whiskey Carrots

EASTER LUNCHEON

Asparagus and Smoked Salmon Timbales, p. 86

*Château Lalandes-Borie
Saint-Julien '83*

Roast Saddle of Lamb Persillé, p. 150

Tomatoes Stuffed with White Bean, Parsley, and Garlic Purée, p. 198

Green Bean and Yellow Bell Pepper Mélange, p. 183

Hearts of Palm, Radish, and Bibb Lettuce Salads, p. 207

Strawberry and Frangipane Tart, p. 251

Oeufs à la Neige à l'Orange, p. 253

Roast Saddle of Lamb Persillé; Tomatoes Stuffed with
White Bean, Parsley, and Garlic Purée; Green Bean and
Yellow Bell Pepper Mélange

Oeufs à la Neige à l'Orange

Cheddar ''Carrots'' and ''Parsnips,'' Caviar ''Raspberries'' and ''Blackberries''

CUISINE COURANTE

APRIL FOOL'S COCKTAIL PARTY

Black Olive and Roasted Red Pepper ''Backgammon Board,'' p. 91

Ham and Mustard Mayonnaise Sandwich ''Playing Cards,'' p. 90

Cocktails
Beaujolais Blanc
Sancerre Rouge

Pumpernickel Cheese ''Dominoes,'' p. 88

Cheddar ''Carrots'' and ''Parsnips,'' p. 87

Caviar ''Raspberries'' and ''Blackberries,'' p. 87

❧

Black Olive and Roasted Red Pepper ''Backgammon Board,''
Ham and Mustard Mayonnaise Sandwich ''Playing Cards,''
Pumpernickel Cheese ''Dominoes''

A CHARLESTON LUNCHEON

Cheddar Straws, *p. 88*

Benne Wafers, *p. 106*

———

Wine Spritzers

Shrimp Creole, *p. 134*

Rice Ring, *p. 134*

Glazed Smithfield Ham, *p. 147*

Bibb and Watercress Salad, *p. 207*

———

Graacher Himmelreich
Riesling Hochgewächs,
Weingut Selbach-Oster '86

Juliette Staats's Pecan Roll, *p. 238*

Caramel Sauce, *p. 239*

Shrimp Creole, Rice Ring, Glazed Smithfield Ham

Juliette Staats's Pecan Roll, Caramel Sauce

Cold Eggedosis Soufflés with Lingonberries,
Ginger Preserve Cookies, Spiced Horseshoe Cookies

A SMORGASBORD

Matjes Herring Salad, p. 203

Lefser Spirals, p. 192

Sardine Deviled Eggs, p. 164

Smørrebrød, p. 95

Aquavit   *Carrot Salad with Lemon Dressing*, p. 212

Pickled Cucumber Salad, p. 213

Beer   *Finnish Dilled Crayfish*, p. 128

Swedish Meatballs, p. 138

Scandinavian Cheeses and Breads and Crackers

Cold Eggedosis Soufflés with Lingonberries, p. 256

Ginger Preserve Cookies, p. 244

Spiced Horseshoe Cookies, p. 246

Cold Eggedosis Soufflés with Lingonberries,
Ginger Preserve Cookies, Spiced Horseshoe Cookies

A SMORGASBORD

Matjes Herring Salad, p. 203

Lefser Spirals, p. 192

Sardine Deviled Eggs, p. 164

Smørrebrød, p. 95

Aquavit   *Carrot Salad with Lemon Dressing*, p. 212

Pickled Cucumber Salad, p. 213

Beer   *Finnish Dilled Crayfish*, p. 128

Swedish Meatballs, p. 138

Scandinavian Cheeses and Breads and Crackers

Cold Eggedosis Soufflés with Lingonberries, p. 256

Ginger Preserve Cookies, p. 244

Spiced Horseshoe Cookies, p. 246

Juliette Staats's Pecan Roll, Caramel Sauce

Stuffed Artichoke Leaves

A SPRING DINNER

Stuffed Artichoke Leaves, p. 181

Valpolicella
Classico '85

Cheese and Chive Ravioli
with Tomato Red Pepper Sauce, p. 176

Tossed Green Salad with Dill Dressing, p. 209

Green Grape Ice, p. 257   *Almond Thins, p. 257*

Cheese and Chive Ravioli with Tomato Red Pepper Sauce,
Tossed Green Salad with Dill Dressing

Clockwise: Carrot Salad with Lemon Dressing, Pickled
Cucumber Salad, Smørrebrød, Sardine Deviled Eggs,
Lefser Spirals, Finnish Dilled Crayfish, Swedish Meatballs

Coffee Almond Ice-Cream Cake with Dark Chocolate Sauce

CUISINE COURANTE

BACHELOR DINNER

Baked Stuffed Clams, p. 128

Kendall-Jackson
Dupratt-DePatie
Zinfandel '84

Rosemary Lamb Kebabs, p. 148

Shredded Potato Pancakes, p. 192

Mixed Greens and Fennel with Balsamic Vinaigrette, p. 209

*Coffee Almond Ice-Cream Cake
with Dark Chocolate Sauce, p. 231*

Rosemary Lamb Kebabs, Shredded Potato Pancakes,
Mixed Greens and Fennel with Balsamic Vinaigrette

A COUNTRY LUNCHEON

Fried Zucchini Blossoms and Bell Pepper Rings, p. 98

Columbia Crest
Washington
Sauvignon Blanc '86

Lemon and Herb Marinated Cornish Hens, p. 158

Vegetable Pasta Salad with Red Pepper Dressing, p. 217

Garden Tomatoes

Spinach and Bibb Lettuce Salad, p. 210

Mango Lime Mousse with Raspberry Sauce, p. 254

Lemon and Herb Marinated Cornish Hens, Vegetable Pasta Salad
with Red Pepper Dressing, Garden Tomatoes

Mango Lime Mousse with Raspberry Sauce

Peach Almond Torte

FOURTH OF JULY DINNER

Beringer Vineyards
Napa Valley
Chardonnay '86

Grilled Salmon with Mustard Mint Sauce, p. 125

Wild Rice Pilaf with Scallions, p. 125

Fireworks Salad, p. 215

Peach Almond Torte, p. 241

Grilled Salmon with Mustard Mint Sauce,
Wild Rice Pilaf with Scallions, Fireworks Salad

Pistachio Tuiles, Chocolate Walnut Bars

LUNCHEONS ON THE VERANDA

Mushroom Salad with Radish and Chives, p. 213

Cahors
Domaine du Cedre '83

Thai-Style Steak and Green Bean Salad
with Spicy Mint Dressing, p. 142

Coconut Parfaits, p. 258

Pistachio Tuiles, p. 245

❧

Vegetables à la Grecque, p. 199

Mâcon-Villages
Blanc '86

Tricolor Scallop Terrine with
Basil, Corn, and Red Pepper, p. 133

Rosé Sorbet, p. 260

Chocolate Walnut Bars, p. 244

❧

Mushroom Salad with Radish and Chives, Thai-Style Steak and
Green Bean Salad with Spicy Mint Dressing, Vegetables à la Grecque,
Tricolor Scallop Terrine with Basil, Corn, and Red Pepper

Marinated Shrimp with Yellow Bell Pepper and Red Onion, Garlic Toast Rounds, Summer Breezes

A COCKTAIL PARTY ALFRESCO

Prosciutto, Pear, and Chive Cornets with Ginger Cream, p. 93

Carrot and Herbed Goat Cheese Spirals, p. 87

Cucumber and Liptauer Spirals, p. 89

Summer Breezes, p. 269

Crab-Salad-Stuffed Cherry Tomatoes, p. 89

Beer

Marinated Shrimp with Yellow Bell Pepper and Red Onion, p. 94

Garlic Toast Rounds, p. 106

Anchovy Lemon Dip with Vegetables, p. 85

Carrot and Herbed Goat Cheese Spirals; Cucumber and Liptauer Spirals;
Crab-Salad-Stuffed Cherry Tomatoes; Anchovy Lemon Dip with Vegetables;
Prosciutto, Pear, and Chive Cornets with Ginger Cream

A MEDITERRANEAN DINNER

Mediterranean Olive Rolls, *p. 100*

Ruffino Cabreo
Bianco '85

Antinori Pèppoli
Chianti Classico '85

Chilled Lemon- and Basil-Marinated Sea Bass, *p. 126*

Herb-Marinated Butterflied Leg of Lamb, *p. 148*

Roasted Quartered Potatoes with Garlic, *p. 149*

Provençal Vegetable Gratin, *p. 201*

Curly Chicory and Red-Leaf Lettuce Salad, *p. 208*

Plum Tarts, *p. 252*

Herb-Marinated Butterflied Leg of Lamb, Roasted Quartered Potatoes with Garlic, Provençal Vegetable Gratin, Curly Chicory and Red-Leaf Lettuce Salad

Plum Tarts

Cold Vanilla-Rum Zabaglione with Fruit

BRUNCH FOR SIX

Lemon Walnut Scones, p. 105

Potato and Leek Frittata, p. 165

Minted Citrus Juice, p. 269 *Cherry Tomato, Bacon, and Basil Salad, p. 216*

Cold Vanilla-Rum Zabaglione with Fruit, p. 254

Coffee *Tea*

Lemon Walnut Scones; Potato and Leek Frittata;
Cherry Tomato, Bacon, and Basil Salad; Coffee

COCKTAILS
IN THE CITY

Spinach, Feta, and Phyllo Purses

Shrimp and Jalapeño Brochettes, Stilton Walnut Tart

Sweet Potato, Crème Fraîche, and Caviar Bites;
Hummus; Toasted Pita Thins

Pizza di Noci e Cioccolata

COLUMBUS DAY DINNER

Gnocchi di Patate al Sugo di Pomodoro
(Potato Dumplings with Tomato Sauce), p. 171

Heitz Cellars
  Napa Valley
    Grignolino Rosé '87

Vitello alla Genovese
(Sautéed Veal Scallops with Sage and Bay Leaves), p. 143

Fagiolini alla Genovese
(Green Beans with Anchovy and Garlic), p. 182

Pizza di Noci e Cioccolata
(Walnut and Chocolate Torte), p. 242

Vitello alla Genovese, Fagiolini alla Genovese

A COUNTRY THANKSGIVING

Herbed Scalloped Oysters, p. 131

Shafer Vineyards
Napa Valley
Merlot '85

Roast Turkey with Chestnut and
Apple Corn Bread Stuffing
and Brandied Giblet Gravy, p. 160

Potato and Turnip Purée, p. 190

Glazed Carrots and Parsnips, p. 185

Peas and Onions with Lemon-Mint Butter, p. 190

Sweet Potato Cloverleaf Rolls, p. 101

Jellied Orange Cranberry Sauce, p. 226

Château DeBaun
Sonoma County
Finale Late Harvest
Symphony '86

Pumpkin Spice Cake Roll, p. 236

Cranberry Walnut Tart, p. 250

Cinnamon Ice Cream, p. 258

Roast Turkey with Chestnut and Apple Corn Bread
Stuffing and Brandied Giblet Gravy,
Sweet Potato Cloverleaf Rolls, Jellied
Orange Cranberry Sauce, Glazed Carrots and Parsnips

Crème Caramel with Sautéed Apples

A SMALL FORMAL THANKSGIVING

Pheasant with Port and Grape Sauce, p. 158

Garlic Toast "Plumes," p. 159

Adelsheim Vineyard
Willamette Valley
Oregon
Pinot Noir '85

Lemon Pecan Wild Rice, p. 179

Butternut Squash Purée, p. 198

Braised Red Cabbage with Mustard Seeds, p. 184

Crème Caramel with Sautéed Apples, p. 252

Pheasant with Port and Grape Sauce, Garlic Toast ''Plumes,'' Lemon Pecan Wild Rice,
Butternut Squash Purée, Braised Red Cabbage with Mustard Seeds

A FORMAL
CHRISTMAS DINNER

Deutz Champagne Cuvée William '82

————————

Essence of Celery Soup, p. 115

*Roast Prime Ribs of Beef
with Herbed Crust and Madeira Sauce*, p. 140

Yorkshire Pudding, p. 140

Cauliflower and Broccoli Timbales, p. 186

*Château Léoville-Las-Cases
Grand Cru Classé
St. Julien '76*

Potato Caraway Croquettes, p. 191

*Fennel and Radish Salad
with Mustard Vinaigrette*, p. 213

Maple Almond Brittle, p. 264

Pineapple Orange Meringue Torte, p. 242

————————

Taylor's 1970 Vintage Port

Pineapple Orange Meringue Torte, Maple Almond Brittle

Roast Prime Ribs of Beef with Herbed Crust, Cauliflower and Broccoli Timbales, Potato Caraway Croquettes

Apricot Citrus Cranberry Compote

CHRISTMAS BREAKFAST

Cranberry Tangerine Juice, p. 269

Apricot Citrus Cranberry Compote, p. 262

Chocolate Pecan Gems, p. 104

Bacon Spirals, p. 143

Cheddar Bread Pudding, p. 162

Coffee   *Tea*

Cheddar Bread Pudding, Bacon Spirals,
Cranberry Tangerine Juice, Chocolate Pecan Gems

A RECIPE COMPENDIUM

ver 500 of the best recipes culled from the past year's issues of *Gourmet* magazine have been brought together in easily readable and reachable cookbook form, in Part Two, A Recipe Compendium. All of the recipes from the Gourmet's Menus and Cuisine Courante columns have been included, as well as recipes from the popular columns: Gastronomie sans Argent, In Short Order, and The Last Touch. You will also find recipes from favorite feature articles of the past year, recipes for such winning delights as chocolate walnut spongecake and *rotelle* with avocado *pesto*.

A platterful of tender spareribs bathed in a richly flavored barbecue sauce: the mere mention of it makes some of us instantly hungry. Looking for innovative-but-inexpensive ways to prepare lamb riblets, beef ribs, and, of course, pork spareribs? From the Gastronomie sans Argent column, you will find spareribs with sauerkraut, noodles, and sour cream, deviled lamb riblets with dill, and crisp beef ribs with horseradish. Or, maybe mussels are a secret passion of your very seasoned palate. These appetizing morsels are among the least expensive of seafood. Sweet in flavor, mussels are high in protein, low in fat, and lend themselves to a variety of preparations. Manhattan-style mussel chowder, spinach- and mushroom-stuffed mussels with curry sauce, mussels steamed in wine with julienne vegetables—from hors d'oeuvres to entrées, there must be a mussel preparation here that will suit your fancy. Elegant-yet-economical potato, pasta, and rice salads are also abundant. Blue cheese and walnut potato salad, for instance, is a wonderful answer to the enduring summer question, ''What to make that is quick and cool?''

Some cooks always seem to be short on time. Recipes from *Gourmet*'s In Short Order column can be prepared in less than forty-five minutes and incorporate ingredients that are readily available. Ingenious combinations have been based on the most refined and inviting of international cuisines. Recipes for two, such as gingered acorn squash soup and pork chops with mustard cheese crust, sound sensational and complex in flavor, but are, in fact, remarkably feasible for a busy couple in the 1980s.

The sweet spray that comes from biting into a crisp, tangy apple is an autumn essence many of us annually treasure. From weekend jaunts in the country, we bring home bushels of apples and pints of cider, and relish the flavors of fall. How can we make our apple adventure last? Creative ideas for apple cookery are featured in recipes from *Gourmet*'s The Last Touch column. A mug of hot mulled cider makes a comforting beverage for curling up before a winter's fire. Apple, walnut, and coconut crisp should certainly appeal to hungry students home for the holidays or friends who have stopped by for conversation and a cup of tea.

Gourmet aficionados may anticipate and cherish the magazine's tried-and-true monthly columns, but also appreciate *Gourmet*'s seasonal features, articles that honor an exotic or everyday fruit, vegetable, or condiment, features that encourage creativity with a certain month's plethora of fresh-from-the-garden produce. This past year, the many beauties of blood oranges were explored. Frequently scorned prunes were celebrated. The cool, refreshing merits of summer drinks were sung. Rich, creamy avocados were studied. Luscious nectarines were given the spotlight.

Vegetables Primavera with Polenta

Ginger was glorified. Some of the exemplary recipes from the magazine's feature articles have been added here with column recipes to truly give you the "best" of *Gourmet, Volume Four*. Won't blood orange sorbet make the perfect dramatic finale at an important dinner party? Don't prune and pecan caramel sticky buns sound unexpectedly tempting? Wouldn't a ruby red margarita be a splendid way to start a long, hot summer weekend? These are just some of the extra, special recipes included here.

Some recipes are intentionally easy. Rosemary lamb kebabs require marinating, but are simply grilled or broiled minutes before serving. Other recipes are a bit more involved. Tricolor scallop terrine with basil, corn, and red pepper, for example, calls upon the cook's mastery of the food processor and dexterity in decorating.

There are recipes for informal as well as formal occasions. Cheese fondue is a comfortable, cozy repast for a spring skiing supper. Sweet potato, crème fraîche, and caviar bites are impressive hors d'oeuvres for a sophisticated city cocktail party.

While most recipe ingredients can be found in your neighborhood supermarket, occasional trips to an Oriental market or specialty foods shop may be necessary, especially if ethnic dishes intrigue. *Gnocchi di patate al sugo di pomodoro* (potato dumplings with tomato sauce) and Oriental snow pea and scallop soup are among this year's original renditions of international recipes.

Locating recipes is simple. Part Two has been divided into thirteen chapters, starting with hors d'oeuvres, canapés, and spreads, and finishing with beverages. Chapters have been conveniently subdivided, and recipes have been arranged in alphabetical order and noted with photo page references. Basic recipes and procedures have been cross-referenced throughout Part Two. There are not one, but three indexes: the General Index, the Index of Recipe Titles, and the Index of 45-Minute Recipes, with microwave recipes highlighted.

A Recipe Compendium should ideally be an invaluable resource. Here, in Part Two of *The Best of Gourmet*, designs for exciting epicurean events are attractively ordered and compiled in one readily accessible section. From savory wild mushroom tartlet beginnings to subtly sweet shortbread, strawberries, and cream endings, the chapters before you present concepts and clear, concise instructions that, we hope, you will find helpful, inspirational, irreplaceable.

HORS D'OEUVRES, CANAPÉS, AND SPREADS

Anchovy Lemon Dip with Vegetables

1 cup plus 2 tablespoons sour cream
a 2-ounce can flat anchovy fillets, drained
2 garlic cloves, minced
1 tablespoon fresh lemon juice
½ pound green beans, trimmed
½ pound wax beans, trimmed
½ pound snow peas, trimmed and
　　strings discarded
thin lemon slices for garnish

In a very small saucepan combine 2 tablespoons of the sour cream, the anchovies, the garlic, and 2 tablespoons water, bring the mixture to a boil, whisking, and cook it at a bare simmer, whisking occasionally, for 10 minutes. Force the mixture through a fine sieve into a small bowl, pressing hard on the solids, whisk in the remaining 1 cup sour cream, the lemon juice, and pepper to taste, and chill the dip, covered, for at least 1 hour or overnight.

In a large kettle of boiling water blanch the green and wax beans for 45 seconds, add the snow peas, and blanch the vegetables for 10 seconds more. Drain the vegetables and plunge them into a bowl of ice and cold water. *The vegetables may be blanched 1 day in advance and kept covered and chilled.* Line a small glass bowl with the lemon slices, fill it to within about 1 inch of the rim with the dip so that the lemon slices show, and arrange the vegetables on a platter around the dip. Makes about 1¼ cups dip.

PHOTO ON PAGE 57

Apple Cheddar Canapés

7 to 9 slices of caraway rye bread
½ large Granny Smith apple, cored, peeled,
　　and minced
1 cup coarsely grated extra-sharp Cheddar
　　(about ¼ pound)
3 tablespoons bottled mayonnaise
1 tablespoon honey
1 teaspoon Dijon-style mustard
¼ teaspoon caraway seeds
freshly ground pepper to taste

Cut out 3 or 4 rounds from each slice of bread with a 2-inch round cutter and on a baking sheet toast them under a preheated broiler about 4 inches from the heat, turning them once, until they are golden. In a large bowl combine the apple, the Cheddar, the mayonnaise, the honey, the mustard, the caraway seeds, the pepper, and salt to taste. Spread each toasted round with a scant teaspoon of the mixture and broil the rounds under the preheated broiler about 4 inches from the heat for 2 minutes, or until the cheese is bubbly. Makes about 28 canapés, serving 6 to 8.

Marinated Artichokes in Green Peppercorn Pimiento Vinaigrette

4 artichokes
1 lemon, halved, plus ¼ cup fresh lemon juice
1 tablespoon vegetable oil
1 tablespoon minced shallot
⅛ teaspoon minced garlic
⅓ cup white-wine vinegar
1 tablespoon Sherry
1 teaspoon Dijon-style mustard
3 teaspoons drained bottled green
    peppercorns, chopped coarse, reserving 2
    teaspoons of the brine
4 teaspoons finely diced drained
    bottled pimiento
½ teaspoon salt, or to taste
⅔ cup olive oil

Cut off the stems of the artichokes with a stainless steel knife, break off the tough outer leaves, and cut off the top quarter of the artichokes. Snip off the tips of the artichokes with a scissors and rub the cut edges with the lemon halves. Arrange the artichokes in one layer in a large saucepan and add enough water to come 2 inches up the side of the pan. Drizzle the artichokes with the vegetable oil and 2 tablespoons of the lemon juice, bring the liquid to a boil, covered, and simmer the artichokes, covered, for 25 to 35 minutes, or until they are tender (test a leaf for doneness).

While the artichokes are cooking, in a blender blend the shallot, the garlic, the vinegar, the remaining 2 tablespoons lemon juice, the Sherry, the mustard, the reserved green peppercorn brine, 1 teaspoon of the pimiento, and the salt until mixture is smooth and with the motor running add the olive oil in a slow stream, blending the dressing until it is emulsified.

Transfer the artichokes with tongs, holding them upside down to drain, to a large heavy-duty sealable plastic bag, drizzle 1 cup of the dressing over them, reserving the remaining dressing, and let the artichokes marinate at room temperature for 30 minutes or chill overnight. Transfer each artichoke with the tongs to a plate, add the dressing in the bag to the reserved dressing, and in the blender blend the dressing until it is emulsified again. Spoon some of the dressing around each artichoke, sprinkle each serving with some of the green peppercorns and the remaining 3 teaspoons pimiento, and serve the remaining dressing separately. Serves 4 as a first course.

Asparagus and Smoked Salmon Timbales

about ¾ pound thinly sliced smoked salmon,
    or enough to line eight ¼-cup ramekins
2 pounds asparagus
1 teaspoon unflavored gelatin
½ cup sour cream
1 teaspoon Dijon-style mustard
2 tablespoons snipped dill plus small sprigs
    for garnish
12 thin lemon slices, halved, for garnish

Line each of eight ¼-cup ramekins, 2¼ inches in diameter by 1¼ inches deep, with some of the smoked salmon, leaving a 1-inch overhang.

Trim the asparagus and in a wide deep skillet of boiling salted water cook it for 3 to 5 minutes, or until the stalks are tender but not limp. Drain the asparagus in a large colander, refresh it under cold water, and pat it dry. Cut off the tips, reserving 24 of them, covered and chilled, for garnish, and cut the stalks and remaining tips into 2-inch lengths. In a small saucepan sprinkle the gelatin over ⅓ cup cold water, let it soften for 5 minutes, and heat the mixture over moderately low heat, stirring, until the gelatin is dissolved. In a food processor blend the 2-inch pieces of asparagus, the sour cream, the mustard, and the snipped dill, pulsing the motor, until the asparagus is chopped fine. With the motor running add the gelatin mixture and blend the mixture until it is just combined.

Fill the lined ramekins with the asparagus mixture, packing it, and fold the overhangs over the tops (the filling need not be covered completely). Chill the timbales, covered with plastic wrap, for at least 2 hours and up to 8 hours.

On each of 8 chilled plates arrange alternately 3 of the lemon half slices and 3 of the reserved asparagus tips, halved lengthwise to make 6 tips. Loosen the timbales with a knife, invert them onto the centers of the plates, and top them with the dill sprigs. Serves 8.

Bacon and Banana Kebabs with Mustard Marinade

2 tablespoons fresh lemon juice
1 tablespoon Dijon-style mustard
2 large firm-ripe bananas
8 slices of lean bacon

Let sixteen 5-inch bamboo skewers soak in water to cover for 30 minutes. In a bowl whisk together the lemon juice, the mustard, and salt and pepper to taste, add the bananas, each cut crosswise diagonally into 8 pieces, and stir them gently to coat them with the marinade. Let the bananas marinate, turning them occasionally, for 15 minutes. In a large skillet cook the bacon over moderate heat, turning it, until it is cooked but still limp, transfer it with a slotted spatula to paper towels to drain, and halve each slice crosswise.

Wrap each piece of banana in a piece of bacon and thread 1 bacon and banana piece onto each skewer. Broil the kebabs on the rack of a broiler pan about 4 inches from the heat, turning them once, for 6 to 8 minutes, or until the bacon is crisp. Serves 8 as an appetizer or an hors d'oeuvre.

Carrot and Herbed Goat Cheese Spirals

5 ounces soft mild goat cheese such as
    Montrachet
3 tablespoons unsalted butter, softened
2 tablespoons snipped fresh dill
1 tablespoon minced fresh parsley leaves
1 tablespoon minced shallot
about 5 carrots, peeled

In a bowl with an electric mixer beat together the cheese, the butter, the dill, the parsley, the shallot, and salt and pepper to taste until the mixture is smooth. *The mixture may be made 1 day in advance and kept covered and chilled. Let the mixture soften before continuing.*

Put 1 carrot on a work surface and with a vegetable peeler cut lengthwise strips, turning the carrot flat side down when the core is reached, cutting more strips, and discarding the core. Spread some of the cheese mixture in a thin layer on each carrot strip and roll the strips into spirals. Continue to make spirals with the remaining carrots, 1 at a time, and cheese mixture in the same manner. On a plate chill the spirals, covered well with plastic wrap, for at least 30 minutes and up to 4 hours. Makes about 50 spirals.

PHOTO ON PAGE 57

Caviar "Raspberries" and "Blackberries"

4 ounces cold cream cheese
about 30 pine nuts, toasted lightly if desired
a 2-ounce jar of red lumpfish caviar
a 2-ounce jar of black lumpfish caviar
small parsley sprigs for garnish

Form a level ½ teaspoon of the cream cheese around each pine nut, forming berry shapes, and chill the shapes on a plate, covered, for 30 minutes. While the shapes are chilling, spread the red caviar and the black caviar gently to avoid breaking the eggs on separate pieces of doubled paper towel and let them drain. Working with 1 berry shape at a time, roll half the shapes in the red caviar and half in the black caviar, pressing the caviar gently onto the cream cheese to help it adhere. Insert the stem of a parsley sprig into each "berry." *The raspberries and blackberries may be made 6 hours in advance and kept covered and chilled.* Makes about 30 hors d'oeuvres.

PHOTO ON PAGE 32

Cheddar "Carrots" and "Parsnips"

½ pound extra-sharp Cheddar, cut into pieces
dill sprigs for garnish
½ teaspoon paprika
⅛ teaspoon cayenne, or to taste

In a food processor purée half the Cheddar until it is just smooth, roll teaspoons of it into parsnip shapes, and insert a dill sprig into the thicker end of each shape to form a "parsnip." In the food processor purée the remaining Cheddar with the paprika and the cayenne and form "carrots" in the same manner as the parsnips. *Chill the carrots and parsnips, covered, for at least 1 hour and up to 24 hours.* Makes about 50 hors d'oeuvres.

PHOTO ON PAGE 32

Cheddar Straws

5 ounces extra-sharp Cheddar at room
  temperature, grated coarse (about 1¾ cups)
½ stick (¼ cup) unsalted butter, cut into pieces
  and softened slightly
½ cup all-purpose flour
⅛ teaspoon salt
⅛ teaspoon cayenne, or to taste

In a food processor blend together the Cheddar and
the butter until the mixture is smooth, stopping the motor occasionally and scraping down the side. Add the
flour, the salt, and the cayenne and blend the mixture
well. Transfer the mixture to a pastry bag fitted with a
¼-inch fluted tip, pipe 3-inch lengths of it onto ungreased baking sheets, spacing them about 1 inch apart,
and bake the Cheddar straws in the middle of a preheated 375° F. oven for 10 to 15 minutes, or until they are
firm to the touch and pale golden. Transfer the Cheddar
straws carefully with a metal spatula to racks and let
them cool. The Cheddar straws keep in an airtight container for 2 weeks. Makes about 100 Cheddar straws.

Pumpernickel Cheese "Dominoes"

12 very thin slices of dark pumpernickel
  bread
¼ pound Saga blue or other semisoft
  spreadable cheese
½ cup bottled mayonnaise

Cut each slice of bread into two 2¼- by 1¼-inch rectangles, spread half the rectangles with the cheese, and
cover the cheese with the remaining rectangles, pressing the sandwiches together and smoothing the cheese
along the edges. *The sandwiches may be prepared up to
this point 8 hours in advance and kept covered with a
dampened paper towel and plastic wrap and chilled.*
Just before serving transfer the mayonnaise to a pastry
bag fitted with a tiny tip or to a wax paper cone, pipe it
decoratively onto the rectangles to form "dominoes,"
and arrange the dominoes decoratively on a platter.
Makes 12 sandwiches.

PHOTO ON PAGE 33

Chicken Liver and Caper Crostini

2 tablespoons minced onion
1 tablespoon unsalted butter
½ cup sliced mushrooms
2 tablespoons drained bottled capers,
  chopped
2 tablespoons dry Marsala
2 tablespoons olive oil
¼ pound chicken livers, trimmed and chopped
  coarse
six ½-inch-thick slices of Italian bread
minced fresh parsley leaves for garnish

In a skillet cook the onion in the butter over moderately low heat, stirring, until it is softened, add the mushrooms, and cook the mixture over moderate heat,
stirring, for 4 to 5 minutes, or until all the liquid the
mushrooms give off is evaporated. Add the capers, the
Marsala, and salt and pepper to taste, simmer the mixture, stirring, until most of the liquid is evaporated, and
transfer it to a food processor. In the skillet, cleaned,
heat 1 tablespoon of the oil over moderately high heat
until it is hot but not smoking and in it sauté the livers,
patted dry and seasoned with salt and pepper, stirring,
for 1 to 2 minutes, or until they are browned on the out-
side but still pink within. Transfer the livers to the food
processor and process the mixture, scraping down the
side, until it is a slightly coarse purée. Brush the bread
slices with the remaining 1 tablespoon oil and toast
them on a baking sheet in the middle of a preheated
350° F. oven for 5 to 7 minutes, or until they are crisp.
Spread the toasts with the liver mixture and sprinkle
them with the parsley. Makes 6 *crostini*.

Minced Clam, Olive, and Cheddar Canapés

a 6½-ounce can minced clams,
  drained well
¼ cup drained pitted black olives, minced
2 tablespoons minced red onion
1 tablespoon mayonnaise
3 slices of homemade-style white bread,
  toasted lightly and crusts discarded
3 tablespoons grated sharp Cheddar

In a bowl combine well the clams, the olives, the onion, and the mayonnaise and spread the mixture on the
toasts. Cut each toast into thirds, sprinkle the canapés
with the Cheddar, and broil them under a preheated
broiler about 4 inches from the heat for 30 seconds,
or until the cheese is melted. Makes 9 canapés.

Crab-Meat Sesame Canapés

10 slices of very thin homemade-type
    white bread
1 tablespoon unsalted butter, melted
¼ pound lump crab meat, picked over
2 tablespoons *tahini* (sesame seed paste,
    available at natural foods stores and many
    supermarkets)
3 tablespoons fresh lemon juice
½ teaspoon minced garlic
¼ teaspoon Tabasco, or to taste
3 tablespoons mayonnaise
2 tablespoons finely chopped scallion
1 teaspoon sesame seeds, toasted

Cut out 10 rounds from the bread with a 2½-inch round cutter, reserving the scraps for another use if desired, brush 1 side of each round with some of the butter, and toast the rounds on a baking sheet in a preheated 400° F. oven for 5 minutes, or until they are golden. In a bowl stir together the crab meat, the *tahini*, the lemon juice, the garlic, the Tabasco, the mayonnaise, the scallion, and salt and pepper to taste until the mixture is combined well, divide the mixture among the toasts, mounding it, and sprinkle it with the sesame seeds. Bake the canapés on the baking sheet in the middle of a 400° F. oven for 10 minutes, or until the crab-meat mixture is heated through. Makes 10 canapés.

Crab-Salad-Stuffed Cherry Tomatoes

½ pound lump crab meat, picked over
2 tablespoons plain yogurt
2 tablespoons mayonnaise
10 black Greek or other brine-cured black
    olives, pitted and chopped
1 teaspoon fresh lemon juice
2 tablespoons finely chopped drained bottled
    roasted red pepper
2 tablespoons minced fresh coriander
about 70 cherry tomatoes

In a bowl combine well the crab, the yogurt, the mayonnaise, the olives, the lemon juice, the red pepper, the coriander, and salt and pepper to taste and chill the salad, covered, while preparing the tomatoes. *The salad may be made 1 day in advance and kept covered and chilled.*

Cut ¼ inch from the stem end of each tomato with a serrated knife and scoop out the pulp and seeds carefully. Sprinkle the tomato shells lightly with salt, invert them on paper towels, and let them drain for 15 minutes. Stuff the tomato shells with the crab salad. Makes about 70 stuffed tomatoes.

PHOTO ON PAGE 57

Cucumber and Liptauer Spirals

For the Liptauer
an 8-ounce package cream cheese,
    softened
2 teaspoons sweet paprika
2 tablespoons minced scallion
2 tablespoons minced *cornichons* (small
    French sour gherkins, available at specialty
    foods shops and some supermarkets)
1 teaspoon fresh lemon juice
⅛ teaspoon Tabasco

2 seedless cucumbers

Make the Liptauer: In a bowl with an electric mixer (do not use a whisk attachment) beat together the cream cheese, the paprika, the scallion, the *cornichons*, the lemon juice, the Tabasco, and salt and pepper to taste until the mixture is combined thoroughly. *The Liptauer may be made 2 days in advance and kept covered and chilled. Let the Liptauer soften before continuing.*

Put the cucumbers on a work surface and with a vegetable peeler cut lengthwise strips, turning the cucumbers flat sides down when the cores are reached, cutting more strips, and discarding the cores. (There should be about 34 strips in all). Discard the 2 peel strips cut from each cucumber, lay the remaining strips in one layer on paper towels, and sprinkle them lightly with salt. Cover the strips with paper towels, pressing them lightly, and let them drain for 15 minutes.

Spread some of the Liptauer in a thin layer on each cucumber strip, roll the strips into spirals, and on a plate chill them, covered with plastic wrap, for 45 minutes. Halve each spiral with a serrated knife, forming 2 spirals, and arrange the spirals, cut sides down, on a plate. *The spirals may be made 4 hours in advance and kept covered and chilled.* Makes about 60 spirals.

PHOTO ON PAGE 57

Fruit Salad with Balsamic Vinegar and Vanilla

2 tablespoons balsamic vinegar
½ teaspoon vanilla
⅛ teaspoon freshly ground pepper
½ honeydew melon, seeds discarded and the
    flesh scooped into balls with a melon-ball
    cutter
1 cup strawberries, hulled and quartered
1 peach, peeled, pitted, and cut into 1-inch
    pieces

In a bowl whisk together the vinegar, the vanilla, the pepper, and salt to taste, add the honeydew, the strawberries, and the peach, and toss the salad until it is combined well. Divide the salad between stemmed glasses. Serves 2 as a first course or dessert.

*Ham and Mustard Mayonnaise Sandwich
"Playing Cards"*

2 teaspoons unflavored gelatin
1 cup bottled mayonnaise
3 tablespoons Dijon-style mustard, or to taste
1 pound thinly sliced cooked ham
14 thin slices of homemade-type white bread,
    cut into 3- by 2-inch rectangles
red bell pepper peel (cut from a bell pepper
    with a vegetable peeler) and ripe black
    olive slices (cut from large olives) cut into
    spade, diamond, heart, and club shapes

In a small saucepan sprinkle the gelatin over 3 tablespoons cold water to soften for 5 minutes and heat the mixture over moderately low heat, stirring, until the gelatin is dissolved. In a bowl whisk together the mayonnaise, the mustard, and the gelatin mixture. Cut the ham slices flush with the bread rectangles and top each rectangle with 2 slices of the ham. Set the rectangles, ham sides up, on racks set over wax paper or foil. Spoon the mayonnaise mixture over the ham, making sure it runs down the sides and covers the top and sides completely. (The mayonnaise mixture should be thick enough, to form a smooth opaque layer but thin enough to run down the sides. If it isn't thin enough, stir in 1 to 2 tablespoons more water.) Decorate the "playing cards" with the spade, diamond, heart, and club shapes and chill them on the racks, uncovered, for 30 minutes, or until the mayonnaise mixture is set. *The playing cards may be made 4 hours in advance and kept covered with-* out touching the surfaces of the cards. Transfer the playing cards to a serving plate. Makes 14 sandwiches.
PHOTO ON PAGE 33

*Hummus
(Chick-Pea Dip with Parsley and Pine Nuts)*

4 garlic cloves
1 teaspoon salt
two 1-pound 3-ounce cans chick-peas,
    drained and rinsed
⅔ cup well stirred *tahini* (sesame seed paste,
    available at specialty foods shops, natural
    foods stores, and some supermarkets)
¼ cup fresh lemon juice, or to taste
½ cup olive oil, or to taste
¼ cup fresh parsley leaves
2 tablespoons pine nuts, toasted lightly
toasted *pita* thins (recipe follows) as an
    accompaniment

On a cutting board mince and mash the garlic to a paste with the salt. In a food processor purée the chick-peas with the garlic paste, the *tahini*, the lemon juice, ¼ cup of the oil, and ½ cup water, scraping down the sides, until the hummus is smooth and add salt to taste. Add water, if necessary, to thin the *hummus* to the desired consistency and transfer the *hummus* to a bowl. In the food processor, cleaned, purée the remaining ¼ cup oil with the parsley until the oil is bright green and the parsley is minced and transfer the parsley oil to a small jar. *The* hummus *and the parsley oil may be made 3 days in advance and kept covered and chilled.* Divide the *hummus* between shallow serving dishes and smooth the tops. Drizzle the *hummus* with the parsley oil and sprinkle it with the pine nuts. Serve the *hummus* with the *pita*. Makes about 4 cups.

PHOTO ON PAGE 66

Toasted Pita Thins

sixteen 4-inch *pita* loaves
⅔ cup olive oil

Halve the *pita* loaves horizontally, forming 32 rounds, and brush the rough side of each round lightly with some of the oil. Cut each round into long thin triangular strips with scissors, bake the strips in one layer in jelly-roll pans in the lower third of a preheated

400° F. oven for 6 to 10 minutes, or until they are golden, and let them cool. *The pita thins may be made 1 week in advance and kept in an airtight container.* Makes about 200 *pita* thins.

PHOTO ON PAGE 66

Black Olive and Roasted Red Pepper "Backgammon Board"

½ cup oil-cured black olives or well drained and patted dry Kalamata olives
8 very thin slices of dark pumpernickel bread
8 very thin slices of homemade-type white bread
¼ pound soft goat cheese, such as Montrachet, or cream cheese at room temperature
two 7-ounce jars roasted red peppers, drained, spread flat on paper towels, and patted dry

Crush the olives lightly with the flat side of a cleaver or large knife on a cutting board, remove and discard the pits, and in a food processor purée the olives well, stopping the motor and scraping down the sides with a spatula several times.

Cut 6 slices of the pumpernickel bread and 6 slices of the white bread into twenty-four 3½- by 1½-inch triangles. With a 1-inch-round cutter cut out rounds from each of the remaining 4 slices of bread. Toast the triangles and rounds lightly, spread the pumpernickel toasts with the olive purée, and spread the white toasts with the cheese. Cut triangles and rounds from the roasted peppers and arrange them on top of the cheese toasts. Arrange the triangles in the design of a backgammon board on a rectangular tray and arrange the black and red round disks around the design. Makes about 30 hors d'oeuvres.

PHOTO ON PAGE 33

Kalamata Olive Butter with Rosemary

⅔ cup drained bottled Kalamata olives or other brine-cured olives
1 stick (½ cup) unsalted butter, softened
1 teaspoon freshly grated lemon rind
¾ teaspoon minced fresh rosemary, or to taste

Crush the olives lightly with the flat side of a large knife on a cutting board, remove and discard the pits,

and in a food processor chop the olives, stopping the motor and scraping down the side with a spatula several times. Add the butter, the rind, and the rosemary and blend the mixture until it is combined well. Serve the butter as an accompaniment to grilled chicken or grilled fish or as a spread for toasted French bread slices. Makes about ¾ cup.

Niçoise Olive and Red Pepper Tapenade

a 7½-ounce jar Niçoise olives (available at specialty foods shops and some supermarkets), drained (about 1½ cups)
½ cup packed drained bottled roasted red peppers (half a 7-ounce jar)
1 tablespoon drained bottled capers

Crush the olives lightly with the flat side of a large knife on a cutting board, discard the pits, and in a food processor purée the olives, stopping the motor and scraping down the side with a spatula several times. Rinse the peppers in a sieve and pat them dry with paper towels. Add the peppers and the capers to the olive purée and purée the mixture until it is combined well. Serve the *tapenade* as a spread for toasted French bread slices or as a filling for cherry tomatoes. Makes about 1 cup.

91

Pimiento-Stuffed Olives in Walnut Cheese Pastry

5 ounces sharp Cheddar, cut into pieces
3 tablespoons cold unsalted butter,
    cut into pieces
¼ cup walnut pieces
½ cup all-purpose flour
about 40 small pimiento-stuffed olives (about
    one-and-a-half 3-ounce jars), drained well
    and patted dry

In a food processor cream together the Cheddar and the butter, add the walnuts, and blend the mixture until the nuts are ground fine. Add the flour and blend the mixture until it is combined well. (The dough will be crumbly but moist.) Coat each olive with a level teaspoon of the dough, rolling it and the dough between the palms to enclose the olive completely, and arrange the pastries 1 inch apart on a baking sheet. *The pastries can be made 2 days in advance and kept covered loosely and chilled.* Bake the olive-stuffed pastries in the lower third of a preheated 375° F. oven for 15 minutes. Makes about 40 hors d'oeuvres.

Ripe Olive, Tomato, and Coriander Salsa

a 6-ounce can pitted ripe olives, drained
    (about 1½ cups) and chopped
1 large tomato, seeded and chopped
½ cup chopped fresh coriander
1 small *jalapeño* chili, seeded and minced
    (wear rubber gloves)
1 garlic clove, minced
3 tablespoons olive oil
2 tablespoons fresh lime juice

In a bowl stir together the olives, the tomato, the coriander, the *jalapeño*, and the garlic until the mixture is combined well, add the oil, the lime juice, and salt and pepper to taste, stirring to combine the *salsa*, and serve the *salsa* as a dip with corn chips or as an accompaniment to grilled meats. Makes 2 cups.

Oysters with Pickled Carrot and Daikon

1 cup fine julienne of carrot
1 cup fine julienne of *daikon* (Oriental white
    radish, available at Oriental markets and
    some supermarkets)

1½ cups distilled white vinegar
2 tablespoons sugar
1 teaspoon salt
60 oysters, shucked (procedure on page 132),
    on the half shell
fresh seaweed (available at most fish markets)
    or rock salt for lining the platters
fresh coriander for garnish

In a heatproof bowl toss together the carrot and the *daikon*. In a saucepan combine the vinegar, ¾ cup water, the sugar, and the salt, bring the liquid to a boil, stirring until the sugar is dissolved, and pour the mixture over the carrot and *daikon* mixture. Let the pickle mixture cool to room temperature and chill it, covered, overnight. *The pickle mixture may be made 2 days in advance and kept covered and chilled.* Arrange the oysters on oyster plates or platters lined with the seaweed. Drain the pickle mixture, divide it among the oysters, and garnish the oysters with the coriander. Serves 12.

PHOTO ON PAGE 12

*Small Potatoes Stuffed with Smoked Salmon,
Scallion, and Yogurt*

10 small red or white potatoes (each the size
    of a walnut), scrubbed, patted dry, and
    rubbed with vegetable oil
3 ounces finely chopped smoked salmon
    (about ½ cup)
½ cup plain yogurt
3 tablespoons minced scallion
2 tablespoons minced fresh
    parsley leaves
20 drained bottled capers for garnish
    if desired

Prick the potatoes with a fork and bake them in the middle of a preheated 425° F. oven for 40 minutes. While the potatoes are baking, in a bowl stir together the salmon, the yogurt, the scallion, and the parsley. While the potatoes are warm, halve them, scoop them out, leaving ⅛-inch-thick shells, and force the scooped-out potato through a ricer or the medium disk of a food mill into the bowl. Combine the mixture well, season it with salt and pepper, and divide it among the potato shells. Top each potato with a caper and serve the potatoes at room temperature. Makes 20 hors d'oeuvres.

Sweet Potato, Crème Fraîche, and Caviar Bites

2 long narrow sweet potatoes (about
    1¼ pounds), scrubbed
about ½ cup *crème fraîche* (available at
    specialty foods shops and many
    supermarkets) or sour cream
1 ounce caviar
tiny dill sprigs for garnish

Cut the sweet potatoes crosswise into ¼-inch slices with a large sharp knife and with a sharp 1- to 1½-inch decorative cutter cut a decorative shape from each slice. Steam the sweet potatoes in a steamer set over boiling water, covered, for 5 to 6 minutes, or until they are just tender, arrange them in one layer on a plate, and let them cool, their surface covered with plastic wrap. Chill the sweet potatoes for at least 1 hour or overnight. *The sweet potatoes may be made 1 day in advance and kept covered and chilled.* Arrange the sweet potatoes, patted dry, on serving plates, top each piece with ½ teaspoon of the *crème fraîche* and ⅛ teaspoon of the caviar, and garnish the "bites" with the dill. Makes about 40 hors d'oeuvres.

PHOTO ON PAGE 66

Prosciutto, Pear, and Chive Cornets
with Ginger Cream

3 ounces cream cheese, softened
1 teaspoon grated peeled fresh gingerroot
1 teaspoon milk
1 teaspoon English-style dry mustard
2 firm-ripe pears
the juice of 1 lemon
20 thin slices of prosciutto (about ½ pound),
    halved crosswise
40 fresh chives, cut into 3-inch lengths

In a bowl with an electric mixer beat together the cream cheese, the gingerroot, the milk, the mustard, and pepper to taste until the mixture is smooth. Halve, core, and cut each pear lengthwise into 20 slices and in a bowl toss the slices gently with the lemon juice, coating them thoroughly. Spread ¼ teaspoon of the ginger cream on 1 piece of prosciutto, arrange 1 pear slice and 3 of the chive lengths in the center, and fold the sides of the prosciutto to enclose the pear and

chives in a cone shape. Continue to make cornets with the remaining ginger cream, prosciutto, pears, and chives in the same manner and arrange them decoratively on a platter. *The cornets may be made 1 hour in advance and kept covered and chilled.* Makes 40 cornets.

PHOTO ON PAGE 57

Red Pepper Spirals with Dill Vinaigrette

⅔ cup cream cheese, softened
2 tablespoons plain yogurt
⅓ cup minced fresh parsley leaves
3 tablespoons minced onion
three 7-ounce jars roasted red peppers (not
    strips), rinsed and patted dry between
    several thicknesses of paper towels
1½ tablespoons red-wine vinegar
6 tablespoons olive oil
soft-leafed lettuce leaves for lining the plates
1 tablespoon snipped fresh dill

In a bowl combine well the cream cheese, the yogurt, the parsley, the onion, and salt and pepper to taste. On a sheet of plastic wrap arrange enough of the red pepper pieces, smooth sides down, trimming the pieces when necessary, to form a 6-inch square and spread half the cream cheese mixture onto the peppers, leaving a ½-inch border on the side farthest from you. Using the plastic wrap as an aid, roll up the pepper layer jelly-roll fashion away from you to enclose the cream cheese mixture. Wrap the pepper roll tightly in the plastic wrap and make another roll in the same manner with the remaining red pepper pieces and cream cheese mixture. Chill the red pepper rolls for at least 6 hours. *The red pepper rolls can be made 1 day in advance and kept wrapped and chilled.*

In a bowl whisk together the vinegar and salt and pepper to taste, add the oil in a stream, whisking, and whisk the vinaigrette until it is emulsified. *The vinaigrette can be made up to this point 1 day in advance and kept covered and chilled.* Discard the plastic wrap, pat the pepper rolls with paper towels, and with a sharp knife cut each roll crosswise into 12 spirals. Line 8 plates with the lettuce and divide the spirals among the plates. Whisk the dill into the vinaigrette and spoon the vinaigrette around the spirals. Serves 8 as a first course.

Shrimp and Jalapeño Brochettes

forty-eight 8-inch wooden skewers
1 garlic clove
½ teaspoon salt
2 tablespoons vegetable oil
a 12-ounce jar pickled whole *jalapeño* peppers, drained
48 small shrimp (about 1 pound), shelled, deveined, rinsed, and drained well

In a shallow dish let the skewers soak in water to cover for 1 hour. On a cutting board mince and mash the garlic to a paste with the salt. In a bowl combine the garlic paste, the oil, and 1 of the *jalapeño* peppers, minced (wear rubber gloves), and combine the mixture well. Add the shrimp, toss them until they are coated with the marinade, and let them marinate for 30 minutes. Cut the remaining *jalapeño* peppers crosswise into forty-eight ¼-inch slices and thread 1 shrimp around 1 *jalapeño* slice on each skewer. *The brochettes may be prepared up to this point 2 hours in advance and kept covered and chilled.* Grill the brochettes on a rack set about 4 inches over glowing coals, turning them once, for 2 to 3 minutes, or until the shrimp are pink and just firm. (Alternatively, the brochettes can be broiled on racks set in jelly-roll pans under a preheated broiler about 4 inches from the heat, turning them once, for 2 to 3 minutes, or until the shrimp are pink and just firm.) Makes 48 hors d'oeuvres.

PHOTO ON PAGE 67

Marinated Shrimp with Yellow Bell Pepper and Red Onion

⅓ cup white-wine vinegar
2 tablespoons medium-dry Sherry
½ teaspoon dried thyme, crumbled
1 teaspoon salt
½ teaspoon sugar
1 teaspoon cracked black peppercorns
⅓ cup extra-virgin olive oil (available at specialty foods shops and most supermarkets)
1 bay leaf
2 tablespoons bottled capers
1 red onion, halved lengthwise and sliced thin crosswise
2 yellow bell peppers, cut into 2-inch strips
1½ pounds medium shrimp (about 40)
garlic toast rounds (page 106) as an accompaniment

In a bowl whisk together the vinegar, the Sherry, the thyme, the salt, the sugar, and the cracked pepper, add the oil in a stream, whisking, and whisk the mixture until it is emulsified. Stir in the bay leaf, the capers, the onion, and the bell peppers until the marinade is combined well.

In a kettle of boiling salted water cook the shrimp for 1 minute, drain them, and shell them, adding them to the marinade as they are shelled. Toss the shrimp with the marinade, transfer the mixture to a sturdy sealable plastic bag, and let the shrimp marinate, chilled, for at least 8 hours or overnight. Drain the shrimp and the vegetables, discarding the bay leaf, arrange them on a platter, and serve them with the garlic toast rounds. Serves 15 to 20.

PHOTO ON PAGE 56

Smoked Salmon, Avocado, and Horseradish Spirals

1 envelope of unflavored gelatin
2 tablespoons fresh lemon juice
½ California avocado
an 8-ounce package cream cheese, softened
3 tablespoons drained bottled horseradish
½ pound thinly sliced smoked salmon
18 thin slices of dense pumpernickel
tiny parsley sprigs for garnish
fresh chives for garnish

In a small saucepan sprinkle the gelatin over the lemon juice, let it soften for 10 minutes, and heat the mixture over moderately low heat, stirring, until the gelatin is dissolved. In a food processor purée the avocado with the cream cheese, the horseradish, and the gelatin mixture until the mixture is smooth. Transfer the mixture to a bowl, set the bowl in a larger bowl of ice and cold water, and stir the mixture until it is thickened to the consistency of thick mayonnaise.

Arrange the smoked salmon slices, overlapping them slightly, on a sheet of plastic wrap to form a 17-by 7-inch rectangle and spread them with the avocado mixture, leaving a ½-inch border. Using the plastic wrap as an aid and beginning with a long side, roll up the smoked salmon jelly-roll fashion, wrap it in the plastic wrap, and twist the ends of the plastic wrap closed. Chill the smoked salmon roll for 3 hours, or until it is firm and the filling is set.

With a 1½-inch round cutter cut out rounds from the pumpernickel, reserving the scraps for another use. Remove the plastic wrap from the salmon roll carefully on a cutting board and with an electric knife or other very sharp knife cut it crosswise into ¼-inch slices. Arrange each salmon roll slice on a pumpernickel round and garnish each canapé with a parsley sprig and 2 short sections of chive. The canapés keep, covered tightly with plastic wrap and chilled, for 2 hours. Makes about 36 canapés.

Smørrebrød
(Danish Open-Faced Sandwiches)

For the spekepølse sandwiches
twelve 4- by 2½-inch ovals of thinly sliced rye
    bread
½ stick (¼ cup) unsalted butter,
    softened
24 small Bibb lettuce leaves,
    ribs discarded
about ¼ pound *spekepølse* (Norwegian
    smoked salted sausage) or salami, sliced
    and cut into twenty-four 1¼-inch-long
    triangles
24 cocktail onions, halved lengthwise
12 *cornichons* (French sour gherkins,
    available at specialty foods shops
    and some supermarkets), sliced
    thin lengthwise

For the smoked salmon sandwiches
twelve 2½-inch squares of lightly toasted
    homemade-type white bread
½ stick (¼ cup) unsalted butter, softened
about 9 ounces thinly sliced smoked salmon,
    cut into twelve 2½-inch squares, piecing it
    together if necessary
¼ cup sour cream
24 slices of ripe olives
12 dill sprigs
For the ham sandwiches
twelve 3-inch rounds of thinly sliced
    rye bread
½ stick (¼ cup) unsalted butter, softened
36 thin slices of seedless cucumber
about ¼ pound thinly sliced boiled ham, cut
    into ¼-inch-wide strips (about 1 cup)
¼ cup minced radish
¼ cup thinly sliced scallion green

Make the *spekepølse* sandwiches: Spread the bread slices with the butter and arrange the lettuce, the *spekepølse*, the onions, and the *cornichons* decoratively on the bread.

Make the smoked salmon sandwiches: Spread the toast with the butter and arrange the smoked salmon, the sour cream, the olives, and the dill decoratively on the toast.

Make the ham sandwiches: Spread the bread with the butter and arrange the cucumber, the ham, the radish, and the scallion green decoratively on the bread.

Arrange the smørrebrød on a platter. Makes 36 smørrebrød.

PHOTO ON PAGE 43

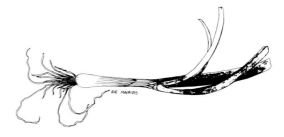

Spinach, Feta, and Phyllo Purses

1½ cups finely chopped onion
½ cup olive oil
two 10-ounce packages frozen spinach,
    cooked, drained, squeezed dry by handfuls,
    and chopped
2 cups grated Feta (about ½ pound)
2 teaspoons dried dill
four 16- by 12-inch sheets of *phyllo*, stacked
    between 2 sheets of wax paper and
    covered with a dampened kitchen towel

In a heavy skillet cook the onion in ¼ cup of the oil over moderately low heat, stirring occasionally, until it is golden, add the spinach, and cook the mixture, stirring, until it is combined well. Remove the skillet from the heat, stir in the Feta and the dill, and let the filling cool.

Lay 1 sheet of the *phyllo* with a long side facing you on a work surface and brush it lightly with some of the remaining ¼ cup oil. Lay another sheet of *phyllo* over the first sheet and brush it lightly with some of the remaining oil. With a sharp knife cut the sheets lengthwise into thirds and cut each length crosswise into fifths, making 15 sections, each approximately 4 by 3⅓ inches. Put a level teaspoon of the filling in the center of each *phyllo* section. Working with 1 section at a time gather the corners of the *phyllo* over the filling and twist the *phyllo* closed gently. Transfer the pastries to an oiled jelly-roll pan and make pastries with the remaining *phyllo*, oil, and filling in the same manner. Bake the pastries in the lower third of a preheated 375° F. oven for 25 minutes, or until they are golden. *The pastries may be baked 1 day in advance and kept covered loosely with plastic wrap and chilled. Reheat the pastries in a 375° F. oven for 10 minutes, or until they are heated through.* Makes 30 hors d'oeuvres.

PHOTO ON PAGE 65

Baked Spinach Balls with Yogurt-Mustard Dipping Sauce

a 10-ounce package frozen leaf spinach
½ cup fine fresh bread crumbs
1 large egg, beaten lightly
¼ cup freshly grated Parmesan
¼ teaspoon ground cumin
2 teaspoons fresh lemon juice
¼ cup plain yogurt
1½ teaspoons Dijon-style mustard
a pinch of cayenne, or to taste

In a saucepan bring 1 cup water to a boil, add the spinach, and cook it for 3 minutes, or until it is just tender. Drain the spinach in a colander, let it cool, and squeeze it dry by the handful. Chop the spinach fine and in a bowl combine it well with the bread crumbs, the egg, the Parmesan, the cumin, the lemon juice, and salt and pepper to taste. Roll the mixture into twelve 1-inch balls and bake the spinach balls on a baking sheet in the middle of a preheated 400° F. oven for 12 minutes, or until they just begin to turn golden.

In a small bowl whisk together the yogurt, the mustard, the cayenne, and salt to taste and serve the baked spinach balls with the yogurt-mustard dipping sauce. Serves 2 as an hors d'oeuvre.

Fried Spinach Won Ton Triangles

½ cup chopped onion
1 large garlic clove, minced
1 tablespoon olive oil
12 cups firmly packed spinach leaves
    removed from the stems (about 2 pounds
    with stems), washed well, spun dry, and
    chopped coarse
¾ cup (about 3½ ounces) minced thinly
    sliced pepperoni
⅛ teaspoon dried thyme, crumbled
⅛ teaspoon dried orégano, crumbled
2 teaspoons fresh lemon juice
1¼ cups (about ¼ pound) coarsely grated
    whole-milk mozzarella
about 32 won ton wrappers (available at
    Oriental markets and many supermarkets,
    thawed if frozen), covered with a
    dampened kitchen towel
1 large egg, beaten lightly
vegetable oil for deep-frying

In a large skillet cook the onion and the garlic in the olive oil over moderately low heat, stirring, until the onion is softened, add the spinach, the pepperoni, the thyme, the orégano, and the lemon juice, and cook the mixture over moderately high heat, stirring, until the spinach is wilted and most of the excess liquid is evaporated. Transfer the mixture to a bowl, let it cool for 5 minutes, and stir in the mozzarella and salt and pepper to taste.

Put 1 won ton wrapper on a work surface with a corner facing you and mound 1 rounded teaspoon of the filling in the center of it. Moisten the edges of the wrapper with some of the egg, fold the corner facing you over the filling to form a triangle, pressing out the air, and pinch the edges together, sealing them well. Make won ton triangles with the remaining wrappers and filling in the same manner.

In a deep fryer or kettle fry the triangles in batches in 2 inches of 360°F. vegetable oil, turning them, for 3 to 4 minutes, or until they are golden brown, and transfer them to paper towels to drain. Makes about 32 won ton triangles.

Stilton Walnut Tarts

2 recipes cream cheese pastry dough
    (recipe follows)
⅔ cup walnuts, ground, plus 14 lightly
    toasted walnut halves for garnish
raw rice for weighting the shells
1¼ cups half-and-half
6 ounces Stilton, crumbled
3 large eggs
watercress sprigs for garnish

Roll half the dough into a ⅛-inch-thick rectangle on a floured surface, fit it into a 14- by 4½-inch rectangular flan form set on a baking sheet, and fold the edges inward, crimping them decoratively. Make another shell with the remaining dough in the same manner. (Alternatively, the shells may be made in two 9-inch tart pans with removable fluted rims.) Sprinkle the ground walnuts evenly in the pie shells and press them gently into the dough. Prick the bottoms of the shells lightly with a fork and chill the shells for 30 minutes. Line the shells with foil, fill the foil with the rice, and bake the shells in the lower third of a preheated 425° F. oven for 10 minutes. Remove the rice and foil carefully, bake the shells for 5 to 6 minutes more, or until they are golden, and let them cool on the baking sheets on racks.

In a saucepan combine the half-and-half and the Stilton, bring the liquid to a simmer, and stir the mixture until the Stilton is just melted. Remove the pan from the heat and let the mixture cool. In a bowl whisk together the Stilton mixture and the eggs, divide the

mixture between the shells, and bake the tarts in the middle of a preheated 375° F. oven for 30 to 35 minutes, or until a knife inserted in the custard ½ inch from the edge comes out clean. (The custard may not be fully set in the center but will continue to cook after the tarts are removed from the oven.) Let the tarts cool to room temperature and remove the flan forms carefully. Transfer the tarts to platters, garnish them with the walnut halves, and garnish the platters with the watercress. To serve the tarts halve them lengthwise and cut them crosswise into sevenths. Makes 28 hors d'oeuvres.

PHOTO ON PAGE 67

Cream Cheese Pastry Dough

¾ stick (6 tablespoons) cold unsalted butter,
    cut into bits
4 ounces cold cream cheese, cut into bits
1 cup all-purpose flour
½ teaspoon salt

In a food processor blend the butter, the cream cheese, the flour, and the salt, pulsing the motor, until the dough just begins to form a ball, gather the dough into a ball, and flatten it slightly. Dust the dough with flour and chill it, wrapped in plastic wrap, for 1 hour. *The dough may be made 1 day in advance and kept wrapped well and chilled.*

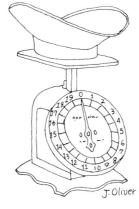

J. Oliver

Tarragon Cheese Spread

8 ounces cream cheese, softened
2 tablespoons sour cream
½ teaspoon minced garlic
3 tablespoons finely chopped fresh tarragon
    leaves
3 tablespoons finely chopped fresh parsley
    leaves
2 teaspoons tarragon vinegar (page 222)

In a food processor blend together well the cream cheese, the sour cream, the garlic, the tarragon, the parsley, the vinegar, and salt and pepper to taste. Makes about 1 cup.

White Bean and Garlic Dip

1 cup canned white beans (*cannellini*), rinsed
    and drained well
2 large garlic cloves, boiled for 5 minutes,
    drained, and peeled
1½ tablespoons olive oil (preferably extra-
    virgin)
½ teaspoon fresh lemon juice
⅛ teaspoon Tabasco, or to taste
assorted vegetables such as celery, carrot, and
    fennel bulb, cut into sticks

In a food processor purée the beans and the garlic with the oil, the lemon juice, the Tabasco, and salt to taste. Transfer the dip to a bowl and serve it with the vegetables. Makes about ¾ cup.

Wild Mushroom Tartlets

pâte brisée (page 248)
raw rice for weighting the shells
1 ounce dried *porcini* or *cèpes* (wild
    mushrooms, available at specialty
    foods shops)
¼ pound shallots, minced
3 tablespoons unsalted butter
1 pound small white mushrooms
½ teaspoon dried tarragon, crumbled
2 tablespoons all-purpose flour
3 tablespoons medium-dry Sherry
½ cup sour cream
fresh lemon juice to taste
¼ cup minced fresh parsley leaves

a 3½-ounce package *enoki-dake* mushrooms
    (available at specialty produce markets and
    some supermarkets)

Roll the dough into a ⅛-inch-thick rectangle on a floured surface and with a floured 3½-inch-long oval cutter cut 20 ovals from it. Fit the ovals into 20 lightly oiled 3¾-inch-long *barquette* tins and chill the tartlet shells for 30 minutes. Weight the shells with empty *barquette* tins or line them with foil, fill the tins or foil with the rice, and bake the shells in a jelly-roll pan in the lower third of a preheated 425° F. oven for 10 minutes. Remove the rice and tins or foil carefully, bake the shells for 5 to 10 minutes more, or until they are golden, and let them cool in the pan on a rack.

In a bowl let the *porcini* soak in boiling water to cover for 30 minutes, or until they are softened, drain them, reserving the soaking liquid for another use, and discard any tough stems. In a large skillet cook the shallots in the butter over moderately low heat, stirring, until they are softened. In a food processor chop fine the *porcini* with the white mushrooms, add the mixture to the shallot mixture, and stir in the tarragon. Cook the mixture, stirring, until the liquid the mushrooms give off is evaporated, stir in the flour, and cook the mixture, stirring, for 2 minutes. Stir in the Sherry, the sour cream, the lemon juice, and salt and pepper to taste and cook the filling, stirring, for 5 minutes, or until it is thickened. Remove the skillet from the heat and let the filling cool. *The filling may be prepared up to this point 2 days in advance and kept covered and chilled.* Stir the parsley into the filling and divide the filling among the shells, smoothing the tops. Bake the tartlets in the lower third of a preheated 375° F. oven for 10 minutes, or until the filling is heated through, arrange 2 of the *enoki-dake*, trimmed, on each tartlet, and bake the tartlets for 2 minutes more. Loosen the tartlets from the tins with the tip of a small sharp knife and transfer them carefully to serving plates. Makes 20 hors d'oeuvres.

Fried Zucchini Blossoms and Bell Pepper Rings

1 cup beer (not dark)
¾ cup plus 2 to 3 tablespoons all-purpose
    flour
⅓ cup rinsed, spun dry, and packed basil
    leaves plus 6 basil sprigs for garnish
½ teaspoon salt

vegetable oil for deep-frying
1 large yellow bell pepper, cut into 6 rings
1 large green bell pepper, cut into 6 rings
6 zucchini blossoms (available seasonally at
    specialty produce markets), rinsed and
    patted dry

In a blender or food processor blend the beer, ¾ cup plus 2 tablespoons of the flour, the ⅓ cup basil leaves, and the salt for 5 seconds. Turn off the motor, scrape down the side, and blend the mixture for 20 seconds more, or until it is just smooth. The batter should be the consistency of pancake batter. (If the batter is too thin add the remaining 1 tablespoon flour and blend the batter for 5 seconds, or until it is just combined.)

Transfer the batter to a bowl, let it stand, covered with plastic wrap, for 1 hour, and stir it until it is combined.

In a large deep skillet heat 2 inches of the oil to 375° F. Dip the bell pepper rings into the batter in batches, letting the excess drip off, fry them in batches in the oil, turning them, for 1 minute and 30 seconds, or until they are golden, and transfer them with tongs as they are fried to paper towels to drain. Dip the zucchini blossoms into the batter in batches, letting the excess drip off, fry them in batches in the oil, turning them, for 1 minute, or until they are golden, and transfer them with tongs as they are fried to paper towels to drain. Divide the bell pepper rings and the zucchini blossoms among 6 plates and garnish each serving with a basil sprig. Serves 6.

BREADS

YEAST BREADS

Chewy Rye Caraway Breadsticks

1¼ cups rye flour (available at natural foods
    stores and some supermarkets)
1¾ cups all-purpose flour
a ¼-ounce package (2½ teaspoons) fast-acting
    yeast
¼ cup light molasses
¾ teaspoon salt
2 tablespoons caraway seeds
cornmeal for sprinkling the baking sheets
an egg wash, made by beating 1 large egg
    with 1 tablespoon water

In a food processor combine the rye flour, ¾ cup of
the all-purpose flour, and the yeast. In a saucepan combine the molasses and ¾ cup water and heat the mixture
over moderate heat, stirring, until a candy thermometer
registers 130° F. With the motor running add the molasses mixture to the flour mixture. Add the salt and ½ cup
of the remaining all-purpose flour and blend the dough
until it begins to form a ball. On a lightly floured surface
knead in 1 tablespoon of the caraway seeds and enough
of the remaining ½ cup all-purpose flour to form a soft,
slightly sticky dough, knead the dough for 5 to 7 minutes, or until it is smooth and elastic, and let it rest on the
lightly floured surface, covered with an inverted bowl,
for 15 minutes. Divide the dough into 16 pieces and
work with 1 piece at a time, keeping the remaining
pieces covered with the bowl. Roll each piece of dough
between the palms of the hands to form a 12-inch-long

rope and arrange the ropes as they are formed 2 inches
apart on 2 baking sheets, sprinkled lightly with the
cornmeal. Let the breadsticks rise, covered loosely, in a
warm place for 20 minutes, brush them lightly with
some of the egg wash, and sprinkle them with the remaining 1 tablespoon caraway seeds. Bake the breadsticks in the upper and lower racks of a preheated
425° F. oven for 10 minutes, switching the baking
sheets halfway through the baking, transfer them to
racks, and let them cool for 30 minutes. Makes 16
breadsticks.

PHOTO ON PAGE 13

Mediterranean Olive Rolls

two ¼-ounce packages (5 teaspoons)
    active dry yeast
1 teaspoon sugar
1 teaspoon freshly ground pepper, or to taste
¾ cup buckwheat flour (available at natural
    foods stores)
3 cups all-purpose flour
1½ cups drained bottled Kalamata or other
    brine-cured black olives, pitted and
    chopped coarse
2 tablespoons extra-virgin olive oil (available
    at specialty foods shops and many
    supermarkets)

In the large bowl of an electric mixer proof the yeast
with 1 cup lukewarm water, the sugar, and the pepper
for 5 to 10 minutes, or until the mixture is foamy. Add

the buckwheat flour, the all-purpose flour, the olives, and the oil and with the electric mixer fitted with the paddle attachment beat the mixture until it forms a soft sticky dough. Knead the dough gently by hand on a floured surface for 2 minutes, dust it lightly with flour, and put it in a large bowl. Let the dough rise, covered tightly with plastic wrap, in a warm place for 45 minutes to 1 hour, or until it is double in bulk. Turn the dough out onto a floured surface, quarter it, forming each quarter into a round, and quarter each round. With floured hands form the pieces of dough into balls, arrange the balls on an oiled baking sheet, and dust them lightly with flour. Let the rolls rise, covered loosely with plastic wrap, in a warm place for 30 to 40 minutes, or until they are almost double in bulk. Make a slash gently with a sharp knife or razor blade ¼ inch deep in the top of each roll and bake the rolls in the lower third of a preheated 400° F. oven for 20 to 25 minutes, or until they sound hollow when the bottoms are tapped. Let the rolls cool on a rack. Makes 16 rolls.

PHOTO ON PAGE 59

Sweet Potato Cloverleaf Rolls

3 tablespoons sugar
a ¼-ounce package (2½ teaspoons) active
    dry yeast
2 large eggs
⅓ cup milk
½ stick (¼ cup) unsalted butter, melted and
    cooled, plus additional melted butter for
    brushing the rolls
1 teaspoon salt

¾ cup mashed cooked sweet potatoes
    (¾ pound sweet potatoes)
3 to 4 cups all-purpose flour

In a small bowl stir together 1 tablespoon of the sugar and ¼ cup warm water, sprinkle the yeast over the mixture, and let it proof for 5 minutes, or until it is foamy. In a large bowl whisk together the eggs, the remaining 2 tablespoons sugar, the milk, the butter, the salt, the sweet potatoes, and the yeast mixture until the mixture is combined well, stir in 3 cups of the flour, 1 cup at a time, and turn the dough out onto a floured surface. Knead the dough, incorporating as much of the remaining 1 cup flour as necessary to prevent the dough from sticking, for 8 to 10 minutes, or until it is smooth and elastic. Form the dough into a ball, put it in a well buttered large bowl, and turn it to coat it with the butter. Let the dough rise, covered with plastic wrap, in a warm place for 1 hour, or until it is double in bulk. Turn the dough out onto a floured surface, cut off pieces of dough about the size of a walnut, and form them into balls. Put 3 balls of dough into each of 18 buttered ⅓-cup muffin tins, brush the tops of the rolls with the additional melted butter, and let the rolls rise, covered loosely, in a warm place for 30 to 45 minutes, or until they are almost double in bulk. Bake the rolls in the middle of a preheated 400° F. oven for 12 to 15 minutes, or until they are golden. *The rolls may be made 1 week in advance and kept wrapped tightly and frozen. Reheat the rolls, wrapped in foil, in a preheated 400° F. oven for 25 to 30 minutes, or until they are heated through.* Makes 18 rolls.

PHOTO ON PAGE 72

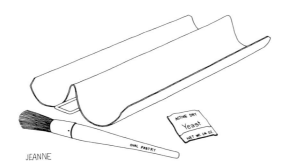

JEANNE

101

Prune and Pecan Caramel Sticky Buns

a ¼-ounce package (2½ teaspoons) active
  dry yeast
¼ cup granulated sugar
2½ cups all-purpose flour
1 teaspoon salt
¼ cup milk
1 teaspoon vanilla
2 large eggs
½ stick (¼ cup) unsalted butter, cut into pieces
  and softened
For the caramel
¾ cup firmly packed light brown sugar
¾ stick (6 tablespoons) unsalted butter,
  melted
2 tablespoons dark corn syrup
For the filling
¾ cup pecans, chopped fine
1½ cups prune purée (recipe follows)

In a small bowl proof the yeast with ¼ teaspoon of the granulated sugar in 6 tablespoons lukewarm water for 5 to 10 minutes, or until the mixture is foamy. In the bowl of an electric mixer fitted with the paddle attachment combine the yeast mixture, the remaining granulated sugar, the flour, the salt, the milk, the vanilla, and the eggs, beat the mixture at low speed until it is combined well, and beat in the butter, a few pieces at a time. Beat the dough at medium speed for 5 to 7 minutes, or until it is smooth and elastic. (The dough will be very sticky.) Scrape the dough from the side of the bowl, sprinkle it lightly with flour, and let it rise, covered with plastic wrap and a kitchen towel, in a warm place for 1 hour, or until it is double in bulk.

Make the caramel while the dough is rising: In a bowl whisk together the brown sugar, the butter, and the syrup until the mixture is combined well and pour the mixture into a buttered 13- by 9-inch baking pan, spreading it evenly.

Make the filling while the dough is rising: In a bowl combine well the pecans and the prune purée.

Punch down the dough and on a well floured surface pat or roll it into a 16- by 12-inch rectangle. Spread the filling on the dough, leaving a ½-inch border on the long sides. With a long side facing you, roll up the dough jelly-roll fashion, brushing off any excess flour, and pinch the edges together firmly to seal the dough. Cut the dough crosswise into 12 pieces with a sharp knife, arrange the pieces cut sides down on the caramel in the pan, and let the buns rise, covered loosely, in a warm place for 45 to 50 minutes, or until they are double in bulk. Bake the buns in the middle of a preheated 350° F. oven for 30 to 35 minutes, or until they are golden, invert them carefully onto a large heatproof platter, and let them cool. Serve the sticky buns warm. Makes 12 buns.

Prune Purée

3 cups (about 1½ pounds) pitted prunes
1½ cups fresh orange juice
½ cup sugar

In a saucepan combine the prunes, the orange juice, and the sugar and cook the mixture, covered, over moderately low heat, stirring occasionally, for 20 to 25 minutes, or until the prunes are tender and the cooking liquid is syrupy. Let the mixture cool to room temperature and in a food processor purée it. Makes about 3 cups.

QUICK BREADS

Bacon and Cheddar Drop Biscuits

¼ cup finely minced onion
4 slices of lean bacon, cooked until crisp,
  reserving 2 tablespoons of the fat
1¾ cups all-purpose flour
2 teaspoons double-acting baking powder
½ teaspoon baking soda
½ teaspoon salt
2 tablespoons cold vegetable shortening
¾ cup coarsely grated extra-sharp Cheddar
  (about 3 ounces)
⅔ cup milk

In a skillet cook the onion in the reserved fat over moderately low heat, stirring, until it is softened and let the mixture cool. In a small bowl combine the onion mixture with the bacon, minced fine, and season the mixture with freshly ground pepper. Into a bowl sift together the flour, the baking powder, the baking soda, and the salt, add the shortening, and blend the mixture until it resembles coarse meal. Stir in the bacon mixture and the Cheddar, add the milk, and stir the mixture until it just forms a soft sticky dough. Drop the dough by rounded tablespoons onto a buttered baking sheet and bake the biscuits in the middle of a preheated 425° F. oven for 15 to 17 minutes, or until they are pale golden. Makes about 16 biscuits.

Ginger Walnut Drop Biscuits

1¾ cups all-purpose flour
2 teaspoons double-acting baking powder
½ teaspoon baking soda
1 teaspoon salt
1 stick (½ cup) cold unsalted butter,
    cut into bits
a ¼-pound piece of fresh gingerroot, peeled,
    chopped, and pressed through a garlic press
    (about ¼ cup purée and juice in all)
½ cup firmly packed brown sugar
1 cup finely chopped walnuts
½ cup milk

Into a bowl sift together the flour, the baking powder, the baking soda, and the salt, add the butter, and blend the mixture until it resembles meal. Stir in the ginger purée and juice, the brown sugar, and the walnuts, add the milk, and stir the mixture until it just forms a soft sticky dough. Drop the dough by rounded tablespoons onto an unbuttered baking sheet and bake the biscuits in the middle of a preheated 425° F. oven for 15 to 17 minutes, or until they are golden. Makes about 18 biscuits.

Monterey Jack and Jalapeño Drop Biscuits

1 cup ail-purpose flour
½ cup yellow cornmeal
2 teaspoons double-acting baking powder
½ teaspoon baking soda
½ teaspoon salt
2 tablespoons cold unsalted butter,
    cut into bits
¼ pound Monterey Jack, grated coarse (about
    1½ cups)
2 pickled 2-inch *jalapeño* peppers, seeds and
    ribs discarded and the peppers minced
    (wear rubber gloves)
2 fresh 2-inch *jalapeño* peppers, seeds and
    ribs discarded and the peppers minced
    (wear rubber gloves)
⅔ cup milk

Into a bowl sift together the flour, the cornmeal, the baking powder, the baking soda, and the salt, add the butter, and blend the mixture until it resembles coarse meal. Stir in the Monterey Jack, the pickled peppers, and the fresh peppers, add the milk, and stir the mixture until it just forms a soft sticky dough. Drop the dough by rounded tablespoons onto a buttered baking sheet and bake the biscuits in the middle of a preheated 425° F. oven for 15 to 17 minutes, or until they are pale golden. Makes about 16 biscuits.

Mustard Biscuits

1 cup all-purpose flour
1½ teaspoons double-acting baking powder
½ teaspoon salt
½ stick (¼ cup) cold unsalted butter,
    cut into bits
¼ cup milk plus additional for brushing the
    rounds
1 tablespoon Dijon-style mustard

Into a bowl sift together the flour, the baking powder, and the salt, add the butter, and blend the mixture until it resembles coarse meal. In a measuring cup combine well ¼ cup of the milk and the mustard, add the milk mixture to the flour mixture, and stir the mixture until it just forms a dough. Gather the dough into a ball, knead it gently 6 times on a lightly floured surface, and roll or pat it out ½ inch thick. Cut out as many rounds as possible with a 2½-inch-round cutter dipped in flour and transfer them to an ungreased baking sheet. Brush the tops of the rounds with the additional milk, bake the biscuits in the middle of a preheated 425° F. oven for 15 minutes, or until they are golden, and transfer them to a rack. Makes about 6 biscuits.

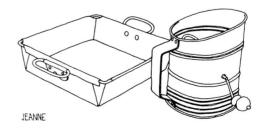

JEANNE

Oatmeal Currant Buttermilk Drop Biscuits

1½ cups all-purpose flour
2 teaspoons double-acting baking powder
½ teaspoon baking soda
2 tablespoons sugar
¾ teaspoon salt
¾ teaspoon cinnamon
1 stick (½ cup) cold unsalted butter,
    cut into bits
¾ cup quick-cooking oats
½ cup dried currants,
    soaked in boiling water
    for 5 minutes and drained well
⅔ cup plus 2 tablespoons buttermilk

Into a bowl sift together the flour, the baking powder, the baking soda, the sugar, the salt, and the cinnamon, add the butter, and blend the mixture until it resembles meal. Stir in the oats and the currants, add the buttermilk, and stir the mixture until it just forms a soft sticky dough. Drop the dough by rounded tablespoons onto a buttered baking sheet and bake the biscuits in the middle of a preheated 425° F. oven for 15 to 17 minutes, or until they are pale golden. Makes about 16 biscuits.

Sour Cream and Dill Drop Biscuits

1¾ cups all-purpose flour
2 teaspoons double-acting baking powder
½ teaspoon baking soda
½ teaspoon salt
½ teaspoon sugar
3 tablespoons snipped fresh dill
4 tablespoons cold vegetable shortening
⅔ cup sour cream
¼ cup milk

Into a bowl sift together the flour, the baking powder, the baking soda, the salt, and the sugar, add the dill and the shortening, and blend the mixture until it resembles meal. Stir in the sour cream and the milk and stir the mixture until it just forms a soft sticky dough. Drop the dough by rounded tablespoons onto a buttered baking sheet and bake the biscuits in the middle of a preheated 425° F. oven for 15 to 17 minutes, or until they are pale golden. Makes about 16 biscuits.

Chocolate Pecan Gems

1 large egg
¼ cup sugar
¼ cup vegetable oil
½ cup plus ⅓ cup all-purpose flour
1 teaspoon double-acting baking powder
¼ teaspoon baking soda
¼ teaspoon salt
1¼ teaspoons cinnamon
1½ ounces fine-quality bittersweet chocolate,
    chopped
¼ cup pecans, toasted and chopped

In a large bowl whisk together the egg, the sugar, and the oil. Into a bowl sift together the flour, the baking powder, the baking soda, the salt, and the cinnamon. Stir the flour mixture into the egg mixture until the batter is just combined, stir in the chocolate and the pecans, and divide the batter among 14 well buttered ⅛-cup gem tins. Bake the muffins in the middle of a preheated 400° F. oven for 12 to 15 minutes, or until a tester comes out clean, and turn them out onto racks. *The muffins may be made 2 days in advance and kept in an airtight container.* Makes 14 muffins.

PHOTO ON PAGE 81

Cherry Orange Sour Cream Muffins

1 cup sour cream
1½ teaspoons freshly grated orange rind
¼ cup fresh orange juice
1 large egg
⅓ cup firmly packed light brown sugar
¼ cup granulated sugar
½ stick (¼ cup) unsalted butter, melted
    and cooled
1½ cups all-purpose flour
2 teaspoons double-acting baking powder
1 teaspoon baking soda
¾ teaspoon salt
1 teaspoon cinnamon
1½ cups (about 6 ounces) dried red tart
    cherries*

In a small bowl whisk together the sour cream, the rind, the orange juice, the egg, the sugars, and the butter until the mixture is combined well. In a bowl whisk together the flour, the baking powder, the baking soda, the salt, and the cinnamon, add the sour cream mixture, and stir the mixture until it is just combined. Stir in the cherries, divide the batter among 12 well buttered ½-cup muffin tins, and bake the muffins in the middle of a preheated 400° F. oven for 15 to 20 minutes, or until they are golden and a tester comes out clean. Let the muffins cool in the tins on a rack for 2 minutes and turn them out onto the rack to cool completely. Makes 12 muffins.

*available year round at specialty food shops and by mail from:

American Spoon Foods
411 East Lake Street
Petoskey, MI 49770
1-800-222-5886

Lemon Walnut Scones

1⅓ cups unbleached all-purpose flour
¼ cup firmly packed light brown sugar
1 tablespoon double-acting baking powder
¾ teaspoon baking soda
1 teaspoon salt
¾ stick (6 tablespoons) cold unsalted butter, cut into bits
⅔ cup whole-wheat flour
⅓ cup miller's bran (available at natural foods stores and some supermarkets)
¾ cup chopped walnuts
⅔ cup raisins
1½ tablespoons freshly grated lemon rind
1 large egg
½ cup buttermilk
an egg wash, made by beating 1 large egg yolk with 1 teaspoon water
softened butter as an accompaniment
assorted jams as accompaniments

Into a bowl sift together the unbleached flour, the brown sugar, the baking powder, the baking soda, and the salt, blend in the butter until the mixture resembles coarse meal, and stir in the whole-wheat flour, the bran, the walnuts, and the raisins until the mixture is combined. In a small bowl whisk together the rind, the egg, and the buttermilk, add the mixture to the flour mixture, and stir the mixture with a fork until it just forms a sticky but manageable dough. Knead the dough lightly on a floured surface for 30 seconds and pat it gently into a ¾-inch-thick round. Cut out rounds with a 2- to 2¼-inch cutter dipped in flour and arrange them on a buttered baking sheet. Form the scraps into a ball, pat the dough into a ¾-inch-thick round, and cut out rounds in the same manner. Arrange the rounds on the baking sheet, brush the tops with the egg wash, and bake the scones in the middle of a preheated 400° F. oven for 15 to 17 minutes, or until they are golden. Serve the scones warm with the butter and the jams. Makes about 12 scones.

PHOTO ON PAGE 63

CRACKERS AND TOASTS

Lemon Pepper Crackers

½ cup all-purpose flour
1 teaspoon coarsely ground black pepper
1 teaspoon freshly grated lemon rind
2 tablespoons cold unsalted butter, cut into pieces
1 tablespoon sour cream
1½ teaspoons fresh lemon juice
coarse salt for sprinkling on the crackers

In a bowl blend the flour, the pepper, the rind, and the butter until the mixture resembles meal, add the sour cream and the lemon juice, and toss the mixture, adding 1 teaspoon water if necessary, until it just forms a dough. Gather the dough into a ball and chill it, wrapped in plastic wrap, for 15 minutes. Roll out the dough 1/16 inch thick on a lightly floured surface and with a 2-inch round cutter cut out 16 rounds. Bake the rounds, sprinkled with the coarse salt, on an ungreased baking sheet in the middle of a preheated 400° F. oven for 12 minutes, or until they are golden. Transfer the crackers to a rack and let them cool for 5 minutes. Makes 16 crackers.

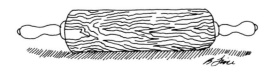

Garlic Jalapeño Cheese Toasts

twelve ¼-inch-thick slices of French or
  Italian bread
1 garlic clove, unpeeled
1 teaspoon minced bottled pickled *jalapeño*
  pepper, including the seeds (wear
  rubber gloves)
2½ tablespoons olive oil
½ cup finely grated Monterey Jack

Toast the bread lightly on the rack of a broiler pan
under a preheated broiler about 4 inches from the heat,
turning it once. In a small saucepan of boiling water
boil the garlic for 5 minutes, peel it, and mash it with
the *jalapeño* pepper to a paste. Brush one side of the
toast with the oil, spread the paste on the oiled sides of
the toast, and sprinkle the Monterey Jack over it. Broil
the toasts on the rack about 4 inches from the heat for
1 to 2 minutes, or until the cheese is bubbling. Makes
12 toasts.

Garlic Toast Rounds

1 long loaf of day-old French or Italian bread
3 garlic cloves, minced
½ teaspoon salt
⅓ cup extra-virgin olive oil (available at
  specialty foods shops and most
  supermarkets)

Cut the bread into ¼-inch slices with a serrated knife
and arrange the slices in one layer on baking sheets.
Mince and mash the garlic with the salt until it forms a
paste. In a small bowl whisk together the oil and the
garlic paste, strain the mixture through a fine sieve into
a bowl, pressing hard on the solids, and brush it on the
bread. Bake the bread in a preheated 350° F. oven for
10 minutes, or until it is golden, and let the toast
rounds cool. *The toast rounds may be made 2 days in
advance and kept in an airtight container.* Makes
about 70 toast rounds.

PHOTO ON PAGE 56

Benne Wafers

¼ cup very fresh sesame (benne) seeds
¾ cup all-purpose flour
¼ teaspoon double-acting baking powder
¼ teaspoon table salt
3 tablespoons cold vegetable shortening
3 tablespoons milk
coarse salt for sprinkling on the cooked wafers

Spread the seeds in a jelly-roll pan and toast them in
the middle of a preheated 350° F. oven, stirring occasionally, for 35 to 45 minutes, or until they are golden
brown. Transfer the seeds to a bowl and chill them, covered, for 20 minutes, or until they are cold. Into a bowl
sift together the flour, the baking powder, and the table
salt, add the shortening, and blend the mixture until it
resembles coarse meal. Add the seeds and the milk and
toss the mixture, adding additional milk if necessary to
form a soft but not sticky dough. Dust the dough lightly
with flour and divide it into thirds. Working with 1 piece
of dough at a time and keeping the others wrapped in
plastic wrap, roll out the dough as thin as possible between sheets of wax paper, peel off the top sheet of paper,
and cut out rounds with a 1-inch cutter. Peel the rounds
from the bottom piece of paper carefully and arrange
them 1 inch apart on ungreased baking sheets. Bake
the wafers in the middle of a preheated 325° F. oven
for 15 to 20 minutes, or until they are very lightly colored. Sprinkle the wafers with the coarse salt, transfer
them to racks, and let them cool. The wafers keep in an
airtight container for 2 weeks. Makes about 60 wafers.

PIZZAS

Broccoli and Ricotta Pizza

4 tablespoons olive oil
¾ pound broccoli, cut into ¾-inch flowerets
  (about 3 cups) and the stems cut into
  ½-inch dice (about 1 cup)
⅔ cup ricotta
1 large egg
2 large garlic cloves
¼ teaspoon salt
⅔ cup freshly grated Parmesan
yellow cornmeal for sprinkling the pan
1 recipe whole-wheat bran pizza dough
  (page 112) or pizza dough (recipe follows)

In a large heavy skillet heat 2 tablespoons of the oil
over moderately high heat until it is hot but not smoking
and in it sauté the broccoli, stirring, for 1 minute, or until it is bright green and well coated with the oil. Add ¼

cup water, cook the broccoli, covered, for 3 minutes, or until it is crisp-tender, and let it stand, uncovered, off the heat. In a bowl whisk together the ricotta and the egg. Mince and mash the garlic with the salt until it forms a paste and whisk it into the ricotta mixture with ⅓ cup of the Parmesan.

Sprinkle an oiled 14-inch black steel pizza pan or black steel baking sheet with the cornmeal. Roll out the dough on a lightly floured surface into a 14-inch round, fit it into the pan, and spread the cheese mixture over it. Transfer the broccoli with a slotted spoon to the pizza, spreading it evenly, sprinkle it with the remaining ⅓ cup Parmesan and salt and pepper to taste, and drizzle the pizza with the remaining 2 tablespoons oil. Bake the pizza on the bottom shelf of a preheated 500° F. electric oven or on the floor of a preheated 500° F. gas oven for 10 to 15 minutes, or until the crust is golden brown. Transfer the pizza with spatulas to a cutting board and cut it into wedges, preferably with a pizza wheel. Serves 2 to 4.

Pizza Dough

a ¼-ounce package (2½ teaspoons) active
   dry yeast
½ teaspoon sugar
2 tablespoons olive oil
2 to 2¼ cups unbleached all-purpose flour
½ teaspoon salt

In a large bowl proof the yeast with the sugar in ⅓ cup lukewarm water for 10 minutes, or until it is foamy. Stir in an additional ⅓ cup lukewarm water, the oil, 2 cups of the flour, and the salt and blend the mixture until it forms a dough. Knead the dough on a floured surface, incorporating as much of the remaining ¼ cup flour as necessary to prevent the dough from sticking, for 5 to 10 minutes, or until it is smooth and elastic.

Alternatively, the dough may be made in a food processor. Proof the yeast as described above and in a food processor combine it with the remaining ingredients. Process the mixture until it forms a ball, adding more water, 1 teaspoon at a time, if it is too dry, or more flour, 1 tablespoon at a time, if it is too wet, and knead the dough by processing it for 15 seconds.

Put the dough, prepared by either method, in an oiled bowl and turn it to coat it with the oil. Let the dough rise, covered with plastic wrap, in a warm place for 1 hour, or until it is double in bulk, and punch it down. The

dough is now ready to be formed into pizzas. Makes enough dough for one 14-inch pizza or four 7-inch pizzas.

Quick Pizza Dough

2 to 2¼ cups unbleached all-purpose flour
a ¼-ounce package fast-acting yeast
½ teaspoon sugar
2 tablespoons olive oil
½ teaspoon salt

In a large bowl whisk together ¾ cup of the flour, the yeast, the sugar, and ⅔ cup hot water (130° F.). Stir in the oil, 1¼ cups of the remaining flour, and the salt and blend the mixture until it forms a dough. Knead the dough on a floured surface, incorporating as much of the remaining ¼ cup flour as necessary to prevent the dough from sticking, for 5 to 10 minutes, or until it is smooth and elastic.

Alternatively, the dough may be made in a food processor. In a food processor combine ¾ cup of the flour, the yeast, and the sugar, with the motor running add ⅔ cup hot water (130° F.), and turn the motor off. Add the oil, 1¼ cups of the remaining flour, and the salt and process the mixture until it forms a ball, adding more water, 1 teaspoon at a time, if it is too dry, or more flour, 1 tablespoon at a time, if it is too wet. Knead the dough by processing it for 15 seconds.

The dough, prepared by either method, may be used immediately, but for better flavor it is best to let it rise once. Put the dough in an oiled bowl and turn it to coat it with the oil. Let the dough rise, covered with plastic wrap, in a warm place for 30 minutes, or until it is double in bulk, and punch it down. This dough may be used instead of the basic pizza dough. Makes enough dough for one 14-inch pizza or four 7-inch pizzas.

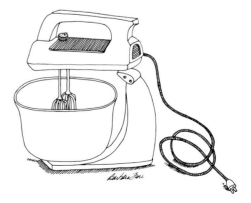

Eggplant Parmigiana Pizza

a 1¼-pound eggplant, cut crosswise into
    ¼-inch slices
6 tablespoons olive oil
yellow cornmeal for sprinkling the pan
1 recipe pizza dough (page 107)
½ cup tomato pizza sauce (recipe follows)
1½ cups grated mozzarella (about 6 ounces)
¼ cup minced fresh parsley leaves
1 tablespoon minced garlic
¾ teaspoon dried thyme
⅓ cup freshly grated Parmesan

Arrange the eggplant slices in one layer on oiled jelly-roll pans and brush them lightly with some of the oil. Broil the slices in batches under a preheated broiler about 2 inches from the heat for 4 to 5 minutes, or until they are golden. Turn the slices, brush them again lightly with some of the remaining oil, reserving 1 tablespoon of the oil, and broil them for 4 to 5 minutes more, or until they are golden.

Sprinkle an oiled 14-inch black steel pizza pan or black steel baking sheet with the cornmeal. Roll out the dough on a lightly floured surface into a 14-inch round and fit it into the pan. Brush the dough with the reserved 1 tablespoon oil and spread it evenly with the tomato sauce. Sprinkle the mozzarella over the sauce and sprinkle the parsley, the garlic, and the thyme over the mozzarella. Arrange the eggplant slices, overlapping them slightly, on the pizza, season the pizza with salt and pepper, and sprinkle it evenly with the Parmesan. Bake the pizza on the bottom shelf of a preheated 500° F. electric oven or on the floor of a preheated 500° F. gas oven for 10 to 15 minutes, or until the crust is golden brown. Transfer the pizza with spatulas to a cutting board and cut it into wedges, preferably with a pizza wheel. Serves 2 to 4.

Tomato Pizza Sauce

1 large garlic clove, minced
¼ teaspoon freshly ground pepper
1 tablespoon olive oil
a 28-ounce can Italian plum tomatoes
    including the juice

In a large heavy saucepan cook the garlic and the pepper in the oil over moderately low heat, stirring, for 2 minutes, or until the mixture is fragrant. Add the tomatoes, squashing them in your hand, with the juice, bring the mixture to a boil, and cook it over moderately low heat, stirring occasionally, for 20 to 30 minutes, or until the sauce is thickened and reduced to about 2 cups. Season the sauce with salt. *The sauce keeps, covered and chilled, for 1 week.* Makes about 2 cups.

Four Cheese Pizza

yellow cornmeal for sprinkling the pan
1 recipe pizza dough (page 107)
    or cornmeal pizza dough (page 111)
½ cup finely diced mozzarella
½ cup finely diced Italian or Danish Fontina
⅓ cup diced Gorgonzola or other blue cheese
⅓ cup freshly grated Parmesan
⅓ cup chopped walnuts
2 tablespoons olive oil
freshly ground pepper to taste

Sprinkle an oiled 14-inch black steel pizza pan or black steel baking sheet with the cornmeal. Roll out the dough on a lightly floured surface into a 14-inch round and fit it into the pan. Sprinkle over the dough the mozzarella, the Fontina, the Gorgonzola, the Parmesan, and the walnuts, drizzle the pizza with the oil, and season it with the pepper. Bake the pizza on the bottom shelf of a preheated 500° F. electric oven or on the floor of a preheated 500° F. gas oven for 10 to 15 minutes, or until the crust is golden brown. Transfer the pizza with spatulas to a cutting board and cut it into wedges, preferably with a pizza wheel. Serves 2 to 4.

Greek Pizza
(Pizza with Tomato, Onion, Peppers, and Feta)

yellow cornmeal for sprinkling the pan
1 recipe pizza dough (page 107)
2 tablespoons olive oil
½ cup tomato pizza sauce (recipe opposite)
¼ pound Feta (preferably fresh), crumbled
    (about ¾ cup)
½ cup thinly sliced red onion
1 green bell pepper, cut crosswise into thin
    rings
¼ cup Kalamata or other brine-cured black
    olives, pitted and sliced
1 tablespoon minced garlic
freshly ground black pepper to taste
1 teaspoon dried orégano

Sprinkle an oiled 14-inch black steel pizza pan or black steel baking sheet with the cornmeal. Roll out the dough on a lightly floured surface into a 14-inch round and fit it into the pan. Brush the dough with 1 tablespoon of the oil and spread it evenly with the tomato sauce. Sprinkle the Feta over the sauce and arrange the onion, the bell pepper, and the olives on the pizza. Sprinkle the pizza with the garlic and the black pepper, crumble the orégano over it, and drizzle the pizza with the remaining 1 tablespoon oil. Bake the pizza on the bottom shelf of a preheated 500° F. electric oven or on the floor of a preheated 500° F. gas oven for 10 to 15 minutes, or until the crust is golden brown. Transfer the pizza with spatulas to a cutting board and cut it into wedges, preferably with a pizza wheel. Serves 2 to 4.

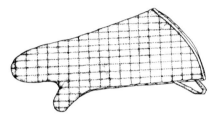

Olive and Basil Pizza with Mozzarella

yellow cornmeal for sprinkling the pan
1 recipe pizza dough (page 107)
1 cup finely diced mozzarella (about
　6 ounces)
½ cup Kalamata or other brine-cured black
　olives, pitted and sliced
1 tablespoon minced garlic
freshly ground pepper to taste
2 tablespoons olive oil
⅓ cup thinly sliced fresh basil leaves

Sprinkle an oiled 14-inch black steel pizza pan or black steel baking sheet with the cornmeal. Roll out the dough on a lightly floured surface into a 14-inch round and fit it into the pan. Sprinkle the dough with the mozzarella, the olives, and the garlic, season the pizza with the pepper and salt to taste, and drizzle it with the oil. Bake the pizza on the bottom shelf of a preheated 500° F. electric oven or on the floor of a preheated 500° F. gas oven for 8 minutes. Sprinkle the basil over the pizza and bake the pizza for 2 to 5 minutes more, or until the crust is golden brown. Transfer the pizza with spatulas to a cutting board and cut it into wedges, preferably with a pizza wheel. Serves 2 to 4.

Pizza Bianca
(*Pizza with Mozzarella, Anchovies, and Garlic*)

yellow cornmeal for sprinkling the pan
1 recipe pizza dough (page 107)
1½ cups grated mozzarella (about 6 ounces)
4 flat anchovy fillets, or to taste, minced
2 large garlic cloves, minced
2 tablespoons freshly grated Parmesan
1 teaspoon dried orégano, crumbled
2 tablespoons olive oil

Sprinkle an oiled 14-inch black steel pizza pan or black steel baking sheet with the cornmeal. Roll out the dough on a lightly floured surface into a 14-inch round and fit it into the pan. In a bowl toss together the mozzarella, the anchovies, and the garlic and spread the mixture on the dough, leaving a ½-inch border. Sprinkle the pizza with the Parmesan, the orégano, and pepper to taste and drizzle it with the oil. Bake the pizza on the bottom shelf of a preheated 500° F. electric oven or on the floor of a preheated 500° F. gas oven for 10 to 15 minutes, or until the crust is golden brown. Transfer the pizza with spatulas to a cutting board and cut it into wedges, preferably with a pizza wheel. Serves 2 to 4.

Pizza Margherita
(*Pizza with Tomato, Mozzarella, and Basil*)

yellow cornmeal for sprinkling the pan
1 recipe pizza dough (page 107)
1½ cups grated mozzarella (about 6 ounces)
1 cup tomato pizza sauce (page 108)
2 large garlic cloves, minced
2 tablespoons olive oil
½ cup thinly sliced fresh basil leaves

Sprinkle an oiled 14-inch black steel pizza pan or black steel baking sheet with the cornmeal. Roll out the dough on a lightly floured surface into a 14-inch round and fit it into the pan. Spread the mozzarella over the dough and spread the tomato sauce evenly over it. Sprinkle the pizza with the garlic and salt and pepper to taste and drizzle the oil over it. Bake the pizza on the bottom shelf of a preheated 500° F. electric oven or on the floor of a preheated 500° F. gas oven for 8 minutes. Sprinkle the basil over the pizza and bake the pizza for 2 to 7 minutes, or until the crust is golden brown. Transfer the pizza with spatulas to a cutting board and cut it into wedges, preferably with a pizza wheel. Serves 2 to 4.

109

Pizza Nissa Socca
(Artichoke, Tomato, and Mushroom Pizza with Capers)

yellow cornmeal for sprinkling the pan
1 recipe pizza dough (page 107)
2 tablespoons olive oil
½ cup tomato pizza sauce (page 108)
a 6-ounce jar marinated artichoke hearts,
    drained and the hearts halved lengthwise
2 large mushrooms,
    sliced very thin
⅔ cup (about ¼ pound) finely diced Cantal
    cheese (available at specialty foods shops)
    or Münster
¼ cup Niçoise black olives or other brine-
    cured black olives
2 teaspoons drained bottled capers (preferably
    large)

Sprinkle an oiled 14-inch black steel pizza pan or black steel baking sheet with the cornmeal. Roll out the dough on a floured surface as thin as possible and fit it into the pan, trimming the excess. Brush the dough with 1 tablespoon of the oil and spread the tomato sauce evenly over it. Arrange on the sauce the artichoke hearts, the mushrooms, the cheese, the olives, and the capers and drizzle the remaining 1 tablespoon oil over the pizza. Bake the pizza on the bottom shelf of a preheated 500° F. electric oven or on the floor of a preheated 500° F. gas oven for 10 minutes, or until the crust is golden brown. Transfer the pizza with spatulas to a cutting board and cut it into wedges, preferably with a pizza wheel. Serves 2 to 4.

Sausage Pizza with Onions and Bell Peppers

1 pound onions, sliced thin
3 tablespoons olive oil
1 small green bell pepper, cut into thin strips
1 small red bell pepper, cut into thin strips
½ pound sweet Italian sausage, casings
    discarded
yellow cornmeal for sprinkling the pan
1 recipe pizza dough (page 107)
6 tablespoons freshly grated Parmesan
1 tablespoon minced garlic
¼ teaspoon dried hot red pepper flakes

In a large heavy skillet cook the onions in the oil, covered, over moderately low heat, stirring occasionally, for 8 minutes. Add the bell peppers and salt and black pepper to taste and cook the mixture, covered, stirring occasionally, for 10 minutes, or until the vegetables are softened.

In a skillet cook the sausage over moderate heat, stirring and breaking up the lumps, just until it is no longer pink and remove the skillet from the heat.

Sprinkle an oiled 14-inch black steel pizza pan or black steel baking sheet with the cornmeal. Roll out the dough on a lightly floured surface into a 14-inch round and fit it into the pan. Sprinkle 4 tablespoons of the Parmesan over the dough and cover it with the onion mixture, spreading it evenly. Transfer the sausage with a slotted spoon to the pizza, spreading it evenly, and sprinkle the pizza with the garlic, the red pepper flakes, and the remaining 2 tablespoons Parmesan. Bake the pizza on the bottom shelf of a preheated 500° F. electric oven or on the floor of a preheated 500° F. gas oven for 10 to 15 minutes, or until the crust is golden brown. Transfer the pizza with spatulas to a cutting board and cut it into wedges, preferably with a pizza wheel. Serves 2 to 4.

Southwestern Pizza
(Spicy Pizza with Monterey Jack, Peppers, and Fresh Coriander)

yellow cornmeal for sprinkling the pan
1 recipe cornmeal pizza dough (recipe
    follows) or pizza dough (page 107)
2 tablespoons olive oil
½ cup tomato pizza sauce (page 108)
¾ teaspoon ground cumin
1 tablespoon minced seeded pickled *jalapeño*
    pepper (wear rubber gloves)
1 cup finely diced Monterey Jack (about ¼
    pound)
½ cup thinly sliced red onion
1 small red bell pepper, cut crosswise into
    thin rings
1 small yellow bell pepper, cut crosswise into
    thin rings
1 tablespoon minced garlic
⅓ cup pitted black olives, sliced crosswise
3 tablespoons chopped fresh coriander,
    or to taste

Sprinkle an oiled 14-inch black steel pizza pan or black steel baking sheet with the cornmeal. Roll out the dough on a lightly floured surface into a 14-inch round, fit it into the pan, and brush it with 1 tablespoon of the oil. In a small bowl whisk together the tomato sauce, the cumin, and the *jalapeño* pepper and spread the mixture evenly on the dough. Sprinkle the Monterey Jack over the mixture and arrange the onion and the bell pepper rings on the pizza. Sprinkle the garlic and the olives on the pizza, season the pizza with salt and pepper, and drizzle it with the remaining 1 tablespoon oil. Bake the pizza on the bottom shelf of a preheated 500° F. electric oven or on the floor of a preheated 500° F. gas oven for 10 to 15 minutes, or until the crust is golden brown. Transfer the pizza with spatulas to a cutting board, sprinkle it with the coriander, and cut it into wedges, preferably with a pizza wheel. Serves 2 to 4.

Cornmeal Pizza Dough

a ¼-ounce package (2½ teaspoons) active dry yeast
½ teaspoon sugar
2 tablespoons olive oil
⅔ cup yellow cornmeal
1¼ to 1½ cups unbleached all-purpose flour
½ teaspoon salt

In a large bowl proof the yeast with the sugar in ⅓ cup lukewarm water for 10 minutes, or until it is foamy. Stir in an additional ⅓ cup lukewarm water, the oil, the cornmeal, 1¼ cups of the flour, and the salt and blend the mixture until it forms a dough. Knead the dough on a floured surface, incorporating as much of the remaining ¼ cup flour as necessary to prevent the dough from sticking, for 5 to 10 minutes, or until it is smooth and elastic.

Alternatively, the dough may be made in a food processor. Proof the yeast as described above and in a food processor combine it with the remaining ingredients. Process the mixture until it forms a ball, adding more lukewarm water, 1 teaspoon at a time, if it is too dry, or more flour, 1 tablespoon at a time, if it is too wet, and

knead the dough by processing it for about 15 seconds.

Put the dough, prepared by either method, in an oiled bowl and turn it to coat it with the oil. Let the dough rise, covered with plastic wrap, in a warm place for 1 hour, or until it is double in bulk, and punch it down. The dough is now ready to be formed into pizzas. Makes enough dough for one 14-inch pizza or four 7-inch pizzas.

Sun-Dried Tomato Pizza with Peppers, Onion, and Garlic Confit

yellow cornmeal for sprinkling the pan
1 recipe pizza dough (page 107) or whole-wheat bran pizza dough (page 112)
1 cup finely diced mozzarella (about 6 ounces)
½ cup thinly sliced red onion
1 small green bell pepper, cut crosswise into thin rings
5 *confit* garlic cloves (page 112), halved lengthwise, or to taste
2 tablespoons freshly grated Parmesan
1 teaspoon dried thyme
1 tablespoon olive oil or oil from a jar of sun-dried tomatoes
12 sun-dried tomatoes packed in oil, drained well and sliced into thin strips

Sprinkle an oiled 14-inch black steel pizza pan or black steel baking sheet with the cornmeal. Roll out the dough on a lightly floured surface into a 14-inch round and fit it into the pan. Sprinkle the mozzarella over the dough and arrange the onion, the bell pepper rings, and the garlic *confit* over the mozzarella. Sprinkle the pizza with the Parmesan and the thyme, drizzle it with the oil, and bake it on the bottom shelf of a preheated 500° F. electric oven or on the floor of a preheated 500° F. gas oven for 7 minutes. Sprinkle the sun-dried tomato strips on the pizza and bake the pizza for 3 to 8 minutes more, or until the crust is golden brown. Transfer the pizza with spatulas to a cutting board and cut it into wedges, preferably with a pizza wheel. Serves 2 to 4.

Whole-Wheat Bran Pizza Dough

a ¼-ounce package (2½ teaspoons) active dry
    yeast
½ teaspoon sugar
2 tablespoons olive oil
¼ cup whole-wheat flour
¼ cup miller's bran (available at natural foods
    stores and many supermarkets)
1⅔ to 2 cups unbleached all-purpose flour
½ teaspoon salt

In a large bowl proof the yeast with the sugar in ⅓ cup lukewarm water for 10 minutes, or until it is foamy. Stir in an additional ⅓ cup lukewarm water, the oil, the whole-wheat flour, the bran, 1⅔ cups of the all-purpose flour, and the salt and blend the mixture until it forms a dough. Knead the dough on a floured surface, incorporating as much of the remaining ¼ cup all-purpose flour as necessary to prevent the dough from sticking, for 5 to 10 minutes, or until it is smooth and elastic.

Alternatively, the dough may be made in a food processor. Proof the yeast as described above and in a food processor combine it with the remaining ingredients. Process the mixture until it forms a ball, adding more lukewarm water, 1 teaspoon at a time, if it is too dry, or more all-purpose flour, 1 tablespoon at a time, if it is too wet, and knead the dough by processing it for 15 seconds.

Put the dough, prepared by either method, in an oiled bowl and turn it to coat it with the oil. Let the dough rise, covered with plastic wrap, in a warm place for 1 hour, or until it is double in bulk, and punch it down. The dough is now ready to be formed into pizzas. Makes enough dough for one 14-inch pizza or four 7-inch pizzas.

Confit Garlic Cloves

1 cup peeled large garlic cloves
¾ to 1 cup olive oil

In a small saucepan combine the garlic with enough of the oil to just cover it, bring the mixture to a simmer, and cook it over moderately low heat for 20 to 25 minutes, or until the garlic is tender. Let the mixture cool and transfer it to a jar. The garlic keeps in the oil, covered and chilled, indefinitely. Makes about 1 cup.

White Clam Pizza

yellow cornmeal for sprinkling the pan
1 recipe pizza dough (page 107)
3 tablespoons olive oil
two 6½-ounce cans minced clams, drained
3 tablespoons minced garlic
¼ teaspoon dried hot red pepper flakes
⅓ cup minced fresh parsley leaves
2 tablespoons freshly grated Parmesan

Sprinkle an oiled 14-inch black steel pizza pan or black steel baking sheet with the cornmeal. Roll out the dough on a lightly floured surface into a 14-inch round and fit it into the pan. Brush the dough with 1 tablespoon of the oil and sprinkle it with the clams, the garlic, the red pepper flakes, the parsley, and the Parmesan. Drizzle the remaining 2 tablespoons oil over the pizza and bake the pizza on the bottom shelf of a preheated 500° F. electric oven or on the floor of a preheated 500° F. gas oven for 10 to 15 minutes, or until the crust is golden brown. Transfer the pizza with spatulas to a cutting board and cut it into wedges, preferably with a pizza wheel. Serves 2 to 4.

SOUPS

Gingered Acorn Squash Soup

1 small acorn squash (about ¾ pound), cut
    into eighths, seeded, peeled with a small
    sharp knife, and cut into ½-inch pieces
1 onion, chopped
3 quarter-size pieces of fresh gingerroot
1 tablespoon unsalted butter
2 cups canned chicken broth
⅓ cup chilled heavy cream
snipped fresh chives or scallion greens
    for garnish

In a saucepan cook the squash, the onion, and the gingerroot in the butter over moderately low heat, stirring occasionally, until the onion is softened. Add the broth, bring the mixture to a boil, and simmer it for 20 to 25 minutes, or until the squash falls apart. Discard the gingerroot and in a blender purée the mixture in batches. Transfer the purée to the pan, cleaned, and heat it over moderate heat, stirring, until it is hot. In a large bowl beat the cream until it holds soft peaks and stir the purée into it until the soup is combined well. Divide the soup between 2 bowls and sprinkle it with the chives. Serve the soup immediately. Makes about 3 cups, serving 2.

Asparagus and Pea Soup with Lemon Butter Toasts

½ pound asparagus, washed well

½ pound unshelled peas,
    washed well and shelled,
    reserving the pods
½ cup canned chicken broth
2 tablespoons unsalted butter, softened
2 teaspoons fresh lemon juice
4 slices of homemade-type white bread, crusts
    removed and the bread halved diagonally to
    form triangles

Cut off and reserve the asparagus tips, snap off and reserve the tough white ends, and reserve the stalks. In a food processor chop coarse the tough white ends and the reserved pea pods. In a saucepan combine the chopped vegetables, the broth, and 3 cups cold water, bring the liquid to a boil, and simmer the mixture for 15 to 20 minutes, or until the liquid is reduced to about 2½ cups. While the mixture is simmering, cut the reserved asparagus tips and stalks into ½-inch pieces. In a small bowl whisk together the butter, the lemon juice, and salt and pepper to taste, divide the butter among the bread triangles, spreading it evenly, and toast the triangles on a baking sheet in the middle of a preheated 400° F. oven for 8 to 10 minutes, or until they are golden. Strain the vegetable mixture through a fine sieve into another saucepan, add the asparagus pieces and the peas, and simmer the vegetables for 4 to 6 minutes, or until they are crisp-tender. Serve the soup with the lemon butter toasts. Makes about 3½ cups, serving 2.

Cold Avgolemono with Cucumber and Mint

5 cups chicken stock (page 123) or canned
   chicken broth
⅓ cup *orzo* (rice-shaped pasta)
¼ cup fresh lemon juice plus additional
   to taste
3 large eggs
1½ cups plain yogurt
white pepper to taste
2 tablespoons minced fresh mint leaves,
   or to taste
1½ cups diced seeded peeled cucumber
lemon slices for garnish
mint sprigs for garnish

In a saucepan combine the stock and 1 cup water and bring the liquid to a boil. Stir in the *orzo* and boil it for 10 minutes, or until it is tender. In a bowl whisk together ¼ cup of the lemon juice and the eggs, add 1 cup of the hot stock mixture in a stream, whisking, and whisk the mixture into the remaining stock mixture. Cook the mixture over moderately low heat, whisking and being careful not to let it boil, for 3 minutes, or until it is thickened slightly, and let it cool. Whisk in the yogurt, the white pepper, and salt to taste and chill the soup, covered, for at least 3 hours or overnight. Stir in the additional lemon juice, the minced mint, and the cucumber, divide the soup among chilled bowls, and garnish it with the lemon slices and the mint sprigs. Makes about 8 cups, serving 6 to 8.

Borscht with Chives

2 pounds beets, trimmed, leaving the roots
   and ½ inch of the stems attached, and
   scrubbed well
3 cups chicken stock (page 123) or canned
   chicken broth
⅔ cup dry red wine
1½ cups chopped onion
3 tablespoons unsalted butter
1 tablespoon firmly packed dark brown sugar
2 tablespoons red-wine vinegar
½ cup sour cream plus additional for garnish
fresh lemon juice to taste
snipped fresh chives for garnish

In a kettle combine the beets, the stock, the wine, and 3 cups water, bring the liquid to a boil, and simmer the mixture, covered, for 30 to 40 minutes, or until the beets are tender. Transfer the beets with a slotted spoon to a bowl, reserving the cooking liquid, let them cool until they can be handled, and peel them. Cut enough of the beets into ½-inch dice to measure 1 cup, reserve them, covered and chilled, and chop coarse the remaining beets. In a large saucepan cook the onion in the butter over moderately low heat, stirring, until it is softened, add the brown sugar and the vinegar, and cook the mixture, stirring, for 2 minutes, or until the sugar is dissolved. Add the coarsely chopped beets and 5 cups of the reserved cooking liquid, strained, bring the liquid to a boil, and simmer the mixture, covered, for 10 minutes. In a blender purée the mixture in batches until it is smooth, transferring it to a bowl, and whisk in ½ cup of the sour cream and salt and pepper to taste. Chill the soup, covered, for at least 4 hours or overnight and stir in the lemon juice. Divide the soup among chilled bowls, top it with the reserved diced beets and the additional sour cream, and garnish it with the chives. Makes about 7 cups, serving 6.

Cool Carrot Orange Soup

⅓ cup chopped onion
2 tablespoons vegetable oil
3 carrots, peeled and sliced thin
½ cup fresh orange juice
white pepper to taste
⅓ cup plain yogurt

In a saucepan cook the onion in the oil over moderately low heat, stirring, until it is softened. Add the carrots and 1 cup boiling water, bring the mixture to a boil, and simmer it, covered partially, for 10 minutes, or until the carrots are very soft. In a blender purée the mixture until it is smooth and transfer the purée to a metal bowl set in a larger metal bowl of ice and cold water. Stir in the orange juice, the white pepper, and salt to taste and stir the mixture until it is cool. Stir in the yogurt, stirring until the soup is smooth, and divide the soup between chilled bowls. Makes about 3 cups, serving 2.

Curried Carrot Vichyssoise

1½ cups chopped leek including 1 inch of the
   green part, washed well and drained
½ cup chopped onion

2 tablespoons unsalted butter
1½ tablespoons curry powder
1½ pounds carrots, sliced thin (about 4 cups)
1 pound boiling potatoes
1 teaspoon salt
2½ cups chicken stock (page 123) or canned
   chicken broth
1 cup milk
1 cup sour cream
white pepper to taste
finely grated blanched carrot for garnish
   if desired

In a heavy kettle cook the leek and the onion in the butter over moderately low heat, stirring, until the vegetables are softened. Stir in the curry powder and cook the mixture, stirring, for 2 minutes. Add the sliced carrots, the potatoes, peeled and cut into ½-inch pieces, the salt, the stock, and 2 cups water, bring the liquid to a boil, and simmer the mixture, covered, for 35 to 40 minutes, or until the potatoes and carrots are very soft. Force the mixture through a food mill fitted with the fine disk into a bowl and force the purée through a fine sieve into another bowl. Whisk in the milk, the sour cream, the white pepper, and salt to taste and chill the soup, covered, for at least 3 hours or overnight. Stir the soup before serving and garnish it with the grated carrot if desired. Makes about 8 cups, serving 6 to 8.

Essence of Celery Soup

11 cups chicken stock (page 123) or canned
   chicken broth
1 cup dry white wine
12 cups chopped celery including the leafy
   tops (about 2 bunches) plus 1 cup thinly
   sliced celery, blanched in boiling salted
   water for 1 minute and drained for
   garnish
2 onions, sliced thin
1 tablespoon celery seeds
2 teaspoons dried thyme
4 large egg whites, beaten lightly
the shells of 4 large eggs, crushed lightly

In a kettle combine the stock, the wine, 6 cups of the chopped celery, and the onions, bring the liquid to a boil, and simmer the mixture, covered, for 30 minutes.

Strain the mixture through a fine sieve set over a large bowl, pressing hard on the solids, and return the liquid to the kettle. Add the remaining 6 cups chopped celery, the celery seeds, the thyme, the whites, and the shells, bring the liquid just to a boil, stirring, and cook the mixture at a bare simmer, undisturbed, for 20 minutes. Ladle the mixture into the fine sieve lined with dampened paper towels set over a large bowl and discard the solids. *The consommé may be made 2 days in advance, cooled uncovered, and kept covered and chilled. Reheat the consommé in the kettle over moderate heat until it is heated through, but do not let it boil.* Put the sliced celery in a heated tureen and ladle the soup into the tureen. Makes about 9 cups, serving 8.

Stracciatella
(Italian Chicken Soup with Egg Strands and Parmesan)

2 large eggs
3 tablespoons Parmesan plus additional
   for sprinkling
1 tablespoon finely chopped fresh
   parsley leaves
1 tablespoon minced scallion including some
   of the green part
about 4 cups wing tip stock (page 123)
   or chicken stock (page 123) or canned
   chicken broth

In a bowl whisk together the eggs, 3 tablespoons of the Parmesan, the parsley, and the scallion. In a saucepan bring the stock to a boil, add the egg mixture in a stream, whisking, and simmer the soup for 2 minutes. Add salt and pepper to taste and serve the soup sprinkled with the additional Parmesan. Makes about 4 cups, serving 4.

Jellied Consommé Madrilène

4½ cups canned beef broth
2½ cups canned chicken broth
3 pounds tomatoes, chopped coarse
1 cup chopped scallion
2 carrots, chopped
1 rib of celery, chopped
½ teaspoon black peppercorns
¼ teaspoon dried thyme, crumbled
1 pound lean ground beef
4 large egg whites plus the shells, crushed
2 tablespoons unflavored gelatin
¼ cup Sercial Madeira
fresh lemon juice to taste
white pepper to taste
Accompaniments
chopped peeled seeded tomato
thinly sliced scallion greens
lemon wedges

In a kettle combine the broths, the tomatoes, the scallion, the carrots, the celery, the peppercorns, the thyme, the beef, and the egg whites and shells, bring the liquid to a boil, stirring, and simmer the mixture, undisturbed, for 1 hour. Ladle the mixture into a sieve lined with a triple thickness of rinsed and squeezed cheesecloth set over a large bowl and skim any fat from the surface. In a small bowl sprinkle the gelatin over the Madeira, let it soften for 5 minutes, and stir the mixture into the hot consommé until the gelatin is dissolved. Let the consommé cool completely, stir in the lemon juice, the white pepper, and salt to taste, and chill the consommé, covered, until it is firm. Divide the consommé among chilled bowls and serve it with the tomato, the scallions, and the lemon wedges. Makes about 5 cups, serving 4 to 6.

Gingered Corn Chowder with Coriander

2 ounces slab bacon (available at many
    butchers' shops and some supermarkets),
    rind discarded and chopped fine
1 onion, chopped coarse
½ teaspoon dried thyme, crumbled
½ teaspoon dried marjoram, crumbled
¼ teaspoon mace
¼ teaspoon freshly ground black pepper
2 tablespoons finely chopped peeled
    fresh gingerroot

½ red bell pepper, chopped fine
½ green bell pepper, chopped fine
3 cups fresh or frozen corn kernels, chopped
    in a food processor for 15 seconds
3½ cups brown stock (page 122) or canned
    beef broth
1 cup heavy cream
⅓ cup chopped fresh coriander

In a large heavy saucepan cook the bacon over low heat, stirring, until all the fat is rendered and transfer the bacon with a slotted spoon to paper towels to drain. Add to the pan the onion, the thyme, the marjoram, the mace, and the black pepper and cook the mixture over moderate heat, stirring, for 3 to 4 minutes, or until the onion is browned lightly. Add the gingerroot and the bell peppers and cook the mixture, stirring occasionally, for 5 minutes. Add the corn and the stock, bring the liquid to a boil, and simmer the mixture, covered, stirring occasionally, for 30 minutes. Add the cream and salt to taste, bring the soup just to a simmer, and stir in the coriander. Serve the soup sprinkled with the bacon. Makes about 7 cups, serving 6.

Mexican Corn Soup

1½ teaspoons minced garlic
3 tablespoons olive oil
1 cup chopped onion
two 2-inch fresh *jalapeño* peppers, seeds and
    ribs discarded and the flesh minced (wear
    rubber gloves)
2 teaspoons ground cumin
1½ teaspoons ground coriander seed
½ cup thinly sliced carrot
½ cup thinly sliced celery
3½ cups chicken stock (page 123) or canned
    chicken broth
8 ears of corn, shucked, the kernels cut off
    the cobs, and the kernels and cobs reserved
    separately
1 red bell pepper, roasted (procedure follows)
    and chopped fine
2 to 3 tablespoons minced fresh coriander or
    parsley leaves, or to taste
cayenne to taste if desired

In a kettle cook the garlic in the oil over moderately low heat, stirring, for 1 minute, add the onion and the

jalapeño peppers, and cook the mixture, stirring, until the onion is softened. Add the cumin, the ground coriander seed, and salt and black pepper to taste and cook the mixture, stirring, for 2 minutes. Add the carrot and the celery and cook the mixture over moderate heat, stirring, for 5 minutes. Add the stock, the corn cobs, and 2½ cups water and simmer the mixture for 15 minutes. Add all but 1 cup of the reserved corn kernels, simmer the mixture for 12 to 15 minutes, or until the kernels are very tender, and discard the cobs. In a blender purée the mixture in batches, blending each batch on high speed for at least 1 minute, or until it is very smooth. (If an even smoother soup is desired, after using the blender force the mixture through a fine sieve set over a bowl, pressing hard on the solids.) Let the soup cool to room temperature. In a small saucepan of boiling water boil the remaining 1 cup reserved corn kernels for 2 to 4 minutes, or until they are tender, drain them in a colander, and refresh them under cold water. Stir the corn into the soup with the roasted bell pepper, the minced coriander, the cayenne, and salt and black pepper to taste and serve the soup at room temperature. Makes about 6 cups, serving 6.

To Roast Bell Peppers or Chilies

Using a long-handled fork char the peppers over an open flame, turning them, for 2 to 3 minutes, or until the skins are blackened. (Or broil the peppers on the rack of a broiler pan under a preheated broiler about 2 inches from the heat, turning them every 5 minutes, for 15 to 25 minutes, or until the skins are blistered and charred.) Transfer the peppers to a bowl and let them steam, covered, until they are cool enough to handle. Keeping the peppers whole, peel them starting at the blossom end, cut off the tops, and discard the seeds and ribs. (Wear rubber gloves when handling chilies.)

Escarole Soup with Meatballs

¼ pound ground veal or lean ground beef
5 tablespoons coarsely grated fresh Parmesan
2 tablespoons finely chopped fresh
    parsley leaves
3 tablespoons fine fresh bread crumbs
¼ teaspoon salt
1 large egg, beaten lightly

3 tablespoons olive oil (preferably extra-
    virgin, available at specialty foods shops,
    some supermarkets, and some natural foods
    stores)
1 cup finely chopped onion
1 teaspoon minced garlic
4 cups packed shredded escarole, rinsed and
    spun dry
2 cups canned chicken broth

In a bowl combine well the veal, 2 tablespoons of the Parmesan, the parsley, the bread crumbs, the salt, half the egg, reserving the remaining egg for another use, and freshly ground pepper to taste and form the mixture into 12 walnut-size balls. (The mixture will be soft.) In a large heavy saucepan heat 1 tablespoon of the oil over moderately high heat until it is hot but not smoking, in it sauté the meatballs, turning them, for 3 minutes, or until they are just firm to the touch and browned lightly, and transfer them with a slotted spoon to a plate. Add the remaining 2 tablespoons oil and the onion to the pan and cook the mixture over moderately low heat, stirring occasionally, until the onion is softened. Add the garlic and cook the mixture, stirring occasionally, for 2 minutes. Add the escarole and cook the mixture, covered, over low heat, stirring occasionally, for 3 minutes, or until the escarole is wilted. Add the broth, the meatballs, and freshly ground pepper to taste, bring the liquid to a boil, and simmer the mixture for 3 minutes. Serve the escarole soup sprinkled with the remaining 3 tablespoons Parmesan. Makes about 3½ cups, serving 2.

Spicy Gazpacho with Shrimp

2 garlic cloves
1 teaspoon salt
enough white bread, crusts removed and the
    bread torn into small pieces, to measure
    1½ cups
¼ cup red-wine vinegar
⅓ cup olive oil
1 teaspoon ground cumin
2½ cups tomato juice
2 pounds tomatoes, peeled, seeded, and
    minced (about 3 cups)
1 green bell pepper, chopped fine (about
    ⅔ cup)
1 red bell pepper, chopped fine (about ⅔ cup)
⅓ cup minced scallion
1 cucumber, peeled, seeded, and minced
⅓ cup minced red onion
½ pound shrimp (about 15), peeled and
    deveined
¼ cup minced fresh parsley, mint, or
    coriander leaves, or a combination
Tabasco to taste
croutons as an accompaniment

On a work surface mince and mash the garlic with the salt until a paste is formed. In a blender combine the garlic paste, the bread, the vinegar, the oil, the cumin, and 1 cup of the tomato juice and blend the mixture until it is smooth. In a large bowl combine well the bread mixture with the tomatoes, the bell peppers, the scallion, the cucumber, and the onion, stir in the remaining 1½ cups tomato juice, and chill the soup, covered, for 3 hours, or until it is very cold. In a saucepan of boiling water boil the shrimp for 30 seconds, or until they are pink and just firm to the touch, transfer them with a slotted spoon to a bowl, and let them cool. Thin the soup with 1 cup ice water, or enough to obtain the desired consistency, add the shrimp, chopped, the parsley, the Tabasco, and salt and black pepper to taste, and serve the soup with the croutons. Makes about 9 cups, serving 6 to 8.

Summer Minestrone

1 tablespoon minced garlic
¼ cup olive oil
1 cup finely chopped red onion
1 bay leaf
¾ teaspoon dried sage, crumbled
¾ teaspoon dried rosemary, crumbled
2½ pounds tomatoes, seeded and chopped
    (about 4 cups)
¼ pound green beans, trimmed and cut into
    ½-inch pieces (about ¾ cup)
1 zucchini, cut into ½-inch dice (about 1 cup)
2 carrots, cut into ¼-inch slices (about ¾ cup)
1 rib of celery, cut into ¼-inch slices
    (about ½ cup)
½ pound boiling potatoes
a 19-ounce can *cannellini* (white beans),
    rinsed and drained well
5 cups chicken stock (page 123) or canned
    chicken broth
½ cup dry white wine
⅓ cup long-grain rice
¼ cup minced fresh basil leaves, or to taste
¼ cup minced fresh parsley leaves, or to taste
freshly grated Parmesan as an accompaniment

In a kettle cook the garlic in the oil over moderately low heat, stirring, for 1 minute, add the onion, the bay leaf, the sage, and the rosemary, and cook the mixture, stirring, until the onion is softened. Add the tomatoes, the green beans, the zucchini, the carrots, the celery, and the potatoes, peeled and cut into ½-inch pieces, and cook the mixture over moderate heat, stirring, for 3 minutes. Add the white beans, the stock, and the wine, bring the mixture to a boil, and simmer it, stirring occasionally, for 15 minutes. Add 1 cup water and the rice, bring the mixture to a boil, and simmer it, covered, for 15 to 20 minutes, or until the rice is tender. Let the soup cool and chill it, covered, for at least 3 hours or overnight. Stir in the basil, the parsley, salt and pepper to taste, and if necessary enough water to obtain the desired consistency. Serve the soup at room temperature with the Parmesan. Makes about 11 cups, serving 6 to 8.

Herbed Ham and Corn Chowder

½ cup chopped onion
2 tablespoons unsalted butter
4 to 6 ounces boneless ham steak,
    cut into ¼-inch dice
¾ pound boiling potatoes
1½ cups milk
½ cup canned chicken broth

¼ teaspoon dried thyme, crumbled, or to taste
a 10-ounce package frozen corn, thawed
¼ cup minced scallion including the
    green part

In a large saucepan cook the onion in the butter over moderately low heat, stirring occasionally, until it is softened, add the ham, the potatoes, peeled and cut into ½-inch dice, the milk, the broth, and the thyme, and bring the mixture to a boil. Simmer the chowder for 10 minutes, stir in the corn and salt and pepper to taste, and simmer the chowder for 10 minutes, or until the potatoes are tender. Stir in the scallion and divide the soup between 2 heated bowls. Makes about 4 cups, serving 2.

Curried Lentil Soup with Tomato and Spinach

⅓ cup finely chopped onion
2 tablespoons vegetable oil
1 garlic clove, minced
1 teaspoon finely grated peeled fresh
    gingerroot
1½ teaspoons curry powder
½ teaspoon ground cumin
½ cup lentils, picked over and rinsed
1¼ cups canned chicken broth
⅓ cup chopped drained canned tomatoes
1 cup firmly packed coarsely chopped
    stemmed spinach leaves, washed well
    and drained
fresh lemon juice to taste

In a large heavy saucepan cook the onion in the oil over moderate heat, stirring, until it is lightly golden, add the garlic and the gingerroot, and cook the mix-ture, stirring, for 1 minute. Add the curry powder and the cumin, cook the mixture, stirring, for 30 seconds, and add the lentils and 1¼ cups water. Bring the liquid to a boil and simmer the mixture, covered, for 5 minutes. Add the broth and simmer the mixture, covered, for 25 minutes. Stir in the tomatoes and the spinach and simmer the soup, stirring occasionally, for 2 minutes. Season the soup with the lemon juice and salt and pepper to taste. Makes 3 cups, serving 2.

Mussel and Parsley Soup

5 pounds mussels
1 cup dry white wine
1 cup minced onion
3 tablespoons unsalted butter
4 large egg yolks
½ cup milk
⅓ cup minced fresh parsley leaves
white pepper to taste
fresh lemon juice to taste

Scrub the mussels well in several changes of water, scrape off the beards, and rinse the mussels. In a large kettle combine the mussels and the wine, bring the wine to a boil over high heat, and steam the mussels, covered, shaking the kettle occasionally, for 4 to 6 minutes, or until the shells have opened. Discard any unopened shells. Drain the mussels in a colander set over a bowl, reserving the liquid, and strain the reserved liquid through a fine sieve lined with several layers of rinsed and squeezed cheesecloth into a large measuring cup. Add enough water to the liquid to measure 4 cups in all and reserve the mussel liquid mixture. Remove the mussels from the shells, discarding all but 8 of the shells, and pull off the mantles (the tough black rims) from the tops of the mussels.

In a large saucepan cook the onion in the butter over moderately low heat, stirring, until it is softened. Add the reserved mussel liquid mixture, bring the mixture to a boil, and simmer the mussel broth for 20 minutes. In a bowl whisk together the yolks and the milk, add about 1 cup of the mussel broth in a stream, whisking, and transfer the mixture to the pan, whisking. Add the pars-ley, the white pepper, and the lemon juice and cook the soup over low heat, stirring, for 5 minutes, but do not let it boil. Stir in the mussels, divide the soup among 4 bowls, and garnish each serving with 2 of the shells if desired. Makes about 5 cups, serving 4.

Manhattan-Style Mussel Chowder

5 pounds mussels
4 slices of lean bacon, cut into ¼-inch pieces
1½ cups chopped onion
1 bay leaf
1 cup chopped green bell pepper
1 cup sliced celery
1 pound boiling potatoes
a 28-ounce can plum tomatoes, drained and
    chopped, reserving the juice
Tabasco to taste

Scrub the mussels well in several changes of water, scrape off the beards, and rinse the mussels. In a kettle steam the mussels with 1 cup water, covered, over moderately high heat for 5 to 7 minutes, or until they are opened. Transfer the mussels with a slotted spoon to a bowl, discard any unopened mussels, and remove the mussels from the shells. Strain the cooking liquid through a fine sieve lined with a triple thickness of rinsed and squeezed cheesecloth and set over a large measuring cup and if necessary add enough water to measure 4 cups liquid.

In the kettle, cleaned, cook the bacon over moderately low heat, stirring, until it is crisp, add the onion and the bay leaf, and cook the mixture, stirring, until the onion is softened. Add the bell pepper and the celery and cook the mixture over moderate heat, stirring, for 2 minutes. Add the potatoes, peeled and cut into ½-inch pieces, the tomatoes with the juice, the mussel cooking liquid, the mussels, and salt and pepper to taste and bring the mixture to a boil. Simmer the chowder, covered, stirring occasionally, for 25 to 30 minutes, or until the potatoes are tender, discard the bay leaf, and season the chowder with the Tabasco. Makes about 12 cups, serving 6 to 8.

Salmon Chowder

½ pound boiling potatoes
½ teaspoon salt
2½ cups milk
¾ cup minced onion
2 tablespoons unsalted butter
½ pound salmon steak, skinned and boned
white pepper to taste
1 tablespoon fresh lemon juice
1 tablespoon all-purpose flour

2 ounces smoked salmon, chopped fine,
    if desired
2 tablespoons snipped fresh dill or 2 teaspoons
    dried
lemon pepper crackers (page 105) as an
    accompaniment

In a saucepan combine the potatoes, peeled and cut into ¼-inch cubes, ¼ teaspoon of the salt, and the milk, bring the liquid to a boil, and simmer the potatoes for 10 minutes, or until they are almost tender. In another saucepan cook the onion in the butter over moderately low heat, stirring occasionally, until it is softened, put the salmon steak on the onion, and sprinkle it with the remaining ¼ teaspoon salt, the white pepper, and the lemon juice. Cook the salmon, its surface covered with a buttered round of wax paper and the pan covered with a lid, turning it once, for 8 to 10 minutes, or until it is just firm to the touch, and transfer it with a slotted spatula to a plate. Sprinkle the flour over the onion and cook the mixture, stirring, for 3 minutes. Add the milk mixture, whisking, and simmer the mixture, stirring occasionally, for 5 minutes. Add the salmon steak, breaking it into chunks, the smoked salmon, the dill, and additional white pepper and salt to taste, cook the chowder over moderate heat, stirring occasionally, until it is heated through, and serve it with the lemon pepper crackers. Makes about 4 cups, serving 2.

Senegalese Soup with Coriander

2 cups canned chicken broth
½ skinless boneless chicken breast
    (about 5 ounces)
1 onion, chopped
¾ cup chopped celery
2 tablespoons vegetable oil
1 tablespoon curry powder
1 teaspoon turmeric
a pinch of cayenne, or to taste
2 tablespoons bottled mango chutney
2 tablespoons minced fresh coriander plus,
    if desired, 2 sprigs for garnish

In a small saucepan bring the broth to a boil and in it poach the chicken at a bare simmer, covered, for 8 minutes, or until it is springy to the touch. While the chicken is poaching, in a saucepan cook the onion and the celery in the oil over moderately low heat, stirring

White Bean Vegetable Soup

2 slices of lean bacon, cut into ¼-inch pieces
1 tablespoon olive oil
⅓ cup finely chopped onion
1 teaspoon minced garlic
1 rib of celery, cut into ¼-inch pieces (about ½ cup)
1 bay leaf
¼ teaspoon crumbled dried rosemary
2 carrots, cut into ¼-inch pieces (about ⅔ cup)
a 19-ounce can white beans, rinsed in a
    colander and drained well
1½ cups canned chicken broth
¼ cup dry white wine
⅓ cup freshly grated Parmesan plus
    additional to taste

In a heavy saucepan cook the bacon over moderate heat, stirring occasionally, until it is crisp, add the oil and the onion, and cook the mixture over moderately low heat, stirring, until the onion is softened. Add the garlic, cook the mixture, stirring, for 1 minute, and add the celery, the bay leaf, and the rosemary. Cook the mixture, covered, over moderate heat, stirring occasionally, for 5 minutes, add the carrots, and cook the mixture, covered, for 5 minutes. In a blender purée 1 cup of the beans with ½ cup of the broth, add the purée to the vegetable mixture with the remaining 1 cup broth, the wine, and salt and pepper to taste, and bring the mixture to a boil. Simmer the mixture, covered, for 10 minutes, stir in the remaining beans, and simmer the soup, covered, stirring occasionally, for 10 minutes, or until the vegetables are tender. Remove the pan from the heat, discard the bay leaf, and add ⅓ cup of the Parmesan, stirring until the cheese is melted. Divide the soup between 2 heated bowls and sprinkle it with the additional Parmesan. Makes about 3 cups, serving 2.

Velvet Pea and Zucchini Soup

¾ pound zucchini, chopped
⅓ cup finely chopped onion
⅓ cup finely chopped white part of scallion
2 tablespoons vegetable oil
⅛ teaspoon dried thyme, crumbled
1½ cups canned chicken broth
2 cups shelled fresh peas (about 2 pounds
    unshelled) or a 10-ounce package frozen
    peas, thawed
sour cream for garnish if desired

In a large heavy saucepan cook the zucchini, the onion, and the scallion in the oil over moderate heat, stirring, for 3 minutes. Add the thyme, the broth, and 1 cup water, bring the liquid to a boil, and simmer the mixture, covered, for 6 minutes. Add the peas and simmer the mixture, uncovered, for 6 minutes, or until the vegetables are tender. Transfer about ⅓ cup of the peas with a slotted spoon to a small bowl, reserving them for garnish, in a blender purée the mixture in batches, and season the soup with salt and pepper. Serve the soup warm or at room temperature in bowls and garnish each bowl with a dollop of the sour cream and some of the reserved peas. Makes about 4 cups, serving 4.

STOCKS

Brown Stock

2 pounds meaty beef shanks, sawed into
    1-inch slices
2 pounds meaty veal shanks, sawed into
    1-inch slices
2 onions, quartered
1 carrot, quartered
2 ribs of celery
1½ teaspoons salt
a cheesecloth bag containing 4 parsley sprigs,
    ½ teaspoon dried thyme, and 1 bay leaf

Spread the beef shanks, the veal shanks, the onions, and the carrot in a flameproof baking pan, brown them well in a preheated 450° F. oven, and transfer them to a kettle. Add 2 cups water to the pan, deglaze the pan over high heat, scraping up the brown bits, and add the liquid to the kettle with 14 cups cold water, the celery, the salt, and the cheesecloth bag. Bring the liquid to a boil and skim the froth. Add ½ cup cold water, bring the mixture to a simmer, and skim any froth. Simmer the mixture, adding boiling water to keep the ingredients barely covered, for 5 to 6 hours, or until the stock is reduced to about 8 cups. Strain the stock through a fine sieve into a bowl, pressing hard on the solids, and let it cool. Chill the brown stock and remove the fat. The brown stock may be frozen. Makes about 8 cups.

occasionally, until the vegetables are softened, stir in the curry powder, the turmeric, and the cayenne, and cook the mixture, stirring, for 2 minutes. Transfer the chicken to a work surface, reserving the broth, and chop it. Add the reserved broth to the vegetable mixture, bring the mixture to a boil, stirring, and simmer it for 5 minutes. In a blender purée the mixture with the chutney and half the chicken until the purée is very smooth and transfer the purée to a metal bowl set in a larger bowl of ice and cold water. Stir the purée until it is cold, stir in the remaining chicken and the minced coriander, and divide the soup between bowls. Garnish each serving with a coriander sprig. Makes about 3 cups, serving 2.

Oriental Snow Pea and Scallop Soup

1½ tablespoons minced peeled fresh
    gingerroot
1 large garlic clove, sliced thin
½ teaspoon black peppercorns
¾ cup thinly sliced scallion
4 cups chicken stock (page 123) or canned
    chicken broth
1 teaspoon soy sauce, or to taste
1½ tablespoons medium-dry Sherry,
    or to taste
1 teaspoon Oriental sesame oil (available at
    specialty foods shops, Oriental markets,
    and most supermarkets), or to taste
¼ pound snow peas, trimmed, discarding the
    strings, and cut crosswise into ½-inch
    pieces
½ pound sea scallops, rinsed, drained well,
    and halved horizontally

In a kettle combine the gingerroot, the garlic, the peppercorns, ½ cup of the scallion, the stock, and 3 cups water, bring the mixture to a boil, and simmer it for 10 minutes. Remove the kettle from the heat, let the mixture cool, and pour it through a fine sieve set over a bowl. Stir in the soy sauce, the Sherry, the oil, and salt and pepper to taste and chill the soup, covered, for at least 3 hours, or until it is cold. In a saucepan of boiling salted water cook the snow peas and the scallops for 1 minute, drain them in a colander, and refresh them under cold water. Stir the snow peas and the scallops into the soup with the remaining ¼ cup scallion. Makes about 7 cups, serving 6.

Spinach Soup with Garlic Croutons

2 cups chicken stock (page 123) or canned
    chicken broth
1 cup sliced scallion including the green part
1 boiling potato (about ½ pound), peeled and
    cut into ¼-inch dice
10 cups firmly packed spinach leaves
    removed from the stems (about 1½ pounds
    with stems), washed well
½ teaspoon sugar
½ teaspoon dried marjoram, crumbled
⅛ teaspoon freshly grated nutmeg
1 tablespoon fresh lemon juice
½ cup heavy cream
garlic croutons (recipe follows)

In a large saucepan combine the stock, 2 cups water, the scallion, and the potato, bring the liquid to a boil, and simmer the mixture for 10 minutes, or until the potato is tender. Stir in the spinach, the sugar, the marjoram, the nutmeg, and the lemon juice and bring the liquid to a boil. Simmer the mixture for 1 minute, or until the spinach is wilted, and stir in the cream. In a blender purée the mixture in batches, transferring it to another large saucepan, and heat the soup over moderate heat, stirring, until it is hot. Divide the soup among heated bowls and sprinkle each serving with some of the croutons. Makes about 7 cups, serving 6.

Garlic Croutons

2 large garlic cloves, halved
2 tablespoons unsalted butter
½ cup ½-inch cubes of pumpernickel bread
    (made from about 2 slices)
½ cup ½-inch cubes of homemade-type white
    bread (made from about 2 slices)

Rub a small heavy skillet with the cut sides of the garlic and in it cook the garlic in the butter over moderately low heat, stirring, for 5 minutes, or until it is golden. Discard the garlic, add the pumpernickel and white bread cubes, and cook them, tossing them, until they are toasted lightly. Sprinkle the croutons with salt to taste and transfer them to paper towels to drain. Makes about 1 cup croutons.

Chicken Stock

a 4-pound fowl including the neck and giblets
   (except the liver)
1 large onion, stuck with 2 cloves
2 leeks, halved lengthwise and washed well
2 carrots
1 rib of celery, halved
2 teaspoons salt
a cheesecloth bag containing 4 parsley sprigs,
   ½ teaspoon dried thyme, 1 unpeeled garlic
   clove, and 1 bay leaf

In a kettle combine the fowl, the neck and giblets, chopped, and 12 cups cold water and bring the water to a boil, skimming the froth. Add ½ cup cold water and bring the mixture to a simmer, skimming the froth. Add the onion, the leeks, the carrots, the celery, the salt, and the cheesecloth bag and simmer the mixture, skimming the froth, for 2 hours. Remove the fowl from the kettle, remove the meat and skin from the carcass, and reserve the meat for another use. Chop the carcass, return it and the skin to the kettle, and simmer the stock, adding boiling water if necessary to keep the ingredients barely covered, for 2 hours more. Strain the stock through a fine sieve into a bowl, pressing hard on the solids, and let it cool. Chill the stock and remove the fat. The stock may be frozen. Makes about 6 cups.

Turkey Giblet Stock

the giblets from 1 turkey (excluding the liver),
   chopped
3 cups chicken stock (recipe precedes)
1 onion stuck with 1 clove
1 carrot, halved
1 rib of celery, chopped
a cheesecloth bag containing 3 sprigs of
   parsley, ¼ teaspoon dried thyme, and
   ½ bay leaf

In a saucepan combine the giblets, the stock, 3 cups water, the onion, the carrot, and the celery, bring the liquid to a boil, and skim the froth as it rises to the surface. Add the cheesecloth bag and cook the mixture over moderately low heat for 1 hour. Strain the stock through a fine sieve into a bowl, pressing hard on the solids, and let it cool. Chill the stock and remove the fat. The stock may be frozen. Makes about 3 cups.

White Fish Stock

1 pound bones and trimmings of any white
   fish such as sole, flounder, or whiting,
   chopped
1 cup sliced onion
12 parsley stems
2 tablespoons fresh lemon juice
½ teaspoon salt
½ cup dry white wine

In a well buttered heavy saucepan combine the fish bones and trimmings, the onion, the parsley, the lemon juice, and the salt and steam the mixture, covered, over moderately high heat for 5 minutes. Add 3½ cups cold water and the wine, bring the liquid to a boil, skimming the froth, and cook the stock over moderate heat for 25 minutes. Strain the stock through a fine sieve into a bowl, pressing hard on the solids, and let it cool. The stock may be frozen. Makes about 3 cups.

J. Oliver

Wing Tip Stock

2½ pounds chicken wing tips (about 125) or
   chicken wings
2 onions, chopped coarse
½ rib of celery, chopped coarse
½ bay leaf
½ teaspoon dried thyme, crumbled
8 parsley stems
1 teaspoon peppercorns

In a large saucepan combine the wing tips with 12 cups cold water, bring the water to a boil, skimming the froth, and simmer the mixture, skimming the froth occasionally, for 15 minutes. Add the onions, the celery, the bay leaf, the thyme, the parsley stems, and the peppercorns and simmer the mixture, skimming the froth occasionally, for 2 hours and 30 minutes. Strain the stock through a fine sieve into a large bowl, pressing hard on the solids, and let it cool. Chill the stock, remove the fat, and in a saucepan boil the stock until it is reduced to about 4 cups. Makes about 4 cups.

FISH AND SHELLFISH

FISH

Bluefish with Lemon Caper Brown-Butter Sauce

two 6-ounce bluefish fillets
1 tablespoon vegetable oil
2 tablespoons unsalted butter
1 tablespoon fresh lemon juice
2 teaspoons drained bottled capers

Season the bluefish with salt and pepper. In a heavy skillet heat the oil over moderately high heat until it is hot but not smoking and in it sauté the bluefish, skin sides down, turning it once, for 6 to 8 minutes, or until it just flakes. While the bluefish is cooking, in a small heavy saucepan cook the butter over moderately high heat, swirling the pan occasionally, until the foam subsides and the butter is nut-brown, remove the pan from the heat, and swirl in the lemon juice and the capers. Transfer the bluefish to 2 heated plates and spoon the butter sauce over it. Serves 2.

Spinach- and Ham-Stuffed Flounder Rolls

½ stick (¼ cup) unsalted butter
1 cup finely chopped cooked ham
8 cups firmly packed spinach leaves removed
   from the stems (about 1 pound with stems),
   washed well, spun dry, and chopped fine
½ cup plus 2 tablespoons dry white wine
¼ teaspoon dried thyme, crumbled
1 tablespoon Dijon-style mustard
4 flounder fillets (about 2 pounds)
2 bay leaves
1½ tablespoons all-purpose flour
2 tablespoons heavy cream
1 teaspoon fresh lemon juice, or to taste

In a large skillet melt 2 tablespoons of the butter over moderate heat, add the ham, the spinach, 2 tablespoons of the wine, the thyme, and the mustard, and cook the mixture, stirring, until the spinach is wilted and most of the excess liquid is evaporated. Transfer the spinach mixture to a bowl, season it with salt and pepper, and let it cool.

Halve the flounder fillets lengthwise along the backbone seam. Lay 1 piece of fish skinned side up on a work surface, season it with salt and pepper, and spread about 2 tablespoons of the spinach mixture over it. Beginning with the wide end, roll up the flounder jelly-roll fashion and secure the roll with a wooden pick. Make rolls with the remaining flounder in the same manner, using about 2 tablespoons of the spinach mixture for each roll and reserving the remaining spinach mixture for the sauce, and arrange the rolls in a buttered saucepan just large enough to hold them in one layer. In a small saucepan combine the remaining ½ cup wine, ½ cup water, and the bay leaves, bring the liquid to a boil, and pour the mixture over the flounder rolls. Poach the flounder rolls, covered, at a bare simmer for 6 to 8 minutes, or until they just flake when tested with a fork, transfer them with a slotted spoon to a platter, reserving the poaching liquid, and keep them warm, covered, in a preheated 150° F. oven.

In a small saucepan melt the remaining 2 tablespoons butter over moderately low heat, add the flour, and cook the *roux*, whisking, for 3 minutes. Whisk in the reserved poaching liquid, the cream, and the reserved spinach mixture, bring the mixture to a boil, whisking, and simmer it, whisking, for 4 minutes. Strain the sauce through a fine sieve set over a small bowl, pressing hard on the solids, and season it with the lemon juice and salt and pepper to taste. Divide the flounder rolls among 4 plates and pour some of the sauce over each serving. Serves 4.

Baked Ocean Perch with Tomato, Black Olives, and Feta

⅓ cup finely chopped onion
2 tablespoons olive oil
2 garlic cloves, minced
¼ cup dry white wine
⅛ teaspoon dried thyme, crumbled
⅛ teaspoon dried orégano, crumbled
a 14- to 16-ounce can whole tomatoes,
    drained, reserving ¼ cup of the liquid, and
    chopped fine
¾ pound ocean perch fillets or other firm-
    fleshed white fish fillets
¼ cup brine-cured black olives such as
    Kalamata, pitted and chopped
⅓ cup crumbled Feta cheese

In a skillet cook the onion in the oil over moderately low heat, stirring, until it is softened, add the garlic, and cook the mixture, stirring, for 1 minute. Add the wine and boil the mixture until almost all the liquid is evaporated. Add the thyme, the orégano, and the tomatoes with the reserved liquid, bring the mixture to a boil, and cook it over moderate heat, stirring occasionally, for 5 minutes, or until it is thickened slightly. Spread half the sauce in the bottom of a gratin dish or baking dish just large enough to hold the perch in one layer, top it with the perch, skin sides down, and spread the remaining sauce over the perch. Sprinkle the olives and the Feta evenly over the sauce and bake the perch in the middle of a preheated 400° F. oven for 15 to 20 minutes, or until it just flakes when tested with a fork. Serves 2.

Grilled Salmon with Mustard Mint Sauce

For the sauce
1½ tablespoons Dijon-style mustard
1½ tablespoons coarse-grained mustard
3 tablespoons white-wine vinegar
¼ cup firmly packed fresh mint leaves,
    or to taste
¾ cup olive oil

a 2½-pound salmon fillet with the skin
vegetable oil for brushing the salmon and
    the grill
wild rice pilaf with scallions (recipe follows)
    as an accompaniment
mint sprigs for garnish

Make the sauce: In a blender blend together well the mustards, the vinegar, and the mint, with the motor running add the oil in a slow stream, and blend the sauce until it is emulsified.

With a sharp knife held at an angle almost parallel to the cutting board cut the salmon, beginning at the narrow end, into cutlets about 1 inch thick, cutting it off the skin. (There should be 12 to 14 cutlets.) Brush 1 side of each cutlet with some of the oil and grill the salmon, oiled sides down, in batches on a well oiled rack set 4 to 5 inches over glowing coals for 1 to 2 minutes, or until the bottom edges change color and appear cooked. Brush the tops of the cutlets with some of the remaining oil, season them with salt and pepper, and turn the cutlets carefully. Grill the cutlets for 1 to 2 minutes more, or until they are barely cooked through. (The salmon will continue to cook off the heat.) Transfer the salmon with spatulas as it is cooked to a platter lined with the wild rice pilaf. Alternatively, the salmon may be cooked in the same manner in a well seasoned ridged grill pan brushed with oil and heated over moderately high heat until the oil begins to smoke.

Just before serving, spoon some of the sauce over the salmon, garnish the platter with the mint sprigs, and serve the remaining sauce separately. Serve the salmon warm or at room temperature. Serves 6.

PHOTO ON PAGE 51

Wild Rice Pilaf with Scallions

1½ cups wild rice, rinsed well and
    drained well
1 tablespoon olive oil
3 cups canned chicken broth
1 tablespoon fresh lemon juice, or to taste
⅔ cup thinly sliced scallion including the
    green part

In a heavy saucepan cook the rice in the oil over moderate heat, stirring, until it is coated well, add the broth, and bring it to a boil. Cook the rice, covered, over low heat for 1 hour to 1 hour and 10 minutes, or until it has absorbed the broth, and stir in the lemon juice, the scallion, and pepper to taste. Serve the rice warm or at room temperature. Serves 6.

PHOTO ON PAGE 51

*Open-Faced Sardine and Egg Salad Sandwiches with
Yogurt Green Peppercorn Dressing*

¾ cup plain yogurt
2 hard-boiled large eggs, sliced thin
    lengthwise, reserving 4 slices for garnish
    and the remaining slices chopped fine
a 3¾-ounce can brisling sardines packed in
    oil, drained, reserving 4 sardines for
    garnish and the remaining sardines
    chopped coarse
2 large iceberg lettuce leaves, rinsed, spun
    dry, and chopped
3 tablespoons finely chopped radish plus
    thinly sliced radish for garnish
2 tablespoons thinly sliced scallion greens
    plus diagonally sliced scallion greens
    for garnish
2 teaspoons Dijon-style mustard
2 teaspoons drained bottled green
    peppercorns, mashed
2 teaspoons drained bottled capers, minced
four 5-inch French rolls

Drain the yogurt in a fine sieve set over a bowl, covered and chilled, for 30 minutes. While the yogurt is
draining, in a bowl combine the chopped egg, the
chopped sardines, the lettuce, the 3 tablespoons
chopped radish, and the 2 tablespoons thinly sliced scallion greens. In a small bowl whisk together the yogurt,
the mustard, the peppercorns, the capers, and salt to
taste and toss the dressing with the salad until the salad
is combined well. Cut a ¾-inch slice from the top of
each roll with a serrated knife, discard the crumb from
the rolls, leaving a ¼-inch shell, and divide the salad
among the shells. Garnish the sandwiches decoratively
with the sliced radish, the reserved egg slices, the diagonally sliced scallion greens, and the reserved sardines.
Serves 2.

Chilled Lemon- and Basil-Marinated Sea Bass

six ½-pound sea bass fillets, skinned and cut
    crosswise into 1¼-inch-wide strips
the rind of 1 lemon, removed in strips with a
    vegetable peeler
½ cup fresh lemon juice
⅓ cup white-wine vinegar
1½ teaspoons salt
½ teaspoon sugar

1½ cups extra-virgin olive oil (available at
    specialty foods shops and many
    supermarkets)
½ cup finely chopped fresh basil leaves plus
    basil sprigs for garnish
2 large garlic cloves, chopped
2 teaspoons dried hot red pepper flakes
1 cup dry white wine
2 bay leaves
2 parsley sprigs
½ cup finely chopped red bell pepper

In the bottom of a shallow dish large enough to hold
the sea bass in one layer arrange the rind evenly. In a
bowl whisk together the lemon juice, the vinegar, ½
teaspoon of the salt, and the sugar, add the oil in a
stream, whisking, and whisk the marinade until it is
emulsified. Whisk in ¼ cup of the chopped basil, the
garlic, and the red pepper flakes. In a large kettle
combine the wine, the bay leaves, the parsley, the
remaining 1 teaspoon salt, and 4 cups water, bring the
liquid to a boil, and reduce the heat to a simmer. Poach
the sea bass, covered, in the liquid in batches for 1½
minutes, or until it is just firm to the touch, and transfer it carefully with a slotted spatula to the dish with
the lemon rind. Pour the marinade over the sea bass
and let the sea bass marinate, covered and chilled, for
at least 8 hours or overnight. Let the sea bass stand at
room temperature for 1 hour, transfer it with a slotted
spatula to small plates, and strain the marinade through
a fine sieve set over a bowl. Whisk the marinade until
it is emulsified and drizzle some of it over each serving. Sprinkle each serving with some of the ¼ cup
chopped basil and some of the red bell pepper and
garnish each serving with a basil sprig. Serves 8 to 10.

Sole with Lemon Ginger Sauce and Fried Leek

1 large leek, trimmed, leaving ½ inch of the green
vegetable oil for deep-frying
2 tablespoons minced shallot
2 teaspoons grated peeled fresh gingerroot
2 tablespoons unsalted butter
½ cup dry white wine
½ teaspoon salt
two 6- to 7-ounce sole fillets
1 teaspoon cornstarch
1 tablespoon strained fresh lemon juice
1 large egg yolk

Remove the 2 outer leaves of the leek by making a lengthwise slit through them from top to bottom and peeling them off. Slice the 2 leaves thin crosswise, reserving the remaining leek for another use. Wash the sliced leek well and let it soak in a bowl of ice and cold water for 10 minutes. Drain the leek and pat it dry. In a saucepan fry the leek carefully, 1 tablespoon at a time, in 1 inch of 360° F. oil for 30 seconds, or until it is browned lightly (the oil will splatter considerably), and transfer it with a slotted spoon to paper towels to drain. Sprinkle the fried leek with salt and keep it warm in a preheated 200° F. oven.

In a small saucepan combine the shallot, the gingerroot, the butter, the wine, the salt, and ½ cup water, bring the liquid to a boil, and boil the mixture for 10 minutes, or until it is reduced to about ¾ cup. Working with 1 sole fillet at a time and holding it skinned side up, fold the ends in on top of the sole, overlapping them, and arrange the fillets folded side up in a small skillet just large enough to hold them in one layer. Strain the wine mixture through a sieve over the sole, pressing hard on the solids and discarding them, and poach the sole, its surface covered with a buttered round of wax paper, at a bare simmer, turning it once, for 3 minutes, or until it just flakes. Pour the cooking liquid carefully into a saucepan and let the sole stand in the skillet off the heat, covered with the wax paper. Boil the cooking liquid until it is reduced to about ½ cup. In a small bowl whisk together the cornstarch and the lemon juice, add the mixture in a stream to the boiling liquid, whisking, and simmer the mixture for 2 minutes. In a bowl whisk together the yolk and 1 teaspoon water, add half the hot liquid in a stream, whisking, and whisk the mixture into the remaining hot liquid. Cook the sauce over moderate heat, stirring, until it is thick enough to coat the spoon, but do not let it boil. Transfer the sole with a slotted spatula to 2 heated plates, nap it with the sauce, and mound the fried leek on top. Serves 2.

Sole Paupiettes with Orange Rosemary Butter Sauce

two 6- to 8-ounce sole fillets, the thicker end
   of each fillet flattened slightly between
   dampened sheets of wax paper
freshly ground white pepper to taste
½ cup dry white wine
1 tablespoon minced shallot
¼ teaspoon salt

For the sauce
2 tablespoons minced shallot
¼ cup white-wine vinegar
¼ cup dry white wine
1 teaspoon freshly grated orange rind
¼ cup fresh orange juice
1 tablespoon minced fresh rosemary
½ stick (¼ cup) cold unsalted butter,
   cut into bits
For garnish
peeled halved orange slices
blanched julienne strips of orange rind
rosemary sprigs

Arrange the fillets, skinned sides up, on a work surface and season them with salt and the white pepper. Cut each fillet lengthwise into thirds. Beginning with the narrow (tail) end of each piece, roll up the pieces jelly-roll fashion and secure them with wooden picks. In a buttered skillet just large enough to hold the *paupiettes* in one layer combine the wine, 2 cups water, the shallot, the salt, and white pepper to taste and bring the liquid to a simmer. Arrange the *paupiettes*, cut sides up, in the skillet and poach them, covered with a buttered round of wax paper, at a bare simmer for 4 to 6 minutes, or until they flake when tested with a fork and are no longer translucent in the center. Transfer the *paupiettes* with a slotted spatula to paper towels to drain and keep them warm, covered, on 2 dinner plates.

Make the sauce: In a small heavy saucepan combine the shallot, the vinegar, the wine, the rind, the orange juice, and the rosemary and cook the mixture over moderately high heat until the liquid is reduced to about 2½ tablespoons. Strain the mixture through a fine sieve into the pan, pressing hard on the solids, and add 1 tablespoon cold water. Whisk in the butter, 1 piece at a time, over low heat, lifting the pan from the heat occasionally to cool the mixture and adding each new piece of butter before the previous one has melted completely. (The sauce must not get hot enough to liquefy.) Season the sauce with salt and white pepper.

Spoon a pool of sauce around the *paupiettes* and garnish the plates with the orange slices, the rind, and the rosemary. Serves 2.

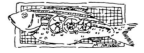

Swordfish with Sesame Seeds and Ginger

2 teaspoons sesame seeds
½ teaspoon ground ginger
½ teaspoon coarse kosher salt
¼ teaspoon freshly ground pepper
two 1-inch-thick swordfish, mako shark, or
    tuna steaks (about ½ pound each)
2 teaspoons vegetable oil
2 scallions including the green part, cut into
    2-inch julienne strips

In a small bowl combine well the sesame seeds, the ginger, the salt, and the pepper and rub the mixture onto both sides of each swordfish steak. In a heavy skillet heat the oil over moderately high heat until it is hot but not smoking and in it cook the swordfish steaks for 5 minutes on each side, or until they are just cooked through. Transfer the steaks with a spatula to heated plates. In the skillet cook the scallions, stirring, for 30 seconds, or until they are just wilted, and divide them between the swordfish steaks. Serves 2.

SHELLFISH

Baked Stuffed Clams

6 slices of lean bacon (about 6 ounces)
2 tablespoons unsalted butter
1 teaspoon minced garlic
1 cup finely chopped onion
⅔ cup finely chopped green bell pepper
48 medium hard-shelled clams, shucked
    (procedure follows), reserving 40 of the
    bottom shells, and chopped fine
1 cup fine dry bread crumbs
½ cup minced fresh parsley leaves
2 tablespoons fresh lemon juice
Tabasco to taste
lemon wedges as an accompaniment

In a large heavy skillet cook the bacon over moderate heat until it is crisp, transfer it to paper towels to drain, and chop it fine. To the fat in the skillet add the butter and the garlic and cook the mixture over moderately low heat, stirring, for 1 minute. Add the onion and the bell pepper and cook the mixture, stirring, until the vegetables are softened. Remove the skillet from the heat and stir in the clams, the bacon, the bread crumbs, the parsley, the lemon juice, the Tabasco, and salt and pepper to taste. Arrange the reserved clam shells in one layer in 2 jelly-roll pans, divide the stuffing among them, and bake the clams in the middle of a preheated 450° F. oven for 12 to 15 minutes, or until they are golden. Serve the clams with the lemon wedges. Serves 8.

To Shuck Hard-Shelled Clams

Scrub the clams thoroughly with a stiff brush under cold water, discarding any that have cracked shells or that are not shut tightly.

Working over a bowl to reserve the liquor hold each clam in the palm of the hand with the hinge against the heel of the palm. Force a clam knife between the shells, cut around the inside edges to sever the connecting muscles, and twist the knife slightly to open the shells.

If the clams are not to be served raw they may be opened in the oven: Arrange the clams in one layer in a baking pan and put the pan in a preheated 450° F. oven for 3 to 5 minutes, or until the shells have opened. Reserve the liquor and discard any unopened clams.

Finnish Dilled Crayfish

3 large bunches of dill, separated into stalks
    and sprigs and the stalks halved crosswise
⅓ cup coarse salt
4 teaspoons sugar
5 pounds live crayfish (available seasonally at
    some fish markets and some specialty foods
    shops), washed well in several changes of
    water and drained, or 2 pounds
    large shrimp

In a large kettle combine 7½ quarts cold water, the dill stalks, the salt, and the sugar, bring the liquid to a boil, covered, and simmer the mixture, covered, for 5 minutes. Bring the liquid to a boil over high heat, add the crayfish, and cook them, covered, stirring occasionally, for 5 to 7 minutes, or until the tail meat is just firm. Transfer the crayfish with a sieve to a large colander, discarding the dill stalks and reserving the cooking liquid, drain them, and let the cooking liquid cool. (If using shrimp, add the shrimp to the boiling cooking liquid, cook them, uncovered, for 1 to 2 minutes, or until they are just firm, and drain them in the same manner.)

Line a large bowl with the dill sprigs, reserving several sprigs for garnish, add the crayfish, and pour in enough of the reserved cooking liquid to just cover them. Let the crayfish marinate, covered and chilled, for at least 8 hours and up to 24 hours. Drain the crayfish, arrange them on a platter, and garnish them with the reserved dill sprigs. Serves 10 to 12.

PHOTO ON PAGE 42

Mussels on the Half Shell with Niçoise Mayonnaise
For the mayonnaise
1 large egg at room temperature
1½ tablespoons fresh lemon juice
1½ teaspoons Dijon-style mustard
1 cup olive oil
1½ tablespoons tomato paste
3 flat anchovy fillets, drained, patted dry, and
   chopped fine
2 garlic cloves, mashed to a paste with
   ½ teaspoon salt
¼ cup drained Kalamata olives or other brine-
   cured black olives, patted dry, pitted, and
   chopped fine

3 pounds mussels
minced fresh basil leaves for garnish
   if desired

Make the mayonnaise: In a blender with the motor on high or in a food processor blend the egg, the lemon juice, and the mustard, add the oil in a slow stream, and turn the motor off. Add the tomato paste, the anchovies, the garlic, the olives, and salt and pepper to taste and blend the mayonnaise until it is combined well. Transfer the mayonnaise to a small bowl and chill it, covered.

Scrub the mussels well in several changes of water, scrape off the beards, and rinse the mussels. In a kettle steam the mussels with 1 cup water, covered, over moderately high heat for 5 to 7 minutes, or until they are opened, transfer them with a slotted spoon to a bowl, and discard any unopened mussels. Remove the mussels from the shells, discarding half the shells, and arrange 1 mussel in each of the remaining shells. Transfer the mussels to a large platter and chill them, covered,

for at least 30 minutes and up to 2 hours. Just before serving spoon about 1 teaspoon of the mayonnaise over each mussel and sprinkle the mussels with the basil. Serves 4 to 6.

Mussels Steamed in Wine with Julienne Vegetables
4 pounds mussels
⅓ cup minced shallot
3 tablespoons olive oil
1 bay leaf
½ teaspoon dried thyme, crumbled
¾ teaspoon fennel seeds, crushed lightly
1½ cups julienne strips of carrot
1½ cups julienne strips of leek, washed well
   in a colander and drained
1 cup dry white wine
3 tablespoons unsalted butter, softened
3 tablespoons all-purpose flour
¼ cup chopped fresh parsley leaves
fresh lemon juice to taste
French bread as an accompaniment

Scrub the mussels well in several changes of water, scrape off the beards, and rinse the mussels. In a kettle cook the shallot in the oil over moderately low heat, stirring, until it is softened, add the bay leaf, the thyme, the fennel seeds, the carrot, and the leek, and cook the mixture over moderate heat, stirring, for 5 to 6 minutes, or until the vegetables are crisp-tender. Add the wine and ½ cup water and bring the mixture to a boil. Add the mussels and steam them, covered, over moderately high heat for 5 to 7 minutes, or until they are opened. Transfer the mussels and the vegetables with a slotted spoon to a heated bowl, discarding any unopened mussels, and keep the mussels covered. Strain the cooking liquid through a fine sieve lined with a triple thickness of rinsed and squeezed cheesecloth and set over a large measuring cup and if necessary add enough water to measure 4 cups liquid. In a saucepan bring the liquid to a boil. In a small bowl knead together the butter and the flour until the mixture is combined well, add the mixture, a little at a time, to the liquid, whisking, and bring the sauce to a boil. Boil the sauce for 2 minutes, whisking, and add the parsley, the lemon juice, and salt and pepper to taste. Divide the mussels and vegetables among 4 heated bowls, pour some of the sauce over each serving, and serve the mussels with the bread. Serves 4.

Deep-Fried Mussels with Tartar Sauce

For the tartar sauce
1 cup mayonnaise (page 220)
¾ teaspoon Dijon-style mustard
1½ tablespoons minced scallion
1½ tablespoons minced onion
¼ cup finely chopped dill pickle
1 hard-boiled large egg, forced through a
    coarse sieve
1½ tablespoons fresh lemon juice, or to taste

3 pounds mussels
1 cup all-purpose flour
cayenne to taste
3 large eggs
3 tablespoons heavy cream
1⅓ cups fine fresh bread crumbs
⅔ cup yellow cornmeal
vegetable oil for deep-frying

Make the tartar sauce: In a bowl stir together the mayonnaise, the mustard, the scallion, the onion, the pickle, the egg, the lemon juice, and salt and pepper to taste and chill the sauce, covered.

Scrub the mussels well in several changes of water, scrape off the beards, and rinse the mussels. Holding the curved side of each mussel against the palm of one hand with the hinged end facing you, insert a small sharp knife carefully between the shells along the flat side and through the broad end and pry the shells apart. Scrape each mussel from its two shells to release it in one piece and transfer the mussels as they are shucked to a sieve. Rinse the mussels well and drain them.

In a shallow bowl stir together the flour, the cayenne, and salt and black pepper to taste. In a bowl whisk together the eggs and the cream and in another bowl stir together well the bread crumbs and the cornmeal. In a deep fryer or large deep kettle heat 2 inches of the oil to 375° F. Working in batches of 6 to 8 mussels, dredge the mussels quickly in the flour mixture, shaking off the excess, dip them in the egg mixture, and roll them in the cornmeal mixture, coating them completely. In a deep fryer fry the mussels in batches in the oil, making sure the oil returns to 375° F. before adding the next batch, for 1 to 2 minutes, or until they are golden and crisp, transfer them as they are fried to a baking sheet lined with paper towels, and keep them warm in a 250° F. oven. Serve the deep-fried mussels with the tartar sauce. Serves 6.

Spinach- and Mushroom-Stuffed Mussels
with Curry Sauce

4 pounds mussels
2 teaspoons minced garlic
1 cup dry white wine
3 tablespoons olive oil
4 teaspoons minced peeled fresh gingerroot
½ cup finely chopped onion
¼ cup minced scallion
½ pound fresh mushrooms, chopped (about
    2 cups)
a 10-ounce package frozen chopped spinach,
    thawed, drained, and squeezed dry
½ cup fresh bread crumbs
½ stick (¼ cup) unsalted butter
6 tablespoons all-purpose flour
2 teaspoons curry powder, or to taste
3 tablespoons chopped fresh coriander if
    desired
fresh lemon juice to taste
cooked rice as an accompaniment

Scrub the mussels well in several changes of water, scrape off the beards, and rinse the mussels. In a kettle combine 1 teaspoon of the garlic, the wine, and 1 cup water, bring the mixture to a boil, and add half the mussels, reserving the remaining mussels, chilled. Steam the mussels, covered, over moderately high heat for 4 to 6 minutes, or until they are opened, transfer them with a slotted spoon to a bowl, and discard any unopened mussels. Remove the mussels from the shells, discarding the shells, chop them fine, and reserve them. Strain the cooking liquid through a fine sieve lined with a triple thickness of rinsed and squeezed cheesecloth and set over a large measuring cup, if necessary add enough water to measure 3 cups liquid, and reserve it. In a large heavy skillet cook the remaining 1 teaspoon garlic in the oil over moderately low heat, stirring, for 1 minute, add 2 teaspoons of the gingerroot, ¼ cup of the onion, and 2 tablespoons of the scallion, and cook the mixture, stirring, until the onion is softened. Add the mushrooms and cook the mixture over moderate heat, stirring, for 5 minutes, or until all the liquid the mushrooms give off is evaporated. Stir in the spinach, the bread crumbs, the reserved chopped mussels, and salt and pepper to taste and remove the skillet from the heat.

Holding the curved side of each of the reserved mussels against the palm of one hand with the hinged end facing you, insert a small sharp knife carefully between the shells along the flat side and through the broad end of the mussel and pry the shells apart, leaving them attached at the hinged end. Stuff each mussel with about 1 tablespoon of the stuffing, pressing the shells together to close them, and tie each mussel closed tightly with kitchen string.

In the kettle, cleaned, cook the remaining ¼ cup onion, the remaining 2 tablespoons scallion, and the remaining 2 teaspoons gingerroot in the butter over moderately low heat, stirring, until the onion is softened, add the flour and the curry powder, and cook the *roux*, stirring, for 3 minutes. Add the reserved mussel cooking liquid in a stream, whisking, and bring the sauce to a boil, whisking. Simmer the sauce, whisking, for 2 minutes, add the mussels, and simmer the mixture, covered, for 20 minutes. Transfer the mussels with a slotted spoon to a large bowl, keep them warm, covered, and add to the sauce the coriander, the lemon juice, and salt and pepper to taste, stirring until the sauce is combined well. Discard the strings from the mussels, arrange the stuffed mussels on the rice, and spoon the sauce over them. Serves 4.

Oyster Stew

½ cup finely chopped onion
1 large garlic clove, minced
2 tablespoons unsalted butter
2 teaspoons all-purpose flour
12 shucked oysters including their liquor
¾ cup half-and-half
¼ cup dry white wine
¼ teaspoon dried thyme, crumbled
2 teaspoons Worcestershire sauce
¼ cup minced fresh parsley leaves

In a saucepan cook the onion and the garlic in the butter over moderately low heat, stirring, until they are softened, add the flour, and cook the *roux*, stirring, for 3 minutes. Drain the oysters in a fine sieve set over a measuring cup and add enough water to the liquor if necessary to measure ¾ cup. Whisk into the pan the oyster liquor, the half-and-half, the wine, the thyme, and the Worcestershire sauce, bring the mixture to a boil, whisking, and simmer it, whisking occasionally, for 4 minutes. Add the oysters, the parsley, and salt and pepper to taste and cook the stew for 1 minute, or until the oysters plump and the edges begin to curl. Makes about 2 cups, serving 2.

Oysters on the Half Shell with Cider Horseradish Cream

12 shucked oysters, reserving the oyster liquor
    and the bottom shells, rinsed and dried
⅓ cup apple cider
2 tablespoons heavy cream
2 tablespoons drained bottled horseradish, or
    to taste
2 teaspoons fresh lemon juice
1 tablespoon minced fresh parsley leaves

In a saucepan combine the reserved oyster liquor and the cider, bring the liquid to a boil, and boil it, skimming the froth, until it is reduced to about ⅓ cup. Add the cream and boil the mixture, stirring, until it is reduced to about ⅓ cup. Set the pan in a bowl of ice and cold water, stir the mixture until it is cold, and stir in the horseradish, the lemon juice, the parsley, and salt and pepper to taste. Arrange the reserved oyster shells on a platter, put 1 oyster in each shell, and spoon the sauce over the oysters. Serves 2 as a first course.

Herbed Scalloped Oysters

1 cup fresh bread crumbs
1 cup fresh cracker crumbs
1 stick (½ cup) unsalted butter, melted
¼ cup minced fresh parsley
    leaves
¼ cup snipped fresh dill
48 oysters, shucked (page 132) reserving
    3 tablespoons of the liquor
1½ tablespoons heavy cream
Tabasco to taste
lemon wedges as an accompaniment
    if desired

In a bowl stir together the bread crumbs, the cracker crumbs, the butter, the parsley, and the dill, spread half the mixture in the bottom of a 13- by 9-inch baking pan, and on it arrange the oysters in one layer. In a small bowl stir together the reserved oyster liquor, the cream, the Tabasco, and salt and pepper to taste and drizzle the liquid evenly over the oysters. Cover the oysters with the remaining crumb mixture, bake them in the middle of a preheated 425° F. oven for 20 to 25 minutes, or until the crumbs are golden, and serve the oysters with the lemon wedges. Serves 8.

To Shuck Oysters

Scrub the oysters thoroughly with a stiff brush under running cold water. Hold each oyster in a kitchen towel in the palm of the hand with the hinged end away from you, force an oyster knife between the shells at the hinged end, pressing down on the knife to pop open the shell, and slide the blade against the flat upper shell to cut the large muscle and free the upper shell. If the shell crumbles and cannot be opened at the hinge, insert the knife between the shells at the curved end of the oyster, pry the shells open, and sever the large muscle. Break off and discard the upper shell and slide the knife under the oyster to release it from the bottom shell.

Bay Scallops with Tomato Sauce and Fried Shallots

¾ pound bay scallops
1 tablespoon all-purpose flour
2 tablespoons olive oil
¼ cup dry white wine
⅓ cup bottled clam juice
⅓ cup tomato juice
vegetable oil for frying
¼ pound shallots, sliced thin crosswise and
    reserved in a bowl of cold water
¼ cup minced fresh parsley leaves

In a bowl toss together the scallops, the flour, and salt and pepper to taste. In a skillet large enough to hold the scallops in one layer without crowding heat the olive oil over high heat until it is hot but not smoking, in it sauté the scallops, stirring, for 1 to 2 minutes, or until they are just firm, and transfer them to a bowl. Add the wine to the skillet, deglaze the skillet, scraping up the brown bits, and stir in the clam juice and the tomato juice. Bring the liquid to a boil and simmer it until it is reduced to about ½ cup. While the liquid is simmering, in a deep heavy skillet heat 1 inch of the vegetable oil until it reg-

isters 375° F. on a deep-fat thermometer, add the shallots carefully, drained well and patted dry, and fry them, stirring, for 1 minute, or until they are golden. Transfer the shallots with a slotted spoon to paper towels to drain and sprinkle them with salt to taste. Add the parsley and the scallops to the tomato sauce, cook the mixture over moderately high heat, stirring, until the scallops are heated through, and serve the scallop mixture with the shallots sprinkled over it. Serves 2.

Foil-Baked Scallops with Ginger, Mushrooms,
and Water Chestnuts

1 teaspoon minced garlic
2 tablespoons unsalted butter
¼ cup thinly sliced scallion
½ teaspoon grated peeled fresh gingerroot
½ teaspoon freshly grated lemon rind
¼ pound mushrooms, sliced (about 1 cup)
⅓ cup thinly sliced drained canned water
    chestnuts
1 tablespoon fresh lemon juice
1 teaspoon Oriental sesame oil (available at
    most supermarkets, specialty foods shops,
    and Oriental markets) plus additional for
    brushing the foil
¾ pound sea scallops, rinsed, drained well,
    and halved horizontally
1 tablespoon minced fresh coriander

In a heavy skillet cook the garlic in the butter over moderately low heat, stirring, for 1 minute, add the scallion, the gingerroot, and the rind, and cook the mixture, stirring, for 1 minute. Add the mushrooms and the water chestnuts, cook the mixture, stirring, for 2 to 3 minutes, or until all the liquid the mushrooms give off is evaporated, and stir in the lemon juice and salt and pepper to taste. Fold 2 pieces of 20- by 12-inch foil in half by bringing the short ends together, unfold each piece, and brush each piece lightly with the additional oil. Arrange half the scallops, seasoned with salt and pepper, just to one side of each fold line and top the scallops with the vegetable mixture. Sprinkle each serving with ½ teaspoon of the remaining oil and 1½ teaspoons of the coriander, fold the foil over the scallop vegetable mixture to enclose it, and fold the edges together to form tightly sealed packets. Bake the packets on a baking sheet in the middle of a preheated 450° F. oven for 10 minutes. Transfer the packets to plates and slit them open at the table or alternatively open them carefully, transfer the scallop vegetable mixtures to plates, and pour the juices over them, discarding the foil. Serves 2.

Grilled Sea Scallops with Sautéed Cabbage

3 cups thinly sliced cabbage
1 tablespoon unsalted butter
1 teaspoon fresh lemon juice
1 teaspoon distilled white vinegar
¾ teaspoon minced fresh thyme or
    ¼ teaspoon dried, crumbled
¾ pound sea scallops
vegetable oil for brushing the scallops

In a large heavy skillet cook the cabbage in the butter, covered, over moderately high heat, stirring occasionally, for 10 to 15 minutes, or until it is crisp-tender, and stir in the lemon juice, the vinegar, the thyme, and salt and pepper to taste. Transfer the cabbage mixture to a platter and keep it warm, covered. Heat a well seasoned ridged grill pan over moderately high heat until it begins to smoke, in it grill the scallops, brushed lightly with the oil, in batches, turning them once, for 3 to 4 minutes, or until they are just cooked through, and arrange them on the cabbage. (Alternatively, the scallops can be sautéed in the heavy skillet.) Serves 2.

Tricolor Scallop Terrine
with Basil, Corn, and Red Pepper

1 cup firmly packed fresh basil leaves,
    washed well and drained, plus 4 small basil
    sprigs for garnish if desired
1 pound sea scallops, rinsed and patted dry
¾ teaspoon salt
white pepper to taste
1⅓ cups well chilled heavy cream
⅓ cup cooked corn kernels (cut from about
    1 ear of corn) or thawed frozen
¼ cup drained bottled roasted red pepper,
    patted dry well on paper towels
4 small soft-leafed lettuce leaves for garnish
    if desired
saffron mayonnaise (page 134) as an
    accompaniment

In a small saucepan steam the basil leaves in the water clinging to them, covered, over moderately high heat for 1 to 2 minutes, or until they are just wilted. Drain the basil in a sieve, rinse it under cold water, and drain it well. Squeeze the basil dry.

Discard the tough bit of muscle clinging to the side of each scallop if necessary and in a food processor purée one third of the scallops with the basil, ¼ teaspoon of the salt, and some of the white pepper. With the motor running add ½ cup of the cream and blend the mixture well. Transfer the basil mixture to a small bowl and chill it, covered, while making the corn and red pepper mixtures.

In the food processor, cleaned, purée the corn with half the remaining scallops, ¼ teaspoon of the remaining salt, and some of the white pepper, with the motor running add ½ cup of the remaining cream, and blend the mixture well. Transfer the corn mixture to another small bowl and chill it, covered, while making the red pepper mixture.

In the food processor, cleaned, purée the red pepper with the remaining scallops, the remaining ¼ teaspoon salt, and some of the white pepper, with the motor running add the remaining ⅓ cup cream, and blend the mixture well.

In a buttered loaf pan, 8 by 4 by 2¾ inches spread the basil mixture in an even layer, top it with the corn mixture, spreading the corn mixture in an even layer, and cover the corn mixture with the red pepper mixture, spreading the red pepper mixture in an even layer. Cover the surface with buttered wax paper and cover the pan with foil. Set the pan in a larger baking pan, add enough hot water to the baking pan to come one fourth of the way up the sides of the loaf pan, and bake the terrine in the middle of a preheated 375° F. oven for 30 to 35 minutes, or until it is firm to the touch and a skewer comes out clean. Transfer the loaf pan to a rack, remove the foil, and let the terrine cool. Remove the paper, invert a platter over the loaf pan, and invert the terrine onto it. Pour off any liquid and chill the terrine, covered with plastic wrap, for at least 2 hours or overnight. *The terrine may be made 1 day in advance and kept covered and chilled.* Cut twelve ½-inch-thick slices from the terrine and arrange 3 slices decoratively on each of 4 plates. Arrange 1 lettuce leaf in the center of each plate, spoon some of the saffron mayonnaise into each leaf, and garnish the mayonnaise with the basil sprigs. Serves 4 with leftovers.

PHOTO ON PAGE 54

Saffron Mayonnaise

a pinch of saffron threads, crumbled
1 teaspoon fresh lemon juice, or to taste
½ cup bottled mayonnaise

In a small bowl combine the saffron and the lemon juice and let the mixture stand, stirring occasionally, for 15 minutes. Add the mayonnaise and blend the mixture well. Makes about ½ cup.

PHOTO ON PAGE 54

Shrimp Creole

1½ pounds (about 44) small shrimp, shelled, reserving the shells, and deveined
½ stick (¼ cup) unsalted butter
2 garlic cloves, halved
⅓ cup finely chopped onion
½ cup finely chopped red bell pepper
½ cup finely chopped green bell pepper
½ cup chopped mushrooms (about 2 ounces)
¼ cup finely chopped celery
2 teaspoons sweet paprika
3 tablespoons all-purpose flour
1 tablespoon tomato paste
2 tablespoons sour cream
¼ teaspoon Tabasco, or to taste
rice ring (recipe follows) as an accompaniment
minced fresh parsley leaves for garnish

Rinse the shrimp well in a colander, drain them, and pat them dry on paper towels. In a bowl rinse the reserved shells well in several changes of cold water, drain them in the colander, and in a small saucepan combine them with 2 cups water. Bring the water to a boil and simmer the mixture for 20 minutes. Strain the broth through a fine sieve set over a large measuring cup. (There should be about 1¼ cups shrimp broth. If not, add enough water to measure 1¼ cups broth or boil the broth until it is reduced to about 1¼ cups.) Reserve the shrimp broth.

In a large heavy skillet melt 2 tablespoons of the butter over moderately low heat and in it cook the garlic, stirring, until it is pale golden. Discard the garlic with a slotted spoon, add the shrimp, and cook them over moderate heat, stirring, for 3 minutes, or until they are barely pink but not cooked through. Transfer the shrimp mixture to a bowl, add the remaining 2 tablespoons but-

ter to the skillet, and in it cook the onion, the bell peppers, the mushrooms, and the celery, stirring, for 5 minutes. Add the paprika and the flour and cook the mixture over moderately low heat, stirring, for 3 minutes. Stir in the tomato paste and the reserved shrimp broth and bring the mixture to a boil. Add the shrimp mixture, including any liquid that has accumulated in the bowl, and simmer the mixture, stirring occasionally, for 3 minutes, or until the shrimp are just cooked through. Stir in the sour cream and the Tabasco, bring the mixture just to a simmer, stirring, and season it with salt and pepper. *The shrimp Creole may be made 1 day in advance and kept covered and chilled. Reheat the shrimp Creole in the skillet over moderately low heat, stirring, until it is heated through, but do not let it boil.* Spoon the shrimp Creole into the center and around the edge of the rice ring and garnish the dish with the parsley. Serves 4.

PHOTO ON PAGE 36

Rice Ring

softened unsalted butter for coating the mold
1½ cups unconverted long-grain rice, cooked in a rice steamer according to the manufacturer's instructions or steamed (page 180)

Butter a 1½-quart ring mold generously, pack it firmly and evenly with the rice while the rice is still hot, and cover it tightly with foil. *The rice ring may be prepared up to this point 1 hour in advance and kept warm in a 250° F. oven.* Invert a heated platter over the mold and invert the rice ring onto it. Serves 4 to 6.

PHOTO ON PAGE 36

Ginger and Bourbon Shrimp on Snow Peas

½ cup julienne strips of peeled fresh gingerroot
2 tablespoons minced shallot
3 tablespoons unsalted butter
1½ pounds (about 20) jumbo shrimp, shelled and deveined
¼ teaspoon dried rosemary, crumbled
a pinch of dried thyme, crumbled
2 tablespoons bourbon

1 tablespoon Grand Marnier

½ cup white fish stock (page 123) or chicken stock (page 123) or canned chicken broth

⅔ cup heavy cream

¾ pound snow peas, trimmed, blanched in boiling salted water for 30 seconds, and drained

In a small saucepan combine the gingerroot with ¾ cup water, bring the water to a boil, and simmer the mixture for 10 minutes. Drain the gingerroot, reserving it and 3 tablespoons of the cooking liquid separately. In a large heavy skillet cook the shallot in 2 tablespoons of the butter over moderately low heat, stirring occasionally, until it is golden, increase the heat to moderately high, and add the shrimp, the rosemary, and the thyme. Sauté the mixture, stirring, for 3 minutes, or until the shrimp are just firm to the touch, and transfer the shrimp with a slotted spoon to a bowl. Add the bourbon and the Grand Marnier to the skillet carefully and deglaze the skillet over moderately high heat, scraping up the brown bits. Add the reserved ginger cooking liquid and the stock and boil the liquid until there is only enough left to coat the bottom of the skillet. Add the cream and boil the mixture until it is reduced by half.

While the cream mixture is being reduced, in another large skillet cook the snow peas in the remaining 1 tablespoon butter over moderately low heat, stirring occasionally, until they are heated through and add salt and pepper to taste. Add to the reduced cream mixture the shrimp and any juices that have accumulated in the bowl and the reserved gingerroot and cook the mixture over moderately low heat, stirring occasionally, until it is heated through. Arrange the snow peas decoratively on 4 heated plates and mound the shrimp mixture on them. Serves 4.

MEAT

BEEF

Blackened Cajun Burger
with Onion and Tomato Relish

1 tomato, chopped fine
1 small red onion, chopped fine
2 teaspoons white-wine vinegar
1 tablespoon vegetable oil
½ teaspoon salt
⅛ teaspoon dried thyme, crumbled
2 teaspoons chili powder
1 teaspoon paprika
½ teaspoon freshly ground black pepper
¼ teaspoon cayenne
¼ teaspoon freshly ground white pepper
¾ pound ground chuck
2 Kaiser or other hard rolls, halved
  horizontally

In a small bowl combine well the tomato, the onion, the vinegar, the oil, ¼ teaspoon of the salt, and the thyme and chill the relish, covered. In another small relish bowl combine well the remaining ¼ teaspoon salt, the chili powder, the paprika, the black pepper, the cayenne, and the white pepper. Halve the chuck, shape each half into a ¾-inch-thick patty, and coat the patties thoroughly with the spice mixture. Heat a well seasoned cast-iron skillet over high heat until it begins to smoke, add the burgers, and reduce the heat to moderately high. Cook the burgers, covered, turning them once, for 6 minutes for medium-rare meat.

Arrange a roll, cut sides up, on each of 2 plates, set a burger on each bottom half, and with a slotted spoon top it with some of the onion and tomato relish. Serve any remaining relish separately. Serves 2.

Piñón
(Caribbean Beef, Egg, and Banana Casserole)

6 slices of lean bacon, chopped coarse
1 pound lean ground beef
2 onions, chopped
1 green bell pepper, chopped
2 garlic cloves, minced
2 hard-boiled large eggs, chopped
4 large pimiento-stuffed olives, chopped
1 cup canned tomato purée
1½ teaspoons dried orégano, crumbled
1 teaspoon salt
1 pound green beans, trimmed, cut into 1-inch
  pieces, blanched in boiling salted water for
  5 minutes, refreshed in a bowl of ice and
  cold water, and drained
2 tablespoons vegetable oil
6 large eggs, beaten lightly with
  1 teaspoon salt
8 firm-ripe bananas

In a large heavy skillet cook the bacon over moderate heat, stirring occasionally, until it is crisp and transfer it with a slotted spoon to paper towels to drain. Add to the skillet the beef, the onions, and the bell pepper, cook the mixture, stirring and breaking up the beef, until the beef is browned lightly, and stir in the garlic. Add the hard-boiled eggs, the olives, the tomato purée, the orégano, the salt, and pepper to taste, cook the mixture over moderately low heat, stirring occasionally, for 10 minutes, and stir in the green beans.

Brush a 10-inch round baking dish (3 inches deep) with the oil. Pour half the beaten eggs into the dish, arrange half the bananas, halved crosswise and halved lengthwise, in one layer on them, and spread half the beef mixture over the bananas. Arrange the remaining bananas on the beef mixture, spread the remaining beef mixture over them, and pour the remaining beaten eggs over the beef mixture. Bake the *piñón* in the middle of a preheated 350° F. oven for 30 to 35 minutes, or until the eggs are set. Serves 8.

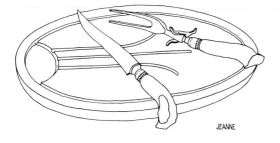

JEANNE

Beef and Green Banana Curry

¼ cup vegetable oil
3 pounds boneless beef chuck pot roast,
    cut into 1½-inch cubes
1 onion, chopped coarse
3 carrots, chopped coarse
1 large garlic clove, minced
1½ teaspoons turmeric
1½ teaspoons ground coriander
1½ teaspoons ground cumin
½ teaspoon cinnamon
½ teaspoon ground ginger
1 cup dry red wine
2 cups canned beef broth
2 cups canned tomato purée
4 large green bananas, cut into 1-inch pieces,
    blanched in simmering salted water for
    2 minutes, and drained well
cooked rice as an accompaniment

In a kettle heat 1 tablespoon of the oil over moderately high heat until it is hot but not smoking and in it brown the beef, patted dry and seasoned with salt and pepper, in batches, adding 2 tablespoons of the remaining oil as necessary and transferring the beef as it is browned to a bowl. To the kettle add the remaining oil, the onion, and the carrots and cook the mixture over moderately high heat, stirring occasionally, until the onion is softened and the vegetables are golden. Add the garlic, the turmeric, the coriander, the cumin, the cinnamon, and the ginger and cook the mixture, stirring, for 30 seconds. Stir in the wine, the broth, the tomato purée, and 1 cup water, bring the liquid to a boil, and simmer the mixture, covered partially, stirring occasionally, for 2 hours to 2 hours and 30 minutes, or until the beef is tender. Stir in the bananas carefully, simmer the curry, covered partially, for 10 to 12 minutes, or until the bananas are tender but not soft, and serve it over the rice. Serves 6 to 8.

Filets Mignons with Mushrooms and Red-Wine Sauce

the white part of 1 leek, sliced thin crosswise,
    rinsed well in a sieve, and drained
1 carrot, halved lengthwise and sliced thin
    crosswise
6 ounces mushrooms, sliced thin
½ teaspoon dried thyme, crumbled
2½ tablespoons olive oil
two 1¾-inch-thick filets mignons (about
    ½ pound each), secured with wooden picks
    if necessary
freshly ground black pepper to taste
⅓ cup dry red wine
½ cup canned beef broth
3 tablespoons cold unsalted butter,
    cut into bits

In a heavy skillet (preferably cast iron) cook the leek, the carrot, the mushrooms, and the thyme in 1½ tablespoons of the oil over moderately low heat, stirring occasionally, until the vegetables are softened, transfer the vegetable mixture to a platter, and keep it warm, covered. In the skillet heat the remaining 1 tablespoon oil over moderately high heat until it is hot but not smoking and in it brown the filets, patted dry and seasoned with the pepper and salt, turning them once, for 2 minutes. Reduce the heat to moderately low, cook the filets, turning them once, for 10 minutes more for medium-rare meat, and transfer them to the platter. Add the wine to the skillet, deglaze the skillet over high heat, scraping up the brown bits, and stir in the broth. Boil the wine mixture until it is reduced to about ⅓ cup, remove the skillet from the heat, and add the butter, swirling the skillet until the butter is incorporated. Season the sauce with salt and pepper and strain it through a fine sieve over the filets. Serves 2.

Filets Mignons with Orange Béarnaise Sauce

the rind of 1 navel orange, removed with a
    vegetable peeler and minced (about 3
    tablespoons), plus additional rind cut into
    fine julienne strips for garnish
2 teaspoons coarsely ground black
    peppercorns
1 teaspoon dried tarragon, crumbled
four 2-inch-thick filets mignons, the edges
    wrapped with thin slices of fresh pork fat or
    bacon secured with kitchen string
2 tablespoons vegetable oil
roasted green beans and roasted scallions
    (pages 183 and 197) as accompaniments
orange béarnaise sauce (recipe follows)

Let the julienne strips of rind stand at room temperature for 3 hours, or until they are curled. On a plate combine well the minced rind, the ground peppercorns, and
the tarragon, press the mixture onto the tops and bottoms of the filets, and chill the filets, wrapped in plastic
wrap, for at least 8 hours or overnight. In a heavy skillet
heat the oil over moderately high heat until it is hot but
not smoking and in it sear the filets, brushed off lightly
and sprinkled with salt to taste, for 2 minutes on each
side. Reduce the heat to moderate and cook the filets,
turning them on all sides, for 15 minutes more for rare
meat. Transfer the filets to a platter, remove the strings,
and garnish the filets with the curled julienne rind. Garnish the platter with some of the roasted green beans and
roasted scallions and serve the remaining roasted green
beans and roasted scallions and the orange béarnaise
sauce separately. Serves 4.

PHOTO ON PAGE 18

Orange Béarnaise Sauce

¼ cup tarragon-wine vinegar (available at
    many supermarkets)
2 tablespoons minced shallot
2 tablespoons minced fresh tarragon or
    2 teaspoons dried
½ teaspoon freshly grated orange rind
3 tablespoons fresh orange juice
¼ teaspoon salt
¼ teaspoon white pepper
3 large egg yolks
2 sticks (1 cup) unsalted butter, melted and
    cooled slightly

In a small heavy saucepan combine the vinegar, the
shallot, the tarragon, the rind, the orange juice, the salt,
and the white pepper, bring the liquid to a boil, and reduce it over moderately high heat to about 2 tablespoons. Transfer the mixture to a blender or food
processor, add the yolks, and turn the motor on and immediately off. With the motor running add the butter in
a stream. Transfer the sauce to a bowl and keep it warm,
its surface covered with a buttered round of wax paper,
in a saucepan of warm water. Makes about 1 cup.

PHOTO ON PAGE 18

Swedish Meatballs

⅔ cup fine dry bread crumbs
1⅓ cups heavy cream
⅔ cup finely chopped onion
1 stick (½ cup) plus 3 tablespoons cold
    unsalted butter
1½ pounds ground round
½ pound ground pork
2 teaspoons salt, or to taste
⅛ teaspoon ground cloves
¼ cup vegetable oil
⅓ cup minced fresh parsley leaves

In a bowl let the bread crumbs soak in the cream for
10 minutes. In a skillet cook the onion in 3 tablespoons
of the butter over moderately low heat until it is softened
and let it cool. In a bowl combine well the bread crumb
mixture, the onion mixture, the ground round, the pork,
the salt, the cloves, and pepper to taste and form rounded teaspoons of the mixture into meatballs. In the skillet
brown the meatballs in batches in the oil over moderate
heat, shaking the skillet to maintain the round shapes,
and transfer them as they are browned to a shallow
flameproof casserole.

Pour off the oil from the skillet, add ¾ cup boiling
water, and deglaze the skillet over high heat, scraping
up the brown bits. Pour the sauce over the meatballs,
bring it to a boil, and simmer the meatballs, covered, for
8 to 10 minutes, or until they are no longer pink within.
Transfer the meatballs with a slotted spoon to a bowl
and keep them covered. Bring the sauce to a boil and
boil it until it is reduced to about 1 cup. Remove the casserole from the heat, add the remaining 1 stick butter,
cut into bits, and swirl the casserole until the butter is
incorporated. Return the meatballs to the casserole. *The
meatballs may be made 1 day in advance and kept cov-*

ered and chilled. Reheat the meatballs, covered, over moderately low heat until they are heated through. Sprinkle the meatballs with the parsley. Serves 10 to 12.

PHOTO ON PAGE 42

Crisp Beef Ribs with Horseradish

1 cup sour cream
¼ cup drained bottled horseradish
1 teaspoon Tabasco
the leftover ribs from a rare to medium-rare
   4-rib roast of beef, separated
2 cups fine dry bread crumbs
3 tablespoons unsalted butter, melted

In a shallow bowl combine the sour cream, the horseradish, the Tabasco, and salt to taste, coat the ribs with the mixture, and dredge them in the bread crumbs. Chill the ribs in one layer on a plate for 30 minutes. Arrange the ribs on the rack of a broiler pan, drizzle them with half the butter, and sprinkle them with salt and freshly ground pepper to taste. Broil the ribs under a preheated broiler about 6 inches from the heat for 5 minutes, or until they are golden. Turn the ribs carefully, drizzle them with the remaining butter, and broil them for 5 minutes more. Serves 2.

Broiled Chili Beef Rib Bones

1 large garlic clove
1 teaspoon salt
½ stick (¼ cup) unsalted butter
1 tablespoon Worcestershire sauce
2 teaspoons chili powder
2 teaspoons ground cumin
12 meaty beef rib bones cut from a
   rib roast, separated

Mince the garlic and mash it with the salt to form a paste. In a small saucepan cook the garlic paste in the butter over moderately low heat until it is softened. Stir in the Worcestershire sauce, the chili powder, and the cumin and remove the pan from the heat. Brush the ribs with some of the sauce and broil them on the rack of a broiler pan under a preheated broiler about 4 inches from the heat, brushing them occasionally with the remaining sauce, for 5 minutes on each side for medium-rare meat. Serves 4.

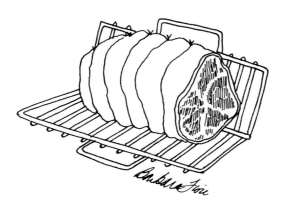

*Roast Prime Ribs of Beef with Herbed Crust and
Madeira Sauce*

a 4-rib standing rib roast (trimmed weight
   10 to 10½ pounds)
1 tablespoon black peppercorns
1½ bay leaves, crumbled (about ¾ teaspoon)
½ stick (¼ cup) unsalted butter, cut into pieces
   and softened
¼ cup plus 1 tablespoon all-purpose flour
2 teaspoons coarsely ground white pepper
1 teaspoon salt
1 pound large shallots (about 1½ inches long),
   peeled, leaving the ends intact
2 heads of garlic, separated into cloves but not
   peeled
For the sauce
½ cup dry red wine
2 cups canned beef broth
⅓ cup Madeira
1 tablespoon cornstarch

parsley sprigs for garnish

Let the rib roast stand at room temperature for 1 hour.
In an electric spice or coffee grinder grind fine the peppercorns and the bay leaves, in a small bowl combine well the butter, the flour, the white pepper, the salt, and the bay leaf mixture, forming a paste, and rub the meat with the paste. In a roasting pan roast the meat, rib side down, in a preheated 500° F. oven for 30 minutes, reduce the heat to 350° F., and roast the meat for 1 hour and 45 minutes to 2 hours more, or until a meat thermometer inserted in a fleshy section registers 130° F. for medium-rare. Forty minutes before the roast is done add the shallots and 30 minutes before the roast is done add the garlic. Transfer the roast to a heated platter and discard the strings if necessary. Transfer the shallots and garlic to paper towels to drain and keep them warm, covered loosely. Let the roast rest for at least 20 minutes and up to 30 minutes before carving.

Make the sauce: Skim the fat from the pan drippings, reserving it for the Yorkshire pudding (recipe follows), add the red wine, and deglaze the pan over moderately high heat, scraping up the brown bits. Boil the liquid until it is reduced by half and transfer it to a saucepan. Add the broth and ¼ cup of the Madeira and boil the mixture for 5 minutes. In a small bowl dissolve the cornstarch in the remaining 4 teaspoons Madeira and add the mixture to the pan in a stream, whisking. Bring the sauce to a boil, whisking, and boil it for 1 minute. Season the sauce with salt and pepper and transfer it to a heated sauceboat.

Arrange the shallots, the garlic, and the parsley around the roast and serve the roast with the sauce. Serves 8 generously.

PHOTO ON PAGE 79

Yorkshire Pudding

1 cup milk at room temperature
2 large eggs at room temperature
¾ teaspoon salt
1 cup all-purpose flour
¼ cup reserved rib-roast pan-drippings fat or
   lard

In a blender blend the milk, the eggs, and the salt for 15 seconds. With the motor running add the flour, a little at a time, and blend the mixture at high speed for 2 minutes. Let the batter stand in the blender at room temperature for 3 hours.

In a 10-inch cast-iron skillet heat the reserved fat in a preheated 450° F. oven for 10 minutes, or until it is just smoking. Blend the batter at high speed for 10 seconds and pour it into the skillet. Bake the pudding in the middle of the 450° F. oven for 20 minutes, reduce the heat to 350° F., and bake the pudding for 10 minutes more. Transfer the pudding to a platter and serve it immediately. Serves 8.

Short Ribs with Rutabagas

3 tablespoons vegetable oil
3 pounds beef chuck short ribs
2 onions, chopped
2 garlic cloves, minced
12 ounces beer (not dark)
1 pound rutabagas, peeled and cut into
   1-inch cubes
1 cup canned beef broth
2 tablespoons tomato paste
2 tablespoons Worcestershire sauce
1 tablespoon cornstarch dissolved in
   2 tablespoons water
¼ cup minced fresh parsley leaves
steamed rice (page 180) as an accompaniment

In a heavy kettle heat the oil over moderately high heat until it is hot but not smoking and in it brown the ribs, patted dry with paper towels, in batches, transferring them to a plate as they are browned. Pour off all but 3 tablespoons of the fat and in the fat remaining in the kettle cook the onions and the garlic over moderately low heat, stirring, until they are softened. Stir in the beer, the rutabagas, the broth, the tomato paste, the Worcestershire sauce, and salt and freshly ground pepper to taste and bring the liquid to a boil. Return the ribs to the kettle and simmer them for 2 hours, or until they and the rutabagas are tender. Skim the fat, bring the liquid to a boil, and stir in the cornstarch mixture. Simmer the mixture for 2 minutes, or until it is thickened, transfer it to a serving dish, and sprinkle it with the parsley. Serve the ribs and the rutabagas with the rice. Serves 4.

Chili Steak with Caper Mayonnaise

a 1-pound boneless sirloin steak, about 1 inch thick
1 teaspoon vegetable oil plus additional for brushing the pan
1½ teaspoons chili powder
½ cup mayonnaise
1 tablespoon minced fresh parsley leaves
1½ tablespoons drained bottled capers
1 teaspoon green peppercorns in brine (available at specialty foods shops and some supermarkets), if desired, drained and chopped
2 teaspoons fresh lemon juice
chopped red onion as an accompaniment
coarsely chopped tomato as an accompaniment

Rub the steak with 1 teaspoon of the oil, sprinkle it with the chili powder, and rub the powder into the steak to coat it thoroughly. Let the steak marinate at room temperature for 15 minutes. While the steak is marinating, in a small bowl combine well the mayonnaise, the parsley, the capers, the green peppercorns, the lemon juice, and salt and black pepper to taste. Heat a well-seasoned ridged grill pan or heavy skillet over moderately high heat until it is smoking, brush it lightly with the additional oil, and in it grill the steak, sprinkled with salt to taste, for 6 minutes on each side for medium-rare meat. Transfer the steak to a work surface and let it

stand for 5 minutes. Holding a knife at a 45° angle, cut the steak across the grain into thin slices, divide the slices between 2 plates, and serve the steak with the caper mayonnaise, the onion, and the tomato. Serves 2.

Sautéed T-Bone Steak
with Onions and Soy Pepper Sauce

4 teaspoons red-wine vinegar
2 teaspoons soy sauce
¼ teaspoon Worcestershire sauce
2 teaspoons freshly ground pepper
2 tablespoons vegetable oil
a 1-inch-thick T-bone or sirloin steak (about 1½ pounds), the fat scored at 1-inch intervals and, if necessary, the tail secured with wooden picks
2 onions, halved lengthwise and sliced thin crosswise

In a bowl whisk together the vinegar, the soy sauce, the Worcestershire sauce, ¼ cup water, the pepper, salt to taste, and 1 tablespoon of the oil. In a large heavy skillet heat the remaining 1 tablespoon oil over moderately high heat until it is hot but not smoking, in it sauté the steak, patted dry, turning it once, for 10 minutes for medium-rare meat, and transfer it to a platter. Pour off all but 2 teaspoons of the fat, in the fat remaining in the skillet sauté the onions over moderately high heat, stirring, until they are golden and softened, and stir in the soy mixture and any juices that have accumulated on the platter. Cook the mixture, stirring, until it is thickened and spoon it over the steak. Serves 2.

*Thai-Style Steak and
Green Bean Salad
with Spicy Mint Dressing*

For the dressing
2 garlic cloves
½ teaspoon salt
½ cup fresh lime juice
3 tablespoons soy sauce
1 tablespoon sugar
two 4-inch fresh hot chilies (preferably red) or
    jalapeño peppers, or to taste, seeded and
    sliced thin crosswise (wear rubber gloves)
⅓ cup thinly sliced fresh mint leaves,
    or to taste

1 pound boneless sirloin steak
    (about 1½ inches thick)
freshly ground black pepper to taste
vegetable oil for brushing the steak and for
    frying the shallot
¾ cup thin lengthwise slices of shallot
¾ pound green beans, trimmed, cut
    diagonally into ¾-inch pieces, and cooked
    until crisp-tender
1¼ cups fresh bean sprouts, rinsed and the
    ends trimmed

Make the dressing: Mince and mash the garlic with
the salt until the mixture forms a paste. In a small bowl
stir together the lime juice, the soy sauce, the sugar,
the garlic paste, the chilies, and the mint until the sugar
is dissolved and let the dressing stand at room temperature for 30 minutes to develop the flavors.

Sprinkle both sides of the steak generously with the
pepper, rubbing the pepper into the meat, and brush
them with some of the oil. Grill the steak, seasoned
with salt, on a well oiled rack set 4 to 5 inches over
glowing coals, turning it once, for 16 to 18 minutes, or
until it is springy to the touch for medium-rare meat.
(Alternatively, the steak may be cooked in the same
manner in a well seasoned ridged grill pan, brushed
with the oil and heated over moderately high heat until
the oil begins to smoke.) Transfer the steak to a cutting
board and let it stand for 15 minutes.

While the steak is grilling, in a skillet heat ½ inch of
the oil over moderately high heat until it is hot but not
smoking and in it fry the shallot, stirring, for 30 seconds to 1 minute, or until it is golden. Transfer the
shallot with a slotted spoon to paper towels and let it

drain. *The shallot may be cooked 1 day in advance and
kept covered and chilled.*

Cut the steak across the grain into ¼-inch-thick
slices and divide the slices among 4 plates, overlapping them in the center. Surround the steak with the
green beans, top the green beans with the bean sprouts,
and sprinkle the bean sprouts with the shallot. Spoon 2
tablespoons of the dressing over each serving of steak
and serve the remaining dressing on the side. Serves 4.
PHOTO ON PAGE 55

Sautéed Calf's Liver with Honey Pear Sauce
1 tablespoon vegetable oil
1 tablespoon unsalted butter
10 ounces calf's liver, sliced ¼ inch thick
1 firm-ripe pear, peeled, quartered, cored,
    and sliced thin crosswise
¼ cup cider vinegar
1 tablespoon honey
1½ teaspoons dried green peppercorns or ½
    teaspoon black peppercorns, crushed with
    the bottom of a heavy saucepan
¼ cup canned chicken broth

In a skillet heat the oil and the butter over moderately
high heat until the foam subsides, in the fat sauté the
calf's liver, patted dry and seasoned with salt, turning it
once, for 30 seconds to 1 minute, or until it is browned
lightly for medium-rare meat, and transfer it with a slotted spatula to a plate. Add the pear to the skillet, sauté it
over moderately high heat, stirring, for 2 minutes, and
transfer it with the spatula to the plate. Add the vinegar,
the honey, and the peppercorns to the skillet, deglaze
the skillet over high heat, scraping up the brown bits,
and boil the mixture until it is reduced by half. Add the
broth and boil the mixture until it is reduced by half.
Add the calf's liver, the pear, and salt to taste and simmer the mixture for 30 seconds. Serves 2.

VEAL

Veal Chop "Schnitzel" with Arugula Salad
two 1-inch-thick veal rib chops, frenched
flour seasoned with salt and pepper for
    dredging
1 large egg, beaten lightly
¾ cup fine fresh bread crumbs

1 large garlic clove, quartered
¼ cup vegetable oil
1 tablespoon unsalted butter
For the salad
1 tablespoon white-wine vinegar
1 teaspoon Dijon-style mustard
⅛ teaspoon dried thyme, crumbled
2 tablespoons olive oil
2 cups loosely packed *arugula* or watercress
   sprigs, washed well and spun dry
4 cherry tomatoes, quartered
1 tablespoon grated carrot

2 lemon wedges

Pound the meat of the chops ½ inch thick between sheets of plastic wrap, being careful not to separate the meat from the bone, pat it dry, and season it with salt and pepper. Dredge the chops in the flour, shaking off the excess, dip them in the egg, letting the excess drip off, and coat them with the bread crumbs. In a large heavy skillet cook the garlic in the oil and the butter over moderately high heat, stirring, until it is golden and discard it. Sauté the chops in the fat, turning them once, for 4 minutes, or until they are golden brown, and transfer them to paper towels to drain.

Make the salad: In a small bowl whisk together the vinegar, the mustard, the thyme, and salt and pepper to taste, add the oil in a stream, whisking, and whisk the dressing until it is emulsified. In a bowl toss the *arugula*, the tomatoes, and the carrot with the dressing.

Arrange each veal chop on a plate, divide the salad between the plates, and garnish each serving with a lemon wedge. Serves 2.

Vitello alla Genovese
(*Sautéed Veal Scallops with Sage and Bay Leaves*)

⅓ cup olive oil
2 pounds veal scallopini (about 18 scallops),
   flattened between sheets of plastic wrap to
   ⅛-inch thickness
¾ cup dry white wine
¾ cup canned chicken broth
¼ cup chopped fresh sage leaves or
   1 tablespoon dried, crumbled, plus whole
   sage leaves for garnish if desired
2 bay leaves, crumbled
green beans with anchovy and garlic
   (page 182) as an accompaniment

In a large heavy skillet heat the oil over moderately high heat until it is hot but not smoking and in it sauté the veal, patted dry and seasoned with salt and pepper, in batches, turning it once, for 45 seconds, transferring it to a plate as it is done. Add the wine and deglaze the skillet, scraping up the brown bits. Add the broth, the chopped sage, the bay leaves, salt and pepper to taste, and any juices that have accumulated on the plate, bring the mixture to a boil, and boil it until it is reduced to about ⅓ cup. Strain the mixture through a fine sieve into a small bowl, pressing hard on the solids. Divide the veal scallops among 6 heated plates, spoon the sauce over them, and garnish the veal with the whole sage leaves. Divide the green beans among the plates. Serves 6.

PHOTO ON PAGE 69

PORK

Bacon Spirals

12 slices of cold bacon

Twist the bacon slices into spirals, arrange them in rows on the rack of a broiler pan, and lay metal skewers across the bacon 1 inch from the top and bottom ends so that the spirals will not untwist while cooking. Bake the spirals in a preheated 375° F. oven for 20 minutes, or until they are crisp, and transfer them to paper towels to drain. Serves 6.

PHOTO ON PAGE 81

Pork Chops with Mustard Cheese Crust

¼ cup finely grated Parmesan
2 tablespoons bottled mango chutney,
   chopped
1 tablespoon Dijon-style mustard
two 1-inch-thick loin pork chops
¾ cup fine dry bread crumbs

In a small bowl combine well the Parmesan, the chutney, the mustard, and salt and pepper to taste, spread the chutney mixture on both sides of the pork chops, and dredge the pork chops in the bread crumbs, shaking off the excess. Broil the pork chops on a lightly oiled rack of a broiler pan under a preheated broiler about 4 inches from the heat, turning them once, for 16 to 18 minutes, or until they are no longer pink within. Serves 2.

Onion- and Sage-Stuffed Pork Chops with Kielbasa and Sauerkraut

For the stuffing

1 cup finely chopped onion
1 garlic clove, minced
2 tablespoons minced fresh sage or
    2 teaspoons dried, crumbled
2 tablespoons unsalted butter
3 tablespoons dry bread crumbs

four 1-inch-thick rib pork chops (about ½
    pound each)
1 tablespoon vegetable oil
½ pound *kielbasa*, cut diagonally into ¾-inch-
    thick slices
1 large onion, sliced
two 1-pound packages of sauerkraut, drained,
    rinsed well, and drained well
¾ cup dry white wine
¼ cup white-wine vinegar
½ cup canned chicken broth
1 bay leaf
2 tablespoons thinly shredded fresh sage
    leaves or 2 teaspoons crumbled dried plus
    fresh whole leaves for garnish if desired
1 tablespoon cornstarch dissolved in
    2 tablespoons cold water
1 tablespoon minced fresh parsley leaves

Make the stuffing: In a heavy skillet cook the onion, the garlic, and the sage in the butter over moderately low heat, stirring, until the onion is softened, remove the skillet from the heat, and stir in the bread crumbs and salt and pepper to taste.

With a sharp paring knife make a ¾-inch-long horizontal incision along the fat side of each chop and cut a deep wide pocket in the chop by moving the knife back and forth carefully through the incision. Fill the chops with the stuffing, distributing it evenly, and pat them dry with paper towels.

In a large flameproof casserole heat the oil over moderately high heat until it is hot but not smoking and in it brown the chops, transferring them with tongs as they are browned to a plate. To the casserole add the *kielbasa*, sauté it, turning it, for 1 minute, or until it is lightly golden, and transfer it with tongs to another plate. Pour off all but 1 tablespoon of the fat from the casserole and in the remaining fat cook the onion over moderately low heat, stirring, until it is softened. Add half the sauer-

kraut, spreading it to form an even layer, and cover it with the chops, seasoned with salt and pepper, and the *kielbasa*. Spread the remaining sauerkraut over the chops and the *kielbasa* and add the wine, the vinegar, the broth, and the bay leaf. Bring the liquid to a boil and simmer the mixture, covered, for 1 hour and 30 minutes, or until the chops are tender. Discard the bay leaf, transfer the chops and *kielbasa* with tongs to a large plate, and keep them warm, covered with foil. Add the shredded sage to the sauerkraut mixture and bring the mixture to a boil, stirring. Stir the cornstarch mixture, add it to the sauerkraut mixture, stirring, and simmer the mixture for 2 minutes. Transfer the sauerkraut mixture to a heated serving dish, nestle the chops and *kielbasa* in it, and sprinkle the dish with the parsley. Garnish the dish with the whole sage leaves. Serves 4.

PHOTO ON PAGE 25

Braised Pork Loin Country-Style Ribs with Apples, Onions, and Garlic

3 pounds pork loin country-style ribs,
    separated
½ cup apple cider
½ cup cider vinegar
¼ cup vegetable oil
4 large garlic cloves, minced
2 large onions, chopped
2 Granny Smith apples, peeled, cored,
    and chopped
1 teaspoon dried thyme, crumbled

In a shallow dish just large enough to hold the ribs in one layer combine the ribs, the cider, and the vinegar and let the ribs marinate, covered and chilled, for at least 2 hours or overnight. Drain the ribs, reserving the marinade, and pat them dry with paper towels. In a heavy flameproof casserole heat the oil over moderately high heat until it is hot but not smoking and in it brown the ribs in batches, transferring them to a plate as they are browned. Pour off all but 2 tablespoons of the fat and in the fat remaining in the casserole cook the garlic, the onions, the apples, and the thyme over moderate heat, stirring occasionally, until the vegetables are softened. Return the ribs to the casserole, add the reserved marinade and salt and pepper to taste, and bring the liquid to a boil. Braise the ribs, covered, in the middle of a preheated 325° F. oven for 1 hour and 30 minutes, or until the meat is tender. Serve the ribs with the apple mixture. Serves 4.

Sautéed Pork Loin with Mustard and Grapes

six ½-inch-thick slices of boneless pork loin
    (about ¾ pound)
flour seasoned with salt and pepper for dredging
2 tablespoons vegetable oil
2 tablespoons minced shallot
½ cup seedless red or green grapes, halved
¼ cup dry white wine
2 teaspoons brandy
¾ cup canned chicken broth
2 teaspoons firmly packed dark brown sugar
1 tablespoon Dijon-style mustard

Pat the pork dry and dredge it in the flour, shaking off the excess. In a large skillet heat the oil over moderately high heat until it is hot but not smoking and in it brown the pork. Transfer the pork with tongs to a plate, add the shallot and the grapes to the skillet, and cook them over moderately low heat, stirring occasionally, for 3 minutes. Add the wine and the brandy and simmer the mixture until almost all the liquid is evaporated. Add the broth and the brown sugar, whisking, and boil the mixture until the liquid is reduced by half. Add the pork and any juices that have accumulated on the plate, simmer the mixture for 2 minutes, or until the pork is just heated through, and transfer the pork with tongs to 2 heated plates. Remove the skillet from the heat, whisk in the mustard and salt and pepper to taste, whisking until the sauce is combined well, and pour the sauce over the pork. Serves 2.

Pork Tenderloin with Apples and Cider Cream Sauce

a ¾-pound pork tenderloin, cut crosswise into
    1-inch slices, reserving 3 inches of the
    narrow end for another use
2 tablespoons unsalted butter
1 Granny Smith apple
1 shallot, minced
¼ teaspoon crumbled dried sage, or to taste
¼ cup apple cider or apple juice
¼ cup cider vinegar
½ cup canned chicken broth
⅓ cup heavy cream
1 tablespoon minced fresh parsley leaves

Flatten the pork slices, cut sides up, to about ¼-inch thickness between sheets of plastic wrap and pat them dry. In a large heavy skillet heat 1 tablespoon of the butter over moderately high heat until the foam begins to subside and in it sauté the pork, seasoned with salt and pepper, turning it once, for 4 minutes. Transfer the pork with tongs to a platter and keep it warm, covered. Peel and core the apple and cut it into 16 wedges. In the skillet cook the apple wedges in the remaining 1 tablespoon butter, covered, over moderate heat, turning them once, for 3 minutes, or until they are golden and just tender. Transfer the apple wedges with tongs to the platter of pork and keep the mixture warm, covered. Add the shallot to the skillet and cook it over moderate heat, stirring, for 30 seconds. Add the sage, the cider, and the vinegar, deglaze the skillet, scraping up the brown bits, and boil the liquid, stirring until it is reduced to about 2 tablespoons. Add the broth and boil the mixture, stirring, until the liquid is reduced by half. Add the cream and the pork with any juices on the platter, leaving the apples on the platter, and boil the mixture, turning the pork for 1 minute, or until the sauce is thickened slightly. Transfer the pork to the platter, pour the sauce over it, and sprinkle the dish with the parsley. Serves 2.

Pork Tenderloin with Scallion Sauce

1 bunch of scallions, cut into ½-inch pieces
    (about 1 cup)
1 cup canned chicken broth
a ¾-pound pork tenderloin
2 tablespoons olive oil
mustard biscuits (page 103) as an
    accompaniment

In a saucepan combine the scallions, the broth, and pepper to taste, bring the broth to a boil, and simmer the scallions for 10 to 15 minutes, or until they are very tender. In a blender purée the mixture, pour the purée into the pan, and boil it until it is thickened. Keep the sauce warm, covered, over low heat.

Cut the tenderloin, beginning at the thick end, into 1-inch-thick slices, folding the thin end under to make the last slice 1 inch thick. In a heavy skillet heat the oil over moderately high heat until it is hot but not smoking, in it sauté the pork slices, patted dry and seasoned with salt and pepper, in batches, turning them once, for 6 to 7 minutes, or until they are just springy to the touch, and transfer them to a platter. Spoon the scallion sauce around the pork and serve the pork with mustard biscuits if desired. Serves 2.

Barbecued Spareribs

5 pounds pork spareribs, the ribs not separated
2 cups chopped onion
3 garlic cloves, minced
¼ cup vegetable oil
an 8-ounce can tomato sauce
⅓ cup firmly packed brown sugar
¼ cup cider vinegar
1 teaspoon salt
½ teaspoon cayenne
1 tablespoon Worcestershire sauce
½ teaspoon freshly ground black pepper

In a kettle of simmering water blanch the spareribs in batches for 30 minutes, drain them, and keep them warm, covered. In a saucepan cook the onion and the garlic in the oil over moderately low heat, stirring occasionally, until they are softened. Stir in the tomato sauce, the brown sugar, the vinegar, the salt, the cayenne, the Worcestershire sauce, and the black pepper, bring the mixture to a boil, and simmer the sauce, stirring occasionally, for 15 minutes. Brush the ribs with some of the sauce and grill them on a well oiled rack set 5 to 6 inches over glowing coals for 10 minutes. Baste them with the remaining sauce, turn them, and grill them for 5 to 10 minutes more, or until they are cooked through. Serves 4.

Spareribs with Sauerkraut, Noodles, and Sour Cream

5 pounds pork spareribs, the ribs not
   separated
1 tablespoon paprika
2¼ cups distilled white vinegar
½ pound spinach noodles
2 tablespoons caraway seeds
½ stick (¼ cup) unsalted butter, softened
a 1-pound package sauerkraut, rinsed and
   drained well
½ cup sour cream

Sprinkle the spareribs with the paprika and salt and pepper to taste and bake them meaty side up in one layer in a large shallow baking pan in the middle of a preheated 350° F. oven for 20 minutes. Turn the ribs meaty side down, pour ½ cup of the vinegar over them, and bake the ribs, covered with foil, basting them with 1½ cups of the remaining vinegar, ½ cup at a time, every 20 minutes, for 1 hour and 20 minutes. While the ribs are baking, in a large saucepan of boiling salted water cook the noodles until they are *al dente*, drain them, and in a 2-quart shallow baking dish toss them with the caraway seeds and the butter until they are coated well with the butter. Stir in the sauerkraut and the sour cream. Arrange the cooked ribs, meaty side up, on the noodle mixture, baste them with the remaining ¼ cup vinegar, and bake the dish, covered, in the middle of the 350° F. oven for 20 to 30 minutes, or until the noodle mixture is heated through. Serves 4 to 6.

Ham and Cauliflower Gratin with Caraway and Dill

1¾ pounds cauliflower, cut into ½-inch
   flowerets
½ pound sliced ham, chopped coarse
4½ tablespoons unsalted butter
¼ cup all-purpose flour
1 teaspoon caraway seeds
2¼ cups milk
½ cup grated Gruyère or Swiss cheese
6 tablespoons freshly grated Parmesan
3 tablespoons snipped fresh dill, or to taste
¾ cup fresh bread crumbs

In a steamer set over boiling water steam the cauliflower, covered, for 4 to 6 minutes, or until it is just tender, and in a bowl toss it with the ham. In a heavy saucepan melt 3 tablespoons of the butter over moderately low heat, add the flour and the caraway seeds, and cook the *roux*, whisking, for 3 minutes. Remove the pan from the heat, add the milk in a stream, whisking, and bring the mixture to a boil, whisking. Simmer the mixture, stirring occasionally, for 3 minutes, add the Gruyère, 4 tablespoons of the Parmesan, and the dill, and cook the mixture over low heat, stirring, until the cheese is just melted and the sauce is smooth, but do not let it boil. Pour the sauce over the ham and cauliflower mixture, stir the mixture until it is combined well, and spread it in a buttered 11- to 12-inch oval gratin dish (or 1½-quart shallow baking dish). In a small bowl combine well the bread crumbs and the remaining 2 tablespoons Parmesan, sprinkle the crumb mixture evenly over the ham and cauliflower mixture, and dot it with the remaining 1½ tablespoons butter, cut into bits. Bake the gratin in the middle of a preheated 425° F. oven for 25 to 30 minutes, or until the topping is golden and the edges are bubbling. Serves 4 as an entrée.

Glazed Smithfield Ham

a fully-cooked 10- to 12-pound Smithfield
  ham*
3 tablespoons Dijon-style mustard
2 tablespoons firmly packed dark brown sugar

*available by mail order from:

  Gwaltney of Smithfield, Ltd.
  P.O. Box 489
  Smithfield, Virginia 23430
  804-357-3131

Trim the ham of excess fat if necessary, leaving a
¼-inch-thick layer of fat, and set it on a rack in a large
foil-lined baking pan. In a small bowl combine well the
mustard and the brown sugar and spread the mixture
over the ham. Bake the ham in the middle of a preheated
400° F. oven for 30 minutes, or until the topping is
browned and bubbly, and transfer it to a cutting board.
If serving the ham warm, let it stand for 15 minutes
before carving it into very thin slices. If serving the ham
at room temperature, let it cool completely before carving it into very thin slices. Arrange the slices, overlapping them, on a large platter around the ham. The
leftover ham and ham slices keep, wrapped tightly and
chilled, for 1 month. The ham slices keep, wrapped
tightly in small packages and frozen, for 6 months.

PHOTO ON PAGE 36

LAMB

Dijon Lamb Chops with Shallot Sauce

4 small double-rib lamb chops, each about
  1½ inches thick
3 tablespoons Dijon-style mustard
½ cup fine dry bread crumbs
⅔ cup dry white wine
1 cup canned beef broth
½ teaspoon dried rosemary,
  crumbled
3 tablespoons minced shallot
2 tablespoons unsalted butter,
  cut into bits

Season the lamb chops with salt and pepper, spread
the mustard all over them, and coat the chops with the
bread crumbs. In a saucepan combine the wine, the
broth, the rosemary, and the shallot, bring the liquid to a
boil, and boil it until it is reduced to about ⅓ cup. Keep
the sauce warm. Broil the chops on the rack of a broiler
pan under a preheated broiler about 4 inches from the
heat for 5 minutes. Turn the chops and broil them for 5
minutes more for medium-rare meat. Transfer the chops
to a platter and let them stand for 5 minutes. Add the
butter to the sauce, swirling the pan until it is incorporated, and serve the sauce with the chops. Serves 2.

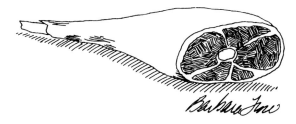

Rosemary Lamb Kebabs

½ cup fresh lemon juice
½ cup dry red wine
3 tablespoons chopped fresh rosemary leaves
    or 1 tablespoon dried, crumbled, plus, if
    desired, 8 rosemary sprigs for garnish
1 tablespoon finely chopped garlic
1 teaspoon dried hot red pepper flakes
1½ teaspoons salt
¾ teaspoon freshly ground black pepper
¾ cup olive oil
4 pounds boneless leg of lamb, trimmed and
    cut into 2-inch pieces
2 zucchini (about 1 pound), quartered
    lengthwise, cut crosswise into 1½-inch
    pieces, and cooked in boiling salted water
    until just tender
4 yellow bell peppers (about 1½ pounds), cut
    into 1½-inch pieces
4 small onions (about 1 pound), each cut into
    8 pieces, the pieces secured with wooden
    picks, and cooked in boiling salted water
    until just tender
1 pint cherry tomatoes
shredded potato pancakes (page 192) as an
    accompaniment

In a large bowl whisk together the lemon juice, the wine, the chopped rosemary, the garlic, the red pepper flakes, the salt, and the black pepper, add the oil in a stream, whisking, and whisk the marinade until it is emulsified. Add the lamb, turn it to coat it thoroughly with the marinade, and let it marinate, covered and chilled, for at least 6 hours or overnight.

In a shallow dish let sixteen 8-inch wooden skewers soak in water to cover for 1 hour. Drain the lamb, reserving the marinade, thread the skewers with the zucchini, the bell peppers, the lamb, the onions, discarding the wooden picks, and the tomatoes, alternating the ingredients in a decorative pattern, and brush the kebabs with some of the reserved marinade. Grill the kebabs on an oiled rack set 5 to 6 inches over glowing coals, basting them often with the reserved marinade and turning them, for 15 to 18 minutes for medium-rare meat. Alternatively, broil the kebabs in jelly-roll pans under a preheated broiler about 4 inches from the heat, basting them often with the reserved marinade and turning them once, for 12 to 15 minutes for medium-rare meat. (Discard any remaining marinade; do not serve it as an accompaniment.) Arrange 2 of the kebabs and 1 potato pancake wedge on each of 8 plates and garnish each plate with a rosemary sprig. Serves 8.

PHOTO ON PAGE 45

Herb-Marinated Butterflied Leg of Lamb

½ cup white-wine vinegar
1 cup olive oil
2 tablespoons fresh thyme leaves or,
    2 teaspoons dried, plus 1 thyme sprig
    for garnish
2 tablespoons fresh rosemary leaves, or
    2 teaspoons dried, plus 1 rosemary sprig
    for garnish
1 tablespoon fresh orégano leaves or
    1 teaspoon dried
½ cup firmly packed fresh mint sprigs or
    1 tablespoon dried
2 large garlic cloves
1 teaspoon freshly ground pepper
a 5- to 6-pound butterflied leg of lamb,
    pricked all over on both sides with the tip of
    a sharp knife
roasted quartered potatoes with garlic (recipe
    follows) as an accompaniment

In a blender blend the vinegar, the oil, the thyme leaves, the rosemary leaves, the orégano, the mint, the garlic, and the pepper until the mixture is smooth and pour the marinade into a dish slightly larger than the lamb. Add the lamb, turn it to coat it well on both sides, and let it marinate, covered and chilled, turning it occasionally, for 24 hours. Let the lamb come to room temperature, transfer it to the rack of a broiling pan, discarding any remaining marinade, and season it with salt. Broil the lamb under a preheated broiler about 4 inches from the heat for 12 to 14 minutes on each side for medium-rare meat. (Alternatively the lamb may be grilled on a rack set 5 to 6 inches over glowing coals for 10 to 12 minutes on each side for medium-rare meat.) Transfer the lamb to a carving board and let it stand for 10 minutes. Holding a sharp knife at a 45° angle, slice the lamb slices thin across the grain. Arrange the lamb with the potatoes on a platter and garnish the platter with the thyme and rosemary sprigs. Serves 8 to 10.

PHOTO ON PAGE 60

Roasted Quartered Potatoes with Garlic

3 pounds small boiling potatoes, quartered
3 tablespoons olive oil
½ teaspoon salt
½ teaspoon freshly ground pepper
3 large garlic cloves, sliced thin
¼ cup minced fresh parsley leaves

In a large roasting pan toss together well the potatoes, the oil, the salt, the pepper, and the garlic and roast the potatoes in a preheated 350° F. oven, tossing them occasionally, for 1 hour, or until they are tender and golden. Add the parsley and toss the mixture well. Serves 8 to 10.

PHOTO ON PAGE 60

Moussaka Gratin
(Lamb and Eggplant Gratin)

1 onion, chopped fine
6 tablespoons olive oil
2 garlic cloves, minced
1 pound ground lean lamb
¼ teaspoon cinnamon
¼ teaspoon ground allspice
a 28-ounce can of Italian plum tomatoes, drained, reserving 1 cup of the juice, and chopped
1 teaspoon dried mint
two 1-pound eggplants, cut crosswise into ⅓-inch slices
For the topping
2½ tablespoons unsalted butter
3½ tablespoons all-purpose flour
1½ cups milk
¼ pound Feta cheese, crumbled
1 large egg, beaten lightly
⅓ cup freshly grated Parmesan

In a large heavy skillet cook the onion in 2 tablespoons of the oil over moderately low heat, stirring, until it is softened, add the garlic, and cook the mixture, stirring, for 1 minute. Add the lamb, cook the mixture over moderate heat, stirring and breaking up the lumps of meat, until the lamb is no longer pink, and stir in the cinnamon and the allspice. Add the tomatoes with the reserved juice, the mint, and salt and pepper to taste, bring the mixture to a boil, and cook it at a strong simmer, stirring occasionally, for 15 minutes, or until it is thickened slightly.

While the lamb mixture is simmering, arrange the eggplant slices in a single layer on oiled baking sheets, brush them lightly with 2 tablespoons of the remaining oil, and broil them under a preheated broiler about 2 inches from the heat for 3 to 5 minutes, or until they are golden brown. Turn the eggplant slices, brush them lightly with the remaining 2 tablespoons oil, and broil them for 3 to 5 minutes more, or until they are golden brown.

Arrange half the eggplant slices, overlapping them, in an oiled 13- to 14-inch gratin dish (or 2-quart shallow baking dish), spread the lamb mixture over them, and cover it with the remaining eggplant slices, overlapping them. *The eggplant and lamb mixture may be made 2 days in advance and kept covered and chilled. Before proceeding with the recipe let the mixture come to room temperature.*

Make the topping: In a heavy saucepan melt the butter over moderately low heat, add the flour, and cook the *roux*, whisking, for 3 minutes. Remove the pan from the heat, add the milk in a stream, whisking, and bring the mixture to a boil, whisking. Simmer the mixture for 3 minutes, add the Feta, and cook the mixture over low heat, whisking, until the cheese is melted, but do not let it boil. Season the mixture with pepper, let it cool, covered, for 5 minutes, and whisk in the egg in a slow stream.

Pour the sauce evenly over the eggplant and lamb mixture, sprinkle it with the Parmesan, and bake the *moussaka* in the middle of a preheated 400° F. oven for 30 minutes, or until it is golden and bubbling. Serves 4 to 6 as an entrée.

Deviled Lamb Riblets with Dill

3 pounds lamb breast riblets, separated
1 large egg, beaten lightly
¼ cup Dijon-style mustard
2 tablespoons red-wine vinegar
1½ cups fine dry bread crumbs
⅓ cup snipped fresh dill
mixed green salad as an accompaniment
   if desired

In a kettle of simmering water blanch the riblets for 20 minutes and drain them. Pat the riblets dry with paper towels and season them with salt and pepper. In a shallow bowl whisk together the egg, the mustard, and the vinegar. In another shallow bowl stir together the bread crumbs and the dill. Dip the riblets in the egg mixture, letting the excess drip off, coat them with the bread crumbs, and arrange them in one layer with ½ inch to 1 inch between them in a jelly-roll pan. Bake the riblets in the middle of a preheated 500° F. oven, turning them once, for 15 to 20 minutes, or until they are crisp and golden. Serve the riblets with the salad. Serves 4.

Grilled Hot Sweet-and-Sour Lamb Riblets

3 pounds lamb breast riblets, separated
1 green bell pepper, chopped
1 teaspoon dried hot red pepper flakes
1⅔ cups sugar
⅔ cup cider vinegar

In a kettle of simmering water blanch the riblets for 20 minutes, drain them, and pat them dry with paper towels. In a food processor purée the bell pepper with the red pepper flakes, the sugar, and the vinegar and transfer the mixture to a small saucepan. Bring the mixture to a boil, stirring, simmer it for 10 minutes, and in a shallow dish just large enough to hold the riblets in one layer let the riblets marinate while they are still warm in the pepper mixture, stirring occasionally, for 1 hour. Drain the riblets, reserving the marinade, and grill them on a well oiled rack set 5 to 6 inches over glowing coals, basting them with the reserved marinade and turning them, for 20 minutes. Serves 4.

Crisp Indian-Style Lamb Riblets with Scallion-Yogurt Sauce

2 cups plain yogurt
2 tablespoons ground cumin
1 tablespoon curry powder
3 pounds lamb breast riblets, separated
⅓ cup minced scallion including
   the green part
1 teaspoon dried mint, crumbled

In a small bowl stir together 1 cup of the yogurt, the cumin, the curry powder, and salt to taste. In a shallow baking dish large enough to hold the riblets in one layer with ½ inch to 1 inch between them toss the riblets with the yogurt mixture to coat them, sprinkle them with salt and pepper to taste, and arrange them in the baking dish. Bake the riblets in the lower third of a preheated 350° F. oven, turning them every 20 minutes, for 1 hour and 30 minutes, or until they are crisp and tender. In a small bowl whisk together the remaining 1 cup yogurt, the scallion, the mint, and salt to taste. Divide the riblets among 4 plates and serve them with the sauce. Serves 4.

Roast Saddle of Lamb Persillé

½ lemon
a 4½- to 5-pound saddle of lamb, trimmed,
   leaving a ¼-inch layer of fat, and tied at
   2-inch intervals
2 tablespoons unsalted butter, softened
2 tablespoons all-purpose flour
¼ cup dry bread crumbs
3 tablespoons minced fresh parsley leaves
   plus sprigs for garnish
1 tablespoon fresh rosemary, minced, or
   1 teaspoon dried, crumbled, plus sprigs for
   garnish if desired
tomatoes stuffed with white bean, parsley,
   and garlic purée and green bean and yellow
   bell pepper mélange (pages 198 and 183
   respectively) as accompaniments

Squeeze the juice of the ½ lemon over the lamb and season the lamb with salt and pepper. In a small bowl knead the butter and the flour together, forming a paste, and spread the *beurre manié* over the fat of the lamb. Roast the lamb on a rack in a shallow roasting pan in a preheated 375° F. oven for 30 minutes. In a bowl blend together the bread crumbs, the minced parsley, and 1 tablespoon of the rosemary, pat the crumb mixture onto the top and sides of the lamb, and roast the lamb for 25 to 40 minutes more, or until a meat thermometer registers 130° F. for medium-rare meat. Transfer the lamb to a heated tray and let it stand in a warm place for 10 minutes. Arrange the stuffed tomatoes, the parsley sprigs, and the rosemary sprigs around the lamb and serve the lamb with the green bean and yellow bell pepper mélange. Serves 8.

PHOTO ON PAGE 30

Warm Lamb Salad
with Potatoes in Bourbon Vinaigrette

For the vinaigrette
1 tablespoon bourbon
1 tablespoon white-wine vinegar
1 teaspoon Dijon-style mustard
¼ cup olive oil
1½ teaspoons minced fresh parsley leaves

¼ cup vegetable oil
¼ cup bourbon
2 tablespoons fresh lemon juice
1 small garlic clove, minced
1 teaspoon firmly packed light brown sugar
⅛ teaspoon dried tarragon, crumbled
⅛ teaspoon dried rosemary, crumbled
⅛ teaspoon dried marjoram, crumbled
two 1½-inch-thick loin lamb chops
    (7 to 8 ounces each), trimmed of all
    but ¼ inch fat
¾ pound (about 9) small boiling potatoes,
    sliced ¼ inch thick and reserved in a bowl
    of cold water
soft-leafed lettuce for lining the plates
2 scallions, sliced thin diagonally

Make the vinaigrette: In a bowl whisk together the bourbon, the vinegar, the mustard, and salt and pepper to taste. Add the oil in a stream, whisking, whisk the vinaigrette until it is emulsified, and stir in the parsley.

In a bowl whisk together the oil, the bourbon, the lemon juice, the garlic, the brown sugar, the herbs, and salt and pepper to taste. In a shallow glass dish pour the marinade over the chops and let the chops marinate at room temperature, turning them once, for 15 minutes.

While the chops are marinating drain the potatoes, in a steamer set over boiling water steam them, covered, for 10 minutes, or until they are just tender, and keep them warm, covered. Preheat a well seasoned ridged grill pan over high heat until water dripped into it sizzles immediately. In the pan sear the chops, patted dry with paper towels, for 1 minute on each side, reduce the heat to moderately high, and cook the chops, turning them once, for 8 minutes for medium-rare meat. (Or broil the chops on the rack of a broiler pan under a preheated broiler about 4 inches from the heat, turning them once, for 5 minutes on each side for medium-rare meat.) Transfer the chops to a cutting board, let them stand for 2 minutes, and slice the meat thin, discarding the fat and bones. Line 2 plates with the lettuce and on the lettuce layer the potatoes, half the scallions, and the lamb slices. Pour the bourbon vinaigrette over the salads and garnish the salads with the remaining scallions. Serves 2.

Lamb Stew with Prunes

¾ pound boneless lamb shoulder, trimmed
    and cut into ¾-inch cubes
a 14- to 16-ounce can tomatoes, drained
    and chopped
½ teaspoon cinnamon
⅛ teaspoon ground cloves
¼ teaspoon crumbled saffron threads
    if desired
2 ounces pitted prunes (⅓ cup packed)

In a 2½-quart glass casserole combine the lamb, the tomatoes, the cinnamon, the cloves, the saffron, and ¼ cup water, cover the surface of the mixture with wax paper, and microwave the mixture at high power (100%) for 8 minutes. Stir in half the prunes, quartered, and microwave the mixture, covered with the wax paper, at medium power (50%) for 20 minutes, or until the lamb is tender. Season the stew with salt and pepper, divide it between 2 heated bowls, and garnish it with the remaining prunes, cut into ¼-inch pieces. Serves 2.

OTHER

Venison Stew with Root Vegetables

6⅔ cups dry red wine
1⅔ cups olive oil
2 bay leaves, broken into large pieces
2 large onions, halved lengthwise and sliced
    thin crosswise
8 pounds venison shoulder, trimmed of sinew
    and cut into 1½-inch pieces, or boneless
    beef chuck (not stew beef), trimmed and
    cut into 1½-inch pieces
1 cup all-purpose flour
2 large garlic cloves, minced
8 cups brown stock (page 122) or canned beef
    broth
2 teaspoons dried thyme, crumbled
3 pounds rutabaga, peeled and cut into
    ½-inch-thick triangles
1½ pounds finger (small) carrots, trimmed
10 ounces (about 38) pearl onions, blanched
    in boiling water for 10 seconds, drained,
    and peeled
1½ cups minced fresh parsley leaves
buttered *spätzle* with scallions (page 178) as
    an accompaniment

In a large bowl stir together the wine, ¼ cup of the oil, the bay leaves, the sliced onions, and salt and pepper to taste, add the venison, and stir the mixture until it is combined well. Let the venison marinate, covered and chilled, for 24 to 48 hours. Strain the mixture through a large colander set over a bowl, reserving the marinade and the onions separately, and discard the bay leaves. In a large heavy skillet heat ⅓ cup of the remaining oil over moderately high heat until it is hot but not smoking and in it brown the venison, patted dry, in batches, transferring it with tongs as it is browned to a heavy kettle and adding up to ⅓ cup of the remaining oil to the skillet as necessary. Pour off any fat remaining in the skillet. Add the remaining ¾ cup oil and the flour to the skillet and cook the *roux* over moderately low heat, stirring constantly with a wooden spatula, for 15 to 20 minutes, or until it is the color of peanut butter. Stir in the reserved onions and cook the mixture, stirring occasionally, until the onions are softened. Transfer the onion mixture to the kettle, add the garlic, the stock, and the thyme, stirring, and bring the liquid to a boil, stirring. In a saucepan bring the reserved marinade to a boil, skimming the froth, and simmer it, skimming the froth, for 5 minutes. Add the marinade to the venison mixture, simmer the mixture, covered partially, for 3 hours to 3 hours and 30 minutes, or until the meat is tender, and skim the fat from the surface. *The venison mixture may be prepared up to this point 2 days in advance. Let the mixture cool completely at room temperature, uncovered, before chilling it, covered. Reheat the mixture over moderately low heat, stirring occasionally.*

While the venison is simmering or reheating, in a large steamer set over boiling water steam the rutabaga, covered, for 10 to 15 minutes, or until it is crisp-tender, and transfer it to a large bowl of ice and cold water. In the same manner steam separately the carrots for 5 to 8 minutes, or until they are crisp-tender, and the pearl onions for 5 to 8 minutes, or until they are crisp-tender, transferring each vegetable as it is steamed to the bowl of ice and cold water. Add the steamed vegetables, drained, and salt and pepper to taste to the venison mixture, simmer the stew, uncovered, stirring occasionally, for 8 to 10 minutes, or until the vegetables are just tender, and stir in the parsley. Serve the stew with the *spätzle*. Serves 12 with leftovers.

PHOTO ON PAGE 13

POULTRY

CHICKEN

Chicken and Leek Shortcakes

For the shortcakes
1 cup all-purpose flour
1½ teaspoons double-acting baking powder
½ teaspoon salt
½ teaspoon dried sage, crumbled
½ teaspoon dried thyme, crumbled
½ stick (¼ cup) cold unsalted butter, cut
    into bits
¼ cup plus 1 tablespoon milk

For the filling
1 skinless boneless chicken breast (about
    ¾ pound), cut into ¾-inch cubes
2 tablespoons unsalted butter
the white part of 1 large leek, split
    lengthwise, cut into ½-inch pieces, washed
    well, and drained
¼ pound mushrooms, sliced
2 tablespoons all-purpose flour
¼ cup dry white wine
1 cup canned chicken broth
⅓ cup plain yogurt

Make the shortcakes: Into a bowl sift together the
flour, the baking powder, and the salt, add the sage, the

thyme, and the butter, and blend the mixture until it resembles coarse meal. Add the milk and stir the mixture
until it just forms a dough. Knead the dough gently on a
lightly floured surface for 30 seconds, roll or pat it out
into a ½-inch-thick round, and with a 3-inch round cutter, dipped in flour, cut out 2 rounds, reserving the
scraps for another use if desired. Bake the shortcakes on
an ungreased baking sheet in a preheated 425° F. oven
for 12 to 15 minutes, or until they are pale golden, transfer them to a rack, and let them cool for 5 minutes.

Make the filling while the shortcakes are baking: In a
skillet cook the chicken in the butter over moderately
high heat, stirring occasionally, for 3 minutes, or until it
is barely firm to the touch, and transfer it with a slotted
spoon to a plate. Add the leek and the mushrooms to the
skillet and cook them over moderate heat, stirring occasionally, until most of the liquid the mushrooms give off
is evaporated. Sprinkle the flour over the vegetables and
cook the mixture over moderately low heat, stirring, for
3 minutes. Add the wine and the broth in a stream,
whisking, and simmer the mixture, whisking occasionally, for 5 minutes. Add the chicken and any juices that
have accumulated on the plate, the yogurt, and salt and
pepper to taste, stirring until the mixture is combined
well, and simmer the mixture for 2 minutes.

Split the shortcakes in half horizontally, divide the
filling between the bottom halves, and top it with the remaining halves. Serves 2.

Curried Chicken and Broccoli Gratin

2 tablespoons vegetable oil
2 garlic cloves, minced
½ teaspoon dried hot red pepper flakes
1 pound broccoli, flowerets cut into ¾-inch
 pieces and stalks cut crosswise into ¼-inch
 slices
2 cups shredded or chopped cooked chicken
 (about 1 pound)
5 tablespoons unsalted butter
1 tablespoon curry powder
4 tablespoons all-purpose flour
2 cups canned chicken broth
⅓ cup thinly sliced scallions
½ cup fresh bread crumbs
⅓ cup freshly grated Parmesan
¼ cup sliced almonds

In a large heavy skillet heat the oil over moderate heat until it is hot but not smoking, add the garlic and the red pepper flakes, and cook the mixture, stirring, for 15 seconds, or until it is fragrant. Add the broccoli and sauté it over moderately high heat, stirring, for 1 minute. Add ⅓ cup water and cook the broccoli, covered, for 4 minutes, or until it is crisp-tender. In a large bowl toss the broccoli mixture with the chicken.

In a heavy saucepan melt 4 tablespoons of the butter over moderately low heat, add the curry powder, and cook it, whisking, for 30 seconds. Add the flour and cook the *roux*, whisking, for 3 minutes. Remove the pan from the heat, add the broth in a stream, whisking, and bring the mixture to a boil, whisking. Simmer the mixture, whisking occasionally, for 3 minutes, add the scallions, and pour the sauce over the broccoli mixture, stirring until the mixture is combined well. Transfer the mixture to a buttered 13- to 14-inch gratin dish (or 2-quart shallow baking dish). *The mixture may be made 1 day in advance and kept covered and chilled. Before proceeding with the recipe let the mixture come to room temperature.*

In a small bowl combine well the bread crumbs and the Parmesan, sprinkle the crumb mixture evenly over the broccoli and chicken mixture, and sprinkle it with the almonds. Dot the top with the remaining 1 tablespoon butter, cut into bits, and bake the gratin in the middle of a preheated 425° F. oven for 20 to 30 minutes, or until the almonds and crumb mixture are golden and the broccoli and chicken mixture is bubbling. Serves 4 to 6 as an entrée.

Chicken Breasts with Fontina, Mushrooms, and Prosciutto

1 whole skinless boneless chicken breast
 (about 10 ounces), halved lengthwise,
 rinsed, and patted dry
flour seasoned with salt and pepper
 for dredging
2 tablespoons unsalted butter
8 small white mushrooms (about 3 ounces),
 sliced thin
½ cup dry white wine
2 ounces prosciutto or smoked ham (about
 2 slices), cut into julienne strips
2 ounces Fontina (preferably Italian),
 sliced thin

Dredge the chicken lightly in the seasoned flour. In a large skillet heat the butter over moderately high heat until the foam subsides and in it sauté the chicken for 3 minutes on each side, or until it is browned lightly. Transfer the chicken with tongs to a plate and keep it warm, covered, in a preheated 250° F. oven. Add the mushrooms to the skillet and sauté them over moderately high heat for 1 minute. Add the wine, bring the liquid to a boil, stirring, and boil the mixture, scraping up the brown bits, for 1 minute. Add the chicken with any juices that have accumulated on the plate and the prosciutto, simmer the mixture, covered, for 5 minutes, or until the chicken is cooked through, and season it with salt and pepper. Transfer the chicken with tongs to a flameproof baking dish, top it with the Fontina, and put the dish under a preheated broiler about 2 inches from the heat for 1 minute, or until the Fontina is melted and browned lightly. Transfer the chicken breasts to 2 plates and spoon the prosciutto mushroom sauce over them. Serves 2.

Lemon-Baked Chicken Breasts

1 tablespoon unsalted butter
1 tablespoon vegetable oil
2 whole chicken breasts, each about
 1¼ pounds, halved
1 cup dry white wine
½ teaspoon dried thyme, crumbled
2 tablespoons fresh lemon juice, or to taste

In a large heavy skillet, preferably cast-iron, heat the butter and the oil over moderately high heat until the foam begins to subside, add the chicken, patted dry, skin side down, without crowding, and sauté it, turning it, until it is golden. Transfer the chicken with tongs to a baking dish and pour off the excess fat from the skillet. Add the wine and the thyme to the skillet, bring the liquid to a boil, scraping up the brown bits, and pour the pan juices over the chicken. Season the chicken with salt and pepper, sprinkle it with the lemon juice, and bake it in the lower third of a preheated 400° F. oven for 30 minutes, or until it is tender. Serves 4.

PHOTO ON PAGE 27

Chicken Gai Yaang
(Thai-Style Grilled Chicken with Spicy
Sweet-and-Sour Sauce)

1 garlic clove
½ teaspoon salt
1 whole chicken breast, halved
½ small red bell pepper, chopped coarse
½ cup distilled white vinegar
⅓ cup sugar
½ teaspoon crushed dried hot red
    pepper flakes
lime wedges for garnish

In a small bowl mash the garlic with the salt. Pat the chicken dry and rub the garlic paste all over it. In a food processor or blender purée the bell pepper with the vinegar, transfer the purée to a small saucepan, and stir in the sugar, the red pepper flakes, and salt to taste. Bring the mixture to a boil, stirring, and simmer the sauce for 5 minutes. Remove the pan from the heat and let the sauce cool. Broil the chicken, skin sides up, on the rack of a broiler pan set about 5 inches from the heat for 10 minutes, or until it is golden brown. Turn the chicken, broil it for 5 to 7 minutes more, or until it is springy to the touch, and let it stand for 5 minutes. Divide the chicken between plates and garnish it with the lime wedges. Divide the sauce between small ramekins and set a ramekin on each plate. Serves 2.

Braised Chicken Legs with Potatoes and Peas

1½ pounds chicken legs (about 3), split into
    drumsticks and thighs
flour seasoned with salt and pepper for
    dredging
1 tablespoon olive oil
1 tablespoon unsalted butter
1 cup chopped onion
¼ teaspoon dried thyme, crumbled
⅛ teaspoon dried sage, crumbled
⅓ cup canned chicken broth
⅓ cup dry white wine
1 cup frozen peas
2 tablespoons vegetable oil
½ pound boiling potatoes (about 2 medium)

Pat the chicken dry and dredge it in the flour, shaking off the excess. In a flameproof casserole heat the olive oil over moderately high heat until it is hot but not smoking, in it brown the chicken, and transfer it with tongs to a plate. To the casserole add the butter, the onion, the thyme, the sage, and salt and pepper to taste and cook the mixture over moderately low heat, stirring, until the onion is softened. Return the chicken, skin sides up, to the casserole, add the broth, the wine, and the peas, and bring the liquid to a boil. Braise the chicken, covered, in the middle of a preheated 450° F. oven for 15 minutes. While the chicken is braising, in a large heavy skillet heat the vegetable oil over high heat until it is hot but not smoking and in it sauté the potatoes, cut crosswise into ¼-inch slices in one layer, turning them, for 5 to 7 minutes, or until they are golden. Season the potatoes with salt and pepper and transfer them to paper towels to drain. Add the potatoes to the casserole and bake the chicken, uncovered, in the 450° F. oven for 10 minutes. Transfer the chicken to a platter and spoon the peas and potatoes over it. Serves 2.

Apricot-Glazed Chicken Wings

1 to 1½ teaspoons black peppercorns,
    or to taste
½ teaspoon fennel seeds
½ cup apricot jam
¼ cup distilled white vinegar
1 tablespoon firmly packed light brown sugar
1 tablespoon soy sauce
1 teaspoon dry mustard
½ teaspoon Oriental sesame oil (available at
    specialty foods shops and some Oriental
    markets) if desired
2 pounds chicken wings, wing tips cut off and
    reserved for another use such as wing tip
    stock (page 123) and the wings halved at
    the joint

In an electric coffee or spice grinder or with the bottom of a small heavy skillet grind medium coarse the peppercorns and the fennel seeds. In a saucepan combine the jam, the vinegar, the brown sugar, the soy sauce, the mustard, and the oil and cook the mixture over moderate heat, stirring, until the jam is melted. In a blender purée the mixture and return it to the pan, cleaned. Stir in the peppercorn mixture and keep the glaze warm, covered, over low heat. Broil the wings on the rack of a broiler pan under a preheated broiler about 2 inches from the heat, turning them, for 20 minutes, or until they are golden. In a bowl toss the wings with salt to taste and three fourths of the glaze until they are coated well. Broil the wings, turning them, for 1 to 2 minutes more, or until they are browned lightly, and serve them with the remaining glaze, heated. Serves 2 as an entrée or 4 to 6 as an hors d'oeuvre.

Barbecued Chicken Wings

1 cup finely chopped onion
2 tablespoons vegetable oil
2 garlic cloves, minced
2 teaspoons firmly packed dark brown sugar
1 tablespoon cider vinegar
2 tablespoons Worcestershire sauce
½ cup ketchup
1 teaspoon Dijon-style mustard
2 pounds chicken wings, wing tips cut off and
    reserved for another use such as wing tip
    stock (page 123) and the wings halved at
    the joint

In a saucepan cook the onion in the oil over moderately low heat, stirring occasionally, until it is softened, add the garlic, and cook the mixture, stirring, for 1 minute. Add the brown sugar, the vinegar, the Worcestershire sauce, and the ketchup and simmer the mixture, stirring, for 5 minutes. Transfer the mixture to a blender and add the mustard and salt and pepper to taste. Purée the sauce, transfer it to the pan, cleaned, and keep it warm, covered, over low heat. Broil the wings on the rack of a broiler pan under a preheated broiler about 2 inches from the heat, turning them, for 20 minutes, or until they are golden. In a bowl toss the wings with half the sauce until they are coated well. Broil the wings, turning them, for 1 to 2 minutes more, or until they are browned lightly, and serve them with the remaining sauce. Serves 2 as an entrée or 4 to 6 as an hors d'oeuvre.

Buffalo Chicken Wings

vegetable oil for deep-frying
2 pounds chicken wings, wing tips cut off and
    reserved for another use such as wing tip
    stock (page 123) and the wings halved at
    the joint
3 tablespoons unsalted butter
2 to 3 tablespoons Tabasco
1 tablespoon white-wine vinegar
blue cheese dressing (recipe follows) and
    celery sticks as accompaniments

In a large deep fryer or large deep kettle heat 2 inches of the oil to 380° F. and in it fry the wings, patted dry, in small batches for 5 to 8 minutes, or until they are golden and crisp, transferring them with tongs as they are fried to paper towels to drain and making sure the oil returns to 380° F. before adding each new batch. In a large skillet melt the butter with the Tabasco, the vinegar, and salt to taste over low heat, stirring, add the wings, and heat them, tossing them to coat them with the mixture. Serve the wings warm or at room temperature with the blue cheese dressing and the celery sticks. Serves 4 to 6 as an hors d'oeuvre.

Blue Cheese Dressing

½ cup mayonnaise
¼ cup sour cream
2 ounces blue cheese, crumbled

In a bowl combine well the mayonnaise, the sour cream, and the blue cheese. Makes about 1 cup.

Indonesian Chicken Wing "Drumsticks"

4¼ pounds chicken wings
¼ cup fresh lime juice
¼ cup vegetable oil
2 garlic cloves, minced
1 tablespoon firmly packed light brown sugar
1 to 2 teaspoons dried hot red pepper flakes,
    or to taste
2 teaspoons salt
1½ cups fine fresh bread crumbs
¾ cup unsalted roasted peanuts, chopped fine

Cut the wings apart at the first joint, separating the "drumstick" (the thickest piece) from the wing tip and second joint, reserving the tips and second joints for another use such as wing tip stock (page 123). Beginning at the narrower end of each drumstick, with a sharp knife cut the tendons and scrape the meat down the bones as far as possible toward the thicker end to make a plump drumstick shape. In a bowl whisk the lime juice, the oil, the garlic, the brown sugar, the red pepper flakes, and 1 teaspoon of the salt, add the wings, tossing them to coat them with the marinade, and let them marinate, covered and chilled, for at least 2 hours and up to 8 hours. In a bowl toss together well the bread crumbs, the peanuts, and the remaining 1 teaspoon salt and coat the wings with the crumb mixture. Bake the wings on a rack in a shallow roasting pan in a preheated 450° F. oven, turning them once, for 30 minutes, or until they are browned lightly. Serves 6 to 8 as an hors d'oeuvre.

Lemon Ginger Chicken Wings

For the marinade
2 garlic cloves, crushed with the flat side of a
    cleaver or large knife
3 quarter-size slices of fresh gingerroot,
    flattened with the flat side of a cleaver
    or large knife
2 tablespoons soy sauce
1 tablespoon Scotch

2 pounds chicken wings, wing tips cut off and
    reserved for another use such as wing tip
    stock (page 123)
For the sauce
½ cup wing tip stock (page 123) or chicken
    stock (page 123) or canned chicken broth
2 tablespoons fresh lemon juice
1 tablespoon plus 1 teaspoon sugar
2 teaspoons soy sauce
1 teaspoon coarsely grated peeled fresh
    gingerroot
1 teaspoon cornstarch dissolved in
    1 tablespoon cold water

2 large egg whites, beaten lightly
1½ cups cornstarch
vegetable oil for deep-frying

Make the marinade: Rub the garlic and the gingerroot on the bottom of a bowl, leaving them in the bowl, add the soy sauce and the Scotch, and whisk the marinade until it is combined well.

In the bowl toss the wings with the marinade until they are coated well, let them marinate, covered and chilled, for at least 1 hour and up to 8 hours, and discard the garlic and the gingerroot.

Make the sauce: In a saucepan combine the stock, the lemon juice, the sugar, the soy sauce, and the gingerroot and bring the mixture to a boil, stirring occasionally. Whisk the cornstarch mixture to combine it and add it to the boiling stock mixture, whisking. Boil the sauce for 2 minutes and keep it warm, covered, over low heat.

Have ready in 2 bowls the egg whites and the cornstarch. Dip the wings in the whites, letting the excess drip off, and dredge them in the cornstarch, making sure that they are coated thoroughly including the loose skin between the joints. In a large deep fryer or large deep kettle heat 2 inches of the oil to 375° F. and in it fry the wings in 2 batches, turning them, for 5 minutes, transferring them with tongs to paper towels to drain as they are fried and making sure the oil returns to 375° F. before adding the second batch. When all the wings are fried heat the oil to 425° F. and in it fry the wings in 2 batches, turning them, for 2 minutes more, or until they are golden and crisp, transferring them with the tongs to paper towels to drain as they are fried. (The second frying crisps the wings.) Sprinkle the wings with salt to taste, transfer them to a bowl, and toss them with the sauce until they are coated lightly. Serves 2 as an entrée or 4 as an hors d'oeuvre.

Puffed Peach Pancakes

3 tablespoons firmly packed dark brown sugar
⅛ teaspoon cinnamon
1 tablespoon fresh lemon juice
1 peach, plum, or nectarine, halved, pitted,
    and sliced thin
2 tablespoons unsalted butter
2 large eggs, beaten lightly
6 tablespoons all-purpose flour
⅛ teaspoon salt
⅓ cup milk
confectioners' sugar for garnish
maple syrup as an accompaniment

In a bowl stir together 1 tablespoon of the brown sugar, the cinnamon, and the lemon juice, add the peach slices, and toss the mixture well. Divide the butter between two 1-cup shallow ovenproof dishes, about 6 by 4 by 1 inch, and heat it in a preheated 425° F. oven for 1 minute, or until it is just melted. In a bowl combine the eggs, the flour, the remaining 2 tablespoons brown sugar, the salt, and the milk and whisk the batter until it is just combined. (The batter will be lumpy.) Divide the batter between the dishes, arrange the peach slices, drained, reserving the brown sugar mixture, in a spoke-like pattern in the centers, and pour 1 teaspoon of the reserved brown sugar mixture over each serving. Bake the pancakes in the middle of the 425° F. oven for 16 to 18 minutes, or until they are puffed and golden brown, sift the confectioners' sugar over them, and serve the pancakes with the maple syrup. Serves 2.

Baked Pear Pancake with Gingered Maple Syrup

2½ tablespoons granulated sugar
½ teaspoon cinnamon
2 ripe small pears (about ¾ pound), peeled,
    quartered lengthwise, cored, and sliced thin
    crosswise
1 tablespoon plus 2 teaspoons fresh lemon
    juice
½ cup all-purpose flour
2 large eggs
⅓ cup milk
2 tablespoons unsalted butter
½ cup maple syrup
1 tablespoon firmly packed light brown sugar
2 teaspoons minced crystallized ginger

¼ cup raisins
confectioners' sugar for sifting over the
    pancake
sour cream as an accompaniment

In a small bowl combine the granulated sugar with the cinnamon. In a bowl toss the pears with 2 teaspoons of the lemon juice and 1 tablespoon of the cinnamon sugar mixture. Into another bowl sift together the flour, 1 tablespoon of the remaining cinnamon sugar mixture, and a pinch of salt. In another small bowl whisk together the eggs and the milk, add the mixture to the flour mixture in a stream, whisking, and whisk the mixture until it is combined well (the batter will be slightly lumpy). Heat 1 tablespoon of the butter in a heavy ovenproof 9-inch skillet, preferably non-stick, over moderate heat, rotating the skillet to coat it, until the foam subsides, pour the batter into the skillet, and sprinkle the pear mixture evenly over it. Cook the pancake for 3 minutes, or until the underside is just set, and bake it in the middle of a preheated 450° F. oven for 10 minutes. While the pancake is baking, in a small saucepan combine the maple syrup, the brown sugar, the ginger, the remaining 1 tablespoon lemon juice, and 2 tablespoons water, bring the mixture to a boil, stirring until the sugar is dissolved, and simmer it for 5 minutes. Add the raisins, simmer the mixture for 1 minute, and remove the pan from the heat. Sprinkle the pancake with the remaining cinnamon sugar mixture, dot it with the remaining 1 tablespoon butter, and bake it in the 450° F. oven for 8 to 10 minutes more, or until it is puffed and golden. Sift the confectioners' sugar over the pancake and serve the pancake immediately with the gingered maple syrup and the sour cream. Serves 2.

Orange Pecan Waffles with Orange Maple Syrup
For the waffles
½ cup pecans, toasted lightly and cooled
1⅓ cups all-purpose flour
2 tablespoons sugar
4 teaspoons double-acting baking powder
½ teaspoon salt
2 teaspoons freshly grated orange rind
2 large eggs
½ stick (¼ cup) unsalted butter, melted
    and cooled
1½ cups very fresh seltzer or club soda
vegetable oil for brushing the waffle iron

6 ounces Brie, the rind discarded and the
  cheese cut into bits and softened
4 slices of lean bacon, cooked until crisp,
  drained, and crumbled
⅓ cup sliced seedless green grapes

In a bowl beat the eggs lightly with salt and pepper to taste. In an 8-inch non-stick skillet or omelet pan heat the butter over moderately high heat until the foam subsides and in it cook the eggs, stirring, for 10 seconds. Reduce the heat to moderate and cook the eggs, lifting the cooked portion and letting the uncooked eggs flow underneath, until they are just set but still soft and moist. Scatter the Brie over the eggs and sprinkle the bacon and the grapes on top. Fold the omelet over, slide it onto a heated plate, and halve it. Serves 2.

Spinach Soufflé

7 cups firmly packed spinach leaves removed
  from the stems (about 1 pound with stems),
  washed well
3 garlic cloves, halved
3 tablespoons unsalted butter
3 tablespoons all-purpose flour
½ cup milk
½ cup chicken stock (page 123) or canned
  chicken broth
¼ cup plus 3 tablespoons freshly grated
  Parmesan
3 large egg yolks, beaten lightly
⅛ teaspoon freshly grated nutmeg
⅛ teaspoon Tabasco, or to taste
1 tablespoon fresh lemon juice
3 large egg whites at room temperature

In a large saucepan cook the spinach in the water clinging to the leaves, covered, over moderate heat, stirring occasionally, for 3 minutes, or until it is wilted. Drain the spinach in a colander, refresh it under cold water, and squeeze it dry by handfuls. Chop the spinach and transfer it to a large bowl. In a small saucepan cook the garlic in the butter over moderately low heat, stirring, for 3 minutes, stir in the flour, and cook the *roux*, stirring, for 3 minutes. Whisk in the milk and the stock, bring the mixture to a boil, whisking, and simmer it, whisking occasionally, for 8 minutes. While the mixture is simmering, butter a 5-cup soufflé dish and sprin-

kle it with 3 tablespoons of the Parmesan. Strain the milk mixture through a fine sieve set over the bowl of spinach, stir in the remaining ¼ cup Parmesan, the yolks, the nutmeg, the Tabasco, the lemon juice, and salt and pepper to taste, and combine the mixture well. Let the mixture cool for 5 minutes. In a bowl with an electric mixer beat the whites with a pinch of salt until they barely hold stiff peaks, stir one fourth of them into the spinach mixture, and fold in the remaining whites gently but thoroughly. Transfer the mixture to the prepared dish, bake it in the middle of a preheated 350° F. oven for 25 to 30 minutes, or until it is puffed and golden and a skewer comes out clean, and serve the soufflé immediately. Serves 6.

BREAKFAST ITEMS

Chocolate-Filled French Toast

two 1-inch-thick diagonal slices of Italian or
  French bread
1½ ounces fine-quality bittersweet chocolate,
  broken into large pieces
1 large egg, beaten lightly
¼ cup milk
1 tablespoon superfine sugar
½ teaspoon vanilla
⅛ teaspoon cinnamon
1½ tablespoons unsalted butter
confectioners' sugar for dusting the
  French toast
coffee or vanilla ice cream as an
  accompaniment

Cut through each slice of bread horizontally with a serrated knife to within ¼ inch of the bottom crust, forming a pocket, and into each pocket stuff half the chocolate, pressing the openings together. In a shallow bowl or pie plate whisk together the egg, the milk, the superfine sugar, the vanilla, the cinnamon, and a pinch of salt, add the filled bread in one layer, and let it soak, turning it once, for 5 to 10 minutes, or until the bread absorbs most of the egg mixture. In a heavy skillet heat the butter over moderately low heat until the foam subsides and in it cook the soaked bread, turning it frequently with a spatula, for 10 minutes, or until it is crisp and golden. Transfer the French toast to heated plates, dust it with the confectioners' sugar, and serve it with the ice cream. Serves 2.

Puffed Peach Pancakes

3 tablespoons firmly packed dark brown sugar
⅛ teaspoon cinnamon
1 tablespoon fresh lemon juice
1 peach, plum, or nectarine, halved, pitted,
  and sliced thin
2 tablespoons unsalted butter
2 large eggs, beaten lightly
6 tablespoons all-purpose flour
⅛ teaspoon salt
⅓ cup milk
confectioners' sugar for garnish
maple syrup as an accompaniment

In a bowl stir together 1 tablespoon of the brown sugar, the cinnamon, and the lemon juice, add the peach slices, and toss the mixture well. Divide the butter between two 1-cup shallow ovenproof dishes, about 6 by 4 by 1 inch, and heat it in a preheated 425° F. oven for 1 minute, or until it is just melted. In a bowl combine the eggs, the flour, the remaining 2 tablespoons brown sugar, the salt, and the milk and whisk the batter until it is just combined. (The batter will be lumpy.) Divide the batter between the dishes, arrange the peach slices, drained, reserving the brown sugar mixture, in a spoke-like pattern in the centers, and pour 1 teaspoon of the reserved brown sugar mixture over each serving. Bake the pancakes in the middle of the 425° F. oven for 16 to 18 minutes, or until they are puffed and golden brown, sift the confectioners' sugar over them, and serve the pancakes with the maple syrup. Serves 2.

Baked Pear Pancake with Gingered Maple Syrup

2½ tablespoons granulated sugar
½ teaspoon cinnamon
2 ripe small pears (about ¾ pound), peeled,
  quartered lengthwise, cored, and sliced thin
  crosswise
1 tablespoon plus 2 teaspoons fresh lemon
  juice
½ cup all-purpose flour
2 large eggs
⅓ cup milk
2 tablespoons unsalted butter
½ cup maple syrup
1 tablespoon firmly packed light brown sugar
2 teaspoons minced crystallized ginger

¼ cup raisins
confectioners' sugar for sifting over the
  pancake
sour cream as an accompaniment

In a small bowl combine the granulated sugar with the cinnamon. In a bowl toss the pears with 2 teaspoons of the lemon juice and 1 tablespoon of the cinnamon sugar mixture. Into another bowl sift together the flour, 1 tablespoon of the remaining cinnamon sugar mixture, and a pinch of salt. In another small bowl whisk together the eggs and the milk, add the mixture to the flour mixture in a stream, whisking, and whisk the mixture until it is combined well (the batter will be slightly lumpy). Heat 1 tablespoon of the butter in a heavy ovenproof 9-inch skillet, preferably non-stick, over moderate heat, rotating the skillet to coat it, until the foam subsides, pour the batter into the skillet, and sprinkle the pear mixture evenly over it. Cook the pancake for 3 minutes, or until the underside is just set, and bake it in the middle of a preheated 450° F. oven for 10 minutes. While the pancake is baking, in a small saucepan combine the maple syrup, the brown sugar, the ginger, the remaining 1 tablespoon lemon juice, and 2 tablespoons water, bring the mixture to a boil, stirring until the sugar is dissolved, and simmer it for 5 minutes. Add the raisins, simmer the mixture for 1 minute, and remove the pan from the heat. Sprinkle the pancake with the remaining cinnamon sugar mixture, dot it with the remaining 1 tablespoon butter, and bake it in the 450° F. oven for 8 to 10 minutes more, or until it is puffed and golden. Sift the confectioners' sugar over the pancake and serve the pancake immediately with the gingered maple syrup and the sour cream. Serves 2.

Orange Pecan Waffles with Orange Maple Syrup
For the waffles

½ cup pecans, toasted lightly and cooled
1⅓ cups all-purpose flour
2 tablespoons sugar
4 teaspoons double-acting baking powder
½ teaspoon salt
2 teaspoons freshly grated orange rind
2 large eggs
½ stick (¼ cup) unsalted butter, melted
  and cooled
1½ cups very fresh seltzer or club soda
vegetable oil for brushing the waffle iron

Huevos Rancheros
(Baked Eggs with Braised Pork and Spicy Tomato Sauce)

For the pork mixture
2 tablespoons olive oil
1½ pounds boneless pork shoulder, cut into
   1½-inch pieces
2 large onions, chopped
4 large garlic cloves, chopped fine
1 tablespoon chili powder
2 teaspoons paprika
1 cup canned chicken broth
2 tablespoons white-wine vinegar
1½ cups drained canned pinto beans, rinsed
   well in a sieve
For the tomato sauce
1 cup chopped onion
2 tablespoons olive oil
3 large garlic cloves, minced
two 28-ounce cans plum tomatoes, drained,
   reserving 1½ cups of the juice, and chopped
a 4-ounce can green chilies, drained and
   chopped fine
2 teaspoons seeded and minced pickled
   jalapeño pepper, or to taste (wear rubber
   gloves)
¾ teaspoon dried orégano, crumbled
¼ teaspoon dried thyme, crumbled
1 teaspoon sugar
1 green bell pepper, chopped fine

6 large eggs at room temperature
minced fresh parsley leaves for garnish
shredded tortilla crisps as an accompaniment
   (recipe follows)

Make the pork mixture: In a large flameproof casserole heat the oil over moderately high heat until it is hot but not smoking and in it brown the pork, patted dry and seasoned with salt and pepper, in batches, transferring it with tongs as it is browned to a plate. Add the onions to the casserole and cook them over moderately low heat, stirring, until they are softened. Add the garlic and cook the mixture, stirring, for 1 minute. Add the chili powder and the paprika and cook the mixture, stirring, for 30 seconds. Add the pork, the broth, and the vinegar, bring the liquid to a boil, and braise the mixture, covered, in a preheated 325° F. oven for 2 hours, or until the pork is very tender. Mash the pork into the cooking liquid with a fork, stirring until the mixture is combined well, and stir in the beans. Spread the mixture evenly in a shallow 2-quart oval baking dish (about 14 inches long). *The pork mixture may be made 2 days in advance and kept covered and chilled.*

Make the tomato sauce while the pork is braising: In a large skillet cook the onion in the oil over moderately low heat, stirring, until it is softened, add the garlic, and cook the mixture, stirring, for 1 minute. Add the tomatoes with the reserved juice, the chilies, the *jalapeño* pepper, the orégano, the thyme, the sugar, and salt and pepper to taste, bring the mixture to a boil, and cook it at a strong simmer, stirring occasionally, for 10 minutes. Add the bell pepper and cook the mixture at a strong simmer, stirring occasionally, for 10 minutes, or until the sauce is thickened. *The tomato sauce may be made 2 days in advance and kept covered and chilled.*

Spoon the tomato sauce over the pork mixture and heat the mixture, covered with foil, in the middle of a preheated 400° F. oven for 30 to 45 minutes, or until it is bubbling. Make 6 large indentations with the back of a large spoon in the mixture, spacing them evenly, and break an egg into each indentation. Bake the mixture in the 400° F. oven for 7 to 10 minutes, or until the whites are set but the yolks are still runny, and sprinkle the dish with the parsley. Serve the *huevos rancheros* with the tortilla crisps. Serves 6.

PHOTO ON PAGE 15

Shredded Tortilla Crisps

twelve 6- to 7-inch corn tortillas
vegetable oil for frying

With scissors or a sharp knife cut the tortillas into ¼-inch-wide strips. In a large skillet heat ¾ inch of the oil to 375° F. and in it fry the tortilla strips in small batches, pinching the strips together loosely with tongs to form curved shapes, for 30 seconds to 1 minute, or until they are crisp and pale golden. Transfer the crisps with a slotted spoon to paper towels to drain and sprinkle them with salt to taste. *The tortilla crisps may be made 1 day in advance and kept in an airtight container.* Serves 6.

PHOTO ON PAGE 15

Brie, Bacon, and Grape Omelet

3 large eggs
1 tablespoon unsalted butter

Make the tomato sauce while the eggplant is draining: In a saucepan cook the onion and the garlic in the oil over moderate heat, stirring occasionally, for 8 minutes, add the tomatoes, breaking them up with a spoon, the thyme, the orégano, the sugar, and salt and pepper to taste, and bring the mixture to a boil. Simmer the sauce, stirring occasionally, for 10 minutes, or until it is thickened slightly.

Dredge the eggplant slices in the flour, shaking off the excess. In a large heavy skillet heat the oil over moderately high heat until it is hot but not smoking and in it sauté the eggplant slices, turning them, for 4 minutes, or until they are browned and tender. Transfer the eggplant slices to a heated platter and keep them warm.

In a large skillet, preferably nonstick, heat the butter over moderately high heat until the foam begins to subside. Add the eggs, season them with salt and pepper, and cook them for 2 minutes, or until the whites are just set. Transfer each egg as it is cooked to an eggplant slice and top with some of the tomato sauce. Sprinkle each serving with half the Parmesan and serve it with half the toast points. Serves 2 as a brunch entrée.

Potato and Leek Frittata

1½ pounds boiling potatoes
3 cups thinly sliced white and pale green part
    of leek, washed well and drained
2 tablespoons unsalted butter
12 large eggs
1 cup freshly grated Parmesan
1 cup coarsely grated Gruyère
2 tablespoons snipped fresh chives
2 tablespoons minced fresh parsley leaves
2 tablespoons olive oil

In a steamer set over boiling water steam the potatoes, covered, for 20 to 25 minutes, or until they are tender, and let them cool until they can be handled. Peel the potatoes and cut them crosswise into thin slices. In a 12-inch non-stick skillet cook the leek in the butter over moderately low heat, stirring, for 12 to 15 minutes, or until it is very soft, and add salt and pepper to taste. In a large bowl whisk together the eggs, add ½ cup of the Parmesan, ½ cup of the Gruyère, the chives, the parsley, and salt and pepper to taste, and whisk the mixture until it is combined well. Stir in the leek and the potatoes. In the skillet, cleaned, heat the oil over moderate heat until it is hot but not smoking, pour in the egg mixture, distributing the potatoes evenly, and cook the *frittata*, without stirring, for 14 to 16 minutes, or until the edge is set but the center is still soft. Sprinkle the remaining ½ cup Parmesan and the remaining ½ cup Gruyère over the top. If the skillet handle is plastic, wrap it in a double thickness of foil. Broil the *frittata* under a preheated broiler about 4 inches from the heat for 4 to 5 minutes, or until the cheese is bubbling and golden. Let the *frittata* cool in the skillet for 5 minutes, run a thin knife around the edge, and slide the *frittata* onto a serving plate. Cut the *frittata* into wedges and serve it warm or at room temperature. Serves 6.

PHOTO ON PAGE 63

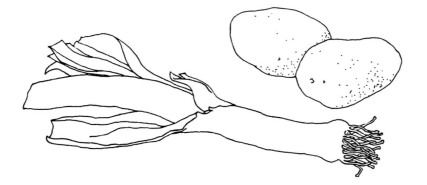

JEANNE

Spanokopita
(Greek Spinach, Feta, and Phyllo Pie)

1½ cups chopped onion
1 tablespoon minced garlic
2 tablespoons olive oil
20 cups firmly packed spinach leaves
    removed from the stems (about 3 pounds
    with stems), washed well, spun dry, and
    chopped
1 tablespoon white-wine vinegar
½ cup firmly packed fresh parsley leaves,
    minced
¼ cup snipped fresh dill
3 large eggs,
    beaten lightly
¾ pound Feta, crumbled
    (about 2 cups)
freshly ground white pepper
1 stick (½ cup) unsalted butter, melted and
    cooled
ten 17- by 12-inch sheets of *phyllo* (thawed if
    frozen), halved crosswise, stacked between
    2 sheets of wax paper, and covered with a
    dampened kitchen towel

In a large deep skillet cook the onion and the garlic in the oil over moderately low heat, stirring, until the vegetables are softened, add the spinach and the vinegar, and cook the mixture, stirring occasionally, until the spinach is wilted. In a bowl combine well the parsley, the dill, and the eggs, stir in the spinach mixture and the Feta, and season the mixture with salt and freshly ground white pepper.

Brush a baking pan, 11 by 7 by 2 inches, with some of the butter, fit 1 of the *phyllo* halves into the pan, pressing it to the bottom and up the sides, and brush it with some of the butter. Fit another *phyllo* half into the pan on top of the first half and brush it with some of the butter. Layer and butter 8 of the remaining *phyllo* halves in the same manner and turn the spinach filling into the pan, spreading it evenly. Cover the filling with 1 of the remaining *phyllo* halves, brush the *phyllo* with some of the remaining butter, and layer and butter the remaining *phyllo* halves in the same manner. Trim the *phyllo* around the edges to fit inside the pan, tucking it in. Bake the *spanokopita* in the middle of a preheated 350° F. oven for 50 to 55 minutes, or until it is crisp and golden. Let the *spanokopita* cool for 10 minutes, and cut it into squares. Serves 6.

EGGS

Sardine Deviled Eggs

12 hard-boiled large eggs, halved lengthwise
½ cup sour cream
2 tablespoons Dijon-style mustard
2 teaspoons drained bottled horseradish
2 teaspoons fresh lemon juice
⅓ cup minced fresh parsley leaves plus whole
    parsley leaves for garnish
a 3¾-ounce can brisling sardines in olive oil,
    drained and chopped coarse

Remove the yolks from the eggs, keeping the egg white halves intact, and force them through a fine sieve into a bowl. Add the sour cream, the mustard, the horseradish, the lemon juice, the minced parsley, and salt and pepper to taste and whisk the mixture until it is combined well. Divide the sardines among the egg white halves and with a pastry bag fitted with a decorative tip pipe the yolk mixture into the egg white halves. Garnish the deviled eggs with the remaining whole parsley leaves. Serves 10 to 12.

PHOTO ON PAGES 42 AND 43

Fried Eggs on Eggplant with Tomato Sauce

four 1-inch-thick crosswise slices of eggplant
    (each about 4 inches in diameter)
For the tomato sauce
1 small onion, chopped
1 garlic clove, minced
1 tablespoon olive oil
a 14½-ounce can tomatoes, drained well
⅛ teaspoon dried thyme, crumbled
⅛ teaspoon dried orégano, crumbled
⅛ teaspoon sugar

flour seasoned with salt and pepper for
    dredging
2 tablespoons olive oil
1 tablespoon butter
4 large eggs
freshly grated Parmesan if desired
toast points as an accompaniment if desired

Sprinkle the eggplant with salt, arrange the slices in one layer between paper towels, and let them drain.

In a small bowl stir the mustard into the Worcestershire sauce until the mixture forms a paste. In a saucepan combine the milk, all but 2 tablespoons of the Cheddar, the bay leaf, the thyme, and the mustard paste, heat the mixture over moderate heat, stirring, until the cheese is melted, and let it cool. Spread the butter on one side of each of the stars and arrange the stars, buttered sides down and overlapping slightly, in a buttered 2-quart gratin dish. In a bowl whisk together the eggs, the Cheddar mixture, the scallion, and salt and pepper to taste and ladle the mixture over the stars. Let the pudding stand at room temperature, covered loosely, for at least 1 hour or let it stand, covered and chilled, overnight. Sprinkle the pudding with the remaining 2 tablespoons Cheddar and bake it in the middle of a preheated 375° F. oven for 25 minutes, or until it is set. Serves 6.

PHOTO ON PAGE 81

Cheese Fondue

¾ pound Gruyère, grated coarse (about
    4 cups)
½ pound Emmenthal or other imported Swiss
    cheese, grated coarse (about 2½ cups)
2 tablespoons cornstarch
2½ cups dry white wine
2 garlic cloves, crushed lightly with the flat
    side of a large knife
2 tablespoons fresh lemon juice plus
    additional to taste
3 tablespoons Sercial Madeira
freshly grated nutmeg to taste
2 crusty loaves of French or Italian bread, cut
    into ¾-inch pieces

In a large bowl toss together well the Gruyère, the Emmenthal, and the cornstarch. In a heavy saucepan or heavy flameproof casserole combine the wine and the garlic, bring the wine to a boil, and simmer the mixture for 5 minutes. Remove and discard the garlic with a slotted spoon and stir in the lemon juice. Add the cheese mixture in small handfuls, stirring with a fork in a figure-eight pattern after each handful is added until the mixture is smooth, stir in the Madeira, the nutmeg, and salt and pepper to taste, and keep the fondue bubbling gently, stirring constantly. Transfer the fondue to a fondue pot if desired. Set the fondue over a portable tabletop gas or alcohol burner and adjust the flame so that the fondue continues to bubble gently. With fondue forks or wooden skewers spear the bread and stir it through the fondue, 1 piece at a time, to coat it with the cheese mixture. Serves 4.

Fried Mozzarella with Roasted Red Pepper Sauce

½ cup fresh bread crumbs
¼ cup pine nuts, toasted
    lightly, cooled, and chopped
    very fine
flour for dredging
1 large egg
an 8-ounce package mozzarella, sliced
    horizontally into four ¼-inch-thick slices
a 7-ounce jar roasted red peppers, drained,
    rinsed, and patted dry
¼ cup olive oil
1½ teaspoons fresh lemon juice
1½ teaspoons red-wine vinegar
cayenne to taste
¼ cup Kalamata or other brine-cured black
    olives, pitted and chopped
2 tablespoons minced fresh parsley leaves
    plus additional for garnish if desired

In a small shallow bowl stir together the bread crumbs, the pine nuts, and salt and pepper to taste. Have ready in 2 separate bowls the flour and the egg, beaten lightly. Working with 1 mozzarella slice at a time, dredge the slices in the flour, shaking off the excess, dip them in the egg, letting the excess drip off, and coat them with the crumb mixture, patting the crumbs gently onto the sides and edges. Line a plate with wax paper and chill the slices in one layer on it for 15 minutes. While the mozzarella is chilling, in a blender blend the peppers, 1 tablespoon of the oil, the lemon juice, the vinegar, the cayenne, 1 tablespoon water, and salt and pepper to taste until the mixture is smooth. Transfer the sauce to a bowl, stir in the olives and 2 tablespoons of the parsley, and divide the sauce between 2 plates. In a large heavy skillet, preferably non-stick, heat the remaining 3 tablespoons oil over moderately high heat until it is hot but not smoking and in it sauté the mozzarella slices, turning them once, for 2 to 3 minutes, or until they are golden. Divide the mozzarella slices between the plates and garnish them with the additional parsley. Serves 2 as a luncheon entrée.

Corn Bread for Stuffing

1 cup all-purpose flour
1⅓ cups yellow cornmeal
1 tablespoon double-acting baking powder
1 teaspoon salt
1 cup milk
1 large egg
3 tablespoons unsalted butter, melted
   and cooled

In a bowl stir together the flour, the cornmeal, the baking powder, and the salt. In a small bowl whisk together the milk, the egg, and the butter, add the milk mixture to the cornmeal mixture, and stir the batter until it is just combined. Pour the batter into a greased 8-inch-square baking pan and bake the corn bread in the middle of a preheated 425° F. oven for 20 to 25 minutes, or until the top is pale golden and a tester inserted in the center comes out clean. Let the corn bread cool in the pan for 5 minutes, invert it onto a rack, and let it cool completely.

PHOTO ON PAGE 72

To Shell and Peel Chestnuts

With a sharp knife cut an X on the round side of each chestnut. Spread the chestnuts in one layer in a jelly-roll pan, add ¼ cup water, and bake the chestnuts in a preheated 450° F. oven for 10 minutes, or until the shells open. Remove the chestnuts, a handful at a time, and shell and peel them while they are still hot.

To Cook Chestnuts

In a deep skillet arrange shelled and peeled chestnuts in one layer, add water to cover, and simmer the chestnuts for 45 minutes, or until they are tender. Drain the chestnuts and pat them dry.

CHEESE, EGGS, AND BREAKFAST ITEMS

CHEESE

Broccoli and Cheese Egg "Crêpes"

3 large eggs
¼ teaspoon dried thyme, crumbled
¼ teaspoon salt
¼ teaspoon freshly ground pepper
vegetable oil for brushing the skillet
¾ cup whole-milk ricotta
½ cup coarsely chopped whole-milk
    mozzarella
1½ cups ½-inch broccoli flowerets, blanched
    for 1 minute, drained, refreshed under cold
    water, and patted dry
2 tablespoons minced shallot
¼ cup freshly grated Parmesan

In a bowl whisk together well the eggs, the thyme, the salt, and the pepper. Brush a non-stick skillet measuring 6 inches across the bottom lightly with the oil and heat the oil over moderately high heat until it is hot but not smoking. Fill a ¼-cup measure three fourths full with the egg mixture and add it to the skillet, swirling it to coat the skillet evenly. Cook the egg "crêpe" for 15 seconds, or until it is set, turn it with a rubber spatula, and cook it for 5 seconds more. Slide the crêpe onto a plate and make 3 more crêpes with the remaining mixture in the same manner, brushing the skillet lightly with the oil each time.

In a bowl combine well the ricotta, the mozzarella, the broccoli, the shallot, 2 tablespoons of the Parmesan, and salt and pepper to taste. Divide the filling among the crêpes, mounding it down the center, and fold the sides over to enclose the filling. Arrange the crêpes in a buttered baking dish just large enough to hold them in one layer, sprinkle them with the remaining 2 tablespoons Parmesan, and bake the crêpes in the middle of a preheated 425° F. oven for 10 to 12 minutes, or until they are browned lightly and heated through. Serves 2.

Cheddar Bread Pudding

8 large slices of seedless rye bread
16 slices of homemade-type white bread
2 teaspoons dry mustard
1 tablespoon Worcestershire sauce
2¾ cups milk
6 ounces extra-sharp Cheddar, grated (about
    1⅔ cups)
½ bay leaf
¼ teaspoon crumbled dried thyme
½ stick (¼ cup) unsalted butter, softened
3 large eggs, beaten lightly
2 tablespoons minced scallion including the
    green part

With a star-shaped cutter measuring 3 inches at its widest point or other 3-inch cutter cut 16 stars from the rye bread and 16 stars from the white bread. Toast the stars in one layer in jelly-roll pans under a preheated broiler about 4 inches from the heat, turning them once, until they are deep golden. Let the stars dry, uncovered, at room temperature overnight. *The stars may be made 2 days in advance and kept in an airtight container.*

For the orange maple syrup
1 cup maple syrup
¼ cup fresh orange juice

1 pound breakfast sausage links, cooked
    according to package instructions, as an
    accompaniment
decorative orange slices for garnish if desired

Make the waffles: In a blender or food processor grind the pecans with the flour, the sugar, the baking powder, and the salt until they are very finely ground and transfer the mixture to a large bowl. *The pecan mixture may be prepared up to this point 1 week in advance and kept tightly sealed in an airtight container or plastic bag and chilled.* Transfer the mixture to a large bowl and stir in the rind. In a small bowl whisk together the eggs and the butter, add the mixture to the pecan mix-

ture with the seltzer, and stir the batter until it is just combined. Heat a well seasoned or non-stick waffle iron until it is hot, brush it lightly with the oil, and pour the batter onto it, using about ½ cup of the batter for each 7-inch round waffle. Cook the waffles according to the manufacturer's instructions, transferring them as they are cooked to a baking sheet and keeping them warm, uncovered, in a preheated 250° F. oven.

Make the orange maple syrup while the waffles are cooking: In a small saucepan combine the maple syrup and the orange juice, heat the mixture over moderately low heat, stirring, until it is hot, and transfer it to a small pitcher.

Arrange the waffles, separated into sections, on a heated platter with the sausage links, garnish the platter with the orange slices, and serve the waffles with the syrup. Makes about 6 waffles, serving 4.

PHOTO ON PAGE 24

PASTA AND GRAINS

PASTA

Fusilli with Kale and Garlic

1 pound kale, stems cut away and discarded
2 large garlic cloves, minced
¼ teaspoon dried hot red pepper flakes
3 tablespoons olive oil
½ pound *fusilli* (spiral-shaped pasta)
freshly grated Parmesan as an accompaniment

Cut the kale crosswise into 1½-inch strips, wash it well, and drain it. In a large heavy skillet cook the garlic and the red pepper flakes in the oil over moderate heat, stirring, until the garlic is golden, add the kale, and cook it, stirring, for 1 minute, or until it is a brighter green. Add ½ cup water and steam the kale, covered, over moderately high heat for 8 minutes, or until it is wilted and just tender.

While the kale is steaming, stir the *fusilli* into a kettle of boiling salted water and boil it for 8 to 10 minutes, or until it is *al dente*. Ladle out ¼ cup of the cooking liquid and add it to the kale mixture. Drain the *fusilli* and add it to the kale mixture. Heat the mixture over moderate heat, stirring, until it is combined well and heated through, season it with salt and pepper, and divide it between 2 heated plates. Serve the *fusilli* with the Parmesan. Serves 2.

Spinach Fusilli with Sautéed Cauliflower and Feta

½ pound spinach *fusilli* (corkscrew-shaped pasta)
¼ cup chopped Kalamata or other brine-cured black olives
⅓ cup julienne strips of pimiento
½ cup crumbled Feta
¼ teaspoon freshly grated lemon rind
1 scallion, chopped fine
2 teaspoons fresh lemon juice
3 tablespoons olive oil
2 cups chopped cauliflower

In a kettle of boiling salted water cook the *fusilli* for 10 to 12 minutes, or until it is *al dente*, and drain it well. While the *fusilli* is cooking, in a bowl combine the olives, the pimiento, the Feta, the rind, the scallion, the lemon juice, and 1 tablespoon of the oil. In a skillet sauté the cauliflower in the remaining 2 tablespoons oil over moderately high heat, stirring, for 3 to 5 minutes, or until it is golden and crisp-tender. To the bowl add the cauliflower with the oil, the *fusilli*, and salt and pepper to taste and toss the mixture until it is combined well. Serves 2.

Gnocchi di Patate al Sugo di Pomodoro
(Potato Dumplings with Tomato Sauce)

2 garlic cloves, minced
2 tablespoons olive oil
two 1-pound 12-ounce cans Italian plum
    tomatoes including the juice
2 teaspoons dried basil, crumbled
1 pound boiling potatoes, unpeeled
½ teaspoon salt
⅓ to ½ cup all-purpose flour
½ cup freshly grated Parmesan
6 sprigs of flat-leafed parsley for garnish
    if desired

In a large heavy saucepan cook the garlic in the oil over moderately low heat, stirring occasionally, until it is golden. Add the tomatoes with the juice and the basil, bring the mixture to a boil, breaking up the tomatoes, and simmer it, stirring occasionally, for 45 to 50 minutes, or until it is thickened. Season the sauce with salt and pepper. *The sauce may be made 2 days in advance, cooled to room temperature, and kept covered and chilled.*

In a large saucepan combine the potatoes with enough cold water to cover them by 2 inches, bring the water to a boil, and add salt to taste. Simmer the potatoes for 20 to 25 minutes, or until they are very tender, drain them, and let them cool until they can be handled. Peel the potatoes, force them through a ricer or the medium disk of a food mill into a bowl, and knead in the salt and ⅓ cup of the flour, or enough to form a soft but not sticky dough. Divide the dough into eighths, on a lightly floured surface roll out each piece of dough into a ½-inch-thick rope, and cut the ropes into 1-inch pieces. (If you prefer to form ridged *gnocchi* put one of the pieces of dough on the tines of a floured fork and press it gently to flatten it slightly. With your index finger roll one end of the dough toward the tip of the tines, forming a slight crease, and roll the other end of the dough toward the fork's handle, forming an overall curled, ridged shape. Make *gnocchi* in the same manner with the remaining dough.) *The* gnocchi, *plain or ridge-shaped, may be prepared up to this point 1 hour in advance and kept on a lightly floured baking sheet at room temperature.*

Heat the tomato sauce over moderately low heat, stirring occasionally, until it is heated through, transfer 2 cups of it to a large bowl, and keep the remaining sauce warm, covered, over low heat. In a kettle of boiling salted water cook the *gnocchi* in 5 batches, boiling them for 8 seconds after they float to the surface, remove them with a slotted spoon, draining them well, and transfer them to the bowl. Toss the *gnocchi* gently with the sauce. Spoon the remaining sauce onto 6 heated plates and divide the *gnocchi* among the plates. Sprinkle the *gnocchi* with the Parmesan and garnish them with the parsley. Serves 6 as a first course.

JEANNE

Roasted Broccoli and Zucchini Lasagne

1 ounce dried *shiitake* mushrooms (Oriental
black mushrooms, available at Oriental
markets and some supermarkets)
2½ pounds broccoli (about 2 bunches), the
flowerets cut into 1-inch pieces and the
stems sliced thin
6 tablespoons olive oil
2 pounds zucchini, washed well and cut into
¼-inch-thick rounds
½ pound shallots, cut crosswise into ¼-inch-
thick pieces
1½ teaspoons dried hot red pepper flakes, or
to taste
1 pound food processor pasta dough (recipe
follows), rolled (procedure follows)
4½ cups béchamel sauce (page 225)
1 pound whole-milk mozzarella, sliced
¼ inch thick
1½ cups freshly grated Parmesan

In a bowl combine the mushrooms with warm water
to cover, let them stand for 20 minutes, and drain them.
Discard the stems, press the mushrooms between layers
of paper towels to remove the excess moisture, and cut
them into ¼-inch strips. Transfer the mushrooms to a
large bowl.

Divide the broccoli between 2 jelly-roll pans, drizzle
it with 3 tablespoons of the oil, and toss the mixture until
it is combined well. Roast the broccoli on the upper and
lower racks of a preheated 500° F. oven for 5 to 6 minutes, or until it is crisp-tender, and transfer it to the
bowl. Divide the zucchini between the 2 pans, drizzle it
with 2 tablespoons of the remaining oil, and toss the
mixture until it is combined well. Roast the zucchini in
the same manner in the 500° F. oven for 3 to 4 minutes,
or until it is crisp-tender, and transfer it to the bowl.
Spread the shallots in 1 of the pans, drizzle them with
the remaining 1 tablespoon oil, and toss the mixture until it is combined well. Roast the shallots in the upper
third of the 500° F. oven, stirring once, for 6 to 7 minutes, or until they are crisp-tender, and transfer them to
the bowl. Sprinkle the red pepper flakes over the vegetable mixture and toss the mixture until it is combined
well.

Cut the dough into 3-inch squares, in a kettle of boiling salted water cook it in batches for 4 to 5 minutes, or
until it is *al dente*, and transfer it with a skimmer to paper towels to drain, patting it dry. Pour 1 cup of the bé-

chamel into a baking pan, 14½ by 10 by 3 inches, cover
it with one third of the pasta, overlapping the squares if
necessary, and spread one third of the vegetable mixture over the pasta. Pour one third of the remaining béchamel over the vegetable mixture, arrange one third of
the mozzarella over the béchamel, and sprinkle it with
¼ cup of the Parmesan. Cover the Parmesan with half
the remaining pasta and spread half the remaining vegetable mixture over the pasta. Pour half the remaining béchamel over the vegetable mixture, arrange half the
remaining mozzarella over the béchamel, and sprinkle
it with ¼ cup of the remaining Parmesan. Layer the remaining ingredients in the same manner, starting with
the pasta and sprinkling the top layer of mozzarella with
the remaining 1 cup Parmesan. *The lasagne may be prepared up to this point 6 hours in advance.* Bake the lasagne in the middle of a preheated 400° F. oven for 30 to
40 minutes, or until the top is golden. Serves 10 to 12.

Food Processor Pasta Dough

2 cups all-purpose flour
2 large eggs, beaten lightly
1 tablespoon olive oil

In a food processor blend the flour, the eggs, the oil,
and 2 tablespoons water until the mixture just begins to
form a ball, adding more water drop by drop if the
dough is too dry. (The dough should be firm and not
sticky.) Blend the dough for 15 seconds more to knead
it. Let the dough stand, covered with an inverted bowl,
at room temperature for 1 hour. Makes 1 pound.

To Roll Pasta Dough

Set the smooth rollers of a pasta machine at the high-
est number. (The rollers will be wide apart.) Divide the
dough into 8 pieces, flatten each piece into a rough rectangle, and cover the rectangles with an inverted bowl.
Dust 1 rectangle with flour and feed it through the
rollers. Fold the rectangle in half and feed it through the
rollers 8 or 9 more times, folding it in half each time and
dusting it with flour if necessary to prevent it from sticking. Turn the dial down one notch and feed the dough
through the rollers without folding. Continue to feed the
dough through the rollers without folding, turning the
dial one notch lower each time, until the lowest notch is
reached. The pasta dough should be a smooth long sheet
about 30 inches long and about 3½ inches wide. Roll the
remaining pieces of pasta dough in the same manner.

Shrimp, Scallop, and Monkfish Lasagne

2½ cups chopped onion
1½ cups chopped green bell pepper
¼ cup olive oil
2 large garlic cloves, minced
two 35-ounce cans Italian plum tomatoes
    including the juice
1½ pounds shrimp, shelled, deveined, and cut
    into ½-inch pieces
1½ pounds sea scallops, halved horizontally
    if large
2 pounds monkfish fillet, trimmed and cut
    into 1-inch pieces
1 pound spinach noodle dough (recipe
    follows), rolled (procedure opposite)
1¾ pounds Gruyère, grated coarse (about
    6 cups)

In a heavy kettle cook the onion and the bell pepper in 3 tablespoons of the oil over moderately low heat, stirring occasionally, until the vegetables are softened, add the garlic, and cook the mixture, stirring, for 1 minute. Stir in the tomatoes with the juice and salt and pepper to taste and bring the mixture to a boil, breaking up the tomatoes. Simmer the mixture, stirring occasionally, for 50 minutes to 1 hour, or until it is very thick.

In a large non-stick skillet cook the shrimp in 1 teaspoon of the remaining oil, covered, over moderate heat, stirring occasionally, for 3 to 4 minutes, or until they are just firm and give off their liquid, transfer them to a large sieve, and let them drain. In the skillet cook the scallops in 1 teaspoon of the remaining oil, covered, stirring occasionally, for 3 to 4 minutes, or until they are just firm and give off their liquid, transfer them to the sieve, and let them drain. In the skillet cook the monkfish in the remaining 1 teaspoon oil, covered, stirring occasionally, for 2 to 3 minutes, or until it is just firm and gives off its liquid, transfer it to the sieve, and let it drain. In a large bowl toss the seafood together until it is combined well.

Cut the dough into 3-inch squares, in a kettle of boiling salted water cook it in batches for 6 to 7 minutes, or until it is *al dente*, and transfer it with a skimmer to paper towels to drain, patting it dry. Pour 1 cup of the tomato sauce into a baking dish, 17 by 12 by 1½ inches, cover it with half the pasta, overlapping the squares if necessary, and spread half the seafood mixture over the pasta. Pour half the remaining sauce over the seafood mixture and sprinkle it with half the Gruyère. Layer the remaining ingredients in the same manner, starting with the pasta, and bake the lasagne in the middle of a preheated 400° F. oven for 25 to 30 minutes, or until the top is golden. Serves 10 to 12.

PHOTO ON PAGE 21

Spinach Noodle Dough

2 cups all-purpose flour
2 large eggs, beaten lightly
½ teaspoon salt
½ pound spinach, cooked, squeezed well,
    and puréed

Sift the flour into a large bowl and make a well in the center. Add the eggs and the salt and blend the mixture slightly. Add the spinach and combine the mixture well, adding 1 to 2 tablespoons warm water, several drops at a time, or enough to make a firm ball of dough. Let the dough stand, covered with an inverted bowl, for 1 hour. Makes 1 pound.

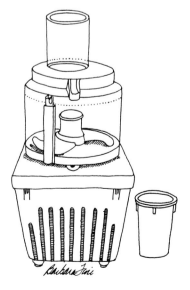

Linguine with Mussel Sauce

4 pounds mussels
⅓ cup dry white wine
1 pound dried *linguine*
1 tablespoon minced garlic
½ cup olive oil
¾ teaspoon dried orégano, crumbled
½ teaspoon dried hot red pepper flakes,
    or to taste
⅓ cup minced fresh parsley leaves (preferably
    flat-leafed)

Scrub the mussels well in several changes of water, scrape off the beards, and rinse the mussels. In a kettle steam the mussels with the wine, covered, over moderately high heat for 5 to 7 minutes, or until they are opened, transfer them with a slotted spoon to a bowl, and discard any unopened mussels. Remove the mussels from the shells and reserve them, discarding the shells. Strain the cooking liquid through a fine sieve lined with a triple thickness of rinsed and squeezed cheesecloth and set over a large measuring cup and if necessary add enough water to measure 1½ cups liquid.

In the kettle, cleaned, cook the *linguine* in boiling salted water for 8 to 10 minutes, or until it is *al dente*, and drain it well. While the *linguine* is cooking, in a skillet cook the garlic in the oil over moderately low heat, stirring, for 1 minute and add the orégano, the red pepper flakes, and the mussel cooking liquid. Bring the mixture to a boil and simmer it, stirring occasionally, for 5 minutes, or until it is reduced by one third. Add the reserved mussels, the parsley, and salt and pepper to taste, cook the sauce until the mussels are heated through, and toss it with the *linguine*. Serves 4 to 6.

Linguine with Shrimp and Saffron Sauce

⅛ teaspoon saffron threads, crumbled
½ cup dry white wine
⅓ pound dried *linguine*
2 teaspoons turmeric
2 tablespoons vegetable oil
½ pound shrimp (about 14), shelled, leaving
    the tail intact, deveined, rinsed, and
    patted dry
1 teaspoon minced garlic
¼ cup minced shallot
½ cup canned chicken broth
¾ cup heavy cream

3 carrots, cut into ribbon-like strands with a
    vegetable peeler, discarding the cores
½ cup thawed frozen green peas
the green part of 4 scallions, sliced very thin
    lengthwise

In a small bowl let the saffron soak in the wine for 5 minutes. In a kettle of boiling salted water cook the *linguine* with the turmeric for 10 to 12 minutes, or until it is *al dente*. While the *linguine* is cooking, in a large skillet heat the oil over moderate heat until it is hot but not smoking and in it cook the shrimp, stirring, for 1 minute. Add the garlic and salt and pepper to taste, cook the mixture, stirring, until the shrimp just turn pink, and transfer the shrimp with tongs to a plate. Add the shallot and the saffron mixture to the skillet and boil the mixture until almost all the liquid is evaporated. Add the broth, the cream, and the carrots and boil the mixture until the liquid is reduced by half. Add the peas, the scallion greens, the *linguine*, drained well, the shrimp and any juices that have accumulated on the plate, and salt and pepper to taste and simmer the mixture until it is just heated through. Serves 2.

Southwestern-Style Macaroni and Cheese

¾ cup dried elbow macaroni
½ cup chopped red bell pepper
½ cup chopped green bell pepper
¼ pound thickly sliced ham, chopped (about
    1 cup)
2 tablespoons vegetable oil
1½ tablespoons all-purpose flour
½ cup milk
½ cup plain yogurt
2 ounces Monterey Jack, chopped (about
    ½ cup)
1 teaspoon minced pickled *jalapeño* pepper
    (wear rubber gloves)
⅓ cup finely crushed taco chips

In a kettle of boiling salted water cook the macaroni for 10 to 12 minutes, or until it is *al dente*, drain it in a colander, and rinse it under warm water. While the macaroni is cooking, in a large saucepan cook the bell peppers and the ham in the oil over moderately high heat, stirring occasionally, for 5 minutes. Reduce the heat to low, add the flour, and cook the mixture, stirring, for 3 minutes. Stir in the milk and the yogurt, bring the mixture to a boil, stirring, and simmer it, stirring occasionally, for 5 minutes. Add the Monterey Jack and the *jalapeño* pepper and cook the mixture over moderately low heat, stirring, until the Monterey Jack is just melted. Add the macaroni and salt and pepper to taste and stir the mixture until it is combined well. Transfer the macaroni and cheese to a shallow flameproof baking dish, sprinkle the taco chips over the top, and broil the macaroni and cheese under a preheated broiler about 2 inches from the heat for 3 to 4 minutes, or until the top is browned lightly. Serves 2.

*Penne with Italian Sausage
and Green Bell Pepper Sauce*

1 onion, chopped
1 tablespoon vegetable oil
two 3-ounce uncooked hot or sweet Italian
  sausages, casings discarded
a 14- to 16-ounce can tomatoes,
  drained and chopped
1 tablespoon tomato paste
¼ cup dry white wine
1 garlic clove, minced
⅓ cup finely chopped green bell pepper
¼ cup minced fresh parsley leaves
½ pound *penne* (quill-shaped pasta)
freshly grated Parmesan as an accompaniment
  if desired

In a large heavy skillet cook the onion in the oil over moderately low heat, stirring, until it is softened. Add the sausage and cook the mixture, stirring and breaking up the lumps, until the meat is no longer pink. Stir in the tomatoes, the tomato paste, the wine, the garlic, and salt and pepper to taste, bring the liquid to a boil, and simmer the mixture, stirring occasionally, for 15 minutes. Stir in the bell pepper and the parsley and simmer the mixture for 5 minutes. While the sauce is cooking, in a large saucepan of boiling salted water cook the *penne* for 10 minutes, or until it is *al dente*, drain it well, and transfer it to a heated bowl. Toss the *penne* with the sauce and serve it with the Parmesan. Serves 2.

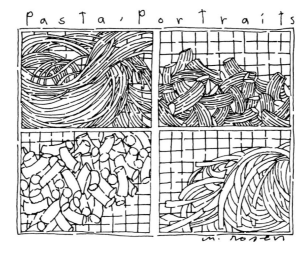

Pasta Portraits

Cheese and Chive Ravioli
with Tomato Red Pepper Sauce

For the sauce
a 28-ounce can plum tomatoes including
 the juice
1 large red bell pepper, chopped coarse
2 large garlic cloves
2 onions, chopped coarse
½ cup chicken stock (page 123) or canned
 chicken broth
For the filling
¾ cup freshly grated Parmesan
4 ounces mozzarella, grated coarse
½ cup ricotta
2 tablespoons snipped fresh chives

1 pound food processor pasta dough
 (page 172)
a 1-inch-thick bunch of chives
freshly grated Parmesan as an accompaniment

Make the sauce: In a saucepan combine the tomatoes with the juice, the bell pepper, the garlic, the onions, and the stock, bring the liquid to a boil, and simmer the mixture, covered, stirring occasionally, for 30 to 40 minutes, or until the vegetables are very tender. Force the mixture through a food mill fitted with the medium disk into another saucepan, add salt and pepper to taste, and simmer the sauce until it is reduced to about 2½ cups.

Make the filling: In a bowl combine well the Parmesan, the mozzarella, the ricotta, the chives, and salt and pepper to taste.

Roll out the dough on a pasta machine, following the procedure on page 172 but rolling and making the ravioli with 1 sheet of dough at a time. After rolling out 1 sheet of dough, trim the ends of the dough and halve the dough crosswise. Cover 1 piece with one third of the chives, arranging them very close together lengthwise over the entire surface of the dough, and press the chives down firmly with a rolling pin. Put the remaining piece of dough on top of the chives and press it down very firmly with a rolling pin. Dust both sides of the chive-layered dough with flour, feed the dough carefully through the rollers set at the fifth-lowest notch, and continue to feed it through the rollers, turning the dial one notch lower each time, until the second-lowest notch is reached. (The chives may break through the dough in spots.) Trim the ends of the dough and cut the dough crosswise into 2 pieces, 1 piece 1½ inches longer than the other. Put heaping tablespoons of the filling in lengthwise rows on the shorter piece, spacing them about 1 inch from the edges with their centers about 3 inches apart. Brush the dough around the filling with water, put the longer piece of dough on top, and press it gently around the mounds of filling, pressing out any air bubbles. With a fluted pastry wheel or knife cut the dough between the rows of filling into about 2½- by 2-inch rectangles. Arrange the ravioli as they are formed in one layer on a lightly floured tray. Continue to make ravioli, 1 sheet of dough at a time, with the remaining dough, chives, reserving a few for garnish, and filling in the same manner. *The ravioli may be kept, uncovered and chilled, for up to 2 hours.*

To 2 kettles of boiling salted water add the ravioli and cook them at a bare simmer, covered partially, for 10 to 12 minutes, or until they are *al dente*. Divide the sauce, heated, among 4 heated dinner plates and arrange the ravioli on the plates. Garnish each portion with some of the reserved chives and serve the ravioli with the Parmesan. Makes about 24 ravioli, serving 4 as a main course or 6 as a first course.

PHOTO ON PAGE 39

Rigatoni with Sausage and Pepper Tomato Sauce

½ pound hot Italian sausage (about 3), casings
 discarded
1 tablespoon olive oil
1 teaspoon minced garlic
½ cup chopped onion
1 green bell pepper, cut into ¼-inch-thick
 strips (about 1 cup)
a 14-ounce can Italian plum tomatoes, drained
 and chopped, reserving the juice
1 teaspoon dried basil, crumbled
½ teaspoon dried orégano, crumbled
¼ teaspoon dried hot red pepper flakes,
 or to taste
¼ cup dry red wine
¼ cup chopped fresh parsley leaves
½ pound rigatoni or other tubular pasta
freshly grated Parmesan to taste

Heat a large heavy skillet over moderate heat until it is hot, in it cook the sausage, stirring and breaking up the lumps, until it is no longer pink, and transfer it with a slotted spoon to a bowl. To the fat remaining in the skillet add the oil and in the fat cook the garlic over moderately low heat, stirring, for 30 seconds. Add the onion and cook the mixture, stirring, until the onion is softened. Add the bell pepper, cook the mixture over moderate heat, stirring, for 4 to 5 minutes, or until the bell pepper is crisp-tender, and add the tomatoes with the reserved juice, the basil, the orégano, the red pepper flakes, the wine, the sausage, and salt and pepper to taste. Simmer the mixture, covered partially, stirring occasionally, for 10 to 12 minutes, or until it is thickened slightly, and stir in the parsley. In a kettle of boiling salted water cook the rigatoni for 8 to 10 minutes, or until it is *al dente*, drain it well, and transfer it to a bowl. Add the sauce, toss the rigatoni with it, and serve the rigatoni with the Parmesan. Serves 2.

Rotelle with Avocado Pesto

For the avocado pesto
2 garlic cloves, halved
1 cup firmly-packed fresh basil leaves
¼ cup firmly-packed fresh parsley leaves (preferably flat-leafed)
2 tablespoons pine nuts
2 tablespoons freshly grated Parmesan
1 ripe avocado (about ½ pound, preferably California)
6 tablespoons olive oil (preferably extra virgin) or avocado oil (both available at specialty foods shops and many supermarkets)

¾ pound *rotelle* (little wheels) or other small round-shaped pasta
¾ pound tomatoes, seeded and chopped
¼ cup pine nuts, toasted lightly

To a food processor with the motor running add the garlic and process it until it is minced. Add the basil, the parsley, the pine nuts, and the Parmesan and blend the mixture until the herbs are chopped fine. Halve lengthwise and pit the avocado, scoop the flesh into the food processor, and purée it. With the motor running add the oil in a stream, blend the *pesto* well, and season it with salt and pepper to taste. *The pesto may be made 2 hours in advance and kept chilled, its surface covered with plastic wrap. Let the pesto come to room temperature before using.*
In a kettle of boiling salted water boil the *rotelle* for

6 to 12 minutes, or until it is *al dente*, drain it, and transfer it to a large serving bowl. Add the *pesto*, toss the mixture well, and stir in the tomatoes and 2 tablespoons of the pine nuts. Sprinkle the *rotelle* with the remaining 2 tablespoons pine nuts. Serves 4.

Spaghetti and Meatballs with Tomato Sauce

1 onion, chopped
1 teaspoon minced garlic
1 tablespoon olive oil
a 28-ounce can Italian plum tomatoes including the juice
½ teaspoon dried thyme, crumbled
½ teaspoon dried orégano, crumbled
½ teaspoon dried basil, crumbled
⅛ teaspoon dried hot red pepper flakes
¼ teaspoon sugar
¼ cup minced fresh parsley leaves
1 slice of homemade-type white bread, torn into pieces
¼ cup heavy cream
¼ pound ground chuck
¼ pound ground pork
¼ cup freshly grated Parmesan plus additional as an accompaniment
½ pound spaghetti

In a heavy saucepan cook the onion and the garlic in the oil over moderate heat, stirring, until the mixture is browned lightly. Add the tomatoes with the juice, breaking them up, the thyme, the orégano, the basil, the red pepper flakes, the sugar, 2 tablespoons of the parsley, and salt and black pepper to taste, bring the sauce to a boil, stirring, and simmer it, stirring occasionally, for 20 minutes. While the sauce is simmering, in a small bowl combine well the bread and the cream, add the chuck, the pork, the Parmesan, the remaining 2 tablespoons parsley, and salt and black pepper to taste, and combine the mixture well. Roll the mixture into balls the size of a walnut, add the meatballs to the sauce, and simmer them, stirring occasionally, for 10 minutes. While the meatballs are simmering, in a kettle of boiling salted water cook the spaghetti for 10 to 12 minutes, or until it is *al dente*, drain it, and transfer it to a heated bowl. Spoon the meatballs and the sauce over the spaghetti and serve the dish with the additional Parmesan. Serves 2.

Buttered Spätzle with Scallions

4½ cups all-purpose flour
1 tablespoon salt
6 large eggs
1½ cups milk
½ stick (¼ cup) unsalted butter, cut into bits
1 cup thinly sliced scallion greens

spätzle maker available by mail order from:
Paprikas Weiss
1546 Second Avenue
New York, New York 10028

In a large bowl whisk together the flour and the salt. In a bowl whisk together the eggs, the milk, and ½ cup water until the mixture is combined well and add the mixture to the flour mixture in a stream, stirring with a wooden spoon until it forms a soft, smooth batter. Set the *spätzle* maker over a large kettle of boiling salted water and working in batches, work cupfuls of the dough through the *spätzle* maker into the water. Stir the noodles gently to separate them, return the water to a boil, and cook the noodles for 5 to 8 minutes, or until they are *al dente*. Drain the *spätzle* and put it in a large bowl of cold water. *The* spätzle *may be kept in the water, covered and chilled, for 2 hours if desired or drained, tossed with 3 tablespoons vegetable oil, and kept covered and chilled overnight. Let the* spätzle *come to room temperature.*

Drain the *spätzle* well and put it in a buttered large shallow baking dish. Dot the *spätzle* with the butter, heat it, covered, in a preheated 350° F. oven for 20 to 30 minutes, or until it is heated through, and toss it with the scallion greens. Serves 12.

PHOTO ON PAGE 12

GRAINS AND WILD RICE

Green Chili Rice Dressing

1 tablespoon salt or ½ teaspoon salt if using
   the microwave (procedure follows)
1½ cups long-grain brown rice
6 slices of lean bacon
1 cup chopped onion
1 teaspoon minced garlic
a 14-ounce can Italian tomatoes,
   drained and chopped
1 cup sour cream
two 4-ounce cans green chilies,
   drained and chopped
¼ pound Monterey Jack, grated
   (about 1½ cups)

In a large saucepan bring 5 quarts water to a boil, add the salt, and sprinkle in the rice, stirring until the water returns to a boil. Boil the rice for 20 minutes, drain it in a large sieve, and rinse it. Set the sieve over a large saucepan of boiling water, steam the rice, covered with a kitchen towel and the lid, for 20 minutes, or until it is fluffy and dry, and let it cool.

In a heavy skillet cook the bacon over moderate heat, turning it, until it is crisp, transfer it to paper towels to drain, and crumble it. Pour off all but 1 tablespoon of the fat from the skillet and in the remaining fat cook the onion over moderate heat, stirring occasionally, until it is softened. Stir in the garlic, cook the mixture, stirring, for 1 minute, and stir in the tomatoes and the sour cream. In a bowl combine well the rice, the tomato mixture, and salt and pepper to taste. In a baking dish, 11 by 7 by 2 inches, spread half the rice mixture, over it sprinkle the bacon, the chilies, and 1 cup of the Monterey Jack, and spread the remaining rice mixture over the cheese. *The rice dressing can be made up to this point 2 days in advance and kept covered and chilled.*

Sprinkle the remaining Monterey Jack over the rice. Heat the dressing, covered with foil, in the upper third of a preheated 400° F. oven for 15 minutes, discard the foil, and heat the dressing for 15 to 20 minutes more, or until the cheese is melted and bubbling. Serves 6 to 8 as a side dish.

The green chili rice dressing can also be made in a microwave oven by using the following procedure.

Note: This recipe was tested in a 600-watt, .8-cubic-foot unit, with interior dimensions of 16 by 10 by 7¼ inches. Cooking times will vary from one manufacturer's product to another, depending on power and size configuration; therefore, it is imperative to refer to the instructions that accompany the appliance and to treat the times given in our recipe as guidelines rather than dicta.

In a 2-quart glass measuring cup or bowl combine the salt, the rice, and 3 cups water, microwave the mixture, covered with microwave-safe plastic wrap, at high power (100%) for 8 to 10 minutes, or until the water begins to boil, and microwave the mixture at medium power (50%) for 25 to 30 minutes, or until the liquid is almost evaporated. Remove the rice from the oven, let it stand, covered, for 10 minutes, or until it is dry, and let it cool.

In a glass baking dish large enough to hold the bacon in one layer arrange the bacon in one layer, cover it with a microwave-safe paper towel, and microwave it at high power (100%) for 5 to 6 minutes, or until it is crisp. Transfer the bacon to paper towels to drain and crumble it. Pour off all but 1 tablespoon of the fat from the baking dish and in the remaining fat microwave the onion at high power (100%), stirring occasionally, for 5 to 7 minutes, or until it is crisp-tender. Stir in the garlic, microwave the mixture at high power (100%) for 2 to 4 minutes, or until the mixture is golden, and stir in the tomatoes and the sour cream. In a bowl combine well the rice, the tomato mixture, and salt and pepper to taste. In a glass baking dish, 11 by 7 by 2 inches, spread half the rice mixture, over it sprinkle the bacon, the chilies, and 1 cup of the Monterey Jack, and spread the remaining rice mixture over the cheese. *The rice dressing can be made up to this point 2 days in advance and kept covered and chilled.*

Sprinkle the remaining Monterey Jack over the rice and microwave the dressing at high power (100%) for 25 to 30 minutes, or until the cheese is melted and bubbling. Serves 6 to 8 as a side dish.

Lemon Pecan Wild Rice

2 cups canned chicken broth
the rind of ½ lemon removed with a vegetable
    peeler and cut into julienne strips (about 1½
    tablespoons)
1 tablespoon fresh lemon juice
1 tablespoon unsalted butter
1 cup wild rice, rinsed well and drained well
½ cup pecans, toasted lightly and chopped
3 tablespoons minced scallion
¼ cup minced fresh parsley leaves

In a heavy saucepan combine the broth, half the rind, the lemon juice, and the butter, bring the mixture to a boil, and stir in the rice. Cook the rice, covered, over low heat for 50 minutes to 1 hour, or until it is tender and has absorbed the liquid, and stir in the pecans, the scallion, the parsley, the remaining rind, and salt and pepper to taste. Serves 4.

PHOTO ON PAGE 75

Minted Sausage Pilaf

¼ pound sweet Italian sausage (about 1 link),
    casing discarded
1 small onion, chopped
1 tablespoon vegetable oil
½ cup converted rice
½ teaspoon salt
¾ teaspoon dried mint, crumbled

In a heavy saucepan cook the sausage and the onion in the oil over moderately high heat, breaking up and stirring the sausage, until the sausage is no longer pink and transfer the mixture with a slotted spoon to a small bowl. Pour off all but 1 tablespoon of the fat and in the pan cook the rice, stirring, for 1 minute. Stir in 1 cup water, the salt, and ½ teaspoon of the mint, bring the liquid to a boil, and cook the mixture, covered, over low heat for 18 to 20 minutes, or until the liquid is absorbed. Stir in the sausage mixture, the remaining ¼ teaspoon mint, and pepper to taste and let the pilaf stand, covered, off the heat for 5 minutes. Serves 2.

ZOË MAVRIDIS

Tomato Rice
with Yellow Squash

2 tomatoes
    (about 1 pound)
¼ cup minced red onion
½ teaspoon minced garlic
1 tablespoon vegetable oil
½ cup converted rice
1 cup canned chicken broth
1 small yellow summer squash
    (about ¼ pound),
    quartered lengthwise and cut crosswise
    into ¼-inch slices
½ tablespoon unsalted butter
2 teaspoons minced fresh coriander
¼ to ½ teaspoon minced fresh *jalapeño* pepper
    (wear rubber gloves)
    if desired

Broil 1 of the tomatoes on a foil-lined shallow pie pan or baking sheet under a preheated broiler about 2 inches from the heat, turning it once, for 12 to 15 minutes, or until it is softened and the skin is blistered and charred. Let the tomato cool and peel and core it over a bowl to catch the juices. In a blender purée the broiled tomato with the juices and strain the purée through a fine sieve into the bowl. In a heavy saucepan cook the onion and the garlic in the oil over moderately low heat, stirring, until the mixture is softened, add the rice, and cook the mixture, stirring, for 2 minutes. Add the tomato purée and cook the mixture, stirring, for 1 minute. Add the broth, heated, bring the liquid to a boil, and cook the mixture, covered, over low heat for 18 to 20 minutes, or until the liquid is absorbed and the rice is tender.

While the rice is cooking, seed and chop the remaining tomato. In a skillet cook the squash in the butter, covered, over moderately low heat, stirring occasionally, for 3 minutes, or until it is just tender, add the chopped tomato, and cook the mixture until it is heated through. Fluff the rice with a fork and let it stand, covered, off the heat for 5 minutes. Stir in the squash mixture, the coriander, and the *jalapeño* pepper and season the mixture with salt and black pepper. Serves 2.

Steamed Rice

1 tablespoon salt
2 cups unconverted long-grain rice

In a large saucepan bring 5 quarts water to a boil with the salt. Sprinkle in the rice, stirring until the water returns to a boil, and boil it for 10 minutes. Drain the rice in a large colander and rinse it. Set the colander over a large saucepan of boiling water and steam the rice, covered with a dish towel and the lid, for 15 minutes, or until it is fluffy and dry. Makes about 6 cups.

Risotto with Peas and Ham

about 5 cups canned chicken broth
1 small onion, minced
¼ pound chopped cooked ham (about 1 cup)
½ stick (¼ cup) unsalted butter
1½ cups unconverted long-grain rice
2 cups shelled fresh peas (about 2 pounds
    unshelled) or a 10-ounce package
    frozen peas, thawed
⅓ cup dry white wine
⅔ cup freshly grated Parmesan

In a saucepan bring the broth to a simmer and keep it at a bare simmer. In a large heavy saucepan cook the onion and the ham in the butter over moderately low heat, stirring, until the onion is softened and add the rice. If using fresh peas, add them at this point and cook the mixture, stirring with a wooden spatula, until the rice is coated well with the butter. Add the wine and cook the mixture over moderately high heat, stirring, until the wine is absorbed. Add about ⅔ cup of the simmering broth and cook the mixture, stirring, until the broth is absorbed. Continue adding the broth, about ⅔ cup at a time, stirring constantly and letting each portion be absorbed before adding the next, until the rice is barely *al dente*. (If using frozen peas, stir them in at this point.) Continue cooking the risotto, adding more broth, about ½ cup at a time, stirring constantly and letting each portion be absorbed before adding the next, until the rice is tender but still *al dente*, a total of about 18 minutes. Remove the pan from the heat and stir in the Parmesan and pepper to taste. Serves 4 to 6.

VEGETABLES

Stuffed Artichoke Leaves

1 large artichoke
2 tablespoons fresh lemon juice
1½ tablespoons plain yogurt
1 tablespoon mayonnaise
2 teaspoons minced fresh basil leaves plus
    28 additional small basil leaves for garnish
¾ ounce thinly sliced prosciutto, chopped fine
    (about 2 tablespoons)
2 hard-boiled large eggs, halved lengthwise
    and sliced thin crosswise
assorted olives as an accompaniment

In a saucepan just large enough to hold the artichoke bring 3 inches salted water with 1 tablespoon of the lemon juice to a boil, add the artichoke, stem discarded, and simmer it, covered, for 25 to 35 minutes, or until it is tender (test a leaf for doneness). Refresh the artichoke in a bowl of ice and cold water and let it drain upside down for 10 minutes. Remove all the outer leaves, reserving them, and pull out the center leaves in one piece, discarding them. Remove the choke with a small spoon and chop fine the artichoke bottom. In a bowl whisk together well the yogurt, the mayonnaise, and the remaining 1 tablespoon lemon juice, add the chopped artichoke bottom, the minced basil, the prosciutto, and salt and pepper to taste, and stir the mixture until it is combined well. Put a slice of hard-boiled egg on each of the 28 largest leaves, mound about ½ teaspoon of the

filling on each slice, and garnish each mound with a basil leaf. Mound about ½ teaspoon of the remaining filling on each of the remaining leaves. Divide the stuffed garnished leaves among 4 small plates and mound some of the olives in the middle of each plate. Serve the remaining stuffed leaves on a small platter. Serves 4.

PHOTO ON PAGE 38

Baked Green Bananas with Lime and Parmesan

2 tablespoons unsalted butter, melted
¼ cup fresh lime juice
½ cup fine dry bread crumbs
½ cup freshly grated Parmesan
4 green bananas

In a shallow dish whisk together the butter, the lime juice, and salt and pepper to taste and in another shallow dish combine well the bread crumbs and the Parmesan. Halve the bananas crosswise and halve them lengthwise. Dip the bananas in the butter mixture, turning them to coat them and reserving the excess butter mixture, dredge them in the bread-crumb mixture, and arrange them in one layer in a buttered shallow baking dish. Bake the bananas in the middle of a preheated 375° F. oven for 20 to 25 minutes, or until they are golden, and drizzle them with the reserved butter mixture. Serves 4 to 6 as a side dish.

Black Bean Burritos with Jalapeño Tomato Sauce

a 14- to 16-ounce can whole tomatoes,
  drained
¼ cup minced white or yellow onion
1 tablespoon minced seeded fresh or pickled
  jalapeño pepper (wear rubber gloves),
  or to taste
four 10-inch flour tortillas
1 cup drained canned black beans
¼ cup finely chopped red onion
1 cup grated Monterey Jack (about ¼ pound)
1 avocado (preferably California)
2 tablespoons chopped fresh coriander leaves
  plus sprigs for garnish if desired

In a blender purée the tomatoes with the white or yellow onion and the *jalapeño* pepper and transfer the sauce to a 1-cup glass measuring cup. Working with 1 tortilla at a time, spread ¼ cup of the beans in a line down the center of each tortilla, top the beans with 1 tablespoon of the red onion and ¼ cup of the Monterey Jack, and roll the tortilla gently around the filling to enclose the filling. Transfer the *burritos* carefully, seam sides down, to a microwave-safe platter or baking dish large enough to hold them in one layer. Cover the platter tightly with microwave-safe plastic wrap and microwave the *burritos* at high power (100%) for 4 minutes. Remove the platter from the oven and keep it covered.

While the *burritos* are cooking, halve and pit the avocado, reserving one half, wrapped tightly in plastic and chilled, for another use. Peel the avocado half and cut it into ½-inch dice. Microwave the tomato sauce, uncovered, at high power (100%) for 2 minutes and stir in 1 tablespoon of the coriander leaves. Transfer the *burritos* with a spatula to 2 heated plates and spoon some of the sauce over them. Top the sauce with the avocado, sprinkle the remaining 1 tablespoon coriander leaves over the avocado, and garnish the servings with the coriander sprigs. Serve the *burritos* with the remaining sauce. Serves 2.

Fagiolini alla Genovese
(*Green Beans with Anchovy and Garlic*)
1½ pounds green beans, trimmed and cut
  diagonally into 1½-inch pieces
½ teaspoon minced garlic
1½ tablespoons unsalted butter
1½ tablespoons olive oil

⅓ cup minced fresh flat-leafed parsley leaves
1½ teaspoons minced anchovy fillet,
  patted dry

In a large saucepan of boiling salted water cook the green beans for 4 to 6 minutes, or until they are crisp-tender, drain them, and plunge them into a bowl of ice and cold water to stop the cooking process. Drain the beans well. In the pan cook the garlic in the butter and the oil over moderately low heat, stirring, until it is golden, add the beans, and cook the mixture, stirring occasionally, until the beans are heated through. Toss the beans with the parsley and the anchovy and season them with salt and pepper. Serves 6.

PHOTO ON PAGE 69

Green Beans with Artichoke Hearts

⅓ cup toasted coarse rye bread crumbs (about
  1 slice of bread)
1 tablespoon unsalted butter, melted
6 ounces green beans, trimmed and cut into
  ½-inch pieces
a 6-ounce jar marinated artichoke hearts,
  drained and chopped

In a bowl toss the bread crumbs with the butter until they are coated well. On the rack of a steamer set over boiling water steam the beans, covered, for 4 to 6 minutes, or until they are crisp-tender. Add to the bread crumbs the beans, the artichoke hearts, and salt and pepper to taste and toss the mixture well. Serves 2.

Green Beans with Walnut Garlic Sauce
¼ cup walnut pieces
1 small garlic clove
¼ cup half-and-half
6 ounces green beans, trimmed

In a food processor or blender purée the walnuts, the garlic, and the half-and-half until the mixture is smooth. In a saucepan of boiling salted water cook the green beans for 5 minutes, or until they are crisp-tender. While the green beans are cooking, in a small saucepan bring the walnut sauce to a simmer over moderate heat, stir in salt and pepper to taste, and simmer the sauce for 3 minutes, or until it is thickened. Drain the green beans, transfer them to a serving dish, and drizzle the sauce over them. Serves 2.

Roasted Green Beans

1½ pounds green beans, trimmed if desired
2 tablespoons vegetable oil

In a large bowl toss the green beans with the oil and salt and pepper to taste until they are coated well, spread them in one layer in a jelly-roll pan, and roast them in a preheated 500° F. oven, stirring once, for 10 minutes. Serves 4.

PHOTO ON PAGE 18

Green Bean and Yellow Bell Pepper Mélange

1½ pounds green beans (preferably *haricots verts*, available at specialty produce markets), trimmed
3 tablespoons unsalted butter
2 large yellow bell peppers, cut into 2- by ¼-inch strips
½ teaspoon dried thyme, crumbled

In a kettle of boiling salted water boil the beans for 3 to 7 minutes, or until they are crisp-tender. Drain the beans in a colander, refresh them under cold water, and drain them well. *The beans may be prepared up to this point 1 day in advance, wrapped in paper towels and plastic wrap, and chilled.* In a large skillet melt the butter over moderately low heat, add the bell peppers and the thyme, and cook the mixture, stirring, for 1 minute. Add the beans and salt and pepper to taste and cook the mixture, stirring occasionally, until the beans are heated through. Serves 8.

PHOTO ON PAGE 30

Sliced Beets with Parsley, Capers, and Lemon

¾ pound beets without the stems (about 1½ pounds with the stems), peeled and sliced ¼ inch thick
2 tablespoons unsalted butter, cut into pieces
1 tablespoon finely chopped fresh parsley leaves
1½ to 2 tablespoons chopped drained bottled capers
2 teaspoons fresh lemon juice

In a large skillet combine the beets with the butter, 1 cup water, and salt to taste, bring the liquid to a boil, and simmer the beets, covered, for 12 minutes. Simmer the beets, uncovered, adding more water if necessary, for 8 to 10 minutes more, or until they are tender and almost all the liquid is evaporated. Add the parsley, the capers, the lemon juice, and salt and pepper to taste and toss the mixture well. Serves 2.

Sweet-and-Sour Beets with Beet Greens

For the dressing

2 tablespoons sugar

¼ teaspoon paprika

¾ teaspoon whole celery seeds

1 tablespoon honey

¼ teaspoon salt

2 teaspoons strained fresh lemon juice,
    or to taste

½ teaspoon freshly grated lemon rind

5 tablespoons distilled white vinegar,
    or to taste

1 tablespoon minced onion

⅓ cup vegetable oil

a 1-pound bunch of beets including the greens
freshly ground pepper to taste

Make the dressing: In a bowl whisk together the sugar, the paprika, the celery seeds, the honey, the salt, the lemon juice, the rind, the vinegar, and the onion, add the oil in a stream, whisking, and whisk the dressing until it is emulsified.

Cut the greens from the beets, leaving 1 inch of the stems attached. Cut the stems from the greens, reserving them, cut the greens crosswise into 1-inch slices, and cut the reserved stems crosswise into 1-inch lengths. Wash well and drain separately the greens and the stems and reserve them. Scrub the beets, put them in a 2½-quart glass casserole with 2 tablespoons water, and microwave them, covered with the lid, at high power (100%), turning them after 5 minutes, for a total of 8 to 12 minutes, depending on the size of the beets, or until they are tender when pierced with a skewer. (If the beets vary in size, remove each beet as it is cooked.) Let the beets cool in a colander for 5 minutes and slip off and discard the skins and the stems.

While the beets are cooling put the reserved beet stems in the casserole with 1 tablespoon hot water and microwave them, covered with the lid, at high power (100%) for 2 to 4 minutes, or until they are barely tender. Add the reserved beet greens and microwave the mixture, covered with the lid, at high power (100%) for 2 to 3 minutes, or until the greens are just tender.

While the greens are cooking cut the beets into ¼-inch slices and in a bowl combine them with half the dressing. Transfer the beet greens mixture with a slot-ted spoon to a serving dish, drizzle the remaining dressing over it, and top the greens with the beets. Season the mixture with the pepper. Serves 2.

Steamed Broccoli with Sesame Cumin Butter

¾ pound broccoli, separated into flowerets
    and the stems reserved for another use

2 teaspoons sesame seeds

1½ tablespoons unsalted butter

¾ teaspoon ground cumin, or to taste

fresh lemon juice to taste

In a steamer set over simmering water steam the broccoli, covered, for 4 minutes, or until it is crisp-tender. In a small heavy skillet toast the sesame seeds over moderate heat, stirring, until they are golden, add the butter, the cumin, and salt to taste, and heat the mixture, stirring, until the butter is melted. Transfer the broccoli to a bowl and add the butter mixture. Toss the broccoli to coat it and sprinkle it with the lemon juice. Serves 2.

Steamed Broccoli with Vinegared Red Onion

½ pound broccoli, cut into 1½-inch flowerets
    and the stems peeled and cut diagonally
    into ⅛-inch slices

½ cup sliced red onion

1 tablespoon unsalted butter

2 tablespoons red-wine vinegar

In a steamer set over boiling water steam the broccoli, covered, for 4 minutes. While the broccoli is steaming, in a small skillet cook the onion in the butter over moderate heat, stirring, for 1 minute, add the vinegar, and cook the mixture, stirring, until the onion is softened and the vinegar is nearly evaporated. Add the broccoli to the skillet and season the mixture with salt and pepper. Serves 2.

Braised Red Cabbage with Mustard Seeds

1¾ pounds red cabbage, sliced thin
    (about 10 cups)

2 large onions, sliced

⅔ cup cider vinegar

¼ cup firmly packed dark brown sugar

3 tablespoons unsalted butter

2 teaspoons mustard seeds

1 bay leaf
1 teaspoon freshly ground pepper
1 teaspoon salt

In a kettle combine 2 cups water, the cabbage, the onions, the vinegar, the brown sugar, the butter, the mustard seeds, the bay leaf, the pepper, and the salt, bring the liquid to a boil, and simmer the mixture, covered, stirring occasionally, for 20 minutes, or until the cabbage is just tender. Simmer the cabbage, uncovered, stirring occasionally, for 20 minutes more and discard the bay leaf. *Leftovers keep in an airtight container, chilled, for 1 week. Reheat the cabbage in a kettle over moderate heat, stirring, until it is hot.* Makes about 6 cups.

PHOTO ON PAGE 75

Carrot and Turnip Gratin

¾ pound carrots, grated coarse in a food
    processor
¾ pound turnips, peeled and grated coarse in a
    food processor
⅓ cup thinly sliced scallion greens
4 tablespoons cornstarch
2 cups milk
½ cup heavy cream
1 large egg
½ cup freshly grated Parmesan
1 tablespoon cold unsalted butter, cut into bits

In a bowl toss together the carrots, the turnips, the scallion greens, and 3 tablespoons of the cornstarch and spread the mixture in a buttered 10-inch round or oval gratin dish (or 1½-quart shallow baking dish), smoothing and tamping it down with a rubber spatula. In a heavy saucepan dissolve the remaining 1 tablespoon cornstarch in ¼ cup of the milk, add the remaining 1¾ cups milk and the cream, and bring the mixture to a boil, whisking. In a bowl whisk the egg, add the milk

mixture in a slow stream, whisking, and pour the custard evenly over the vegetables. Sprinkle the top with the Parmesan, dot it with the butter, and bake the gratin in the middle of a preheated 375° F. oven for 45 minutes, or until it is golden and bubbling. Let the gratin stand for 10 minutes before serving. Serves 6.

Glazed Carrots and Parsnips

1¼ cups canned chicken broth
½ stick (¼ cup) unsalted butter
3 tablespoons sugar
1 teaspoon salt
2 pounds carrots, cut into sticks,
    2 by ¼ by ¼ inches (about 4 cups)
2 pounds parsnips, peeled and cut into sticks,
    2 by ¼ by ¼ inches (about 4 cups)
3 tablespoons minced fresh parsley leaves

In a large saucepan combine the broth, the butter, the sugar, and the salt and bring the mixture to a boil. Add the carrots and cook the mixture, covered, over moderately high heat for 1 minute. Add the parsnips and cook the mixture, covered, for 4 to 5 minutes, or until the vegetables are tender. Transfer the vegetables with a slotted spoon to a bowl and keep them warm, covered. Boil the cooking liquid until it is reduced to about ⅓ cup and pour it over the vegetables. *The vegetables may be prepared up to this point 1 day in advance, kept covered and chilled, and reheated.* Add the parsley and salt and pepper to taste and toss the mixture gently. Serves 8.

PHOTO ON PAGE 73

Irish Whiskey Carrots

2 tablespoons unsalted butter
¾ pound carrots, cut into
    2- by ¼- by ¼-inch sticks
2 teaspoons sugar
½ cup Irish whiskey

In a heavy skillet melt the butter, add the carrots, the sugar, and salt to taste, and stir the mixture until the carrots are coated with the butter. Add the whiskey, bring the liquid to a boil, and simmer the carrots, covered, for 5 minutes. Remove the lid and simmer the carrots, stirring occasionally, for 4 to 5 minutes, or until they are tender and the liquid is evaporated. Serves 4.

PHOTO ON PAGE 27

Orange-Glazed Carrots with Garlic and Coriander

3 carrots, sliced diagonally ¼ inch thick
¼ cup strained fresh orange juice
1 tablespoon unsalted butter
¼ teaspoon minced garlic
1 tablespoon small fresh coriander leaves

In a small skillet combine the carrots, the orange juice, the butter, the garlic, salt to taste, and 1 cup water, bring the liquid to a boil, and simmer the mixture, covered, for 20 to 25 minutes, or until the carrots are almost tender. Bring the liquid to a boil, uncovered, boil it until almost all of it is evaporated, and sprinkle the coriander over the carrots. Serves 2.

Cauliflower and Broccoli Timbales

6 cups cauliflower flowerets (about 1 head)
4½ cups broccoli flowerets plus 8 small
    flowerets for garnish (1 to 2 bunches)
⅔ cup heavy cream
3 large eggs

On a steamer rack set over a large saucepan of boiling water steam the cauliflower, covered, for 10 to 12 minutes, or until it is very tender, transfer it to a large bowl, and let it cool. On the rack set over the pan of boiling water steam 4½ cups of the broccoli, covered, for 7 to 9 minutes, or until it is very tender, transfer it to a bowl, and let it cool. In another bowl whisk together the cream, the eggs, and salt and pepper to taste. In a food processor purée the caulilflower with two thirds of the cream mixture until the mixture is smooth and transfer the mixture to the large bowl. In the food processor, cleaned, purée the broccoli with the remaining cream mixture until the mixture is smooth and transfer the mixture to a bowl. Divide the cauliflower mixture among 8 buttered ¾-cup timbale molds, smoothing the tops, and divide the broccoli mixture over the cauliflower, smoothing the tops. Put the molds in a baking dish, add enough hot water to the dish to reach halfway up the sides of the molds, and bake the timbales in the middle of a preheated 375° F. oven for 25 to 30 minutes, or until a knife comes out clean.

While the timbales are baking, in a small saucepan of boiling salted water blanch the remaining 8 broccoli flowerets for 10 seconds, drain them, and plunge them into a bowl of ice and cold water to stop the cooking.

Drain the broccoli well and, if making the timbales in advance, reserve it. *The timbales may be made 1 day in advance and kept covered and chilled. To reheat the timbales unmold them into a baking dish just large enough to hold them in one layer, add about 2 tablespoons hot water to the dish, or enough to barely cover the bottom, and reheat the timbales, covered with foil, in a preheated 500° F. oven for 15 minutes.* Run a thin knife around the inside of the molds, invert the timbales onto a platter, and arrange a broccoli floweret on each timbale. Serves 8.

PHOTO ON PAGE 79

Corn Custards

⅓ cup finely chopped red onion
1½ teaspoons unsalted butter
¼ teaspoon cornstarch
½ cup heavy cream
¾ cup fresh corn kernels (cut from about
    1½ ears of corn) or thawed frozen
1 large whole egg
1 large egg yolk
⅛ teaspoon salt
freshly ground white pepper to taste
⅛ teaspoon dried thyme, crumbled
½ teaspoon snipped fresh chives
2 buttered toast rounds as an accompaniment

In a skillet cook the onion in the butter over moderate heat, stirring, until it is softened and let it cool. In a bowl combine the cornstarch and the cream and stir the mixture until the cornstarch is dissolved. In a blender purée the onion mixture, the corn, the whole egg, the yolk, and the cream mixture, strain the custard mixture through a fine sieve into a bowl, pressing hard on the solids, and stir in the salt, the white pepper, the thyme, and the chives. Divide the custard between 2 well buttered ¾-cup ramekins and steam the custards, covered with buttered rounds of wax paper, in a steamer set over simmering water, covered, for 20 to 22 minutes, or until a knife inserted in the center comes out clean. Transfer the custards with tongs to a rack, remove the wax paper, and let the custards cool for 5 minutes. Run a thin knife around the sides of the ramekins and invert the custards onto the toast rounds. Serves 2.

Ham and Carrot Cornmeal Fritters with Yogurt Sauce

½ cup plain yogurt
¼ teaspoon ground cumin
¼ teaspoon ground coriander
1 large egg yolk
5 tablespoons milk
2 large egg whites
½ cup yellow cornmeal
¼ cup all-purpose flour
1¼ teaspoons double-acting baking powder
½ cup coarsely grated carrot
½ cup diced cooked ham
¼ cup chopped scallion
vegetable oil for deep-frying

In a small bowl whisk together the yogurt, the cumin, the coriander, and salt and pepper to taste and chill the sauce, covered. In a bowl whisk together the egg yolk and the milk and in another bowl beat the egg whites until they hold soft peaks. Sift together the cornmeal, the flour, and the baking powder into the milk mixture, whisk the mixture until it is combined well, and whisk in the egg whites. Stir in the carrot, the ham, the scallion, and salt and pepper to taste.

In a deep skillet heat 1½ inches of the oil to 340° F. on a deep-fat thermometer, in it fry ¼ cup mounds of the batter in batches, turning the fritters, for 5 minutes, or until the fritters are golden, and transfer the fritters with a slotted spoon as they are fried to paper towels to drain. Serve the fritters with the yogurt sauce. Makes about 6 fritters, serving 2.

*Sautéed Eggplant in Pita Pockets
with Tahini Yogurt Sauce*

1 purple eggplant (about ¾ pound), peeled
    and cut into ¼-inch-thick rounds
1 small red bell pepper, quartered lengthwise
    and seeds and ribs discarded
¼ cup plus 1 teaspoon olive oil
½ onion, sliced thin
1 tomato, seeded and chopped
two 5- to 6-inch whole-wheat *pita* loaves
tahini yogurt sauce (recipe follows)

Arrange the eggplant and the bell pepper in one layer on a lightly oiled jelly-roll pan, brush the vegetables with 2 tablespoons of the oil, and broil them under a preheated broiler about 4 inches from the heat for 4 to 6 minutes, or until they are golden. Turn the vegetables, brush them with 2 tablespoons of the remaining oil, and broil them for 4 to 6 minutes more, or until they are golden. Transfer the eggplant to paper towels to drain. Broil the bell pepper, turning it once, for 5 minutes more, or until the skin is blistered and charred, transfer it to a bowl, and let it steam, covered, until it is cool enough to handle.

While the bell pepper is broiling, in a skillet sauté the onion in the remaining 1 teaspoon oil over moderately low heat until it is soft. Peel the bell pepper, cut it into julienne strips, and add it to the skillet. Add the tomato and cook the mixture over moderate heat until it is heated through. Cut a ½-inch-wide slice from each *pita* to form a 4- to 5-inch opening, microwave the *pita* pockets, wrapped in paper towels, at high power (100%) for 45 seconds, or until they are heated through, and keep them warm. (Or heat the *pita* pockets, wrapped in foil, in a preheated 250° F. oven until they are warm.) Divide the eggplant and the vegetable mixture between the *pita* pockets, pour half the *tahini* yogurt sauce into each pocket, and season the sandwiches with salt and black pepper. Serves 2.

Tahini Yogurt Sauce

1 garlic clove
½ teaspoon salt
¼ cup well stirred *tahini* (sesame seed paste,
    available at natural foods stores and many
    supermarkets)
2 tablespoons fresh lemon juice, or to taste
2 tablespoons plain yogurt
freshly ground black pepper to taste
a pinch of cayenne, or to taste
1 teaspoon minced fresh parsley leaves

Mince and mash the garlic with the salt until a paste is formed. In a bowl combine the garlic paste and the *tahini* and add the lemon juice, stirring. (The mixture will be very thick.) Add 3 tablespoons water slowly, stirring, and stir in the yogurt, the black pepper, the cayenne, and the parsley. (The sauce should be about the consistency of mayonnaise.) Makes about ⅔ cup.

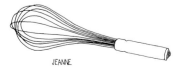

JEANNE

Creamed Leeks

2 tablespoons unsalted butter
the white and pale green parts of 4 large
    leeks, cut crosswise into ½-inch slices,
    separated into rings, rinsed well, and
    soaked in cold salted water to cover for
    30 minutes
½ cup heavy cream
⅓ cup canned chicken broth
freshly grated nutmeg to taste
white pepper to taste

In a large heavy skillet heat the butter over moderate heat until the foam begins to subside, add the leeks, drained well, and stir them to coat them with the butter. Add the cream and the broth, bring the liquid to a boil, stirring, and cook the mixture over moderate heat, stirring occasionally, for 10 to 15 minutes, or until it is thickened. Season the mixture with the nutmeg, the white pepper, and salt to taste. Serves 4.

PHOTO ON PAGE 27

Grilled Okra and Onion with Garlic Oil

1 large garlic clove, minced
¼ teaspoon salt
3 tablespoons olive oil
½ pound small okra,
    rinsed and patted dry
1 onion, cut into ¼-inch-thick slices
2 teaspoons fresh lemon juice
lemon wedges as an accompaniment

In a mortar with a pestle mash the garlic with the salt until the mixture forms a paste, add the oil, and combine the mixture well. Strain the mixture through a fine sieve set over a bowl, pressing hard on the solids. Brush the okra and the onion slices with some of the garlic oil, grill the vegetables on a well oiled rack set over glowing coals, covered, turning them occasionally, for 8 to 10 minutes, or until they are just tender, and transfer them to a platter. (Alternatively the vegetables may be grilled in a ridged cast-iron grill pan, covered, over moderately high heat.) Season the vegetables with the remaining garlic oil, the lemon juice, and salt and pepper, toss the mixture until it is combined well, and serve it with the lemon wedges. Serves 2.

Onion Gratin with Gruyère Toasts

3 tablespoons vegetable oil
4 pounds large onions, halved lengthwise and
    sliced thin crosswise
3 tablespoons medium-dry Sherry
½ stick plus 1 tablespoon (5 tablespoons)
    unsalted butter
3½ tablespoons all-purpose flour
¼ teaspoon dried thyme,
    crumbled
2 cups canned beef broth
2 tablespoons Dijon-style mustard
about eighteen ¼-inch-thick slices of French
    or Italian bread

1½ cups coarsely grated Gruyère or Swiss
    cheese

In a heavy kettle heat the oil over moderately high heat until it is hot but not smoking, add the onions, seasoned with salt and pepper, and cook them, stirring frequently, for 20 to 30 minutes, or until they are golden. Add the Sherry and cook the mixture, stirring, until almost all the liquid is evaporated.

While the onions are cooking, in a saucepan melt 2 tablespoons of the butter over moderately low heat, add the flour and the thyme, and cook the *roux*, whisking, for 3 minutes. Remove the pan from the heat, add the broth in a stream, whisking, and bring the mixture to a boil, whisking. Simmer the mixture, stirring occasionally, for 2 minutes, remove the pan from the heat, and whisk in the mustard. In a large bowl combine well the onions and the sauce and spread the mixture in a buttered 14- to 15-inch oval gratin dish (or 2-quart shallow baking dish). *The onion mixture may be made 2 days in advance and kept covered and chilled. Before proceeding with the recipe reheat the mixture, covered with foil, in a preheated 425° F. oven for 20 minutes, or until it is heated through.*

Butter 1 side of each slice of bread with the remaining 3 tablespoons butter, softened, and arrange the slices buttered sides up, overlapping them slightly, on the onion mixture. Bake the gratin in the middle of a preheated 425° F. oven for 10 to 15 minutes, or until the bread is golden, sprinkle the Gruyère over the toasts, and bake the gratin for 5 to 8 minutes more, or until the cheese is melted and bubbling. Serves 6 as a luncheon entrée or 8 to 10 as a side dish.

Parsnip Purée with Peas

¾ pound parsnips, peeled and
   cut into 1-inch pieces
1 large boiling potato (about 5 ounces), peeled
   and cut into 1-inch pieces
½ cup frozen peas
1 tablespoon minced scallion
2 tablespoons unsalted butter, cut into bits
   and softened
3 tablespoons milk at room temperature

To a saucepan of cold water add the parsnips and the potato, bring the water to a boil, and add salt to taste. Boil the vegetables for 8 to 10 minutes, or until they are tender. While the vegetables are cooking, in a saucepan of boiling salted water cook the peas for 1 minute, drain them, and transfer them to a bowl. Add to the bowl the scallion, the butter, and the milk. Drain the root vegetables, return them to the pan, and steam them over moderate heat, stirring, for 30 seconds to evaporate any excess liquid. Force the root vegetables through a ricer or food mill fitted with the medium disk into the bowl, add salt and pepper to taste, and combine the mixture well. Serves 2.

Pea and Goat Cheese Tart

For the shell
pâte brisée (page 248)
3 cups raw rice or beans for weighting the
   shell
For the custard
¼ pound mild goat cheese, such as
   Montrachet
½ cup ricotta
1 large egg
2 tablespoons milk
⅓ cup firmly packed fresh mint leaves
For the topping
2 cups shelled fresh peas (about 2 pounds
   unshelled), cooked (recipe follows) or a
   10-ounce package frozen peas, thawed
¼ cup minced radish
¼ cup minced scallion
1 tablespoon fresh lemon juice
1 teaspoon Dijon-style mustard
3 tablespoons olive oil

about 4 radishes, sliced very thin, plus 1
small radish, sliced very thin, leaving the
   stem end intact, and fanned, for garnish if
   desired

Make the shell: Roll out the dough into a round ⅛ inch thick on a lightly floured surface, fit it into a 9-inch tart pan with a removable fluted rim, and crimp the edge decoratively. Prick the bottom of the shell lightly with a fork and chill the shell for 30 minutes. Line the shell with foil, fill the foil with the rice, and bake the shell in the lower third of a preheated 425° F. oven for 15 minutes. Remove the rice and the foil carefully, bake the shell for 8 to 10 minutes more, or until it is golden, and let it cool in the pan on a rack.

Make the custard: In a food processor or blender purée the goat cheese with the ricotta, the egg, the milk, and the mint and season the custard with salt and pepper to taste.

Pour the custard into the shell and bake the tart in the middle of a preheated 375° F. oven for 25 minutes, or until the filling is set and pale golden. Let the tart cool on a rack for 15 minutes and remove the rim carefully.

Make the topping while the tart is cooling: In a bowl toss together the peas, the radish, and the scallion. In a small bowl whisk together the lemon juice, the mustard, and salt and pepper to taste, add the olive oil in a stream, whisking, and whisk the dressing until it is emulsified. Pour the dressing over the pea mixture and toss the topping well.

Spoon the topping onto the tart and arrange the radish slices and the fanned radish decoratively on it. Serves 4 as a luncheon entrée or 6 as a first course.

To Cook Fresh Peas

To simmer shelled fresh peas: For each cup of shelled fresh peas bring to a boil 1 cup water with 4 empty pea pods, add ½ teaspoon sugar, ¼ teaspoon salt, and the 1 cup peas, and simmer the peas for 3 to 8 minutes, or until they are tender. Drain the peas in a colander and discard the pods. Refresh the peas under cold water and drain them well.

To steam shelled fresh peas: In a steamer set over boiling water steam the peas, covered partially, for 5 to 12 minutes, or until they are tender. Transfer the peas to a colander, refresh them under cold water, and drain them well.

Peas and Onions with Lemon-Mint Butter

1 pound pearl onions (about 40), blanched in
   boiling water for 3 minutes, drained,
   and peeled
½ stick (¼ cup) unsalted butter
2 teaspoons freshly grated lemon rind
1 teaspoon dried mint, crumbled
two 10-ounce packages frozen peas

Trim and cut an X into the root end of each onion and
in a steamer set over boiling water steam the onions,
covered, for 15 to 20 minutes, or until they are tender.
While the onions are steaming, in a small saucepan melt
the butter over low heat, stir in the rind, the mint, and
salt and pepper to taste, and keep the mixture warm,
covered. In a saucepan bring 1 cup water to a boil, add
the peas, and return the water to a boil, breaking up the
peas with a fork. Simmer the peas, covered, for 4 to 5
minutes, or until they are heated through, drain them
well, and transfer them to a heated serving dish. Add the
onions and the butter mixture and toss the mixture well.
Serves 8.

Curried Pea Fritters
with Coriander Yogurt Dipping Sauce

For the sauce
½ cup plain yogurt
2 tablespoons chopped fresh coriander
1 teaspoon fresh lime juice
For the fritters
½ cup all-purpose flour
2 teaspoons curry powder
1 teaspoon ground cumin
¼ teaspoon cayenne
½ teaspoon double-acting baking powder
¼ teaspoon salt
½ cup plus 2 tablespoons seltzer
¼ cup finely chopped scallion
1 cup shelled fresh peas (about 1 pound
   unshelled), cooked (page 189),
   or half a 10-ounce package frozen
   peas, thawed
vegetable oil for frying

Make the sauce: In a small bowl stir together the yogurt, the coriander, the lime juice, and salt to taste.
Make the fritters: In a bowl stir together well the
flour, the curry powder, the cumin, the cayenne, the

baking powder, and the salt, add the seltzer, and stir the
batter until it is combined well. Stir in the scallion and
the peas. In a large deep skillet heat 1 inch of the oil to
375° F. on a deep-fat thermometer, in it fry tablespoons
of the batter in batches, turning the fritters, for 2 minutes, or until they are golden and crisp, and transfer
them as they are cooked to paper towels to drain. Sprinkle the fritters with salt if desired and serve them with
the dipping sauce. Makes about 30 fritters, serving 6 as
an hors d'oeuvre.

Creamed Peas and Cucumber with Dill

2 tablespoons unsalted butter
1 pound cucumbers, peeled, quartered
   lengthwise, seeded, and cut into ½-inch
   pieces
2 cups shelled fresh peas (about 2 pounds
   unshelled) or a 10-ounce package frozen
   peas, thawed
⅓ cup heavy cream
3 tablespoons snipped fresh dill
fresh lemon juice to taste

In a large heavy skillet heat the butter over moderately high heat until the foam subsides, add the cucumber
and salt to taste, and sauté the cucumber, stirring, for 5
minutes. Add the peas and ⅓ cup water and simmer the
mixture, covered, for 5 minutes, or until the peas are
tender. Add the cream and boil the mixture, uncovered,
for 2 to 3 minutes, or until the liquid is thickened slightly. Stir in the dill, the lemon juice, and salt and pepper to
taste and transfer the mixture to a heated serving dish.
Serves 6.

Potato and Turnip Purée

3 pounds russet (baking) potatoes
2 pounds turnips, peeled and cut into 1-inch pieces
½ stick (¼ cup) unsalted butter, softened
freshly ground white pepper to taste

In a large saucepan combine the potatoes, peeled and
cut into 1-inch pieces, with enough cold water to cover
them by 1 inch, bring the water to a boil, and simmer the
potatoes for 10 to 15 minutes, or until they are tender.
While the potatoes are cooking, in a steamer set over
boiling water steam the turnips, covered, for 12 to 15
minutes, or until they are very tender. In a food proces-

sor purée the turnips. Drain the potatoes in a large colander, return them to the pan, and cook them over moderate heat, shaking the pan, for 30 seconds to evaporate any excess liquid. Force the potatoes through a ricer or the medium disk of a food mill into a bowl, add the butter, stirring until it is melted, and stir in the turnip purée, the white pepper, and salt to taste. *The purée may be made 1 day in advance, kept covered and chilled, and reheated.* Makes about 6 cups, serving 8.

Potato Caraway Croquettes

⅓ cup minced onion
1 tablespoon unsalted butter
1½ tablespoons all-purpose flour plus
    additional for dredging the croquettes
½ cup milk
1 teaspoon caraway seeds
½ cup sour cream
1 pound russet (baking) potatoes
1 large egg beaten with 2 tablespoons milk
2 cups fine dry bread crumbs
vegetable oil for deep-frying

In a saucepan cook the onion in the butter over moderately low heat, stirring, until it is softened, stir in 1½ tablespoons of the flour, and cook the *roux* over low heat, stirring, for 3 minutes. Remove the pan from the heat and add the milk, scalded, in a stream, whisking vigorously until the mixture is thick and smooth. Add salt and pepper to taste, simmer the mixture, whisking, for 5 minutes, and whisk in the caraway seeds and the sour cream, whisking until the sauce is smooth. Let the sauce cool, its surface covered with plastic wrap. In a kettle combine the potatoes with enough cold water to cover them by 2 inches, bring the water to a boil, and simmer the potatoes for 10 to 15 minutes, or until they are barely tender. Drain the potatoes and steam them in the dry kettle, covered, over low heat, shaking the kettle gently, for 1 minute. Let the potatoes cool, peel them, and grate them coarse. Add the potatoes to the sauce, combine the mixture well, and chill it for 4 hours.

Shape 2 tablespoons of the potato mixture into cork-shaped croquettes, transferring each croquette as it is shaped to a jelly-roll pan lined with plastic wrap. Have ready in separate bowls the additional flour, the egg mixture, and the bread crumbs. Dredge the croquettes in the flour, dip them into the egg mixture, and coat them with the bread crumbs, transferring them to a rack as they are coated. Chill the croquettes, covered loosely, for 1 hour on the rack. *The croquettes may be prepared up to this point 1 day in advance and kept covered loosely and chilled on the rack.* In a deep skillet heat 1 inch of the oil until a deep-fat thermometer registers 360° F., in it fry the croquettes in batches for 30 seconds to 1 minute, or until they are golden, and transfer them with a slotted spoon to paper towels to drain. Transfer the croquettes to a heated vegetable dish. Makes about 18 croquettes.

PHOTO ON PAGE 79

Country Potato Gratin

1 large garlic clove, halved lengthwise
1½ pounds boiling potatoes
1 cup coarsely grated Gruyère or Swiss cheese
freshly grated nutmeg to taste
1 large egg
2 cups milk
2 tablespoons cold unsalted butter,
    cut into bits

Rub a 13- to 14-inch oval gratin dish (or 2-quart shallow baking dish, preferably ceramic) with the garlic and butter it. Peel the potatoes, slice them thin crosswise, using a *mandoline* or food processor, and in the dish arrange them in 4 layers, overlapping them and sprinkling each layer with ¼ cup of the Gruyère, some of the nutmeg, and salt and pepper to taste. In a small bowl whisk the egg, add the milk, scalded, in a stream, whisking, and pour the custard evenly over the potato and cheese mixture. Sprinkle the top with the remaining ¼ cup Gruyère, dot it with the butter, and bake the gratin in the middle of a preheated 375° F. oven for 45 minutes, or until it is golden and bubbling and the potatoes are tender. Serves 6 to 8 as a side dish.

Lefser
(Norwegian Potato Pancakes)

1½ pounds russet (baking) potatoes
2 tablespoons unsalted butter,
   cut into bits and softened
2 tablespoons milk
1 teaspoon salt
⅛ teaspoon pepper
1 cup all-purpose flour

In a large saucepan combine the potatoes with enough cold water to cover them by 2 inches, bring the water to a boil, and add salt to taste. Simmer the potatoes, covered partially, for 30 to 40 minutes, or until they are tender, and drain them. Return the potatoes to the pan and steam them dry, covered, shaking the pan occasionally, for 3 minutes. Let the potatoes cool until they can be handled, peel them, and force them through a ricer or food mill fitted with the medium disk into a bowl. Add the butter, the milk, the salt, and the pepper, beat the mixture until it is smooth, and chill it, covered, for 2 to 4 hours, or until it is chilled well.

Add the flour to the potato mixture and combine the mixture to form a smooth dough. Form ¼ cup of the dough into a ball, flatten the ball slightly on a lightly floured surface, and roll the dough into a 7- to 8-inch round. Heat an ungreased well seasoned griddle, preferably cast-iron, over moderate heat until it is hot, transfer the potato round carefully with a large metal spatula to the griddle, and cook the *lefse*, turning it once, for 2 to 3 minutes, or until it is browned lightly and dry on both sides but still tender and pliable. Transfer the *lefse* with the spatula to a kitchen towel and let it cool. Make *lefser* with the remaining dough in the same manner, wiping the griddle after each *lefse* has been cooked. The *lefser* may be stacked and kept in an airtight container overnight or they may be wrapped well in plastic wrap and frozen. Makes about ten 8-inch *lefser*.

PHOTO ON PAGES 42 AND 43

Lefser Spirals
(Norwegian Potato Pancakes with Salt Cod Filling)

½ pound salt cod
½ cup minced red bell pepper
1 cup minced cabbage
1 tablespoon minced white part of scallion
   plus ¼ cup minced scallion green
1 tablespoon unsalted butter
2 cups cream-style cottage cheese, puréed in a
   food processor or forced through a fine
   sieve into a bowl
1½ tablespoons fresh lemon juice
six 8-inch *lefser* (recipe opposite)

In a glass bowl combine the cod with cold water to cover, let it soak, covered and chilled, changing the water several times, for 24 hours, and drain it. In a kettle combine the cod with cold water to cover, bring the water to a boil, and simmer the cod, covered, for 25 to 30 minutes, or until it flakes easily when tested with a fork. Drain the cod in a colander, refresh it under cold water, and discard any skin and bones. Flake the cod with a fork and transfer it to a bowl.

In a skillet cook the bell pepper, the cabbage, and the white part of scallion in the butter over moderately low heat, stirring occasionally, until the vegetables are crisp-tender and toss the mixture with the cod. Add the cottage cheese, the lemon juice, the scallion green, and salt and pepper to taste and combine the mixture well. Spread ½ cup of the filling on 1 *lefse*, roll up the *lefse*, and cut it diagonally into ½-inch-thick slices. Continue to make spirals in the same manner with the remaining 5 *lefser* and the remaining filling and arrange the spirals on a platter. Makes about 36 spirals.

PHOTO ON PAGES 42 AND 43

Shredded Potato Pancakes

3 pounds (about 6 large) russet (baking)
   potatoes
4 tablespoons vegetable oil
2 tablespoons unsalted butter

Peel the potatoes and grate them coarse (preferably in a food processor). In a 10-inch non-stick skillet heat 1 tablespoon of the oil and 1 tablespoon of the butter over moderately high heat until the foam subsides. Working with half the potatoes (about 4 cups) and keeping the remaining potatoes in a bowl of cold water, squeeze the potatoes in paper towels to remove any excess moisture and spread them evenly in the skillet. Cook the pancake, tamping it down firmly with a spatula, for 10 minutes, or until the underside is golden, and season it with salt and pepper. Invert a baking sheet over the skillet and invert the pancake onto the baking sheet. Add 1 tablespoon of the remaining oil to the skillet and slide the pancake carefully back into the skillet. Cook the pancake over moderately high heat for 10 minutes more, or until the underside is golden, transfer it to a baking sheet, and keep it warm in a preheated 250° F. oven while making a second pancake in the same manner with the remaining oil, butter, and potatoes, drained well and squeezed of excess moisture. Cut each pancake into 4 wedges. Serves 8.

PHOTO ON PAGE 45

Baked Puffed Potato Slices with Parmesan

1 large baking potato, scrubbed
1 garlic clove, chopped
1½ tablespoons olive oil (preferably virgin)
¼ cup freshly grated Parmesan
2 tablespoons minced fresh parsley leaves

Cut the potato lengthwise into 4 slices, rub the cut sides together until the starchy white liquid appears on the surface (the starch on the potato slices will make them puff), and bake the slices, cut sides up, in an oiled jelly-roll pan in the middle of a preheated 400° F. oven for 30 to 35 minutes, or until they are tender and puffed. While the potatoes are baking, in a small saucepan cook the garlic in the oil over moderately low heat, stirring occasionally, for 2 minutes and strain the oil through a fine sieve into a bowl, pressing hard on the garlic and reserving the oil. Sprinkle the Parmesan on the potatoes and bake the potatoes in the 400° F. oven for 1 to 2 minutes, or until the cheese is melted. Season the potatoes with salt and pepper, sprinkle them with the parsley, and drizzle them with the reserved oil. Serves 2.

Fried Potato Thins

3 large long white (boiling) potatoes (about
    1½ pounds)
vegetable oil for deep-frying
coarse salt to taste

Cut the potatoes lengthwise into ½-inch slices and with a vegetable peeler shave the slices in long thin strips into a bowl of ice and cold water. Let the potatoes soak for 15 minutes, drain them, and pat them dry. In a deep fryer or kettle fry the potatoes in batches in 2 inches of 350° F. oil, making sure the oil returns to 350° before adding each new batch, for 1 minute, or until they are just golden, and transfer them to paper towels to drain. Sprinkle the potatoes with the salt. Serves 4.

PHOTO ON PAGE 18

Stuffed Potato with
Baked Egg, Bacon, and Cheddar

2 slices of lean bacon
two ¾-pound russet (baking) potatoes
2 tablespoons unsalted butter, cut into bits
¼ cup milk
¼ cup sour cream
2 large eggs
2 tablespoons chopped scallion green
¼ cup finely grated sharp Cheddar

Arrange the bacon in one layer on a double thickness of microwave-safe paper towels in an 8-inch-square baking dish and microwave it, covered with a double thickness of microwave-safe paper towels, at high power (100%) for 4 to 6 minutes, or until crisp. Drain and cool the bacon on paper towels, and crumble it.

Prick each potato on one side with a fork, arrange the potatoes 1 inch apart on a microwave-safe paper towel in the microwave oven, and microwave them at high power (100%), turning them over after 3 minutes, for 5 to 7 minutes, or until they are barely tender when squeezed. Remove the potatoes from the oven and let them stand, wrapped in a kitchen towel, for 5 minutes. (The potatoes will continue to cook as they stand.)

While the potatoes are standing, in a 2-cup glass measuring cup combine the butter and the milk, microwave the mixture at high power (100%) for 30 seconds to 1 minute, or until the butter is just melted, and whisk in the sour cream. Cut off a ½-inch-thick lengthwise slice from the pricked side of each potato, reserving the slices for another use if desired, scoop out each potato, leaving a ¼-inch-thick shell, and chop the scooped-out potato.

Break an egg into each potato shell, prick the yolk membrane lightly in three places, being careful not to break the yolk, and season the eggs with salt and pepper. Wrap the potatoes with plastic wrap and microwave them 1 inch apart on the paper towel at medium power (50%) for 2 minutes to 2 minutes and 30 seconds, or until the egg whites begin to turn opaque.

In a bowl combine well the bacon, the sour cream mixture, the chopped potato, the scallion, and salt and pepper to taste. Fill the potatoes with the bacon mixture, being careful not to break the yolks, sprinkle them with the Cheddar, and microwave them 1 inch apart on the paper towel at medium power (50%) for 1 minute and 30 seconds to 2 minutes, or until the cheese is melted. Serves 2.

O'Brien Potatoes in Crisp Potato Shells
(Potatoes Stuffed with Pimiento, Green Pepper, and Onion)

2 russet (baking) potatoes (about ½ pound
    each), scrubbed, patted dry, and rubbed
    with vegetable oil
1 cup chopped onion
5 tablespoons unsalted butter
1 green bell pepper, chopped coarse
a 4-ounce jar pimientos,
    drained and chopped

Prick the potatoes a few times with a fork and bake them in the middle of a preheated 450° F. oven for 1 hour and 30 minutes. In a large heavy skillet cook the onion in the butter over moderately low heat, stirring occasionally, until it is softened, add the bell pepper, and cook the mixture for 2 minutes. Remove the skillet from the heat. While the potatoes are warm, halve them lengthwise, scoop them out, leaving crisp shells, and chop the scooped-out potato coarse. Add the chopped potato to the skillet and cook the mixture over moderately high heat, stirring, until the potato is browned slightly. Stir in the pimientos, cook the mixture for 1 minute, and divide it among the potato shells. Serves 4.

Roasted Potatoes Provençale

1 pound red boiling potatoes, cut into ½-
    inch dice
2 garlic cloves, chopped
2 tablespoons olive oil
10 Kalamata or other brine-cured black
    olives, pitted and chopped
1½ tablespoons minced fresh parsley leaves

In a baking pan toss together well the potatoes, the garlic, and the oil and roast the mixture in a preheated 425° F. oven, stirring occasionally, for 25 minutes, or until it is golden. Transfer the mixture to a serving dish and stir in the olives, the parsley, and salt and pepper to taste. Serves 2.

Salade Niçoise-Stuffed Potatoes

2 russet (baking) potatoes (about
    ½ pound each)

vegetable oil for rubbing the potatoes and for
    deep-frying
2 teaspoons Dijon-style mustard
1 tablespoon red-wine vinegar
3 tablespoons olive oil
¼ pound green beans, trimmed and cut into
    1-inch lengths
a 6½-ounce can chunk light tuna, drained
1 tomato, chopped
¼ cup pitted and halved Niçoise, Kalamata, or
    other brine-cured black olives
2 tablespoons minced fresh parsley leaves

To bake the potatoes in a conventional oven: Scrub the potatoes, pat them dry, and rub them with the vegetable oil. Prick the potatoes a few times with a fork and bake them in the middle of a preheated 425° F. oven for 1 hour. *The potatoes may be baked 8 hours in advance.* Or bake the potatoes in a microwave oven according to the procedure that follows. In a small bowl whisk together the mustard, the vinegar, and salt and pepper to taste, add the olive oil in a stream, whisking, and whisk the dressing until it is emulsified.

In a saucepan of boiling salted water cook the green beans for 2 minutes, or until they are crisp-tender, drain them, and transfer them to a bowl of ice and cold water. In a bowl combine the green beans, drained well, the tuna, the tomato, the olives, the parsley, and the dressing and toss the salad well. *The salad may be made 8 hours in advance and kept covered and chilled.* Halve the potatoes lengthwise and with a melon-ball cutter scoop the potatoes into balls, leaving ¼-inch-thick shells. In a heavy saucepan or deep-fryer fry the potato balls in 1½ inches of 375° F. vegetable oil for 5 minutes, or until they are golden, transfer them with a slotted spoon to paper towels to drain, and sprinkle them with salt to taste. Add the potato balls to the salad, toss the salad well, and divide it among the potato shells. Serves 4.

To Microwave Baking Potatoes

For two ½-pound potatoes: Scrub the potatoes and leave them wet. Prick each potato once with a fork and wrap it in a sheet of microwave-safe paper towel, tucking in the ends. Arrange the potatoes in the microwave, end to end 1-inch apart with the tucked-in ends down, microwave them at high power (100%) for 8 to 10 minutes, or until they yield to gentle pressure, and let them stand, wrapped, for 5 minutes.

To microwave more than 2 baking potatoes, arrange the potatoes, wrapped separately, end to end 1-inch apart in a circle: for 3 potatoes, microwave them for 12 to 15 minutes; for 4 potatoes, microwave them for 17 to 20 minutes.

Note: These procedures were tested in a 600-watt, .8-cubic-foot unit, with interior dimensions of 16 by 10 by 7¼ inches. Cooking times will vary from one manufacturer's product to another, depending on power and size configuration; therefore, it is imperative to refer to the instructions that accompany the appliance.

Twice-Baked Potatoes with Parmesan

3 russet (baking) potatoes
  (about ½ pound each)
vegetable oil for rubbing the potatoes
3 tablespoons unsalted butter, softened
½ cup sour cream
1 large egg yolk
⅓ cup minced fresh parsley leaves
4 tablespoons freshly grated Parmesan
1 to 2 tablespoons milk
sweet paprika for sprinkling the potatoes

To bake the potatoes in a conventional oven: Scrub the potatoes, pat them dry, and rub them with the oil. Prick the potatoes a few times with a fork and bake them in the middle of a preheated 425° F. oven for 1 hour. To bake the potatoes in a microwave oven: Follow the procedure opposite. While the potatoes are baking, in a bowl whisk together 2 tablespoons of the butter, the sour cream, the egg yolk, the parsley, 3 tablespoons of the Parmesan, and 1 tablespoon of the milk. While the potatoes are warm, halve them lengthwise, scoop them out, leaving the shells as thin as possible, and force the scooped-out potato through a ricer or the medium disk of a food mill into the bowl. Combine the mixture well, adding additional milk if necessary to reach the desired consistency, transfer it to a pastry bag fitted with a large star tip, and pipe it decoratively into the potato shells. Sprinkle the potatoes with the remaining 1 tablespoon Parmesan and bake them in a baking dish in the middle of a preheated 425° F. oven for 12 to 15 minutes, or until they are browned lightly. Cut the remaining 1 tablespoon butter into 6 pieces, top each potato with 1 piece, and sprinkle the potatoes lightly with the paprika. Serves 6.

Herbed New Potatoes

¾ pound small boiling potatoes, quartered
1 tablespoon minced fresh parsley leaves
1 tablespoon minced fresh mint
1 tablespoon snipped fresh chives
2 tablespoons unsalted butter, softened

In a steamer set over boiling water steam the potatoes, covered, for 10 minutes, or until they are just tender. In a bowl toss the potatoes gently with the parsley, the mint, the chives, the butter, and salt and pepper to taste. Serves 2.

Sweet Potato and Apricot Purée

1¼ pounds sweet potatoes, peeled and cut
  crosswise into ½-inch slices
⅛ cup packed dried apricots, chopped fine
2 tablespoons unsalted butter, softened
freshly ground white pepper to taste

In a steamer set over boiling water steam the sweet potatoes and the apricots, covered, for 20 minutes, or until the potatoes are very tender, and in a food processor purée the mixture with 1 tablespoon of the butter, the white pepper, and salt to taste until the purée is smooth. Divide the purée between 2 heated plates, make a depression with the back of a spoon in each serving, and divide the remaining 1 tablespoon butter between the servings. Serves 2.

Lemon Sweet Potato Purée

2 pounds sweet potatoes or yams, scrubbed well
½ stick (¼ cup) unsalted butter, softened
3 tablespoons fresh lemon juice, or to taste

In a large saucepan combine the sweet potatoes with
enough salted water to cover them by 2 inches, bring the
water to a boil, and simmer the sweet potatoes, covered,
for 20 to 30 minutes, or until they are tender. Drain the
sweet potatoes, let them cool until they can be handled,
and peel them. Force the sweet potatoes through a ricer
or food mill fitted with a medium disk into the pan, add
3 tablespoons of the butter, the lemon juice, and ¼ cup
water, and heat the purée over moderately low heat,
stirring, until it is hot, adding more water if necessary to
thin it to the desired consistency. Season the purée with
salt and pepper, mound it in a heated serving dish, making a small well in the center, and fill the well with the
remaining 1 tablespoon butter. Serves 4.

PHOTO ON PAGE 25

Fried White and Sweet Shoestring Potatoes

1 russet (baking) potato
1 small sweet potato (about ½ pound)
vegetable oil for deep-frying
1 tablespoon minced scallion green
lime wedges as an accompaniment

Peel the russet potato, cut it into ¼-inch-thick shoestring sticks, and reserve the sticks in a bowl of cold
water. Peel the sweet potato and cut it into ¼-inch-
thick shoestring sticks. In a deep skillet heat 2 inches
of the oil to 375° F. on a deep-fat thermometer, in it fry
the sweet potato sticks in batches for 1 to 2 minutes, or
until they are golden, and transfer them with a slotted
spoon to paper towels to drain. In the 375° F. oil fry
the russet potato sticks, drained and patted dry between several thicknesses of paper towels, in batches
for 2 to 3 minutes, or until they are golden, and transfer them with the spoon to paper towels to drain. Season the shoestring potatoes with salt and pepper,
arrange them on a platter, and sprinkle the scallion
over them. Serve the potatoes with the lime. Serves 2.

Rutabaga and Rosemary Gratin

1 pound rutabaga, peeled, halved lengthwise,
   and sliced thin crosswise, preferably using

a *mandoline* or food processor
2 tablespoons all-purpose flour
¼ teaspoon dried rosemary, crumbled
1 cup freshly grated Parmesan
1 cup heavy cream
½ cup canned chicken broth

In a steamer set over boiling water steam the rutabaga, covered, for 3 to 4 minutes, or until it is barely
tender, let it cool, and pat it dry. In a buttered 11- to 12-
inch oval gratin dish (or 1½-quart shallow baking dish)
arrange one third of the rutabaga in an even layer and
sprinkle it with 1 tablespoon of the flour, ⅛ teaspoon of
the rosemary, ⅓ cup of the Parmesan, and salt and pepper to taste. Arrange half the remaining rutabaga in an
even layer over the Parmesan and sprinkle it with the remaining 1 tablespoon flour, the remaining ⅛ teaspoon
rosemary, ⅓ cup of the remaining Parmesan, and salt
and pepper to taste. Arrange the remaining rutabaga in
an even layer over the Parmesan and season it with salt
and pepper. In a small saucepan combine the cream and
the broth, bring the mixture just to a boil, and pour it
evenly over the rutabaga mixture. Sprinkle the top with
the remaining ⅓ cup Parmesan and bake the gratin, covered with foil, in the middle of a preheated 375° F. oven
for 30 minutes. Remove the foil and bake the gratin, uncovered, for 20 minutes more, or until it is golden
brown and the rutabaga is tender. Let the gratin stand for
5 minutes before serving. Serves 6 as a side dish.

Rutabagas in Cream with Caramelized Onions

2 pounds onions, halved lengthwise and sliced
   thin crosswise
½ stick (¼ cup) unsalted butter
2 pounds rutabagas, peeled and cut into
   ½-inch dice
1 cup heavy cream

In a large saucepan cook the onions in the butter over
moderate heat, stirring occasionally, for 20 to 25 minutes, or until they are golden brown, stir in the rutabagas, the cream, and ¾ cup water, and cook the mixture
over moderately low heat, stirring occasionally, for 15
to 20 minutes, or until the rutabagas are tender. Season
the mixture with salt and pepper. *The rutabagas can be
made 2 days in advance, kept covered and chilled, and
reheated in a saucepan over moderately low heat.*
Serves 6 to 8.

Roasted Scallions

24 scallions, trimmed into 8-inch lengths
1½ tablespoons vegetable oil

Coat the scallions with the oil, arrange them in one layer in a jelly-roll pan, and sprinkle them with salt and pepper to taste. Roast the scallions in a preheated 500° F. oven for 5 to 7 minutes, or until they are just tender. Serves 4.

PHOTO ON PAGE 18

Creamed Spinach with Sour Cream

20 cups firmly packed spinach leaves
    removed from the stems (about 3 pounds
    with stems), washed well
½ cup canned chicken broth
⅓ cup minced shallot
2 tablespoons unsalted butter
½ cup sour cream
1 teaspoon fresh lemon juice
⅛ teaspoon sugar
⅛ teaspoon freshly grated nutmeg
¼ cup sliced almonds, toasted lightly

In a kettle cook the spinach in the water clinging to the leaves, covered, over moderate heat, stirring occasionally, for 3 minutes, or until it is wilted. Drain the spinach in a colander, refresh it under cold water, and squeeze it dry by handfuls. Transfer the spinach to a blender or food processor, add the broth, and purée the mixture. In a large skillet cook the shallot in the butter over moderately low heat, stirring, until it is softened, add the spinach purée and the sour cream, and combine the mixture well. Stir in the lemon juice, the sugar, the nutmeg, and salt and pepper to taste and cook the mixture, stirring, until it is just heated through. Transfer the mixture to a heated serving dish and sprinkle it with the almonds. Serves 6.

Indian-Spiced Sautéed Spinach with Fried Potatoes

1¼ pounds boiling potatoes
1 teaspoon vegetable oil plus additional for
    deep-frying
2 large garlic cloves, minced
1½ teaspoons cuminseed
½ teaspoon dried hot red pepper flakes
2 tablespoons unsalted butter
½ teaspoon ground cardamom
½ teaspoon ground coriander seeds
14 cups firmly packed spinach leaves
    removed from the stems (about 2 pounds
    with stems), washed well and spun dry
1 tablespoon fresh lemon juice

Peel the potatoes and cut them into ½-inch dice. In a deep fryer or deep skillet fry the potatoes, patted dry, in batches in 1 inch of 375°F. oil for 4 to 5 minutes, or until they are browned, transferring them with a slotted spoon to paper towels to drain, and sprinkle them generously with salt.

In a large kettle cook the garlic, the cuminseed, and the red pepper flakes in the butter and 1 teaspoon of the oil over moderately low heat, stirring, for 3 minutes, add the cardamom and the coriander, and cook the mixture, stirring, until the garlic and the cuminseed just begin to color. Add the spinach, sauté it over moderately high heat, stirring, until it is just tender, and stir in the lemon juice. Season the spinach mixture with salt, transfer it with a slotted spoon to a heated serving dish, and sprinkle the fried potatoes on top. Serves 4 to 6.

Acorn Squash and Apple Purée

1 acorn squash, halved and the seeds and
    strings discarded
1 Golden Delicious apple, cut into 1-inch
    pieces
1½ tablespoons unsalted butter
freshly grated nutmeg to taste if desired

Arrange the squash, cut sides down, in a glass dish, prick the skin all over with the tip of a sharp knife, and microwave the squash at high power (100%) for 10 minutes. Put the apple in a 1- or 2-cup glass measuring cup, cover it with microwave-safe plastic wrap, and microwave it and the squash at high power (100%) for 4 to 6 minutes, or until they are tender. Scoop out the squash, discarding the skin, pour off any liquid from the apple, and force the squash and the apple through the medium disk of a food mill into a bowl. Stir in the butter, the nutmeg, and salt and pepper to taste. Serves 2.

Butternut Squash, Apple, and Onion Gratin

1 pound onions, halved lengthwise and sliced
    thin crosswise
2 tablespoons unsalted butter
¾ pound Granny Smith apples (about 2)
3 tablespoons all-purpose flour
1 pound butternut squash, peeled, halved
    lengthwise, seeds and strings discarded,
    and the flesh sliced thin crosswise,
    preferably using a *mandoline* or food
    processor
½ cup canned chicken broth
¾ cup fresh bread crumbs
¾ cup coarsely grated sharp Cheddar
6 slices of lean bacon, cooked crisp and
    crumbled

In a heavy skillet cook the onions in the butter over moderate heat, stirring, until they are softened. Peel, quarter, and slice thin the apples and in a bowl toss them with the flour. In a buttered 13- to 14-inch oval gratin dish (or 2-quart shallow baking dish) arrange the apples and the squash in layers, seasoning each layer with salt and pepper, and top the mixture with the onions, spreading them in an even layer. Add the broth, heated, and bake the mixture, covered tightly with foil, in the middle of a preheated 375° F. oven for 45 to 55 minutes, or until the squash is tender. While the mixture is baking, in a small bowl toss together well the bread crumbs, the Cheddar, and the bacon. Remove the foil from the squash mixture, sprinkle the top evenly with the crumb mixture, and bake the gratin, uncovered, in the middle of the 375° F. oven for 20 minutes, or until the topping is golden. Serves 6 to 8 as a side dish.

Butternut Squash Purée

2 butternut squash (about 3½ pounds total),
    halved lengthwise, seeds and strings
    discarded, and the squash peeled and cut
    into 1-inch pieces (about 8 cups)
¼ cup plain yogurt
2 tablespoons unsalted butter, softened
⅛ teaspoon freshly grated nutmeg, or to taste

In a steamer set over boiling water steam the squash, covered, for 10 to 12 minutes, or until it is tender, remove the steamer from over the water, and let the squash stand for 5 minutes. Force the squash through the medium disk of a food mill set over a bowl and stir in the yogurt, the butter, the nutmeg, and salt and pepper to taste. *The purée may be made 1 day in advance, cooled, and kept covered and chilled. Reheat the purée in a baking dish, covered, in a preheated 350° F. oven for 20 minutes, or until it is hot.* Serves 4.

PHOTO ON PAGE 75

Tomatoes Stuffed with White Bean, Parsley, and Garlic Purée

2 cups dried white beans, such as Great
    Northern
1 cup parsley sprigs
2 to 3 garlic cloves, or to taste, minced and
    mashed to a paste
2 to 4 tablespoons extra-virgin olive oil
    (available at specialty foods shops and
    some supermarkets), or to taste
8 small tomatoes

In a large saucepan combine the beans with enough hot water to cover them by 4 inches, bring the water to a boil, and boil the beans for 2 minutes. Remove the pan from the heat, let the beans soak for 1 hour, and drain them. In the saucepan combine the beans with enough cold water to cover them by 4 inches, bring the water to a boil, and simmer the beans for 40 minutes, or until they are tender. Drain the beans in a colander set over a bowl, reserving the cooking liquid.

In a food processor purée the beans, the parsley, the garlic, the oil, and salt to taste until the mixture is smooth and with the motor running add about ¼ cup of the reserved cooking liquid, or enough to thin the purée to the consistency of mashed potatoes. *The purée may be made 2 days in advance and kept in a bowl, covered and chilled.*

Halve the tomatoes horizontally and with a melon-ball cutter scoop out and discard the seeds and pulp, leaving a ¼-inch shell. Sprinkle the shells with salt and pepper, invert them onto a triple thickness of paper towels, and let them drain for 10 minutes. Transfer the purée to a large pastry bag fitted with a large star tip and pipe it into the shells, mounding it. Arrange the tomatoes in an oiled shallow baking dish and bake them in the lower third of a preheated 375° F. oven for 15 to 20 minutes, or until the purée is heated through. Makes 16 stuffed tomatoes, serving 8.

PHOTO ON PAGE 30

Vegetables à la Grecque

½ cup olive oil (preferably extra-virgin,
   available at specialty foods shops and many
   supermarkets)
⅓ cup fresh lemon juice
4 garlic cloves
1 shallot, chopped fine
2 teaspoons coriander seeds
2 teaspoons fennel seeds
½ teaspoon black peppercorns
½ teaspoon salt
1 bay leaf
8 small white onions (about ¼ pound), peeled
1 fennel bulb, trimmed and quartered
   lengthwise
12 baby carrots or 2 large carrots, trimmed,
   peeled, and cut crosswise into ⅓-inch slices
1 cup small cauliflower flowerets (about
   ¼ pound)
12 baby yellow summer squash or ¼ pound
   yellow summer squash or zucchini, cut
   crosswise into ⅓-inch slices
⅓ cup finely diced tomato for garnish

In a large saucepan combine 2½ cups water with the oil, the lemon juice, the garlic, the shallot, the coriander seeds, the fennel seeds, the peppercorns, the salt, and the bay leaf, bring the mixture to a boil, covered, and simmer it, covered, for 10 minutes. Add the onions and cook the mixture, uncovered, at a slow boil for 5 minutes. Add the fennel bulb and the carrots and cook the mixture at a slow boil for 5 minutes. Add the cauliflower and cook the mixture at a slow boil for 5 minutes. Add the squash and cook the mixture at a slow boil for 5 minutes, or until the vegetables are just tender. Transfer the vegetables with a slotted spoon to a wide shallow bowl large enough to hold them in one layer. Bring the cooking liquid to a boil, boil it, stirring occasionally, until it is emulsified and reduced to about 1 cup, and strain it through a fine sieve over the vegetables. Let the mixture cool and chill it, covered, for at least 4 hours or overnight. Divide the vegetables, transferring them with a slotted spoon, among 4 small plates, spoon a little of the cooking liquid over them, and sprinkle some of the tomato over each serving. Serves 4 as a first course.

PHOTO ON PAGE 54

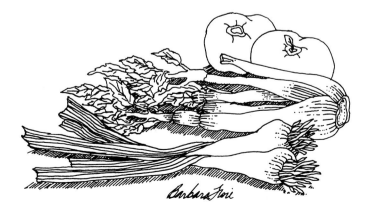

199

Vegetables Primavera with Polenta

3 tablespoons unsalted butter

¼ pound thin sliced prosciutto, cut crosswise into 1-inch pieces

¼ teaspoon dried sage, crumbled

2 cups canned chicken broth

⅔ cup yellow cornmeal

2 ounces green beans, cut into 1-inch pieces

2 ounces baby carrots, trimmed

¼ cup olive oil

2 ounces baby zucchini, cut diagonally into ¼-inch pieces

2 ounces baby summer squash, cut diagonally into ¼-inch slices

⅓ cup shredded cabbage

1 small tomato, seeded and cut into ¼-inch dice

3 tablespoons freshly grated Parmesan

In a 2-quart glass casserole or measuring cup combine 1 tablespoon of the butter, the prosciutto, and 1 tablespoon water and microwave the mixture at high power (100%) for 1 minute. Stir in the sage, the broth, and the cornmeal, stirring until the mixture is smooth, and microwave the mixture, covered, at high power (100%) for 6 minutes. Stir the mixture well to remove any lumps and microwave it, covered, at high power, for 7 minutes. Pour the polenta into a buttered shallow 3-cup dish and smooth the top. Chill the polenta, its surface covered with plastic wrap, for 1 hour or overnight. Cut the polenta into pieces.

In a saucepan of boiling salted water cook the beans for 4 minutes, or until they are just tender, and with a slotted spoon transfer them to a bowl of ice and cold water to refresh them. In the saucepan cook the carrots for 5 minutes, or until they are just tender, and with a slotted spoon transfer them to a bowl of ice and cold water to refresh them.

In a skillet heat 2 tablespoons of the olive oil over moderately high heat until it is hot but not smoking and in it sauté the polenta pieces, turning them once, until they are heated through and just beginning to color. Transfer the polenta with a slotted spatula to a plate and keep it warm in a 200° F. oven. In the skillet heat the remaining 2 tablespoons oil and 2 tablespoons butter over moderately high heat until it is hot but not smoking, add the zucchini and the summer squash, and sauté the vegetables, stirring, for 2 minutes, or until they are barely tender. Add the cabbage and sauté

the mixture for 1 minute. Add the tomato, the beans, drained, and the carrots, drained, sauté the vegetables, stirring, until they are heated through, and toss them with 1 tablespoon of the Parmesan and salt and pepper to taste. Divide the polenta between 2 heated plates, spoon some of the vegetables over it, and sprinkle the servings with the remaining Parmesan. Serves 2 as a luncheon entrée or 4 as a first course.

PHOTO ON PAGE 82

Summer Vegetable Dumplings with Jalapeño Vinegar

2 tablespoons white-wine vinegar

1 teaspoon minced drained bottled pickled *jalapeño* pepper

¼ teaspoon sugar, or to taste

3 tablespoons minced scallion

½ cup cooked fresh corn or thawed frozen

¼ cup finely chopped seeded tomato

¼ cup finely chopped green bell pepper

2 tablespoons cream cheese, softened

12 won ton wrappers (available at Oriental markets and many supermarkets), thawed if frozen, covered with a dampened kitchen towel

1 tablespoon vegetable oil

In a small bowl combine well the vinegar, the *jalapeño* pepper, the sugar, 1 tablespoon of the scallion, and salt and black pepper to taste. In a bowl combine well the corn, the tomato, the bell pepper, the cream cheese, the remaining 2 tablespoons scallion, and salt and black pepper to taste. Put 1 won ton wrapper on a work surface, moisten the edges lightly with water, and mound 2 level teaspoons of the corn mixture in the center. Fold the wrapper over the filling to form a triangle, pressing out the air and pinching the edges firmly to seal them well, and cover the dumpling with a dampened kitchen towel. Make dumplings with the remaining wrappers and filling in the same manner, covering them as they are made. In a non-stick skillet large enough to hold the dumplings in one layer heat the oil over high heat until it is hot but not smoking, arrange the dumplings in the skillet so that each stands upright on its folded edge, and cook them over moderately high heat, shaking the skillet occasionally, for 2 minutes, or until the undersides are golden brown and crisped. Add ¼ cup water to the skillet and steam the dumplings, covered, for 5 minutes. Remove the lid and continue to cook the dumplings until all of the liquid is evaporated and the undersides are recrisped. Transfer the dumplings to a heated platter and pour the *jalapeño* vinegar over them. Serves 2 as a first course or luncheon entrée.

Provençal Vegetable Gratin

4 cups thinly sliced fennel bulb (about 2½ pounds)
6 cups thinly sliced white and pale green part of leek (about 6), washed well and drained well
¾ stick (6 tablespoons) unsalted butter
2 large garlic cloves, minced
⅓ cup plus 1 tablespoon freshly grated Parmesan
1 tablespoon minced fresh thyme leaves or ½ teaspoon crumbled dried
a 1½-pound eggplant, halved lengthwise and cut crosswise into ½-inch slices
3 tomatoes (about 1½ pounds), halved lengthwise and cut crosswise into ½-inch slices
4 small zucchini (about 1 pound), cut crosswise into ½-inch slices
3 tablespoons olive oil

In a large kettle or deep heavy skillet cook the fennel and the leek in the butter, covered, over moderate heat, stirring occasionally, for 30 to 40 minutes, or until the vegetables are soft. Remove the kettle from the heat and stir in the garlic and salt and pepper to taste. *The leek mixture may be made 1 day in advance and kept covered and chilled. Reheat the mixture over low heat, stirring, before continuing.* Divide the mixture between two 10-inch round baking dishes, spreading it evenly, or spread it in 1 large baking dish, such as an oval gratin dish measuring 15 by 10½ inches, and

sprinkle ⅓ cup of the Parmesan and the minced thyme on top. Arrange the eggplant, the tomatoes, and the zucchini, alternating the vegetables in concentric circles, on top of the leek mixture, working toward the center. Brush the vegetables with the oil and sprinkle them with the remaining 1 tablespoon Parmesan and salt and pepper to taste. Bake the gratin in a preheated 350° F. oven for 1 hour. Serves 8 to 10.

PHOTO ON PAGE 60

Yam and Potato Gratin with Jarlsberg

¾ pound boiling potatoes
¾ pound yams or sweet potatoes, peeled and sliced thin crosswise, using a *mandoline* or food processor
1 cup coarsely grated Jarlsberg
freshly grated nutmeg to taste
1½ tablespoons all-purpose flour
1 large egg
2 cups milk
2 tablespoons cold unsalted butter, cut into bits

Peel the potatoes and, using a *mandoline* or food processor, slice them thin. In a buttered 13- to 14-inch oval gratin dish (or 2-quart shallow baking dish) arrange the potatoes and the yams in a total of 4 alternating layers, beginning with a potato layer, sprinkling each potato layer with ⅓ cup of the Jarlsberg, some of the nutmeg, and salt and pepper, and sprinkling the yam layers with the flour. In a bowl whisk the egg, add the milk, scalded, in a stream, whisking, and pour the custard evenly over the yam and potato layers. Sprinkle the remaining ⅓ cup Jarlsberg on top, dot it with the butter, and bake the gratin in the middle of a preheated 375° F. oven for 45 minutes, or until it is golden and bubbling and the potatoes are tender. Let the gratin stand for 5 minutes before serving. Serves 6 to 8 as a side dish.

SALADS AND SALAD DRESSINGS

ENTRÉE SALADS

Avocado and Chicken Salad Mediterranean-Style
For the dressing
1 tablespoon plus 1 teaspoon fresh
    lemon juice
¼ teaspoon Tabasco
½ teaspoon dried orégano, crumbled
5 tablespoons extra-virgin olive oil (available
    at specialty foods shops and many
    supermarkets)
¼ cup finely chopped red onion

1½ pounds boneless chicken breasts
    with the skin
1 tablespoon olive oil
½ teaspoon dried orégano, crumbled
½ cup oil-cured black olives (available at
    specialty foods shops and many
    supermarkets), pitted and halved
¼ cup chopped fresh mint leaves
3 tablespoons chopped fresh flat-leafed
    parsley leaves
1 tomato, cut into ¼-inch pieces
2 firm-ripe avocados (about 1¼ pounds in all,
    preferably California)
about 16 leaves of Boston or other soft-leafed
    lettuce

Make the dressing: In a large bowl whisk together the lemon juice, the Tabasco, and the orégano, add the oil in a stream, whisking, and whisk the dressing until it is emulsified. Stir in the onion.

Heat a well seasoned ridged grill pan over moderately high heat until it is hot or prepare a charcoal grill. Pat the chicken dry, rub the skinless side with the oil, and sprinkle it with the orégano and salt and pepper to taste. Grill the chicken, skin side down, pressing the thickest part occasionally with a metal spatula, for 7 minutes, turn it, and grill it in the same manner for 7 minutes more, or until it is cooked through. Transfer the chicken with tongs to a plate, let it cool to room temperature, and discard the skin and any juices that accumulate on the plate. Cut the chicken into ¾-inch pieces, add it to the dressing, and let it marinate at room temperature, stirring occasionally, for 1 hour. Add the olives, the mint, the parsley, and the tomato and toss the salad well. Halve lengthwise and pit the avocados, with a 1-inch melon-ball cutter scoop the flesh into balls, and add it to the salad. Toss the salad gently and season it with salt and pepper. *The salad may be made 1 hour in advance and kept covered tightly and chilled.* Divide the lettuce leaves among 4 plates and top them with the salad. Serves 4.

Fried Chicken and Potato Salad with Carrot
1 cup plain yogurt
2 tablespoons ground cumin
2 teaspoons Worcestershire sauce
3½ teaspoons Tabasco
1 pound boneless skinless chicken thighs,
    cut into ¾-inch pieces
2 pounds boiling potatoes, peeled, cut into
    ¼-inch-thick sticks, and reserved in a bowl
    of cold water
¾ pound carrots, cut into
    ¼-inch-thick sticks
2½ cups fine dry bread crumbs
3½ tablespoons white-wine vinegar
freshly ground white pepper to taste
1 cup olive oil
½ cup minced fresh parsley leaves
vegetable oil for deep-frying
½ cup thinly sliced scallion

In a bowl whisk together the yogurt, the cumin, the Worcestershire sauce, 2 teaspoons of the Tabasco, and salt and black pepper to taste, add the chicken, and combine the mixture well. Let the chicken marinate, covered and chilled, for at least 8 hours or overnight.

In a kettle of boiling salted water cook the potatoes for 4 to 6 minutes, or until they are just tender, transfer them with a sieve to a bowl of ice and cold water to stop the cooking, and drain them well. In the boiling water cook the carrots for 2 to 4 minutes, or until they are crisp-tender, drain them, and plunge them into a bowl of ice and cold water to stop the cooking. Drain the carrots well and in a bowl combine them with the potatoes. *The salad may be prepared up to this point 1 day in advance and kept covered and chilled.*

In a large plastic bag combine the bread crumbs and the chicken, drained, shake the bag to coat the chicken with the bread crumbs, and transfer the chicken to a rack set in a jelly-roll pan. Chill the chicken, uncovered, for 30 minutes. In a bowl whisk together the vinegar, the white pepper, and the remaining 1½ teaspoons Tabasco, add the olive oil in a stream, whisking, and whisk the dressing until it is emulsified. Whisk in the parsley. In a deep skillet heat 1½ inches of the vegetable oil to 375° F. on a deep-fat thermometer, in it fry the chicken in batches for 30 seconds to 1 minute, or until it is no longer pink within, and transfer it with a slotted spoon to paper towels to drain. To the potato mixture add the chicken, the scallion, and the dressing, whisked, and toss the salad well. *Do not finish making the salad more than 1 hour in advance.* Serves 4 to 6.

Matjes Herring Salad

½ cup minced white onion
½ cup minced red onion
½ cup finely grated carrot
¼ cup white-wine vinegar
2 large egg yolks
freshly ground black pepper to taste
1 cup vegetable oil
four 6-ounce jars *matjes* herring in spiced
    sauce, drained and chopped
1½ cups minced drained pickled beets
1 cup minced drained dill pickles
1 cup drained bottled capers
parsley sprigs for garnish
rye crackers as an accompaniment

In a bowl combine the white onion and the red onion with enough cold water to cover them by 1 inch and let the onions soak for 15 minutes. Drain the onions, pat them dry with paper towels, and in the bowl toss them with the carrot. In another bowl whisk together the vinegar, the yolks, the pepper, and salt to taste, add the oil in a stream, whisking, and whisk the dressing until it is emulsified. Arrange the onion mixture, the herring, the beets, the pickles, and the capers decoratively on a platter, spoon the dressing over the salad, and garnish the salad with the parsley. Serve the salad with the crackers. Serves 10 to 12.

Lobster Salad with Dill and Lemon Mayonnaise

two 1¼-pound live lobsters
2 tablespoons fresh lemon juice
1 large egg yolk
⅛ teaspoon Tabasco
⅓ cup olive oil
¼ cup snipped fresh dill
1 cup chopped celery
⅓ cup finely chopped drained bottled
    pimiento
¼ cup minced scallion
soft-leafed lettuce leaves, rinsed and spun
    dry, for lining the plates

Into a large kettle of boiling salted water plunge the lobsters and boil them, covered, for 8 minutes from the time the water returns to a boil. Transfer the lobsters with tongs to a cutting board and let them cool until they can be handled. Break off the claws at the body and crack them. Remove the claw meat and cut it into ¾-inch pieces. Halve the lobsters lengthwise along the undersides, remove the meat from the tails, and cut it into ¾-inch pieces. In a bowl combine the claw and tail meat. Break off the legs at the body, reserving them for another use, remove the meat from the body cavities near the leg joints, and add it to the bowl.

In a blender blend the lemon juice, the yolk, and the Tabasco until the mixture is combined and with the motor running add the oil in a slow stream. Add the dill and salt and pepper to taste and blend the mayonnaise until the dill is puréed. To the lobster meat add the celery, the pimiento, the scallion, and the mayonnaise, combine the salad well, and season it with salt and pepper. Line 2 plates with the lettuce leaves and divide the salad between them. Serves 2.

Meatball and Fusilli Salad

¾ pound ground chuck
¼ pound ground pork
1 cup coarsely grated extra-sharp Cheddar
¼ cup fine fresh bread crumbs
1 large egg, beaten lightly
2 tablespoons vegetable oil
1 onion, chopped
1 green bell pepper, chopped
1 cup canned beef broth
⅓ cup sour cream
1 pound *fusilli* (corkscrew-shaped pasta)
1 cup thinly sliced scallion green

In a bowl combine well the chuck, the pork, the Cheddar, the bread crumbs, the egg, and salt and black pepper to taste. (Test the seasoning by cooking a small amount of the meat mixture.) Form rounded teaspoons of the mixture into meatballs, in a large heavy skillet heat the oil over moderately high heat until it is hot but not smoking, and in it brown the meatballs in batches, shaking the skillet to maintain the round shapes. Transfer the meatballs with a slotted spoon as they are browned to a bowl. In the oil remaining in the skillet cook the onion and the bell pepper, stirring, until the vegetables are browned and softened, stir in the broth, and deglaze the skillet, scraping up the brown bits. Bring the liquid to a boil, add the meatballs, and simmer them for 2 to 3 minutes, or until they are no longer pink within. Stir in the sour cream, remove the skillet from the heat, and cover it. In a kettle of boiling salted water cook the *fusilli* for 6 to 8 minutes, or until it is *al dente*, drain it well, and in a large bowl toss it with the meatball mixture, the scallion green, and salt and pepper to taste. *The salad may be made 1 day in advance and kept covered and chilled. Let the salad come to room temperature before serving.* Serves 4 to 6.

Mussel and Potato Salad
with Lemon Herb Vinaigrette

For the vinaigrette
4 tablespoons fresh lemon juice
2 teaspoons Dijon-style mustard
¾ cup olive oil
1 tablespoon minced fresh basil leaves or
  1 teaspoon dried, crumbled
½ teaspoon dried tarragon,
  crumbled

3 tablespoons minced fresh parsley leaves

2 pounds boiling potatoes, peeled, quartered
  lengthwise, and cut crosswise into ¾-inch
  pieces
5 pounds mussels
1½ cups thinly sliced celery
1 cup cooked fresh peas (about 1 pound
  unshelled) or half a 10-ounce package
  frozen peas, thawed
2 cups cherry tomatoes, halved
¼ cup chopped scallion greens
  plus additional for garnish
  if desired
Boston lettuce leaves for lining the platter

Make the vinaigrette: In a bowl whisk together the lemon juice, the mustard, and salt and pepper to taste, add the oil in a stream, whisking, and whisk the vinaigrette until it is emulsified. Whisk in the basil, the tarragon, and the parsley.

In a steamer set over boiling water steam the potatoes, covered, for 8 to 10 minutes, or until they are just tender, and transfer them to a large bowl. Toss the potatoes with ½ cup of the vinaigrette and let them cool. Scrub the mussels well in several changes of water, scrape off the beards, and rinse the mussels. In a kettle steam the mussels with 1 cup water, covered, over moderately high heat for 5 to 7 minutes, or until they are opened, transfer them with a slotted spoon to a bowl, and let them cool. Discard any unopened mussels and remove the mussels from the shells, reserving 8 shells for garnish if desired. To the potatoes add the mussels, the celery, the peas, the tomatoes, ¼ cup of the scallion greens, the remaining vinaigrette, and salt and pepper to taste and toss the salad well. Line a large platter with the lettuce leaves and mound the salad in the center. Arrange the reserved mussel shells around the salad and sprinkle the salad with the additional scallion greens. Serves 6.

Marinated Seafood and Blood Orange Salad

three 2½- by ½-inch strips of blood orange
  rind, removed with a vegetable peeler
a 2½- by ½-inch strip of lemon rind, removed
  with a vegetable peeler
12 coriander sprigs
2 quarter-size slices of fresh gingerroot

6 black peppercorns
½ teaspoon salt
¾ pound large shrimp, shelled and deveined
¾ pound sea scallops, halved horizontally
    if large
3 blood oranges plus ¼ cup blood orange juice
¼ cup fresh lime juice
For the Maltaise mayonnaise
1 tablespoon blood orange juice
1 tablespoon fresh lime juice
1 large egg yolk
1 teaspoon Dijon-style mustard
¼ teaspoon minced garlic if desired
¼ teaspoon crushed fresh gingerroot (forced
    through a garlic press) if desired
¼ cup vegetable oil
¼ cup olive oil

½ cup minced red or green bell pepper
⅓ cup minced red onion or scallion
1 tablespoon minced fresh coriander plus
    additional whole leaves for garnish
red-leaf lettuce leaves for lining the platter

In a saucepan combine the orange rind, the lemon rind, the coriander sprigs, the gingerroot, the peppercorns, and the salt with 3 cups water, bring the water to a boil, and simmer the mixture, covered, for 15 minutes. Let the mixture cool to room temperature and strain it through a sieve into a saucepan. Add the shrimp and the scallops, bring the liquid just to a simmer, stirring, and drain the seafood in a colander. In a bowl combine the orange juice and the lime juice, add the seafood, and let it marinate, covered loosely, stirring occasionally to coat it with the marinade, for 3 hours.

Using a zester or the fine side of a grater grate the rind from 2 of the oranges, keeping it in long shreds, and reserve it, wrapped in a dampened paper towel. With a serrated knife cut away the pith from the 2 oranges and cut away the rind and pith from the remaining orange. Cut the oranges crosswise into thin slices and reserve them, covered and chilled.

Make the Maltaise mayonnaise: In a blender or food processor blend together the orange juice, the lime juice, the yolk, the mustard, the garlic, the gingerroot, and salt and pepper to taste, with the motor running add the oils in a stream, and blend the mayonnaise until it is emulsified.

In a bowl combine the seafood, drained, the bell pep-

per, the onion, the minced coriander, and the reserved rind, add the mayonnaise, and toss the mixture gently to coat it lightly with the mayonnaise. Arrange the salad on a platter lined with the lettuce and garnish it with the reserved orange slices and the additional coriander. Serves 4 as a luncheon entrée or 6 as a first course.

Shrimp, Cucumber, and Celery Salad in Dill Dressing
    ½ pound small shrimp (about 24)
    ¼ cup plain yogurt
    2 tablespoons mayonnaise
    2 tablespoons snipped fresh dill
    1 teaspoon Dijon-style mustard
    1 teaspoon fresh lemon juice, or to taste
    ½ cucumber, halved lengthwise, seeded, and
        cut into ½-inch pieces
    ½ cup thinly sliced celery

To a saucepan of boiling salted water add the shrimp, remove the pan from the heat, and let the shrimp stand, covered, for 5 minutes. Drain the shrimp and refresh them under cold water until they are cool. Shell the shrimp and, if desired, devein them. In a bowl whisk together the yogurt, the mayonnaise, the dill, the mustard, the lemon juice, and salt and pepper to taste and stir in the shrimp, the cucumber, and the celery. Serves 2.

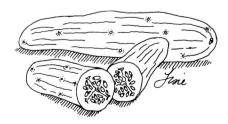

Lemon- and Garlic-Marinated Shrimp
with Green Beans and Endive

3 tablespoons fresh lemon juice
2 large garlic cloves, crushed and chopped
¼ teaspoon salt
¼ teaspoon sugar
6 tablespoons olive oil (preferably extra virgin, available at specialty foods shops and many supermarkets)
1 pound large shrimp, shelled, rinsed, and patted dry on paper towels
¼ pound green beans (preferably *haricots verts*, available at specialty produce markets)
¼ pound (about 1 large) endive
1 large egg yolk
1 small tomato, sliced
2 decorative slices of lemon
snipped fresh chives for garnish

In a bowl whisk together the lemon juice, the garlic, the salt, and the sugar, add 4 tablespoons of the olive oil in a stream, whisking, and whisk the marinade until it is emulsified. In a large heavy skillet cook the shrimp in the remaining 2 tablespoons olive oil over moderately low heat, covered, turning them occasionally, for 4 to 5 minutes, or until they are just cooked through and transfer them with a slotted spoon to another bowl. Whisk the olive oil mixture remaining in the skillet into the marinade and in a sturdy and sealable plastic bag combine the shrimp and the marinade. Let the shrimp marinate, chilled, for 8 hours or overnight.

In a saucepan of salted boiling water boil the beans for 2 to 3 minutes, or until they are crisp-tender, drain them in a colander, and plunge them into a bowl of ice and cold water to stop the cooking. Drain the beans and pat them dry on paper towels. Cut the endive lengthwise into thin slices, discarding the core, arrange the endive spears in a fan design on a platter, and top the endive fan design with the green beans. Remove the shrimp from the marinade, reserving the marinade and scraping off any garlic clinging to the shrimp, and arrange the shrimp on the platter at the base of the fan. Strain the reserved marinade through a fine sieve into a small bowl. In a blender blend the egg yolk, with the motor running add the reserved marinade in a stream, and blend the dressing until it is emulsified. Arrange the tomato and lemon slices deco-ratively on either side of the shrimp, sprinkle the shrimp with the chives, and serve the dressing on the side. Serves 2.

PHOTO ON FRONT JACKET

Snow Pea and Shrimp Salad
with Lemon Sesame Vinaigrette

½ pound snow peas, trimmed and strings discarded
3 tablespoons fresh lemon juice
¼ cup plus 2 tablespoons olive oil
1½ teaspoons Oriental sesame oil (available at specialty foods shops, Oriental markets, and most supermarkets)
¾ pound shrimp (about 22), shelled and deveined
2 tablespoons minced drained bottled pimiento
2 teaspoons sesame seeds, toasted lightly

In a large saucepan of boiling salted water blanch the snow peas for 30 seconds, drain them well, and plunge them into a bowl of ice and cold water to stop the cooking. Drain the snow peas, pat them dry, and cut them lengthwise into julienne strips. Reserve the snow peas, covered and chilled.

In a bowl whisk together the lemon juice and salt and pepper to taste, add ¼ cup of the olive oil and the sesame oil in a stream, whisking, and whisk the vinaigrette until it is emulsified. In a large skillet, preferably non-stick, heat 1 tablespoon of the remaining olive oil over moderately high heat until it is hot but not smoking and in it sauté half the shrimp, turning them once, for 1 minute, or until they are just firm. Transfer the shrimp with a slotted spoon to a plate and sauté the remaining shrimp in the remaining 1 tablespoon oil in the same manner.

Arrange the reserved snow peas on 2 plates, divide the shrimp between the plates, and sprinkle the snow peas with the pimiento and the sesame seeds. Whisk the vinaigrette and drizzle it over the salads. Serves 2 as a luncheon entrée.

Tortellini Salad with Arugula

1 teaspoon Dijon-style mustard
2 tablespoons red-wine vinegar
⅓ cup olive oil

½ zucchini, scored lengthwise with the tines
of a fork, quartered lengthwise, and cut
crosswise into ¼-inch slices
9 ounces fresh *tortellini*
1 small red bell pepper,
cut into ½- by ⅛-inch pieces
2 tablespoons freshly grated Parmesan
2 tablespoons minced fresh parsley leaves
4 cups loosely packed *arugula* or watercress,
coarse stems discarded, washed well and
spun dry

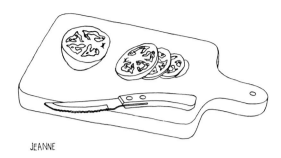

JEANNE

In a small bowl whisk together the mustard, the vine-gar, and salt to taste, add the oil in a stream, whisking, and whisk the dressing until it is emulsified. In a sauce-pan of boiling salted water blanch the zucchini for 1 minute, or until it just begins to turn translucent, drain it, and refresh it in a bowl of ice and cold water. In a large saucepan cook the *tortellini* in boiling salted water for 5 minutes, or until they are *al dente*, drain them, and refresh them under cold water. Drain the zucchini and the *tortellini* well and in a bowl combine them with the bell pepper, the Parmesan, the parsley, three fourths of the dressing, and salt and pepper to taste, tossing the in-gredients well to coat them with the dressing. In another bowl toss the *arugula* with the remaining dressing and divide it and the *tortellini* between plates. Serves 2.

SALADS WITH GREENS

Bibb and Watercress Salad

5 cups loosely packed Bibb lettuce leaves
(about 2 to 3 heads), rinsed and spun dry
1 bunch of watercress, coarse stems
discarded, rinsed and spun dry
2 to 3 tablespoons extra-virgin olive oil
(available at specialty foods shops and
many supermarkets), or to taste
1½ teaspoons fresh lemon juice plus
additional to taste

In a salad bowl toss together the Bibb lettuce and the watercress, drizzle the greens with 2 tablespoons of the oil, and toss the salad until it is combined well. Drizzle the salad with the lemon juice, season it with salt and pepper, and toss it until it is combined well. Season the salad if desired with the remaining 1 tablespoon oil, the additional lemon juice, and salt and pepper, tossing the salad well after each addition. Serves 4.

Hearts of Palm, Radish, and Bibb Lettuce Salads

a 14-ounce can hearts of palm, drained
48 Bibb lettuce leaves (about 4 heads),
rinsed and spun dry
6 large radishes, sliced thin
2 cups loosely packed watercress sprigs,
rinsed and spun dry
2 hard-boiled large egg yolks, forced through
a coarse sieve into a bowl
½ teaspoon Dijon-style mustard
2 tablespoons wine vinegar
2 tablespoons walnut oil*
4 tablespoons extra-virgin olive oil*

*available at specialty foods shops and some
supermarkets

Halve crosswise 6 of the hearts of palm, quarter them lengthwise, and cut the remaining hearts of palm cross-wise into ¼-inch slices. On each of 8 salad plates ar-range 6 of the hearts of palm quarters alternately with 6 of the lettuce leaves and top each lettuce leaf with 2 overlapping radish slices. Mound ¼ cup of the water-cress in the middle of each plate, top it with some of the sliced hearts of palm, and sprinkle the salads with the yolks. (Alternatively, in a salad bowl toss the hearts of palm, all sliced, with the lettuce, the radishes, the wa-tercress, and the yolks.)

In a small bowl whisk together the mustard, the vine-gar, and salt to taste, add the oils in a stream, whisking, and whisk the dressing until it is emulsified. Drizzle the salads with the dressing. Serves 8.

*Boston Lettuce and Cherry Tomatoes
with Citrus Vinaigrette*

¼ cup strained fresh orange juice
2 tablespoons strained fresh lemon juice
¼ cup olive oil
5 cups bite-size pieces of rinsed and spun-dry
    Boston lettuce
⅔ cup cherry tomatoes, halved
⅓ cup julienne strips of yellow or red bell
    pepper

In a small saucepan bring the orange juice and the lemon juice to a boil, simmer the mixture until it is reduced to about 2 tablespoons, and let it cool. In a bowl whisk together the juice mixture and salt and black pepper to taste, add the oil in a stream, whisking, and whisk the vinaigrette until it is emulsified. In another bowl toss the lettuce, the tomatoes, and the bell pepper with the vinaigrette until the salad is combined well. Serves 2.

Caesar Salads on Garlic Croutons

1 large garlic clove, halved
2 tablespoons fresh lemon juice
½ teaspoon English-style dry mustard
2 flat anchovy fillets, minced
¼ cup olive oil (preferably extra-virgin)
    plus additional for brushing the bread
6 cups lightly packed torn romaine, rinsed
    and spun dry
two ½-inch-thick horizontal slices from a
    round loaf of bread
2 poached eggs (procedure follows) if
    desired
2 tablespoons freshly grated Parmesan

Rub the bottom of a large bowl with half of the garlic clove dipped in salt, add the lemon juice, the mustard, the anchovies, and salt and pepper to taste, and whisk the mixture until it is combined well. Add ¼ cup of the oil in a stream, whisking, and whisk the dressing until it is emulsified. Add the romaine and toss the salad well. Brush the bread lightly with the additional oil and on a baking sheet toast the bread lightly on both sides under a preheated broiler about 3 inches from the heat. Rub 1 side of each crouton with the remaining half clove of garlic and put each crouton on a plate. Top the croutons with the salad, top the salads with the poached eggs, and

sprinkle each serving with half the Parmesan. Serves 2 as a main course or side dish.

To Poach Eggs

2 tablespoons distilled white vinegar
very fresh eggs at room temperature

Fill a wide 3-inch-deep pan three-fourths full with water. Add the vinegar, bring the liquid to a rolling boil over high heat, and reduce the heat to a bare simmer. Break the eggs, 1 at a time, into a saucer and slide them into the pan. As each egg is dropped in, push the white back immediately toward the yolk with a large slotted spoon, moving the egg gently. Simmer the eggs for 3 minutes, transfer them with the slotted spoon to a pan of cold water, and let them stand until they are needed. Drain the eggs carefully in the slotted spoon, blot them carefully with paper towels, and trim them. If poached correctly the yolk will be covered completely by the white and the egg will have returned approximately to its original oval shape. To serve the eggs hot, heat them in a saucepan of simmering water to cover for 30 seconds, or until they are heated through.

Curly Chicory and Red-Leaf Lettuce Salad

3 tablespoons tarragon vinegar
1 teaspoon Dijon-style mustard
1½ tablespoons minced fresh tarragon or
    1 teaspoon dried, crumbled
½ cup olive oil
8 cups torn curly chicory (preferably *frisée*,
    available at specialty produce markets),
    rinsed and spun dry
4 cups torn red-leaf lettuce, rinsed and
    spun dry

In a bowl whisk together the vinegar, the mustard, the tarragon, and salt and pepper to taste, add the oil in a stream, whisking, and whisk the dressing until it is emulsified. In a large bowl toss the curly chicory and the red-leaf lettuce with the dressing. Serves 8 to 10.

PHOTO ON PAGE 60

Endive Salad with Mustard Caraway Dressing

2 teaspoons Dijon-style mustard
1 teaspoon caraway seeds
1 tablespoon cider vinegar

⅛ teaspoon salt
¼ cup vegetable oil
2 large Belgian endives, trimmed

In a bowl whisk together the mustard, the caraway seeds, the vinegar, the salt, and pepper to taste, add the oil in a very slow stream, whisking, and whisk the dressing until it is emulsified. Quarter the endives lengthwise, arrange 4 quarters on each of 2 plates, and drizzle half the dressing over each salad. Serves 2.

Escarole Salad with Pine Nuts

¼ pound escarole, torn into bite-size pieces, washed well, and spun dry (about 4 cups loosely packed)
2 tablespoons pine nuts
2 tablespoons olive oil
2 teaspoons fresh lemon juice
2 tablespoons minced fresh parsley leaves

Put the escarole in a heatproof salad bowl. In a small skillet cook the pine nuts in the oil over moderate heat, stirring, until they are golden. Working quickly transfer the pine nuts with a slotted spoon to the escarole, stirring the escarole, and drizzle the salad with the hot oil, tossing it well. Drizzle the salad with the lemon juice, tossing it well, season it with salt and pepper, and sprinkle it with the parsley. Serves 2.

Tossed Green Salad with Dill Dressing

½ teaspoon Dijon-style mustard
1 tablespoon white-wine vinegar
1 tablespoon snipped fresh dill
¼ cup olive oil
¼ bunch of watercress, coarse stems discarded, rinsed and spun dry
2 cups loosely packed torn red-leaf lettuce, rinsed and spun dry
3 cups loosely packed torn Boston lettuce, rinsed and spun dry

In a small bowl whisk together the mustard, the vinegar, the dill, and salt and pepper to taste, add the oil in a stream, whisking, and whisk the dressing until it is emulsified. In a bowl toss together well the watercress, the red-leaf lettuce, and the Boston lettuce with the dressing and divide the salad among 4 plates. Serves 4.

PHOTO ON PAGE 39

Mixed Greens and Fennel with Balsamic Vinaigrette

1 bunch of curly endive (chicory), washed, spun dry, and torn into bite-size pieces (about 4 cups)
2 bunches of *arugula*, stems discarded, washed well and spun dry (about 4 cups)
2 heads of Boston lettuce, rinsed, spun dry, and torn into bite-size pieces (about 6 cups)
3 cups sliced fennel or celery
⅓ cup pine nuts, toasted lightly
½ cup coarsely grated fresh Parmesan if desired
¼ cup balsamic vinegar*
¾ cup extra-virgin olive oil*

*available at specialty foods shops and some supermarkets

In a large bowl combine the curly endive, the *arugula*, the Boston lettuce, the fennel, the pine nuts, and the Parmesan. In a small bowl whisk together the vinegar and salt and pepper to taste, add the oil in a stream, whisking, and whisk the dressing until it is emulsified. Pour the dressing over the salad and toss the salad until it is combined well. Serves 8.

PHOTO ON PAGE 45

Radicchio and Romaine Salad with Sunflower Seeds and Mustard Vinaigrette

3 cups thinly sliced *radicchio*
1 large head of romaine, rinsed, spun dry, and torn into bite-size pieces (about 14 cups)
⅓ cup raw sunflower seeds (available at natural foods stores and many supermarkets), toasted lightly and cooled
1 tablespoon Dijon-style mustard
2½ tablespoons white-wine vinegar
⅔ cup olive oil

In a large bowl combine the *radicchio*, the romaine, and the sunflower seeds. In a bowl whisk together the mustard, the vinegar, and salt and pepper to taste, add the oil in a stream, whisking, and whisk the dressing until it is emulsified. Pour the dressing over the *radicchio* and romaine mixture and toss the salad until it is combined well. Serves 10 to 12.

Romaine and Red-Leaf Lettuce Salad with Scallion Vinaigrette

For the vinaigrette
¼ cup sliced scallion including the green part
1½ tablespoons white-wine vinegar
¼ cup olive oil

4 cups torn bite-size pieces of romaine, rinsed
  and spun dry
4 cups torn bite-size pieces of red-leaf lettuce,
  rinsed and spun dry
¾ cup loosely packed fresh flat-leafed parsley
  leaves or chopped fresh curly parsley leaves

Make the vinaigrette: In a blender purée the scallion with the vinegar, the oil, and salt and pepper to taste until the dressing is emulsified.

In a salad bowl toss together the romaine, the red-leaf lettuce, and the parsley, drizzle the dressing over the greens, and toss the salad gently until it is combined well. Serves 4.

Spinach and Bibb Lettuce Salad

enough well washed and spun-dry spinach
  leaves cut crosswise into ½-inch shreds to
  measure 3 cups
enough washed and spun-dry Bibb lettuce
  leaves torn into bite-size pieces to measure
  3 cups
3 tablespoons minced scallion greens
⅓ cup extra-virgin olive oil (available at
  specialty foods shops and some
  supermarkets)
3 to 5 tablespoons fresh lime juice, or to taste

In a salad bowl toss together the spinach, the Bibb lettuce, and the scallion, drizzle the greens with the oil, and toss them until they are coated well. Add the lime juice and salt and pepper to taste and toss the salad until it is combined well. Serves 6.

Spinach, Blue Cheese, and Bacon Salad with Grapefruit Walnut Dressing

8 cups firmly packed spinach leaves removed
  from the stems (about 1 pound with stems),
  washed well, spun dry, and torn into pieces
⅓ cup crumbled blue cheese
8 slices of lean bacon, cooked until crisp
  and crumbled
½ small red onion, sliced thin
For the dressing
1 grapefruit, rind and pith cut away with a
  serrated knife and the grapefruit cut into
  sections and seeded
¼ cup walnuts, toasted lightly and the loose
  skin rubbed off
2 teaspoons white-wine vinegar
½ cup olive oil

In a large bowl toss together the spinach, the blue cheese, the bacon, and the onion.

Make the dressing: In a blender blend together the grapefruit, the walnuts, the vinegar, and salt and pepper to taste until the mixture is smooth, with the motor running add the oil in a stream, and blend the dressing until it is emulsified.

Pour the dressing over the spinach mixture and toss the salad well. Serves 6 to 8.

Watercress and Bibb Salad with Parsley Dressing

2 bunches of watercress, coarse stems
  discarded, leaves rinsed and spun dry
  (about 9 cups)
4 heads of Bibb lettuce, rinsed, spun dry, and
  torn into bite-size pieces (about 9 cups)
1½ cups julienne strips of red bell pepper
1¾ cups lightly packed fresh parsley leaves
¾ cup olive oil
3 tablespoons red-wine vinegar

In a large bowl combine the watercress, the Bibb lettuce, and the bell pepper. In a blender purée the parsley with the oil, the vinegar, and salt and pepper to taste, pour the dressing over the watercress mixture, and toss the salad until it is combined well. Serves 10 to 12.

PHOTO ON PAGE 21

Watercress and Carrot Salad with Pistachio Dressing

1½ tablespoons white-wine vinegar
1 tablespoon shelled natural pistachio nuts,
  the skins rubbed off
2 tablespoons olive oil
½ teaspoon honey

2 cups loosely packed watercress sprigs,
  rinsed and spun dry
½ cup coarsely grated carrot

In a blender blend together the vinegar, the pistachios, the oil, the honey, and salt and pepper to taste. In a bowl combine the watercress and the carrot, add the dressing, and toss the salad until it is combined well. Serves 2.

Watercress, Mushroom, and Radish Salad

½ teaspoon Dijon-style mustard
2 to 3 teaspoons fresh lemon juice, or to taste
2 tablespoons walnut oil (available at
  specialty foods shops and some
  supermarkets)
2 tablespoons vegetable oil
1 bunch of watercress, coarse stems
  discarded, the sprigs washed well and spun
  dry (about 5 cups loosely packed sprigs)
3 firm white mushrooms, sliced thin
8 radishes, sliced thin

In a salad bowl whisk together the mustard, the lemon juice, and salt to taste, add the oils in a stream, whisking, and whisk the dressing until it is emulsified. Add the watercress, the mushrooms, and the radishes and toss the salad well. Serves 4.

Apple, Watercress, and Blue Cheese Salad

2 tablespoons fresh lemon juice
¼ cup olive oil (preferably extra-virgin)
freshly ground pepper to taste
2 Granny Smith apples
1 bunch of watercress (about 6 ounces),
  washed well, spun dry, and coarse stems
  discarded
1 rib of celery, sliced thin
½ red onion, sliced thin
¼ pound blue cheese, crumbled

In a small bowl whisk together the lemon juice, the oil, the pepper, and salt to taste. In a large bowl combine the apples, cored and cut into ⅓-inch cubes, the watercress, the celery, the onion, and the blue cheese. Toss the apple mixture with the dressing and season the salad with salt and pepper. Serves 4.

Apple, Fennel, and Blue Cheese Salad with Toasted Walnuts

1 small Granny Smith apple
1 tablespoon fresh lemon juice
1 cup thinly sliced fennel bulb or celery
1 small head of Boston lettuce, separated into
  leaves, rinsed, and spun dry (about 3 cups
  packed loosely)
¼ cup walnuts, toasted lightly and chopped
1½ ounces blue cheese (preferably
  Roquefort), crumbled (about ⅓ cup)
1 tablespoon white-wine vinegar
½ teaspoon Dijon-style mustard
2 tablespoons sour cream
2 tablespoons olive oil

In a bowl toss the apple, cored and chopped, with 2 teaspoons of the lemon juice, add the fennel, the lettuce, and the walnuts, and toss the mixture until it is combined. In a blender blend together the blue cheese, the vinegar, the remaining 1 teaspoon lemon juice, the mustard, the sour cream, the oil, 2 tablespoons water, and salt and pepper to taste, scraping down the sides, until the dressing is smooth, pour the dressing over the apple mixture, and toss the salad until it is combined well. Serves 2.

VEGETABLE SALADS AND SLAWS

Avocado Salad with Red Onion and Coriander

3 avocados (preferably California)
1 lemon, halved crosswise, plus 2 tablespoons
  fresh lemon juice, or to taste
3 tablespoons olive oil, or to taste
½ cup finely chopped red onion
½ cup loosely packed fresh coriander,
  or to taste

Peel the avocados and halve them lengthwise, discarding the pits. Rub the avocados well with the cut sides of the lemon and slice them thin crosswise. Arrange the avocado slices, overlapping them, on a platter, drizzle them with the lemon juice and the oil, and season them with salt and pepper. Sprinkle the onion over the avocados and mound the coriander in the center of the salad. Serves 6.

PHOTO ON PAGE 15

Blue Cheese and Walnut Potato Salad

2 pounds small red potatoes, cut into
   1-inch pieces
¼ pound (about ½ cup) blue cheese
⅓ cup mayonnaise
⅓ cup plain yogurt
1½ tablespoons fresh lemon juice, or to taste
1½ cups finely chopped celery
½ cup walnuts, chopped coarse, toasted
   lightly, and cooled
¼ cup finely chopped dill pickle
1 teaspoon celery seeds

In a steamer set over boiling water steam the potatoes, covered, for 8 to 10 minutes, or until they are just
tender, transfer them to a bowl, and let them cool. In a
blender purée the blue cheese with the mayonnaise, the
yogurt, the lemon juice, and salt and pepper to taste.
To the potatoes add the celery, the walnuts, the pickle,
the celery seeds, and the dressing and toss the salad
until it is combined well. Serves 4 to 6.

Warm Shredded Brussels Sprout Salad with Bacon

3 tablespoons vegetable oil
¾ pint Brussels sprouts, trimmed, halved
   lengthwise, and sliced thin crosswise
1 teaspoon caraway seeds
2 tablespoons red-wine vinegar
a pinch of sugar
2 slices of lean bacon, cooked crisp and
   crumbled

In a skillet heat the oil over moderately high heat until
it is hot but not smoking and in it sauté the Brussels
sprouts and the caraway seeds, stirring, for 1 to 2 minutes, or until the Brussels sprouts are crisp-tender and
browned lightly. Remove the skillet from the heat, add
the vinegar, the sugar, and salt and pepper to taste, and
stir the salad until it is combined well. Sprinkle the salad
with the bacon. Serves 2.

*Red Cabbage and Carrot Coleslaw with
Mustard Yogurt Dressing*

1½ cups thinly sliced red cabbage
1 cup coarsely grated carrot
1½ teaspoons Dijon-style mustard
½ teaspoon sugar
1 tablespoon red-wine vinegar

¼ cup plain yogurt
1 tablespoon vegetable oil

In a bowl toss the cabbage and the carrot together
until the mixture is combined well. In a small bowl
whisk together the mustard, the sugar, the vinegar, the
yogurt, and salt to taste, add the oil in a stream, whisking, and whisk the dressing until it is combined well.
Pour the dressing over the coleslaw and toss the salad
to coat it well. Serves 2.

Red Cabbage and Celery Slaw

2 pounds red cabbage, halved lengthwise
   and sliced thin
5 ribs of celery, peeled and sliced thin
   crosswise
5 tablespoons cider vinegar
4 teaspoons honey
¾ cup vegetable oil

In a large bowl toss together the cabbage and the celery. In a small bowl whisk together the vinegar, the
honey, and salt and pepper to taste and whisk the mixture until the honey is dissolved. Add the oil in a stream,
whisking, and whisk the dressing until it is emulsified.
Add the dressing to the cabbage mixture and toss the
slaw until it is combined well. Serves 12.

PHOTO ON PAGE 12

Carrot Salad with Lemon Dressing

2 pounds carrots, grated coarse (preferably in
   a food processor, about 10 cups)
5 tablespoons fresh lemon juice
freshly ground black pepper to taste
¾ cup vegetable oil

In a kettle of boiling salted water blanch the grated
carrots for 15 seconds, drain them in a colander, and refresh them in a bowl of ice and cold water. Drain the carrots well again and transfer them to a bowl. *The carrots
may be prepared up to this point 1 day in advance and
kept covered and chilled.* In a bowl whisk together the
lemon juice, the pepper, and salt to taste, add the oil in a
stream, whisking, and whisk the dressing until it is
emulsified. Toss the carrots with the dressing until they
are coated well and transfer the salad to a serving bowl.
Serves 10 to 12.

PHOTO ON PAGES 42 AND 43

Cucumber Salad with Sour Cream and Dill Dressing

2 cucumbers (¾ pound), peeled, halved
    lengthwise, seeded, and cut diagonally into
    ¼-inch slices
½ teaspoon salt
½ cup sour cream
1 tablespoon distilled white vinegar, or
    to taste
1 small onion, chopped fine
1 tablespoon snipped fresh dill
2 hard-boiled large eggs, chopped
freshly ground pepper to taste
soft-leafed lettuce for lining the plates

In a bowl toss the cucumbers with the salt and let them stand for 20 minutes. In a bowl whisk together the sour cream, the vinegar, the onion, and the dill. Drain the cucumbers in a colander, rinse them under cold water, and pat them dry. Stir the cucumbers, the eggs, the pepper, and salt to taste into the sour cream mixture and stir the salad until it is combined well. Line 2 chilled salad plates with the lettuce and divide the salad between them. Serves 2.

Pickled Cucumber Salad

3 cups cider vinegar
¾ cup plus 2 tablespoons sugar
6 tablespoons salt
1½ tablespoons freshly ground white pepper
two 15-inch seedless cucumbers, the skin
    scored with the tines of a fork and the
    cucumbers sliced very thin (about 10 cups)

In a large bowl stir together the vinegar, the sugar, the salt, and the pepper, add the cucumbers, and combine the salad well. Chill the salad, covered, for at least 3 hours or overnight and transfer the cucumbers and some of the liquid to a serving bowl. Serves 10 to 12.

PHOTO ON PAGE 43

*Fennel and Radish Salad
with Mustard Vinaigrette*

3 tablespoons Dijon-style mustard
2 tablespoons white-wine vinegar
¾ cup olive oil
4 fennel bulbs, trimmed and sliced thin
    crosswise (about 4 cups)

2 tablespoons minced fresh parsley leaves
24 radishes, trimmed and sliced thin
    crosswise (about 2 cups)
16 red-leaf lettuce leaves, rinsed
    and spun dry

In a blender blend together the mustard, the vinegar, and salt and pepper to taste, with the motor running add the oil in a stream, and blend the vinaigrette until it is emulsified. In a bowl toss the fennel and the parsley with half the vinaigrette and in another bowl toss the radishes with the remaining vinaigrette. On each of 8 salad plates arrange 2 of the lettuce leaves and divide the fennel and radish mixtures among the plates. Serves 8.

Mushroom Salad with Radish and Chives

½ pound firm white mushrooms, stems
    trimmed flush with the caps
½ cup thinly sliced radish
⅓ cup plain yogurt
1½ teaspoons fresh lemon juice, or to taste
3 tablespoons snipped fresh chives
freshly ground pepper to taste
12 Bibb lettuce or other small soft-leafed
    lettuce leaves, rinsed and spun dry

Slice the mushrooms thin with a sharp knife and in a bowl toss them with the radish, the yogurt, the lemon juice, the chives, the pepper, and salt to taste. Arrange 3 lettuce leaves on each of 4 small plates and divide the mushroom salad among the plates. Serves 4 as a first course.

PHOTO ON PAGE 55

Mushroom Sesame Salad

2 teaspoons white-wine vinegar
½ teaspoon soy sauce
¼ teaspoon Dijon-style mustard
3 tablespoons vegetable oil
½ pound firm white mushrooms, sliced thin
1½ tablespoons sesame seeds, toasted lightly
2 tablespoons minced scallion including some
    of the green part
2 Boston lettuce leaves, rinsed and spun dry

In a bowl whisk together the vinegar, the soy sauce, the mustard, and salt and pepper to taste, add the oil in a stream, whisking, and whisk the dressing until it is emulsified. Add the mushrooms, the sesame seeds, and the scallion and toss the salad until it is combined well. Arrange a lettuce leaf on each of 2 chilled plates and fill each leaf with half the salad. Serves 2.

Pea and Potato Salad with Bacon Dressing

1½ pounds red potatoes
1 small red onion, chopped fine
¼ pound sliced lean bacon, chopped
2 teaspoons all-purpose flour
1½ teaspoons sugar
¼ cup cider vinegar
1 tablespoon Dijon-style mustard
3 hard-boiled large eggs, chopped
2 cups shelled fresh peas (about 2 pounds
    unshelled), cooked (procedure on page 189),
    or a 10-ounce package frozen peas, thawed
3 tablespoons minced fresh parsley leaves

Cut the potatoes into pea-size cubes and in a steamer set over boiling water steam them, covered, for 4 to 8 minutes, or until they are just tender. Transfer the potatoes to a bowl, add the onion, and toss the mixture with salt and pepper to taste. In a skillet cook the bacon over moderately low heat, stirring, until it is crisp and transfer it with a slotted spoon to paper towels to drain. Pour off all but 2 tablespoons of the fat from the skillet, to the remaining fat add the flour and the sugar, and cook the mixture, stirring, for 30 seconds. Add the vinegar and ¼ cup water, bring the mixture to a boil, whisking, and whisk in the mustard. Pour the dressing over the potato mixture, add the eggs, the peas, the parsley, and the bacon, and toss the salad well. Serve the salad warm or at room temperature. Serves 6.

Fresh Pea and Pepper Salad

1½ cups shelled fresh peas (about 1½ pounds
    unshelled), chopped coarse
1 red bell pepper, diced fine
¾ cup finely chopped celery
¼ cup finely chopped red onion
¼ cup mayonnaise, or to taste
1 teaspoon fresh lemon juice, or to taste
Bibb or Boston lettuce leaves for lining
    the plates

In a bowl toss together the peas, the bell pepper, the celery, and the onion, add the mayonnaise, the lemon juice, and salt and pepper to taste, and blend the mixture well. Divide the salad among plates lined with the lettuce. Serves 4 to 6.

Oriental Pea and Noodle Salad with
Spicy Peanut Sauce

For the sauce
⅓ cup smooth peanut butter
1½ tablespoons soy sauce
1 tablespoon minced peeled fresh gingerroot
2 tablespoons fresh lemon juice, or to taste
1 garlic clove, minced
½ teaspoon dried hot red pepper flakes
¼ teaspoon sugar

½ pound small tubular pasta or
    small shells
2 cups shelled fresh peas (about 2 pounds
    unshelled), cooked (page 189), or a
    10-ounce package frozen peas, thawed
⅓ cup finely chopped scallion
¼ cup roasted peanuts, chopped

Make the peanut sauce: In a blender blend the peanut butter with the soy sauce, the gingerroot, the lemon juice, the garlic, the red pepper flakes, the sugar, and ⅓ cup water until the mixture is smooth.
In a kettle of boiling salted water boil the pasta for 8 to 12 minutes, or until it is just tender, drain it in a colander, and rinse it under cold water. Drain the pasta well, transfer it to a large bowl, and toss it with the peas and the scallion. Add the peanut sauce, toss the salad well, and sprinkle it with the roasted peanuts. Serves 4 to 6.

Fireworks Salad
(Snow Pea, Bell Pepper, and Daikon Salad
with Ginger Dressing)

¾ pound snow peas, trimmed and strings
  discarded
1 large red bell pepper, cut into 1½-inch
  julienne strips
1 large yellow bell pepper, cut into 1½-inch
  julienne strips
1⅓ cups 1½-inch julienne strips of peeled
  daikon (Oriental white radish, available at
  specialty produce markets)
2 tablespoons fresh lemon juice
2 teaspoons grated peeled fresh gingerroot,
  or to taste
⅓ cup olive oil

In a large saucepan of boiling water blanch the snow
peas for 15 seconds, drain them, and plunge them into a
bowl of ice and cold water to stop the cooking. Drain the
snow peas well and cut them diagonally into thin
slices. In a bowl toss the snow peas with the bell
peppers and the *daikon.* In a small bowl whisk together
the lemon juice, the gingerroot, and salt and pepper
to taste, add the oil in a slow stream, whisking,
and whisk the dressing until it is emulsified. Pour
the dressing over the salad and toss the salad well.
Serves 6.

PHOTO ON PAGE 51

Greek-Style Potato Salad

3 pounds small red potatoes, halved and sliced
  crosswise ¼ inch thick
1½ cups Kalamata or other brine-cured black
  olives, cut into slivers
2 unpeeled garlic cloves
1 tablespoon chopped fresh orégano or
  1 teaspoon crumbled dried
2 tablespoons red-wine vinegar
½ cup olive oil
1 cup (about ½ pound) crumbled Feta
½ cup finely chopped fresh parsley leaves
freshly ground pepper to taste

In a steamer set over boiling water steam the potatoes in batches, covered, for 6 to 8 minutes, or until
they are just tender and in a large bowl combine them
with the olives. In a small saucepan of boiling water

boil the garlic for 5 minutes and peel it. In a blender
purée the garlic with the orégano, the vinegar, and the
oil, add the Feta, and blend the dressing until it is
combined well. Toss the potato mixture with the dressing, the parsley, the pepper, and salt to taste. Serves
6 to 8.

Two Potato and Bacon Salad
with Lime-Mayonnaise Dressing

1 large egg at room temperature
2 tablespoons fresh lime juice
½ teaspoon freshly grated lime rind
1 teaspoon Dijon-style mustard, or to taste
¼ teaspoon salt
¼ teaspoon white pepper
1 cup olive oil, vegetable oil, or a
  combination of both
1 teaspoon honey
2 teaspoons distilled white vinegar
1½ pounds sweet potatoes or yams, peeled
  and cut into ½-inch dice
1½ pounds boiling potatoes, peeled, cut into
  ½-inch dice, and reserved in a bowl of
  cold water
2 ribs of celery including the leaves, strings
  discarded, sliced crosswise ¼ inch thick
6 slices (6 ounces) of lean bacon, chopped,
  cooked until crisp, and drained

In a food processor or blender with the motor on
high blend the egg, the lime juice, the rind, the mustard, the salt, and the pepper, add the oil in a slow
stream, and turn the motor off. Transfer the mayonnaise to a bowl, whisk in the honey and the vinegar
until the dressing is combined well, and reserve the
dressing, its surface covered with a piece of plastic
wrap. In a steamer set over boiling water steam the
sweet potatoes for 6 to 8 minutes, or until they are just
tender, and transfer them to a large bowl. In a steamer
steam the boiling potatoes, drained, for 6 to 8 minutes,
or until they are just tender, and transfer them to the
bowl. To the potato mixture add the celery, the bacon,
and the dressing and toss the salad until it is combined
well. Serves 4 to 6.

Warm Potato Salad with Red Onion and Dill

½ cup finely chopped red onion
¾ pound red potatoes, cut into ¾-inch cubes
1 tablespoon balsamic vinegar (available at
    specialty foods shops and most
    supermarkets) or red-wine vinegar,
    or to taste
2 tablespoons olive oil
2 tablespoons snipped fresh dill

In a small bowl let the onion soak in ice water to cover for 10 minutes, drain it well in a sieve, and transfer it to a larger bowl. While the onion is soaking, in a steamer set over boiling water steam the potatoes, covered, for 8 to 10 minutes, or until they are just tender, transfer them to the bowl of onion, and drizzle the mixture with the vinegar, tossing it. Add the oil and the dill, toss the salad well, and season it with salt and pepper. Serves 2.

Cherry Tomato, Bacon, and Basil Salad

5 cups cherry tomatoes, halved
6 slices of lean bacon, cooked until crisp
    and crumbled
⅓ cup finely chopped fresh basil leaves, or to
    taste, plus 6 basil sprigs
2 tablespoons red-wine vinegar
4 tablespoons extra-virgin olive oil (available
    at specialty foods shops and some
    supermarkets)

In a bowl toss together the tomatoes, the bacon, and the chopped basil until the mixture is combined well. In a small bowl whisk together the vinegar and salt and pepper to taste, add the oil in a stream, whisking, and whisk the dressing until it is emulsified. Pour the dressing over the tomato mixture, toss the salad lightly until it is coated well with the dressing, and garnish it with the basil sprigs. Serves 6.

PHOTO ON PAGE 63

Pasta, Tomato, and Corn Salad with Basil Dressing

1 pound *rosetti** (rose-shaped pasta) or other
    pasta such as small shells or wagon wheels
2 tablespoons plus 2 teaspoons red-wine
    vinegar, or to taste

½ cup thinly sliced fresh basil leaves
freshly ground pepper to taste
¾ cup olive oil
1 pint (¾ pound) cherry tomatoes, halved
1½ cups cooked fresh corn kernels (cut from
    about 3 ears of corn) or a 10-ounce package
    frozen corn, thawed and drained

In a kettle of boiling salted water cook the *rosetti* for 18 to 20 minutes, or until it is just tender, and drain it well. Rinse the *rosetti* and drain it well. In a small bowl whisk together the vinegar, the basil, the pepper, and salt to taste, add the oil in a stream, whisking, and whisk the dressing until it is emulsified. In a large bowl combine the *rosetti*, the tomatoes, and the corn, add the dressing, and toss the salad well. Serves 4 to 6.

*available at some specialty foods shops and by mail order from:

Morisi's Macaroni Store
647 Fifth Avenue
Brooklyn, NY 11215
718-788-2299

Grilled Vegetable and Pasta Salad
with Red Bell Pepper Dressing

2 large red bell peppers
2½ tablespoons red-wine vinegar
1½ teaspoons dried rosemary
½ cup olive oil
3 zucchini (about 1½ pounds), cut lengthwise
    into ¼-inch-thick slices
3 yellow summer squash (about 1½ pounds),
    cut lengthwise into ¼-inch-thick slices
3 red onions, cut into ¼-inch-thick slices
1 pound *penne* or *ziti* (tubular pastas)

On a well oiled rack set 5 to 6 inches over glowing coals grill the bell peppers, turning them every 5 minutes, for 20 to 25 minutes, or until the skins are blistered and charred, transfer them to a bowl, and let them steam, covered, until they are cool enough to handle. Working over the bowl, peel the peppers starting at the blossom end, cut off the tops, and discard the seeds and ribs. In a blender or food processor purée the peppers with any juices that have accumulated in the bowl, the vinegar, the rosemary, and salt and black pepper to taste, add the oil in a slow stream, and blend the dressing until it is combined well.

On the well oiled rack grill the zucchini, the summer squash, and the onions, turning them, for 8 to 10 minutes, or until they are just tender, and cut them into ¼-inch-thick strips. In a kettle of boiling salted water cook the *penne* for 6 to 8 minutes, or until it is *al dente*, drain it well, and in a bowl toss it with the grilled vegetables, the dressing, and salt and black pepper to taste. Serves 8 to 10.

it under running cold water. Drain the *rotelle* well and in a bowl toss it with the red pepper dressing. In a saucepan of boiling salted water blanch the zucchini for 2 minutes, or until it just begins to turn translucent, drain it in the colander, and refresh it under running cold water. Pat the zucchini dry and stir it into the pasta salad with the peas and salt and pepper to taste. Serves 6.

PHOTO ON PAGE 48

Vegetable Pasta Salad with Red Pepper Dressing

a 7-ounce jar roasted red peppers, drained and patted dry
1 large egg yolk
⅛ teaspoon cayenne, or to taste
1 tablespoon white-wine vinegar
¼ cup olive oil
¼ cup plain yogurt
1 pound *rotelle* (spiral-shaped pasta)
¾ pound small zucchini, scrubbed and cut into ¼-inch slices
2 cups shelled fresh peas (about 2 pounds unshelled), cooked in boiling water until just tender and drained, or a 10-ounce package frozen peas, thawed

In a blender or food processor purée the red peppers, the yolk, the cayenne, the vinegar, and salt to taste until the mixture is smooth and with the motor running add the oil in a stream. Turn off the motor, scrape down the side, and blend in the yogurt. In a kettle of boiling salted water cook the *rotelle* for 12 minutes, or until it is just tender, drain it in a colander, and refresh

Warm Chopped Vegetable Salad with Goat Cheese

1 tablespoon white-wine vinegar
½ teaspoon Dijon-style mustard
freshly ground white pepper to taste
2 tablespoons olive oil
¼ cup dry white wine
1 bay leaf
1 large carrot, cut into ¼-inch dice
1 cup chopped broccoli
⅓ cup chopped celery
3 tablespoons chopped or crumbled goat cheese

In a small bowl whisk together the vinegar, the mustard, the white pepper, and salt to taste, add the oil in a stream, whisking, and whisk the dressing until it is emulsified. In a small saucepan combine 1½ cups water, the wine, and the bay leaf, bring the liquid to a boil, and add the carrot and the broccoli. Cook the vegetables for 1½ minutes, or until they are crisp-tender, and drain them well, discarding the bay leaf. Transfer the vegetables to a bowl, add the celery, the goat cheese, and the dressing, and toss the salad well. Serves 2.

JEANNE

GRAIN SALADS

Rice and Broccoli Salad with Sunflower Seed Dressing

1 tablespoon salt
2 cups unconverted long-grain rice
1 bunch of broccoli, the stems peeled and
   sliced thin diagonally and the flowerets cut
   into 1-inch pieces (about 5 cups)
1 cup slivered blanched almonds,
   toasted lightly
½ cup thinly sliced scallion green
⅓ cup shelled raw sunflower seeds (available
   at natural foods stores, specialty foods
   shops, and many supermarkets),
   toasted lightly
4 teaspoons white-wine vinegar
½ cup vegetable oil
5 teaspoons Oriental sesame oil (available at
   Oriental markets, specialty foods shops,
   and many supermarkets)

In a large saucepan bring 5 quarts water to a boil, add the salt, and sprinkle in the rice, stirring until the water returns to a boil. Boil the rice for 10 minutes, drain it in a large sieve, and rinse it. Set the sieve over a large saucepan of boiling water, steam the rice, covered with a dish towel and the lid, for 15 minutes, or until it is fluffy and dry, and transfer it to a large bowl. In a large saucepan of boiling salted water cook the broccoli for 2 to 3 minutes, or until it is crisp-tender, drain it well, and refresh it in a bowl of ice and cold water. Drain the broccoli well and pat it dry. To the rice add the broccoli, the almonds, and the scallion green and combine the mixture well. In a blender purée the sunflower seeds with the vinegar, the oils, and salt and pepper to taste, add 1 cup water in a stream, and blend the dressing until it is emulsified. Toss the salad with the dressing until it is combined well. Serves 4 to 6.

Curried Rice Salad with Beef and Ginger

1 tablespoon salt
1½ cups unconverted long-grain rice
1 tablespoon cornstarch
1 teaspoon sugar
3 tablespoons soy sauce
4 teaspoons white-wine vinegar
3 tablespoons vegetable oil
1 pound boneless beef chuck top blade steaks
   (about ½ inch thick), trimmed and cut into
   ¼-inch-wide strips
¾ pound carrots, sliced thin diagonally
1 onion, chopped
1 tablespoon minced peeled fresh gingerroot
1½ teaspoons curry powder
½ cup thinly sliced scallion green

In a large saucepan bring 5 quarts water to a boil, add the salt, and sprinkle in the rice, stirring until the water returns to a boil. Boil the rice for 10 minutes, drain it in a large sieve, and rinse it. Set the sieve over a large saucepan of boiling water, steam the rice, covered with a dish towel and the lid, for 15 minutes, or until it is fluffy and dry, and transfer it to a large bowl. In a bowl combine the cornstarch, the sugar, the soy sauce, the vinegar, and 1½ cups water, stir the mixture until the cornstarch is dissolved, and reserve it.

In a large heavy skillet heat 2 tablespoons of the oil over moderately high heat until it is hot but not smoking and in it sauté the beef, patted dry and seasoned with salt and pepper, in batches, stirring, for 1 minute, transferring it as it is browned to a bowl. Add the remaining 1 tablespoon oil to the skillet, heat it until it is hot but not smoking, and in it cook the carrots and the onion, stirring occasionally, until the carrots are browned and crisp-tender. Add the gingerroot and the curry powder, cook the mixture, stirring, for 30 seconds, and stir in the reserved soy mixture and any juices that have accumulated with the beef. Bring the mixture to a boil, simmer it, stirring occasionally, for 2 minutes, or until the sauce is thickened, and stir in the beef. Spoon the beef mixture over the rice, add the scallion green and salt and pepper to taste, and combine the salad well. Serve the salad warm or at room temperature. Serves 4 to 6.

Indonesian-Style Brown Rice Salad with Tofu and Peanut Sauce

½ pound firm tofu, rinsed
1 tablespoon salt
1½ cups long-grain brown rice
½ pound green beans, trimmed and cut into
   1-inch pieces
vegetable oil for deep-frying
3 large garlic cloves, sliced thin lengthwise

3 hard-boiled large eggs, sliced lengthwise
¾ cup unsalted dry-roasted peanuts,
 ground coarse
1½ teaspoons salt
3 tablespoons sugar
2½ teaspoons distilled white vinegar

Wrap the tofu in several thicknesses of paper towels, in a bowl weight it with a 2-pound weight, and chill it for at least 4 hours or overnight.

In a large saucepan bring 5 quarts water to a boil, add the salt, and sprinkle in the rice, stirring until the water returns to a boil. Boil the rice for 20 minutes, drain it in a large sieve, and rinse it. Set the sieve over a large saucepan of boiling water and steam the rice, covered with a dish towel and the lid, for 20 minutes, or until it is fluffy and dry.

In a large saucepan of boiling salted water cook the green beans for 2 to 3 minutes, or until they are crisp-tender, drain them, and refresh them in a bowl of ice and cold water. Drain them well and pat them dry with paper towels.

Cut the tofu into ¼-inch-thick strips and pat the strips between paper towels. In a large deep skillet heat 1 inch of the oil to 375° F. on a deep-fat thermometer, in it fry the tofu in batches, turning it, for 3 to 4 minutes, or until it is pale golden, and transfer it with a slotted spoon to paper towels to drain. In the skillet fry the garlic for 15 to 30 seconds, or until it is golden, and transfer it with a slotted spoon to paper towels to drain. Sprinkle the tofu and the garlic with salt and pepper to taste.

On a platter mound the rice, arrange the green beans, the tofu, and the egg slices decoratively on it, and scatter the garlic over the salad.

Pour off the oil from the skillet, to the skillet add the peanuts, the salt, the sugar, the vinegar, and 1½ cups water, and bring the mixture to a boil, stirring constantly. Boil the mixture, stirring occasionally, until it is reduced to about 1¼ cups and spoon the sauce over the salad. Serves 6 to 8.

SALAD DRESSINGS

Buttermilk Roquefort Dressing with Chives

¾ cup buttermilk
½ cup olive oil
⅓ cup snipped fresh chives
¼ pound Roquefort, crumbled

In a food processor or blender blend the buttermilk, the oil, the chives, and half the Roquefort for 30 seconds, add the remaining cheese, and blend the dressing for 5 seconds. Makes about 1¾ cups.

Herbed Cream Cheese Dressing

8 ounces cream cheese, softened
½ cup sour cream
½ cup loosely packed fresh parsley leaves
½ cup loosely packed dill sprigs, coarse
 stems discarded
½ cup chopped scallion
1 tablespoon white-wine vinegar
¼ cup vegetable oil
2 teaspoons Worcestershire sauce, or to taste
2 tablespoons half-and-half or milk

In a food processor blend the cream cheese, the sour cream, the parsley, the dill, and the scallion, scraping down the side, until the mixture is smooth. With the motor running add the vinegar, the oil, the Worcestershire sauce, the half-and-half, and salt and pepper to taste and blend the dressing until it is combined well. Makes about 2 cups.

Herbed Cottage Cheese Dressing

½ cup cottage cheese
1½ tablespoons fresh lemon juice, or to taste
¼ teaspoon dried tarragon
a pinch of dried thyme
⅛ teaspoon celery salt, or to taste
⅓ cup vegetable oil

In a blender or food processor blend the cottage cheese, the lemon juice, the tarragon, the thyme, the celery salt, pepper to taste, and 2 tablespoons water, scraping down the sides, until the mixture is smooth. With the motor running add the oil in a stream and blend the dressing until it is emulsified. Makes about ¾ cup.

Cucumber Dill Sour Cream Dressing

½ cucumber, peeled, seeded, and grated
    coarse (about ½ cup)
¼ teaspoon salt
2 teaspoons Dijon-style mustard
1 tablespoon white-wine vinegar or fresh
    lemon juice, or to taste
white pepper to taste
½ cup sour cream
¼ cup plain yogurt
1 tablespoon snipped fresh dill

In a small sieve set over a bowl toss the cucumber with the salt and let the mixture drain for 10 minutes. In a blender or food processor blend the mustard, the vinegar, the white pepper, and salt to taste until the mixture is combined, add the sour cream, the yogurt, and the dill, and blend the mixture, scraping down the sides, until it is smooth. Add the cucumber and blend the dressing until it is just combined well. Makes about 1¼ cups.

Garlic Mint Dressing

1 garlic clove, crushed
2 tablespoons fresh lime juice, or to taste
1 teaspoon Dijon-style mustard
½ teaspoon dried mint
⅛ teaspoon sugar
¼ teaspoon salt
⅓ cup vegetable oil

In a blender or food processor blend the garlic, the lime juice, the mustard, the mint, the sugar, and the salt, scraping down the sides, until the mixture is smooth. With the motor running add the oil in a stream and blend the dressing until it is emulsified. Makes about ½ cup.

Creamy Tarragon Dressing

2 teaspoons egg yolk
2 tablespoons tarragon vinegar (page 222) or
    Sherry vinegar (available at specialty foods
    shops and some supermarkets)
2 tablespoons finely chopped fresh
    tarragon leaves
½ cup vegetable oil or olive oil

In a blender blend the yolk, the vinegar, the tarragon, and salt and pepper to taste, with the motor running add the oil in a slow stream, and turn the motor off. The dressing keeps, covered and chilled, for 5 days. Makes about ½ cup.

Mayonnaise

2 large egg yolks at room temperature
2 teaspoons wine vinegar
1 teaspoon Dijon-style mustard
¼ teaspoon salt
white pepper to taste
1½ cups olive oil, vegetable oil, or a
    combination of both
fresh lemon juice to taste
cream to thin the mayonnaise if desired

Rinse a mixing bowl with hot water and dry it well. In the bowl combine the yolks, 1 teaspoon of the vinegar, the mustard, the salt, and the white pepper, beat the mixture vigorously with a whisk or an electric mixer at high speed until it is combined, and add ½ cup of the oil, drop by drop, beating constantly. Add the remaining 1 teaspoon vinegar and the remaining 1 cup oil in a stream, beating constantly. Add the lemon juice, white pepper, and salt to taste and thin the mayonnaise with the cream or water. Makes about 2 cups.

Chipotle Mayonnaise

1½ cups mayonnaise
3 canned *chipotle* chilies (available at
    Hispanic markets and some specialty foods
    shops and supermarkets), minced (wear
    rubber gloves), reserving 1 teaspoon of
    the liquid
1½ teaspoons ground cumin

In a bowl stir together the mayonnaise, the chilies with the reserved liquid, the cumin, and salt to taste until the mixture is combined well. Serve the mayonnaise with grilled meats. Makes about 1¾ cups.

Herbed Mayonnaise

1 cup mayonnaise
½ cup plain yogurt
2 tablespoons dry white wine
½ cup minced fresh parsley leaves

¼ cup snipped fresh chives

1½ teaspoons minced fresh tarragon leaves or
½ teaspoon dried, crumbled

1½ teaspoons minced fresh thyme leaves or
½ teaspoon dried, crumbled

In a bowl stir together the mayonnaise, the yogurt, the wine, the parsley, the chives, the tarragon, the thyme, and salt and pepper to taste until the mixture is combined well. Serve the mayonnaise with poached fish. Makes about 2 cups.

Horseradish Mayonnaise

1 cup mayonnaise

2 tablespoons drained bottled horseradish

1 tablespoon minced pimiento-stuffed olives

½ teaspoon Tabasco, or to taste

In a bowl stir together the mayonnaise, the horseradish, the olives, the Tabasco, and salt to taste until the mixture is combined well. Serve the mayonnaise with grilled meats. Makes about 1¼ cups.

Quick Mayonnaise

1 large egg at room temperature

5 teaspoons fresh lemon juice

1 teaspoon Dijon-style mustard

¼ teaspoon salt

¼ teaspoon white pepper

1 cup olive oil, vegetable oil, or a
combination of both

In a food processor or blender with the motor on high blend the egg, the lemon juice, the mustard, the salt, and the white pepper, add the oil in a slow stream, and turn the motor off. Thin the mayonnaise with water if desired. Makes about 1 cup.

Tarragon Mayonnaise

2 scallions including 3 inches of the green
part, chopped coarse

1 cup firmly packed fresh spinach leaves,
washed well and drained

⅓ cup firmly packed fresh tarragon leaves

1 tablespoon tarragon vinegar (page 222)

1 cup bottled mayonnaise

In a saucepan of boiling salted water blanch the scallions for 30 seconds, add the spinach, and blanch the vegetables for 30 seconds. Drain the vegetables in a sieve, pressing hard to remove the excess liquid, and in a blender purée the vegetables with the tarragon, the vinegar, 2 tablespoons of the mayonnaise, and freshly ground pepper to taste. In a bowl stir together well the purée and the remaining mayonnaise. Serve the mayonnaise with chilled poached fish or chicken or toss it with sliced boiled potatoes. Makes about 1¼ cups.

Tomato Mayonnaise

¼ cup minced onion

¼ cup minced red bell pepper

1 tablespoon vegetable oil

½ cup canned tomato purée

2 cups mayonnaise

In a small heavy saucepan cook the onion and the bell pepper in the oil over moderately low heat, stirring occasionally, until the vegetables are softened. Add the tomato purée and cook the mixture over moderately high heat, stirring, until most of the liquid is evaporated. Let the mixture cool and in a bowl combine it well with the mayonnaise and salt and pepper to taste. Serve the mayonnaise with cooked vegetables or grilled meats. Makes about 2½ cups.

Herbed Vinaigrette

2 tablespoons white-wine vinegar or fresh
lemon juice

½ teaspoon Dijon-style mustard

⅓ cup olive oil

1½ teaspoons minced fresh parsley leaves

1½ teaspoons snipped fresh chives

1½ teaspoons minced fresh tarragon or
½ teaspoon dried, crumbled

1½ teaspoons minced fresh chervil or
½ teaspoon dried, crumbled

In a bowl whisk together the vinegar, the mustard, and salt and pepper to taste, add the oil in a stream, whisking, and whisk the vinaigrette until it is emulsified. Stir in the parsley, the chives, the tarragon, and the chervil. Makes about ⅔ cup.

Warm Herbed Vinaigrette with Egg

4 tablespoons white-wine vinegar or fresh
  lemon juice
⅔ cup olive oil
2 hard-boiled large eggs, minced
1 tablespoon minced celery leaves
1 tablespoon minced fresh parsley leaves
1 tablespoon snipped fresh chives
1 teaspoon English-style dry mustard
½ teaspoon Worcestershire sauce

In a saucepan combine the vinegar and the oil, bring the mixture to a boil, and remove the pan from the heat. Stir in the eggs, the celery leaves, the parsley, the chives, the mustard, the Worcestershire sauce, and salt and pepper to taste. Makes about 1½ cups.

Tarragon Vinaigrette

3 tablespoons tarragon vinegar (recipe follows)
¼ teaspoon salt, or to taste
¼ teaspoon freshly ground pepper, or to taste
½ cup olive oil
3 tablespoons minced fresh tarragon or
  1 tablespoon dried, crumbled

In a bowl whisk together the vinegar, the salt, and the pepper, add the oil in a stream, whisking, and whisk the vinaigrette until it is emulsified. Stir in the tarragon. Makes about ¾ cup.

Tarragon Vinegar

½ cup firmly packed fresh tarragon leaves
1⅞ cups distilled white vinegar
1 branch fresh tarragon just large enough to fit
  in a 1-pint jar for garnish if desired

Bruise the tarragon leaves slightly on a work surface by rolling a heavy rolling pin over them and transfer them to a sterilized 1-pint jar (sterilizing procedure follows) with a tight-fitting lid. In a saucepan heat the vinegar over moderate heat until it is hot and pour it through a funnel into the jar. Seal the jar tightly with the lid and let the vinegar stand for at least 3 days and up to 10 days. Strain the vinegar through a fine sieve into a measuring cup, reserving the leaves for another use if desired, pour it into a sterilized 1-pint jar with a tight-fitting lid over the branch of fresh tarragon, and seal the jar tightly with the lid. Makes 1 pint.

SAUCES

SAVORY BUTTERS, MARINADES, AND SAUCES

Aïoli
(Garlic Mayonnaise)

3 garlic cloves, chopped
½ teaspoon salt
2 large egg yolks at room temperature
¼ teaspoon white pepper
1 cup olive oil
2 tablespoons fresh lemon juice

In a mortar with a pestle mash the garlic with the salt until the mixture forms a paste. In a bowl with an electric mixer beat the garlic paste, the yolks, and the white pepper at high speed for 5 to 7 minutes, or until the mixture is thick and pale. Add ⅓ cup of the oil, drop by drop, beating constantly, beat in the lemon juice and 1 teaspoon lukewarm water, and add the remaining ⅔ cup oil in a stream, beating constantly. Serve the *aïoli* with *crudités* or hard-boiled eggs. Makes about 1¼ cups.

Avocado Aïoli
(Avocado Garlic Mayonnaise)

2 large garlic cloves, halved lengthwise and
   any inner green sprouts discarded
¼ teaspoon salt, or to taste
1 firm-ripe avocado (about ½ pound,
   preferably California)
1 large egg yolk at room temperature
1 to 2 tablespoons fresh lemon juice
¼ cup olive oil
½ cup vegetable oil
cayenne to taste

Mince and mash the garlic to a paste with the salt. Alternatively, to a food processor with the motor running add the garlic, process it until it is minced, and add the salt, blending the mixture until it is combined. Halve lengthwise, pit, and peel the avocado and in a food processor purée it with the garlic mixture, the yolk, and 1 tablespoon of the lemon juice. With the motor running add the oils in a slow stream, stopping the motor occasionally and scraping down the side. Season the *aïoli* with the cayenne, salt, black pepper, and up to 1 tablespoon of the remaining lemon juice to taste. *The aïoli may be made 8 hours in advance and kept chilled, its surface covered with plastic wrap.* Serve the sauce at room temperature with cooked vegetables or cold poached or grilled fish. Makes about 1½ cups.

Lemon Tarragon Butter

2 tablespoons minced red onion
1 stick (½ cup) unsalted butter, softened
3 tablespoons minced fresh tarragon leaves
1 teaspoon grated lemon rind
1½ teaspoons fresh lemon juice
1 tablespoon minced fresh parsley leaves

In a small bowl let the onion soak in ½ cup cold water for 15 minutes, drain it, and pat it dry. In a bowl cream together the butter, the onion, the tarragon, the rind, the lemon juice, the parsley, and salt and pepper to taste. Let the butter stand, covered, in a cool place for at least 1 hour. Serve the butter with grilled fish, chicken, or vegetables. Makes about ½ cup.

Lemon Pepper Marinade

2 teaspoons dried hot red pepper flakes
2 teaspoons dried orégano
½ cup fresh lemon juice
1 tablespoon coarsely ground black pepper
⅓ cup olive oil

In a blender grind the red pepper flakes and the orégano with the lemon juice, the black pepper, the oil, and salt to taste until the marinade is combined well. Use the marinade to marinate beef or pork, covered and chilled, for at least 4 hours and up to 8 hours. Baste the meat with the marinade as it is grilled. Makes about ⅔ cup.

Mint and Yogurt Marinade

¼ cup minced fresh mint leaves
1 teaspoon sugar
1 teaspoon minced garlic
2 teaspoons fresh lemon juice
2 tablespoons vegetable oil
1 cup plain yogurt

In a bowl with a fork mash the mint with the sugar and the garlic and stir in the lemon juice, the oil, the yogurt, and salt to taste. Use the marinade to marinate lamb, beef, or chicken, covered and chilled, overnight. Makes about 1 cup.

Mustard and Bourbon Marinade

½ cup Dijon-style mustard
¼ cup plus 2 tablespoons bourbon
¼ cup soy sauce
½ cup firmly packed dark brown sugar
2 teaspoons Worcestershire sauce
⅓ cup minced scallion

In a bowl stir together the mustard, the bourbon, the soy sauce, the brown sugar, the Worcestershire sauce, and the scallion. Use the marinade to marinate shrimp or scallops, covered, at room temperature for 1 hour, or beef, chicken, or pork, covered and chilled, overnight. Baste the shellfish or meat with the marinade as it is grilled. Makes about 1⅓ cups.

Teriyaki Marinade

⅔ cup soy sauce
¼ cup *mirin* (sweet Japanese rice wine, available at Oriental markets and some supermarkets) or sweet Sherry
5 tablespoons cider vinegar
½ cup sugar
2 tablespoons chopped fresh gingerroot

In a saucepan combine the soy sauce, the *mirin*, the vinegar, the sugar, and the gingerroot, bring the mixture to a boil, stirring, and simmer it until it is reduced to about 1 cup. Strain the mixture through a fine sieve into a bowl and let it cool. Use the marinade to marinate chicken, beef, or shrimp, covered and chilled, overnight. Baste the meat or shellfish with the marinade as it is grilled. Makes about 1 cup.

Bacon Cheddar Dipping Sauce

5 slices of lean bacon
½ cup finely chopped onion
2 tablespoons all-purpose flour
½ cup milk
½ cup beer (not dark)
1 teaspoon Worcestershire sauce, or to taste
cayenne to taste
½ pound sharp Cheddar, grated coarse (about 2 cups)

In a heavy skillet cook the bacon over moderately low heat, turning it, until it is crisp, transfer it with tongs to paper towels to drain, and reserve it. Pour off all but 2 tablespoons of the fat from the skillet and in the remaining fat cook the onion over moderately low heat, stirring occasionally, for 5 minutes. Stir in the flour and cook the *roux* over moderately low heat, stirring, for 3 minutes. Add the milk and the beer in a stream, whisking, whisk in the Worcestershire sauce, the cayenne, and salt and pepper to taste, and bring the liquid to a boil. Boil the mixture, stirring, for 2 minutes, remove the skillet from the heat, and add the Cheddar and the bacon, chopped fine. Stir the mixture over low heat until the Cheddar is melted and serve the sauce immediately as a dip for breadsticks or French bread. Makes about 1½ cups.

Quick Béarnaise Sauce

⅓ cup tarragon vinegar (page 222)
¼ cup dry white wine
2 tablespoons minced shallot
1 tablespoon dried tarragon
½ teaspoon salt
3 large egg yolks at room temperature
2 sticks (1 cup) unsalted butter, melted and
   cooled to warm
2 tablespoons minced fresh tarragon leaves

In a small heavy saucepan combine the vinegar, the wine, the shallot, the dried tarragon, and the salt, bring the mixture to a boil, and cook it at a bare simmer until the liquid is reduced to about 1 tablespoon. Transfer the mixture to a blender or food processor, add the yolks, and blend the mixture well. With the motor running add the butter in a slow stream, add the fresh tarragon and freshly ground pepper to taste, and blend the mixture well. The sauce may be kept warm in a small bowl, its surface covered with buttered wax paper, in a pan of warm water, or in a vacuum bottle. Makes about 1 cup.

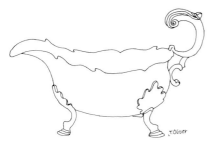

Béchamel Sauce

1 tablespoon minced onion
3 tablespoons unsalted butter
¼ cup all-purpose flour
3 cups milk
¼ teaspoon salt
white pepper to taste

In a saucepan cook the onion in the butter over moderate heat, stirring, until it is softened. Stir in the flour and cook the *roux* over low heat, stirring, for 3 minutes.

Remove the pan from the heat and add the milk, scalded, in a stream, whisking vigorously until the mixture is thick and smooth. Add the salt and white pepper and simmer the sauce for 10 to 15 minutes, or until it is thickened to the desired consistency. Strain the sauce through a fine sieve into a bowl and cover the surface with a buttered round of wax paper. Makes about 2¼ cups.

Malaysian-Style Fiery Chili Basting Sauce

two 2-inch *jalapeño* peppers, chopped (wear
   rubber gloves) including some of the seeds
   (about ¼ cup total)
½ cup chopped shallot
1 large garlic clove, minced
¼ cup finely chopped fresh coriander stems
1 tablespoon minced peeled fresh gingerroot
½ teaspoon turmeric
¾ cup canned tomato purée
2 tablespoons fresh lime juice

In a blender purée the *jalapeño* peppers, the shallot, the garlic, the coriander, the gingerroot, the turmeric, the tomato purée, the lime juice, and salt to taste. Use the sauce to baste shrimp, crab, or beef during the last third of its grilling time. Makes about 1½ cups.

Curried Mango Chutney and Coriander Dipping Sauce

2½ tablespoons bottled mango chutney,
   or to taste
⅓ cup salted roasted cashews
2 to 3 tablespoons fresh lime juice, or to taste
8 ounces cream cheese, softened
¼ cup mayonnaise
¼ cup plain yogurt
1 teaspoon curry powder, or to taste
2 tablespoons chopped fresh coriander,
   or to taste

In a food processor blend together the chutney, the cashews, and the lime juice, scraping down the side, until the mixture is chopped fine. Add the cream cheese, the mayonnaise, the yogurt, the curry powder, the coriander, and salt to taste and blend the mixture until it is combined well. Chill the sauce, covered, for 1 hour and serve it as a dip for raw vegetables or toasted *pita* triangles. Makes about 2 cups.

Minted Cucumber Yogurt Dipping Sauce

1 cup plain yogurt
2 cucumbers, peeled, seeded, and grated
  coarse (about 1½ cups)
1 garlic clove, mashed to a paste with
  1 teaspoon salt
2 teaspoons fresh lemon juice, or to taste
2 teaspoons olive oil
1 tablespoon snipped fresh dill or
  1 teaspoon dried
1 tablespoon chopped fresh mint leaves
  or 1 teaspoon dried, crumbled

In a bowl whisk together the yogurt, the cucumbers, the garlic mixture, the lemon juice, the oil, the dill, the mint, and salt and pepper to taste. Chill the sauce, covered, for 1 hour and serve it as a dip for raw vegetables, fried eggplant, or chilled cooked shrimp. Makes about 2 cups.

Ripe Olive and Clam Sauce for Pasta

a 6½-ounce can minced clams
¼ cup olive oil
¼ cup dry white wine
a 6-ounce can pitted ripe olives, drained
  (about 1½ cups) and chopped
½ cup sliced scallion including the green part

Drain the liquid from the clams into a small saucepan and reserve the clams. To the pan add the oil and the wine, bring the liquid to a boil, and simmer it for 5 minutes. Stir in the reserved clams, the olives, and the scallion. Serve the sauce with ½ pound pasta, such as *rotelle*, *fusilli*, or macaroni, cooked, drained, and rinsed, and sprinkle it with freshly grated Parmesan. Makes about 1 cup.

Jellied Orange Cranberry Sauce

1½ cups fresh orange juice
1½ cups sugar
a 12-ounce bag (3¼ cups) cranberries, picked
  over and rinsed
1 tablespoon freshly grated orange rind

In a large saucepan combine the orange juice and the sugar, bring the mixture to a boil, stirring until the sugar is dissolved, and add the cranberries. Bring the mixture back to a boil and simmer it, stirring occasionally, for 20 to 30 minutes, or until it is reduced to about 2 cups. Stir in the rind and pour the mixture into a well oiled 2-cup decorative mold. Let the cranberry sauce cool to room temperature and chill it, covered, for at least 1 day and up to 3 days. Dip the mold in a pan of hot water for 1 minute, invert it onto a serving plate, and shake it gently to release the cranberry sauce. Makes about 2 cups, serving 8.

PHOTO ON PAGE 73

Plum Basting Sauce

1 onion, chopped
1 pound plums, pitted and chopped (about
  3 cups)
1 tablespoon vegetable oil
1 teaspoon dry mustard
2 tablespoons fresh lime juice
1 tablespoon Dijon-style mustard
2 teaspoons soy sauce
2 tablespoons sugar

In a heavy saucepan cook the onion and the plums in the oil over moderately low heat, stirring occasionally, until the onion is softened. Stir in the dry mustard, the lime juice, the Dijon-style mustard, the soy sauce, the sugar, and ½ cup water, bring the mixture to a boil, and simmer it, stirring occasionally, for 25 to 30 minutes, or until it is very thick. (If the mixture begins to stick add ½ cup more water.) Force the mixture through a fine sieve into a bowl, pressing hard on the solids. Use half the sauce to baste shrimp, ham steak, or chicken during the last third of its grilling time and serve the remaining sauce separately. Makes about 1½ cups.

Spicy Red Pepper and Tomato Dipping Sauce

a 7-ounce jar roasted red peppers, drained,
  patted dry, and chopped
a 14-ounce can plum tomatoes, drained in a
  colander and chopped
1 small green bell pepper, chopped
½ teaspoon minced garlic, or to taste
1 tablespoon red-wine vinegar
2 tablespoons olive oil
¼ cup sliced scallion
2 tablespoons chopped fresh parsley leaves

1½ to 2 tablespoons drained bottled horseradish
Tabasco to taste

In a food processor blend together the red peppers, the tomatoes, the green bell pepper, the garlic, the vinegar, the oil, the scallion, the parsley, the horseradish, the Tabasco, and salt and pepper to taste until the mixture is a coarse purée. Chill the sauce, covered, for 1 hour and serve it as a dip for chilled cooked shrimp, raw clams, or raw oysters. Makes about 1½ cups.

Smoked Salmon Dipping Sauce

8 ounces cream cheese, softened
½ cup sour cream
1 tablespoon fresh lemon juice, or to taste
¼ pound smoked salmon, chopped fine
1½ tablespoons snipped fresh chives
white pepper to taste

In a food processor blend together the cream cheese, the sour cream, and the lemon juice until the mixture is smooth, add the salmon, the chives, the white pepper, and salt to taste, and blend the mixture until it is combined well. Serve the sauce as a dip for raw vegetables or dark bread. Makes about 2 cups.

Tartar Sauce

4 sweet gherkins, minced
3 shallots, minced
the yolk of 1 hard-boiled large egg, minced
1 tablespoon minced capers
1 tablespoon minced fresh parsley leaves
1 tablespoon grated onion
1 tablespoon minced fresh tarragon or
    1 teaspoon dried, crumbled
1 tablespoon minced fresh chervil or
    1 teaspoon dried, crumbled
1 teaspoon Dijon-style mustard
1 teaspoon fresh lemon juice
1 teaspoon sugar
white pepper to taste
1½ cups mayonnaise (page 220)

Fold the gherkins, the shallots, the egg yolk, the capers, the parsley, the onion, the tarragon, the chervil, the mustard, the lemon juice, the sugar, the white pepper, and salt to taste into the mayonnaise. Makes about 2 cups.

Quick Tomato Barbecue Sauce

1 onion, chopped (about 1 cup)
1 tablespoon minced garlic
1 dill pickle, chopped (about ½ cup)
1½ cups distilled white vinegar
¼ cup firmly packed dark brown sugar
2 tablespoons Dijon-style mustard
2 tablespoons Worcestershire sauce
2 teaspoons Tabasco
1 cup ketchup
¼ cup vegetable oil

In a blender purée the onion, the garlic, and the pickle with the vinegar, add the brown sugar, the mustard, the Worcestershire sauce, the Tabasco, the ketchup, and the oil, and blend the mixture until it is smooth. Transfer the mixture to a saucepan and simmer it, stirring occasionally, for 20 to 25 minutes, or until it is reduced to about 2 cups. Use the sauce to baste shrimp, beef, or chicken during the last third of its grilling time. Makes about 2 cups.

CONDIMENTS: RELISHES AND SPICES

Sweet Cranberry Applesauce

6 McIntosh apples, cored and cut into eighths
¼ pound (about 1¼ cups) cranberries, picked
    over and rinsed
½ cup apple cider
a 2-inch cinnamon stick
⅓ cup firmly packed light brown sugar,
    or to taste
1 tablespoon unsalted butter
¼ teaspoon cinnamon
a pinch of freshly ground nutmeg

In a large heavy saucepan combine the apples, the cranberries, the cider, and the cinnamon stick, bring the liquid to a boil, and simmer the mixture, covered, stirring occasionally, for 15 to 18 minutes, or until the apples are very tender. Discard the cinnamon stick, force the mixture through a food mill fitted with a fine disk or through a sieve into a bowl, and stir in the brown sugar, the butter, the cinnamon, and the nutmeg. Makes about 2½ cups.

Savory Red Onion and Garlic Applesauce

5 large garlic cloves, peeled and left whole,
 or to taste
6 McIntosh apples, cored and cut into eighths
½ cup canned chicken broth
2 tablespoons white-wine vinegar
1 red onion, chopped
2 tablespoons unsalted butter
freshly ground pepper to taste

In a large saucepan combine the garlic, the apples, the broth, and the vinegar, bring the liquid to a boil, and simmer the mixture, covered, stirring occasionally, for 15 to 18 minutes, or until the apples are tender. While the apples are cooking, in a skillet cook the onion in the butter over moderately low heat, stirring, until it is soft and transfer it to a large bowl. Add the apple mixture, combine the mixture well, and force it through a food mill fitted with a fine disk into a bowl, mashing the garlic to force it through the disk. Season the applesauce with the pepper and salt. Makes 3 cups.

East Indian Banana and Coconut Salad

⅓ cup milk
a 3½-ounce can sweetened flaked coconut
½ teaspoon cuminseed
an 8-ounce container plain yogurt, drained in
 a fine sieve set over a bowl and covered and
 chilled overnight
⅔ cup well chilled heavy cream
2 teaspoons fresh lime juice
½ teaspoon dried mint, crumbled
½ cup raw sunflower seeds (available at
 natural foods stores and most
 supermarkets), toasted lightly and cooled
2 firm-ripe bananas

In a shallow baking dish stir together the milk and ⅓ cup water, add the coconut, and let the mixture stand, covered, stirring occasionally, for 2 hours. Drain the coconut mixture in a fine sieve, transfer it to paper towels, and pat it until it is moist-dry. In a dry small heavy skillet toast the cuminseed over moderate heat, swirling the skillet, for 3 to 4 minutes, or until it turns several shades darker and begins to pop. In an electric spice or coffee grinder pulverize the cuminseed. In a bowl whisk together the yogurt, the ground cuminseed, ⅓ cup of the cream, the lime juice, the mint, and salt to taste and stir

in the coconut, the sunflower seeds, and the bananas, sliced thin. In a small bowl beat the remaining ⅓ cup cream until it holds soft peaks and fold it into the salad. Serves 6 to 8 as an accompaniment to curry.

Honey Tarragon Mustard

1 cup Dijon-style mustard
3 tablespoons honey
3 tablespoons finely chopped fresh tarragon
 leaves

In a blender or food processor blend together the mustard, the honey, and the tarragon. Makes about 1 cup.

Onion and Cranberry Confit

2 pounds onions, halved lengthwise and sliced
 thin crosswise
½ cup sugar
½ stick (¼ cup) unsalted butter
1½ teaspoons minced garlic
½ cup red-wine vinegar
1 cup fresh or frozen cranberries, picked over
½ bay leaf
½ teaspoon dried rosemary, crumbled

In a heavy saucepan cook the onions and the sugar in the butter over moderate heat, stirring occasionally, for 10 minutes, or until the onions are golden, add the garlic, and cook the mixture, stirring, for 1 minute. Stir in the vinegar, the cranberries, the bay leaf, the rosemary, and ¼ cup water, cook the mixture, stirring occasionally, for 15 minutes, or until the *confit* is thickened, and discard the bay leaf. *The* confit *can be made 1 week in advance and kept covered and chilled.* Serve the *confit* with roasted meats or poultry. Makes about 2 cups.

Cajun Spice Powder

2 tablespoons sweet paprika
1½ tablespoons powdered thyme
1 tablespoon garlic powder
1 tablespoon celery salt
1 tablespoon cayenne
2 teaspoons white pepper
2 teaspoons black pepper

In a bowl combine well the paprika, the thyme, the garlic powder, the celery salt, the cayenne, the white pepper, and the black pepper. The Cajun spice mixture keeps in a tightly sealed jar in a cool dark place for up to 6 months. Use the Cajun spice mixture to season fish, gumbos, and stews. Makes about ⅓ cup.

Chinese Five-Spice Powder

1 tablespoon Szechwan peppercorns*
8 star anise*
6 cloves
a 1½-inch piece cinnamon stick, crushed
   coarse
1 tablespoon fennel seeds

*available at Oriental markets and some
   specialty foods shops and supermarkets

In a jelly-roll pan combine the Szechwan peppercorns, the star anise, the cloves, the cinnamon, and the fennel seeds, toast the mixture in a preheated 250° F. oven for 20 minutes, and let it cool to room temperature. In an electric spice or coffee grinder pulverize the mixture and strain it through a sieve into a bowl. The Chinese five-spice powder keeps in a tightly sealed jar in a cool dark place for up to 6 months. Use the Chinese five-spice powder to season poultry and meats. Makes about ¼ cup.

Curry Powder

3 tablespoons coriander seeds
2 tablespoons cuminseed
2 tablespoons turmeric
1 tablespoon mustard seeds
2½ teaspoons fennel seeds
the seeds from 8 cardamom pods
8 cloves
1½ teaspoons ground ginger
1½ teaspoons black peppercorns
¼ teaspoon freshly grated nutmeg
¼ teaspoon cayenne

In a jelly-roll pan combine the coriander seeds, the cuminseed, the turmeric, the mustard seeds, the fennel seeds, the cardamom seeds, the cloves, the ginger, the black peppercorns, the nutmeg, and the cayenne, toast the mixture in a preheated 250° F. oven for 20 minutes,

and let it cool to room temperature. In an electric spice or coffee grinder pulverize the spice mixture in batches and strain it through a sieve into a bowl. The curry powder keeps in a tightly sealed jar in a cool dark place for up to 6 months. Use the curry powder to season soups and stews. Makes about ½ cup.

Fines Herbes

½ cup firmly packed fresh parsley leaves
   (preferably flat-leafed)
2 teaspoons dried chervil, crumbled
2 teaspoons dried chives
1½ teaspoons dried tarragon, crumbled

Chop coarse the parsley, add to it the chervil, the chives, and the tarragon, and chop the mixture until the parsley is chopped fine. (The moisture from the parsley rehydrates the dried herbs.) The *fines herbes* keeps covered and chilled for 2 days. Use the *fines herbes* to season egg and poultry dishes. Makes about ¼ cup.

Herbes de Provence

2 tablespoons dried thyme
2 teaspoons dried basil
2 teaspoons dried summer savory
2 teaspoons dried rosemary
1 teaspoon dried marjoram
½ bay leaf

In an electric spice or coffee grinder pulverize the thyme, the basil, the summer savory, the rosemary, the marjoram, and the bay leaf. The *herbes de Provence* keeps in a tightly sealed jar in a cool dark place for up to 6 months. Use the *herbes de Provence* to season meats, stews, and sauces. Makes about 3 tablespoons.

Quatre Epices
(Four Spices)

3 tablespoons white peppercorns
1 whole nutmeg, crushed coarse
12 cloves
1 tablespoon ground ginger

In an electric spice or coffee grinder pulverize the white peppercorns, the nutmeg, and the cloves. Strain the mixture through a sieve into a bowl, add the ginger, and stir the mixture until it is combined well. The *quatre épices* keeps in a tightly sealed jar in a cool dark place for 6 months. Use the *quatre épices* to season pâtés, sausages, and sauces. Makes about ⅓ cup.

Pickling Spice

2 tablespoons mustard seeds
1 tablespoon whole allspice
2 teaspoons coriander seeds
2 teaspoons black peppercorns
2 teaspoons dill seeds
2 teaspoons cloves
1 teaspoon ground ginger
1 teaspoon dried hot red pepper flakes
1 bay leaf, crumbled
a 2-inch piece cinnamon stick, crushed fine

In a bowl combine well the mustard seeds, the allspice, the coriander seeds, the black peppercorns, the dill seeds, the cloves, the ginger, the red pepper flakes, the bay leaf, and the cinnamon. The pickling spice keeps in a tightly sealed jar in a cool dark place for up to 6 months. Use the pickling spice to season the brine for pickles or the cooking liquid for shellfish. Makes about ⅓ cup.

DESSERT SAUCES

Cinnamon Sour Cream Dipping Sauce

1½ cups sour cream
2 to 3 tablespoons firmly packed light brown
    sugar, or to taste
½ teaspoon cinnamon, or to taste
¼ teaspoon ground ginger, or to taste
a pinch of freshly grated nutmeg
fresh lemon juice to taste

In a bowl whisk together the sour cream and the brown sugar until the sugar is dissolved, add the cinnamon, the ginger, the nutmeg, the lemon juice, and a pinch of salt, and whisk the mixture until it is combined well. Serve the sauce as a dip for fresh fruit. Makes about 1½ cups.

Sour Cherry Jam

4 cups coarsely chopped pitted sour cherries
    (about 3 pounds unpitted)
1 teaspoon freshly grated orange rind
¼ cup fresh lemon juice
a 1¾-ounce box powdered pectin
5 cups sugar
½ cup Cognac or other brandy if desired

In a large heavy kettle stir together the cherries, the rind, the lemon juice, and the pectin until the mixture is combined well and bring the mixture to a full boil, stirring. Stir in the sugar, bring the mixture to a rolling boil that cannot be stirred down, and boil it, stirring constantly, for 1 minute. Remove the kettle from the heat, skim off any foam, and stir in the Cognac. Ladle the mixture into 6 sterilized ½-pint Mason-type jars (sterilizing procedure follows), filling the jars to within ⅛ inch of the tops, wipe the rims with a dampened cloth, and seal the jars with the lids. Put the jars in a water bath canner or on a rack set in a deep kettle, add enough hot water to the canner to cover the jars by 1 to 2 inches, and bring it to a boil. Process the jars, covered, for 5 minutes, transfer them with tongs to a rack, and let them cool completely. Store the jars in a cool dark place. Makes 6 half pints.

To Sterilize Jars and Glasses for Pickling
and Preserving

Wash the jars in hot suds and rinse them in scalding water. Put the jars in a kettle and cover them with hot water. Bring the water to a boil, covered, and boil the jars for 15 minutes from the time that steam emerges from the kettle. Turn off the heat and let the jars stand in the hot water. Just before they are to be filled invert the jars onto a kitchen towel to dry. The jars should be filled while they are still hot. Sterilize the jar lids for 5 minutes, or according to the manufacturer's instructions.

DESSERTS

CAKES

Coffee Almond Ice-Cream Cake with Dark Chocolate Sauce

1½ cups chocolate wafer crumbs (about 30 wafers)
½ stick (¼ cup) unsalted butter, melted
1½ pints coffee ice cream
1½ cups well chilled heavy cream
1 teaspoon vanilla
1½ cups crushed *amaretti* (Italian almond macaroons, available at specialty foods shops and some supermarkets)
½ cup sliced blanched almonds, toasted lightly
dark chocolate sauce (recipe follows)

In a bowl with a fork stir together the crumbs and the butter until the mixture is combined well, pat the mixture onto the bottom and 1 inch up the side of a lightly oiled 8-inch springform pan, 2½ inches deep, and freeze the crust for 30 minutes, or until it is firm. Spread the ice cream, softened, evenly on the crust and return the pan to the freezer for 30 minutes, or until the ice cream is firm. In a bowl with an electric mixer beat the cream with the vanilla until it holds stiff peaks, fold in the *amaretti* thoroughly, and spread the mixture over the ice cream. Smooth the top of the cake, sprinkle it with the almonds, and freeze the cake for 30 to 45 minutes, or until the top is firm. Freeze the cake, covered

with plastic wrap and foil, for at least 4 hours or overnight. Just before serving wrap a warm dampened kitchen towel around the side of the pan, remove the side, and transfer the cake to a serving plate. Cut the cake into wedges with a knife dipped in hot water and serve it with the chocolate sauce.

PHOTO ON PAGE 44

Dark Chocolate Sauce

1½ cups heavy cream
⅔ cup firmly packed dark brown sugar
4 ounces bittersweet chocolate, chopped
3 ounces unsweetened chocolate, chopped
½ stick (¼ cup) unsalted butter, softened
3 to 4 tablespoons Amaretto, or to taste

In a small heavy saucepan combine the cream and the brown sugar, bring the mixture to a boil over moderately high heat, whisking occasionally, and whisk it until the brown sugar is dissolved. Remove the pan from the heat, add the bittersweet chocolate and the unsweetened chocolate, and whisk the mixture until the chocolate is melted. Whisk in the butter and the Amaretto until the sauce is smooth and let the sauce cool slightly. *The chocolate sauce may be made 1 week in advance and kept covered and chilled. Reheat the chocolate sauce over very low heat, stirring occasionally, until it is warm.* Makes about 3 cups.

PHOTO ON PAGE 44

231

Ginger Pound Cake

4 cups sifted cake flour (not self-rising)
1 teaspoon double-acting baking powder
1½ teaspoons ground ginger
¼ teaspoon mace
¼ teaspoon salt
4 sticks (2 cups) cold unsalted butter,
    cut into pieces
1 teaspoon freshly grated orange rind
3 cups sugar
6 large eggs at room temperature
½ cup packed minced peeled fresh gingerroot
¾ cup milk at room temperature
Accompaniments
sliced peaches tossed with fresh lemon juice
    and sugar to taste
fresh raspberries
whipped cream
crystallized ginger (recipe follows), chopped

Butter and flour well a 10-inch tube pan, 4 inches deep. Into a bowl sift the flour twice with the baking powder, the ground ginger, the mace, and the salt. In the bowl of an electric mixer cream the butter with the rind at moderately high speed for 10 minutes, or until it is very light and fluffy, and add the sugar, 2 tablespoons at a time, beating well after each addition. Add the eggs, 1 at a time, beating well after each addition, add the gingerroot, and beat the batter until it is combined well. With the mixer at low speed add the flour mixture alternately with the milk, beginning and ending with the flour mixture, using 6 additions for the flour mixture and 5 for the milk and beating the batter after each addition until it is just combined. Pour the batter into the prepared pan and bake it in the middle of a preheated 300° F. oven for 1 hour and 45 minutes to 2 hours, or until a skewer comes out clean. Let the cake cool in the pan on a rack for 15 minutes and run a long thin knife around the side. Invert the cake onto the rack and let it cool completely.

Serve the cake with the peaches, the raspberries, the whipped cream, and the crystallized ginger.

PHOTO ON BACK JACKET

Crystallized Ginger

1½ pounds large pieces of very fresh
    gingerroot (preferably "young" ginger,
    available at some Oriental markets in
    January and February, July and August)

three 3- by ½-inch strips of orange rind
    removed with a vegetable peeler
three 3- by ½-inch strips of lemon rind
    removed with a vegetable peeler
3½ cups sugar

Trim the small knobs from the gingerroot, reserving them for another use if desired, and cut the gingerroot into 1½- to 2-inch pieces (there should be about 4½ cups). Peel the gingerroot and slice it lengthwise ⅛ inch thick. In a large heavy saucepan combine the gingerroot with 8 cups cold water and the rinds, bring the water to a boil, and cook the mixture at a bare simmer for 1 hour. In another large heavy saucepan combine 3 cups of the sugar with 1½ cups water and cook the mixture over moderately low heat, stirring, until the sugar is dissolved. Drain the gingerroot well and add it to the sugar syrup. Bring the mixture to a boil and cook it at a bare simmer for 2 hours, or until the gingerroot is translucent and a candy thermometer registers 230° F. Transfer the gingerroot with a skimmer immediately to a piece of foil, discarding the syrup, let the gingerroot cool until it can be handled, and roll it in the remaining ½ cup sugar, coating it well. The ginger keeps in an airtight container for 1 month. Makes about 1 pound.

PHOTO ON BACK JACKET

Frozen Hazelnut Praline Meringue Cake

For the meringue
1 cup hazelnuts, toasted and skinned
    (procedure follows)
1⅓ cups sugar
¼ teaspoon salt
⅔ cup (about 5) large egg whites at room
    temperature
For the caramel and praline
1 cup sugar
¾ cup hazelnuts, toasted and skinned
For the ganache and filling
3½ cups well chilled heavy cream
5 ounces semisweet chocolate, chopped
⅓ cup sugar
3 tablespoons Kahlúa

Line 2 buttered baking sheets with parchment paper or foil and with the bottom of a 9½-inch springform pan as a guide trace 1 circle on each sheet of parchment.

Make the meringue: In a food processor grind together fine the hazelnuts, ⅓ cup of the sugar, and the salt, being careful not to grind the mixture to a paste, transfer the mixture to a bowl, and stir in ⅓ cup of the remaining sugar. In a large bowl with an electric mixer beat the whites with a pinch of salt until they hold soft peaks, add the remaining ⅔ cup sugar gradually, beating, and beat the whites until they hold stiff glossy peaks. Fold in the hazelnut mixture gently but thoroughly and transfer the meringue to a pastry bag fitted with a ½-inch plain tip. Starting in the middle of each parchment circle, pipe the meringue in a tight spiral to fill in the circles, pipe the remaining meringue into 1½-inch mounds around the circles, and bake the meringue in a preheated 275° F. oven for 50 to 55 minutes, or until it is firm when touched lightly and a mound releases easily from the parchment. Remove the parchment from the baking sheets, let the meringues cool on it, and peel off the parchment carefully. With a serrated knife and the bottom of the springform pan as a guide trim the meringue layers to fit into the springform pan. Reserve the trimmings and the mounds for the filling. *The meringues may be made 1 day in advance and kept wrapped well in plastic wrap at room temperature.*

Make the caramel and praline: In a small heavy saucepan combine the sugar and ¼ cup hot water, bring the mixture to a boil, covered, over moderately low heat, stirring occasionally until the sugar is dissolved, and simmer it, uncovered and undisturbed, tilting and rotating the pan, until it is a medium caramel. Pour one fourth of the caramel immediately onto a sheet of foil, stir the hazelnuts into the remaining caramel, and turn the praline out onto another sheet of foil. Let the caramel and the praline cool completely. Break the caramel into small pieces and reserve it in a plastic bag for garnish. Break the praline into pieces, in a food processor grind it coarse, and reserve it in another plastic bag. *The caramel and the praline may be made 1 day in advance and kept tightly sealed in airtight containers at room temperature.*

Make the *ganache* and filling: In a small saucepan combine ½ cup of the cream and the chocolate and heat the *ganache* over moderately low heat, stirring, until it is smooth. Reserve 3 tablespoons of the *ganache* for garnish and spread the remaining *ganache* on the undersides of the meringue layers. In the large bowl of an electric mixer beat the remaining 3 cups cream with the sugar and the Kahlúa until the mixture just holds stiff peaks, fold in the reserved meringue trimmings and mounds, crumbled coarse, and fold in 1 cup of the reserved praline, folding the filling until it is combined.

Fit 1 of the meringue layers *ganache* side up carefully into the bottom of the 9½-inch springform pan, fill the pan with the filling, smoothing the top, and add the remaining meringue layer *ganache* side down. Freeze the meringue cake, covered, overnight. *The meringue cake may be prepared up to this point 2 days in advance and kept covered and frozen.*

Let the cake stand at room temperature for 10 minutes and remove the side of the pan. Coat the side of the cake with the remaining reserved praline and transfer the cake to a platter. Make a cone out of parchment paper, leaving a hole as small as possible at the narrow end, transfer the reserved 3 tablespoons *ganache*, warmed, to the cone, and pipe the *ganache* decoratively on top of the cake. Garnish the frozen hazelnut praline meringue cake and the platter with the reserved caramel pieces and let the cake stand in the refrigerator for 2 hours before serving.

PHOTO ON PAGE 16

To Toast and Skin Hazelnuts

Toast the hazelnuts in one layer in a baking pan in a preheated 350° F. oven for 10 to 15 minutes, or until they are colored lightly and the skins blister. Wrap the nuts in a kitchen towel and let them steam for 1 minute. Rub the nuts in the towel to remove the skins and let them cool.

*Peanut Butter Train Cake with
Milk Chocolate Frosting*

For the cake
2 cups all-purpose flour
1½ teaspoons baking soda
¾ teaspoon double-acting baking powder
1 teaspoon salt
2 cups sugar
2 tablespoons unsalted butter, softened
½ cup chunky peanut butter
2 large eggs
1 cup sour cream
1 tablespoon vanilla
For the frosting
⅔ cup heavy cream
¼ cup confectioners' sugar
1 pound milk chocolate, broken into pieces

assorted candy and nuts for decoration, such
   as thick and thin licorice for the track;
   nonpareils for the wheels; and M & M's,
   jujubes, and slivered almonds for the cargo
vanilla ice cream as an accompaniment

Line the bottoms of 10 buttered small loaf pans, 4 by 2 by 2 inches, with wax paper, butter the paper, and dust the pans with flour, shaking out the excess.

Make the cake: Into a small bowl sift together the flour, the baking soda, the baking powder, and the salt. In a large bowl with an electric mixer preferably fitted with the paddle attachment beat together the sugar, the butter, and the peanut butter until the mixture is light and combined well, add the eggs, 1 at a time, beating well after each addition, and beat in the sour cream, the vanilla, and ⅔ cup water. Add the flour mixture and beat the batter for 2 minutes. Divide the batter evenly among the pans, smoothing the tops, and bake the cakes in the middle of a preheated 350° F. oven for 30 to 35 minutes, or until a tester comes out clean. Let the cakes cool in the pans on racks for 2 minutes. Run a thin knife around the edges of the pans, invert the cakes onto the racks, discarding the paper, and let them cool completely. (Alternatively the cake may be made in a buttered baking pan, 13 by 9 by 2 inches. Line the bottom of the pan with wax paper, butter the paper, and dust the pan with flour, shaking out the excess. Pour the batter into the pan, smoothing the top, rap the pan 3 times on a hard surface to expel any air bubbles, and pull a knife in a rectangle through the batter ½ inch from the edge of the pan. Bake the cake in the middle of a preheated 350° F. oven for 45 to 50 minutes, or until a tester comes out clean. Run a thin knife around the edges of the pan, invert the cake onto a rack, discarding the paper, and let it cool. With a serrated knife cut the cake into ten 4- by 2½-inch rectangles.) *The cakes may be made 1 day in advance and kept wrapped well.*

Make the frosting: In the top of a double boiler set over barely simmering water whisk together the cream and the confectioners' sugar, sifted, add the chocolate, and heat the mixture, whisking occasionally, until it is smooth. Remove the pan from the heat, leaving the top of the double boiler set over the water.

Assemble the "train": Cut a ¼-inch-thick slice from one end of 2 of the cakes, stack the slices on top of each other, spreading some of the frosting between them to secure them, and arrange the stacked slices on top of one end of another cake to form the "engine car," spreading some of the frosting on the cake to secure them. Spread the engine car and the remaining cakes with the remaining frosting, arrange the cakes frosting sides up like a train on a licorice "track," and decorate them with the candy and nuts. Serve the cake with the ice cream. Serves 10.

PHOTO ON PAGE 19

Treacle Cake with Cinnamon Applesauce

2¾ cups all-purpose flour
1 tablespoon ground ginger
2 teaspoons cinnamon
¼ teaspoon freshly grated nutmeg
1 teaspoon ground allspice
½ teaspoon salt
1 cup vegetable shortening at room
   temperature
1½ cups firmly packed dark brown sugar
1 cup dark unsulfured molasses
2 teaspoons baking soda
4 large eggs
confectioners' sugar for sifting over the cake
cinnamon applesauce (recipe follows) as an
   accompaniment

Into a bowl sift together the flour, the ginger, the cinnamon, the nutmeg, the allspice, and the salt. In another bowl with an electric mixer cream the shortening, add the brown sugar, beating, and beat the mixture until it is light and fluffy. Add the molasses in a stream and beat the mixture until it is combined well. In a measuring cup stir the baking soda into ⅔ cup boiling water and add the mixture to the molasses mixture in a stream, beating. (The batter will separate at this point.) Beat in the flour mixture and the eggs and beat the mixture until it is just combined. Pour the batter into a buttered and floured 10-inch springform pan and bake the cake in the lower third of a preheated 350° F. oven for 1 hour and 5 minutes to 1 hour and 10 minutes, or until a tester comes out clean. Let the cake cool in the pan on a rack for 5 minutes, remove the side of the pan, and let the cake cool completely. *The cake improves in flavor if made 24 hours in advance.* Invert the cake onto a serving plate, put a paper doily on top of it, and sift the confectioners' sugar over the doily. Remove the doily carefully and serve the cake with the cinnamon applesauce.

PHOTO ON PAGE 26

Cinnamon Applesauce

2 tablespoons unsalted butter
4 McIntosh apples
  (about 1½ pounds)
2 to 3 tablespoons sugar,
  or to taste
¼ teaspoon cinnamon

In a heavy skillet melt the butter over moderate heat, add the apples, sliced but not peeled or cored, and stir them to coat them with the butter. Stir in ½ cup water, the sugar, and the cinnamon and simmer the mixture, covered, stirring occasionally, for 20 minutes. Purée the mixture through a food mill fitted with the coarse blade into a bowl and serve it warm or at room temperature. Makes about 2 cups.

PHOTO ON PAGE 26

Pumpkin Spice Cake Roll

For the filling
2 envelopes unflavored gelatin
¼ cup Cognac or other brandy
2 large eggs
1½ cups canned pumpkin purée
½ cup firmly packed light brown sugar
½ cup milk
¼ teaspoon salt
¾ teaspoon cinnamon
¼ teaspoon freshly grated nutmeg
⅔ cup heavy cream
For the cake
5 large eggs, separated, the whites at room
    temperature
⅓ cup granulated sugar
3 tablespoons light molasses
½ teaspoon freshly grated lemon rind
½ cup cake flour (not self-rising)
¾ teaspoon ground ginger
½ teaspoon cinnamon
⅛ teaspoon ground cloves
¼ teaspoon salt
confectioners' sugar for dusting the towel

confectioners' sugar for sifting over the
    cake roll

Make the filling: In a small bowl sprinkle the gelatin over the Cognac and let it soften for 5 minutes. In a large saucepan whisk together the eggs, the pumpkin, the brown sugar, the milk, the salt, the cinnamon, and the nutmeg until the mixture is smooth and cook the mixture over moderately low heat, whisking and being careful not to let it boil, for 5 minutes, or until it is heated through. Whisk in the gelatin mixture and cook the mixture, whisking, for 1 minute, or until the gelatin is dissolved completely. Transfer the mixture to a metal bowl set in a larger bowl of ice and cold water and let it cool, stirring, for 5 minutes, or until it is the consistency of raw egg white. In a bowl with the electric mixer beat the cream until it just holds stiff peaks, whisk about one third of it into the pumpkin mixture to lighten it, and fold in the remaining cream gently but thoroughly. Chill the filling, covered, for at least 1 hour and up to 12 hours.

Make the cake: Line a jelly-roll pan, 15½ by 10½ by 1 inches, with foil, grease the foil, and dust it with flour, knocking out the excess. In a bowl with an electric mixer beat the yolks, the granulated sugar, the molasses, and the rind until the mixture is thick and pale and forms a ribbon when the beaters are lifted. In another bowl with the beaters, cleaned, beat the whites with a pinch of salt until they just hold stiff peaks, stir about one third of the whites into the yolk mixture, and fold in the remaining whites gently but thoroughly. Sift the flour, the ginger, the cinnamon, the cloves, and the salt over the egg mixture, fold in the dry ingredients until the mixture is just combined, and spread the batter evenly in the pan. Rap the pan on a hard surface to eliminate any air bubbles and bake the cake in the middle of a preheated 350° F. oven for 12 to 15 minutes, or until it is colored lightly and springs back when pressed lightly. Invert the cake onto a large kitchen towel that has been dusted generously with the confectioners' sugar and peel the foil carefully from the cake. Roll up the cake gently in the towel, starting with a long side, and let the cake roll cool completely on a rack.

Assemble the cake: Unroll the cake and spread it evenly with the filling, reserving about ¾ cup of the filling for decoration. Reroll the cake carefully, transfer the cake roll to a platter, and trim the ends diagonally. *The cake roll may be prepared up to this point 6 hours in advance and kept covered and chilled.*

Sift the confectioners' sugar over the cake roll, transfer the reserved filling to a pastry bag fitted with a fluted tip, and pipe it decoratively down the center of the cake roll.

Lemon Cherry Cheesecake

For the crust
1½ cups graham cracker crumbs
1 teaspoon cinnamon
1 stick (½ cup) unsalted butter, melted
For the filling
1½ pounds cream cheese, softened
1⅓ cups sugar
5 large eggs
⅔ cup sour cream
1½ teaspoons vanilla
1½ teaspoons freshly grated lemon rind
¼ cup fresh lemon juice
½ teaspoon salt
For the garnish
⅔ cup apricot preserves

about 20 dark sweet cherries,
  pitted and halved
about 10 yellow sweet cherries,
  pitted and halved

cherry sauce (recipe follows)
  as an accompaniment

Make the crust: In a bowl stir together the crumbs, the cinnamon, and the butter until the mixture is combined well and pat the mixture onto the bottom and halfway up the side of a 9-inch springform pan (2½ inches deep). Chill the crust for at least 30 minutes and up to 1 hour.

Make the filling: In a bowl with an electric mixer beat the cream cheese until it is light and fluffy, add the sugar gradually, beating, and beat the mixture until it is combined well. Add the eggs, 1 at a time, beating well after each addition, and beat in the sour cream, the vanilla, the rind, the lemon juice, and the salt, beating the mixture until it is combined well.

Pour the filling into the crust, smooth the top, and bake the cheesecake in the middle of a preheated 325° F. oven for 1 hour and 10 minutes. Turn the oven off, let the cheesecake cool completely in the oven with the door propped open about 6 inches, and chill it, covered, overnight.

Prepare the garnish: In a small saucepan combine the preserves with 1 tablespoon water, heat the mixture over moderately low heat, stirring, until it is heated through, and force the preserves through a fine sieve into a small bowl. Remove the side of the springform pan and transfer the cheesecake to a serving plate. Arrange the dark cherries in 2 concentric circles around the outer edge of the top of the cake and arrange the yellow cherries in the center. Brush the cherries evenly with the apricot glaze and serve the cheesecake with the cherry sauce.

Cherry Sauce

1 cup dry red wine
½ cup sugar
¼ cup fresh lemon juice plus additional
  to taste
3 cups (about 1 pound) dark sweet cherries,
  pitted and halved
2 tablespoons cornstarch
1½ tablespoons kirsch plus additional to taste

In a saucepan combine the wine, the sugar, ¼ cup of the lemon juice, a pinch of salt, and 1 cup water and bring the mixture to a boil, stirring until the sugar is dissolved. Add the cherries and simmer the mixture for 5 minutes, or until the cherries are tender. In a small bowl stir together the cornstarch and 4 tablespoons cold water until the cornstarch is dissolved, add the mixture to the cherry mixture, stirring, and bring the sauce to a boil. Boil the sauce, stirring, for 2 minutes, remove the pan from the heat, and stir in 1½ tablespoons of the kirsch. Let the sauce cool completely, chill it, covered, for at least 3 hours or overnight, and add the additional lemon juice and kirsch. Makes 3½ cups.

Almond Cheesecakes with Amaretti Crumbs

¾ cup (6½ ounces) cream cheese
¼ cup sugar
2 tablespoons sour cream
1 large egg
¼ teaspoon vanilla
¼ teaspoon almond extract
2 *amaretti* (Italian almond macaroons,
  available at specialty foods shops and some
  supermarkets)

In a bowl with an electric mixer cream together the cream cheese and the sugar, add the sour cream, the egg, the vanilla, the almond extract, and a pinch of salt, and beat the mixture until it is smooth. Butter the insides of two 1-cup glass measuring cups, divide the mixture between the cups, and microwave it at low power (20%) for 14 to 18 minutes, or until it is just set. Chill the cups in a bowl of ice and cold water in the refrigerator for 15 minutes, or until they are chilled. Run a thin knife around each cheesecake, invert each cheesecake onto a small plate, and top it with 1 of the *amaretti*, crushed. Serves 2.

Chocolate Roll with Banana Rum Ice Cream

For the ice cream

⅓ cup sugar

1½ teaspoons cornstarch

2 large egg yolks

¾ cup milk

1 cup mashed ripe banana (about 3 bananas)

3 tablespoons dark rum

¾ cup well chilled heavy cream

For the chocolate roll

½ cup unsweetened cocoa powder

2 tablespoons cornstarch

2 tablespoons all-purpose flour

5 large eggs, separated, the whites at room
temperature

½ cup plus 3 tablespoons sugar

⅛ teaspoon salt

⅛ teaspoon cream of tartar

For the syrup

½ cup sugar

2 tablespoons dark rum

1 firm-ripe banana

unsweetened cocoa powder for sifting over
the chocolate roll

Make the ice cream: In a bowl whisk together the sugar, the cornstarch, and the yolks until the mixture is combined well and add the milk, scalded, in a slow stream, stirring the custard with the whisk. In a heavy saucepan cook the custard over moderate heat, stirring constantly with the whisk, until it comes to a boil, boil it, whisking constantly, for 2 minutes, and strain it through a fine sieve into a metal bowl set in a larger bowl of ice and cold water. Stir in the banana and the rum, let the mixture cool, stirring, and chill it, its surface covered with plastic wrap, until it is cold. Stir in the cream until the mixture is combined well and freeze the mixture in an ice-cream freezer according to the manufacturer's instructions.

Make the chocolate roll: Line a lightly greased 15½- by 10½-inch jelly-roll pan with foil, leaving a 1-inch overhang on the short sides, and grease the foil. Line the foil with wax paper, grease the paper, and flour it lightly, shaking out the excess. Into a bowl sift together the cocoa, the cornstarch, and the flour and in a large bowl with an electric mixer beat the yolks and ½ cup of the sugar for 5 minutes, or until the mixture is thick and pale and forms ribbons when the beater is lifted. In an-

other bowl with cleaned beaters beat the whites with the salt until they are frothy, add the cream of tartar, and beat the whites until they hold soft peaks. Add the remaining 3 tablespoons sugar, a little at a time, and beat the whites until they barely hold stiff peaks. Fold one fourth of the whites into the yolk mixture, spoon the yolk mixture onto the remaining whites, and sift the cocoa mixture over the yolk mixture. Fold the mixture together gently but thoroughly, pour the batter into the prepared pan, and spread it evenly with a metal spatula. Bake the cake in the middle of a preheated 400° F. oven for 7 to 9 minutes, or until it is puffed and a tester comes out clean. Invert a baking sheet over the cake and invert the cake onto it. Peel off the paper carefully and fit another piece of paper over the cake, leaving a 1-inch overhang. Invert the cake, paper side down, onto a rack and let it cool.

Let the ice cream soften slightly, spread it over the cake, leaving a ¼-inch border all around, and with a long side facing you and using the paper as an aid, roll up the cake jelly-roll fashion, keeping it wrapped in the paper. (The cake may crack but it will hold together.) Freeze the cake, wrapped in the paper, on the baking sheet for at least 6 hours or overnight.

Make the syrup: In a small skillet combine the sugar, the rum, and ½ cup water, bring the liquid to a boil, stirring until the sugar is dissolved, and simmer the syrup for 4 minutes.

Cut the banana diagonally into ¼-inch slices. Add the banana slices to the syrup in batches, poach them at a bare simmer for 10 seconds, and transfer them with a slotted spoon to wax paper. Bring the remaining syrup to a boil, boil it until it is reduced to about ⅓ cup, and strain it through a fine sieve into a small bowl.

Remove the wax paper from the chocolate roll and transfer the roll to a work surface. Trim the ends on the diagonal if desired, sift the cocoa over the chocolate roll, and transfer the roll to a platter. Add the banana slices to the syrup and transfer them with a fork, letting the excess syrup drip off, to the chocolate roll.

Juliette Staats's Pecan Roll

For the cake

6 extra-large eggs, separated, the whites at
room temperature

¾ cup firmly packed light brown sugar

6 tablespoons cake flour (not self-rising)

1 teaspoon double-acting baking powder

2 teaspoons vanilla
1½ cups pecans, minced very fine (do not use
   a food processor)
¼ teaspoon salt
confectioners' sugar for dusting the cake and
   the wax paper
For the filling
1¼ cups well chilled heavy cream
1 tablespoon confectioners' sugar
1 teaspoon vanilla

pecan halves for decoration
caramel sauce (recipe follows) as an
   accompaniment

Make the cake: Line a lightly oiled jelly-roll pan, 15½ by 10½ by 1 inches, with a long sheet of wax paper, leaving a 1-inch overhang on the short sides. Oil the paper lightly and dust it with flour, knocking out the excess. In a bowl with an electric mixer beat the yolks with the brown sugar until the mixture is thick and pale, add the flour and the baking powder, and beat the mixture until it is combined well. Add the vanilla and the minced pecans and blend the mixture well. (The mixture will be very thick.) In another bowl with the electric mixer and cleaned beaters beat the whites with the salt until they just hold stiff peaks, stir one third of them into the pecan mixture to lighten it, and fold in the remaining whites gently but thoroughly. Spread the batter evenly in the jelly-roll pan and bake the cake in the middle of a preheated 325° F. oven for 18 minutes, or until it is pale golden. Spread a kitchen towel on a large flat surface, top it with a sheet of wax paper, and dust the paper lightly with the confectioners' sugar. Invert the cake onto the paper and peel off the sheet of paper it baked in. Trim the edges of the cake and dust the surface lightly with the confectioners' sugar. With a long side facing you and using the paper and the towel as a guide, roll up the cake jelly-roll fashion, keeping it wrapped in the paper and the towel, and let the roll cool. *The roll may be prepared up to this point 3 hours in advance and kept covered at room temperature.*

Make the filling: In a chilled bowl beat the cream with the confectioners' sugar and the vanilla until it holds stiff peaks and reserve about ½ cup of the whipped cream, chilled, for decoration.

Unroll the cake partially, being careful not to open it so far that it cracks, spread the inside of the roll with the filling, and reroll the cake gently in the paper. Transfer the roll to a platter, remove the paper, and trim the ends on the diagonal. *The pecan roll may be prepared up to this point 4 hours in advance and kept covered and chilled.* Transfer the reserved whipped cream to a pastry bag fitted with a fluted tip and pipe rosettes on the roll. Decorate the pecan roll with the pecan halves and serve it with the caramel sauce.

PHOTO ON PAGE 37

Caramel Sauce

1 cup sugar
1 cup heavy cream

In a large heavy skillet cook the sugar over moderately high heat, stirring constantly with a fork, until it is melted completely and turns a deep golden caramel. Remove the skillet from the heat and stir the caramel to prevent further darkening. Pour the cream into the side of the skillet carefully (the caramel will harden when the cream is added), cook the caramel mixture over moderate heat, stirring, until the caramel is dissolved, and let the sauce cool to lukewarm. The sauce keeps, covered and chilled, for 1 month. Makes about 1⅓ cups.

PHOTO ON PAGE 37

JEANNE

Chocolate Walnut Spongecake

9 large eggs, separated, at room temperature
1½ cups sugar
2 tablespoons fresh orange juice
1 tablespoon fresh lemon juice
⅓ cup potato starch
⅓ cup matzo cake meal
⅓ cup unsweetened cocoa powder
¼ teaspoon salt
½ cup ground walnuts

In a large bowl with an electric mixer beat the yolks until they are thick and pale, add 1 cup of the sugar gradually, beating, and beat the mixture until it is very thick. Beat in the orange juice and the lemon juice and beat the mixture until it is combined well. Into a small bowl sift together the potato starch, the matzo cake meal, and the cocoa powder, add the mixture gradually to the yolk mixture, beating, and beat the mixture until it is just combined. In a bowl with the beaters, cleaned, beat the whites with the salt until they hold soft peaks, add the remaining ½ cup sugar, a little at a time, beating, and beat the whites until they just hold stiff peaks. Stir 1 cup of the whites into the chocolate mixture, fold in the remaining whites gently but thoroughly, and fold in the walnuts carefully. Pour the batter into an ungreased 10-inch tube pan (4¼ inches deep) with a removable bottom and bake the spongecake in the middle of a preheated 325° F. oven for 55 to 60 minutes, or until a tester comes out clean. Invert the pan over the neck of a bottle and let it cool upside down. Run a thin knife around the edge and tube of the pan and remove the side of the pan. Run the knife under the bottom of the spongecake to release it and transfer the spongecake carefully with 2 spatulas to a serving plate.

Almond Lemon Torte

For the torte rounds
1 cup blanched whole almonds
1 cup confectioners' sugar
1½ cups all-purpose flour
2 sticks (1 cup) cold unsalted butter,
   cut into bits
For the filling
¾ cup sweetened condensed milk
2 large egg yolks
⅓ cup plus 1 tablespoon fresh lemon juice

1 teaspoon freshly grated lemon rind
¾ cup slivered almonds, toasted lightly
   and cooled
For the glaze
1 cup plus 2 tablespoons confectioners' sugar
1½ tablespoons fresh lemon juice

¼ cup slivered almonds, toasted lightly and
   cooled, for garnish

Make the torte rounds: In a food processor grind fine the almonds with the confectioners' sugar, add the flour, and blend the mixture until it is combined well. Add the butter, blend the mixture until it resembles coarse meal, and on a work surface knead the dough lightly with the heel of the hand to distribute the butter evenly. Form the dough into a ball and dust it lightly with flour. Wrap the dough in plastic wrap and chill it for at least 1 hour or overnight. Divide the dough into 4 pieces and on 2 baking sheets press each piece into an 8-inch round. Bake the rounds in the middle of a preheated 375° F. oven, 1 sheet at a time, for 10 to 12 minutes, or until they are golden, and let them cool on the sheets on racks. With a narrow metal spatula loosen the rounds carefully and transfer them to a work surface. *The torte rounds may be made 1 day in advance and kept wrapped well in plastic wrap.*

Make the filling: In a bowl whisk together the condensed milk and the yolks until the mixture is combined well, add the lemon juice and the rind, and whisk the mixture until it is thickened. *The filling may be prepared up to this point 1 day in advance and kept covered and chilled.* Stir in the almonds until they are combined well.

On a serving dish arrange 1 torte round, spread it with one third of the filling, and layer the remaining rounds and the remaining filling in the same manner.

Make the glaze: In a bowl whisk together the confectioners' sugar, the lemon juice, and 1½ tablespoons hot water until the mixture is shiny and smooth. Pour the glaze onto the torte immediately, letting the excess drip down the side.

Arrange the almonds decoratively on the glaze and let the torte stand for at least 30 minutes, or until the glaze is set. *The torte may be made 6 hours in advance in order to achieve a softer, more cake-like consistency and may be chilled but in this case the glaze will lose its shine.*

PHOTO ON PAGE 20

Peach Almond Torte

For the torte
1 cup blanched whole almonds
1 cup superfine sugar
⅓ cup all-purpose flour
1 stick (½ cup) unsalted butter, melted
2 tablespoons peach schnapps
¼ teaspoon almond extract
¾ cup egg whites (about 5 large egg whites)
    at room temperature
¼ teaspoon salt

2 peaches
2 tablespoons apple jelly
1 tablespoon peach schnapps or peach brandy
vanilla or peach ice cream as an
    accompaniment if desired

Make the torte: In a food processor or blender grind fine the almonds with ¾ cup of the sugar, transfer the mixture to a bowl, and stir in the flour, the butter, the schnapps, and the almond extract. In another bowl beat the whites with the salt until they barely hold soft peaks, add the remaining ¼ cup sugar gradually, and beat the whites until they just hold stiff peaks. Stir one third of the whites into the almond mixture and fold in the remaining whites gently but thoroughly. Pour the batter into a buttered 9-inch springform pan and bake the torte in the middle of a preheated 375° F. oven for 40 minutes, or until it is golden brown and a tester comes out clean. Let the torte cool in the pan on a rack for 10 minutes, remove the side of the pan, and invert the torte onto the rack. Remove the bottom of the pan from the torte and let the torte cool completely. *The torte may be prepared up to this point 1 day in advance and kept wrapped in plastic wrap at room temperature.*

In a saucepan of boiling water blanch the peaches for 15 seconds, transfer them with a slotted spoon to a colander, and refresh them under cold water. Peel the peaches, halve and pit them, and cut 3 of the halves crosswise into thin slices, reserving the remaining half, wrapped tightly in plastic wrap, for another use.

Arrange the peach slices decoratively on the torte. In a small saucepan combine the apple jelly and the schnapps, bring the mixture to a boil, stirring, and simmer the glaze, stirring occasionally, for 2 minutes. Brush the glaze over the peaches and let it cool. *The torte may be topped and glazed 2 hours in advance and kept at room temperature.* Serve the torte with the ice cream.

PHOTO ON PAGE 50

Orange Walnut Torte

6 large eggs, separated, at room temperature
1⅓ cups granulated sugar
¼ cup fresh orange juice
3 tablespoons fresh lemon juice
2 teaspoons freshly grated orange rind
½ cup matzo cake meal
½ cup potato starch
1 cup finely chopped walnuts
confectioners' sugar for sprinkling the torte

In a large bowl with an electric mixer beat the yolks until they are thick and pale, add the granulated sugar gradually, beating, and beat the mixture until it is very thick. Beat in the orange juice, the lemon juice, and the rind, add the matzo cake meal and the potato starch gradually, beating, and beat the mixture until it is combined well. In a bowl with the beaters, cleaned, beat the whites with a pinch of salt until they just hold stiff peaks, stir 1 cup of them into the orange mixture, and fold in the remaining whites gently but thoroughly. Fold in the walnuts carefully, pour the batter into an ungreased 9-inch tube pan (3½ inches deep) with a removable bottom, and bake the torte in the middle of a preheated 325° F. oven for 55 to 60 minutes, or until a tester comes out clean. Invert the pan over the neck of a bottle and let the torte cool upside down. Run a thin knife around the edge and tube of the pan and remove the side of the pan. Run the knife under the bottom of the torte to release it, transfer the torte carefully with 2 spatulas to a serving plate, and sprinkle it with the confectioners' sugar, sifted.

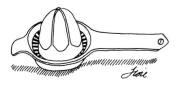

Pineapple Orange Meringue Torte

For the meringue layers
1¾ cups superfine sugar
2½ teaspoons cornstarch
8 large egg whites at room temperature
1 teaspoon vanilla
For the pastry cream
8 large egg yolks
⅓ cup sugar
5 tablespoons cornstarch
2½ cups milk
2 teaspoons freshly grated orange rind
1 teaspoon vanilla
2 tablespoons fresh lemon juice
three 8-ounce cans crushed pineapple in juice,
   drained well and squeezed dry between
   several thicknesses of paper towels
For the meringue topping
6 large egg whites
1½ cups sugar
¼ teaspoon salt

2 tablespoons finely chopped mixed glacéed
   fruit, such as cherries, pineapple, and
   angelica, for garnish

Line 2 baking sheets with foil, trace two 8-inch circles on each sheet of foil, leaving a ½-inch space between them, and oil them lightly.

Make the meringue layers: In a bowl combine well the sugar and the cornstarch. In another bowl with an electric mixer beat the whites with a pinch of salt until they are frothy, beat in 2 tablespoons of the sugar mixture, and beat the whites until they hold soft peaks. Beat in the vanilla and the remaining sugar mixture, a little at a time, and beat the meringue until it holds stiff glossy peaks. Transfer the meringue mixture to a pastry bag fitted with a ½-inch plain tip and pipe it in a spiral pattern onto the prepared foil, filling in the circles. Bake the meringues in a preheated 250° F. oven, turning the baking sheets around after 1 hour, for 2 hours to 2 hours and 15 minutes, or until they are dry. Invert the meringue layers onto racks, peeling off the foil carefully, let them cool, and trim them with a sharp knife so that the edges are even. *The meringue layers may be made 1 day in advance and kept in an airtight container.*

Make the pastry cream: In a bowl whisk together the yolks, over them sift together the sugar and the cornstarch, and whisk the mixture until it is combined well.

Add the milk, scalded, in a stream, whisking. In a heavy saucepan bring the mixture to a boil over moderate heat, whisking, and boil the custard, whisking, for 2 minutes. Whisk in the rind and the vanilla and let the custard cool, its surface covered with plastic wrap. *The pastry cream may be prepared up to this point 1 day in advance and kept covered and chilled.* Stir in the lemon juice and the pineapple just before filling the meringue layers.

Make the meringue topping: In the bowl of an electric mixer whisk together the whites, the sugar, and the salt, set the bowl over a pan of simmering water, and stir the mixture until the sugar is dissolved. Remove the bowl from the pan and with the beaters beat the mixture until it holds stiff glossy peaks.

Center 1 meringue layer on a 9-inch round metal tart pan bottom without the rim, set on a baking sheet, spread it with one fourth of the pastry cream, and top the pastry cream with a second meringue layer. Continue to layer the remaining pastry cream and meringue layers, ending with the pastry cream. Working quickly, with a long metal spatula spread the side of the torte with a generous covering of the meringue topping. Transfer the remaining meringue topping to a pastry bag fitted with a decorative tip and pipe it on and around the dessert, covering the metal round completely. Bake the torte on the baking sheet in the middle of a preheated 450° F. oven for 3 to 4 minutes, or until it is golden, transfer it on the metal round to a cake plate, and sprinkle the glacéed fruit over the center.

PHOTO ON PAGE 78

Pizza di Noci e Cioccolata
(Walnut and Chocolate Torte)

fine dry bread crumbs for dusting the pan
1⅔ cups walnut pieces (about ½ pound)
⅔ cup sugar
6 ounces fine-quality bittersweet chocolate,
   chopped fine
¼ cup finely chopped candied orange rind
¼ teaspoon grated fresh lemon rind
5 large egg yolks
6 large egg whites at room temperature
whipped cream as an accompaniment
chocolate curls for garnish if desired

Dust a buttered 10-inch tart pan with a removable rim with the bread crumbs. In a food processor grind fine the walnuts with ⅓ cup of the sugar and in a bowl combine well the walnut mixture, the chopped chocolate, the candied orange rind, and the lemon rind. In a large bowl with an electric mixer beat the egg yolks with the remaining ⅓ cup sugar until the mixture is thick and pale and forms a ribbon when the beaters are lifted and in another large bowl with the beaters, cleaned, beat the egg whites until they just hold stiff peaks. Stir the walnut mixture and one third of the whites into the yolk mixture and fold in the remaining whites gently but thoroughly. Pour the batter into the prepared pan and bake the torte in the middle of a preheated 375° F. oven for 30 to 35 minutes, or until a tester comes out clean. Transfer the torte in the pan to a rack and let it cool. Remove the rim and serve the torte with the whipped cream and the chocolate curls.

PHOTO ON PAGE 68

COOKIES

Chocolate Chip Almond Meringue Cookies

¾ cup (about 4 ounces) blanched whole
   almonds, toasted lightly and cooled
½ cup plus 2 tablespoons sugar
3 large egg whites at room temperature
¼ teaspoon cream of tartar
⅛ teaspoon almond extract
1 cup (6 ounces) miniature semisweet
   chocolate chips

In a food processor grind fine the almonds with 2 tablespoons of the sugar. In a large bowl beat the whites with a pinch of salt and the cream of tartar until they hold soft peaks, beat in the remaining ½ cup sugar, a little at a time, and beat the meringue until it holds stiff glossy peaks. Beat in the almond extract and fold in the almond mixture and the chocolate chips. Spoon rounded tablespoons of the mixture 1 inch apart onto a large foil-lined baking sheet and bake the meringues in the middle of a preheated 350° F. oven for 20 to 25 minutes, or until they are pale golden and firm to the touch. Slide the foil off the baking sheet onto a rack and let the meringues cool on the foil for 5 minutes. Peel the meringues gently from the foil and let them cool completely on the rack. The meringues may be stored in an airtight container for 2 days. Makes about 24 meringues.

Cherry Nut Chocolate Chip Cookies

2 sticks (1 cup) unsalted butter, softened
1 cup firmly packed dark brown sugar
½ cup granulated sugar
2 large eggs
1½ teaspoons vanilla
2 cups all-purpose flour
1 teaspoon salt
¾ teaspoon baking soda
2 cups (about ½ pound) dried red tart
   cherries*
1 cup coarsely chopped walnuts
2 cups semisweet chocolate chips

In a bowl with an electric mixer cream the butter, add the sugars, and beat the mixture until it is light and fluffy. Beat in the eggs, 1 at a time, beating well after each addition, and beat in the vanilla. In another bowl whisk together the flour, the salt, and the baking soda until the mixture is combined well, add the mixture to the butter mixture gradually, beating, and beat the mixture until it is just combined. Stir in the cherries, the walnuts, and the chocolate chips, drop rounded tablespoons of the batter 2 inches apart onto lightly buttered baking sheets, and bake the cookies in the middle of a preheated 375° F. oven for 12 to 15 minutes, or until they are golden. Transfer the cookies to racks and let them cool. The cookies may be stored in airtight containers for 5 days. Makes about 48 cookies.

*available year round at specialty foods shops and by mail from:

American Spoon Foods
411 East Lake Street
Petoskey, MI 49770
1-800-222-5886

Peanut Butter Chocolate Chip Bars

2 sticks (1 cup) unsalted butter, softened
1 cup firmly packed light brown sugar
1 cup chunky-style peanut butter
1 large egg
1½ teaspoons vanilla
½ teaspoon salt
1½ cups all-purpose flour
2 cups (12 ounces) semisweet chocolate chips

In a large bowl with an electric mixer cream the butter, add the brown sugar, and beat the mixture until it is light and fluffy. Add the peanut butter, beat the mixture until it is combined well, and beat in the egg, the vanilla, and the salt. Add the flour gradually, beating, beat the batter until it is just combined, and stir in the chocolate chips. Spread the batter evenly in a buttered jelly-roll pan, 15½ by 10½ by 1 inches, and bake it in the middle of a preheated 350° F. oven for 20 to 25 minutes, or until a tester comes out clean. Let the mixture cool in the pan on a rack and cut it into 36 bars. The cookies keep in an airtight container for 3 days. Makes 36 cookies.

Toasted Coconut Chocolate Chip Cookies

2 sticks (1 cup) unsalted butter, softened
1⅓ cups firmly packed dark brown sugar
2 large eggs
1 teaspoon vanilla
2 cups all-purpose flour
¾ teaspoon baking soda
1 teaspoon salt
2 cups sweetened flaked coconut, toasted
    lightly and cooled
2 cups (12 ounces) semisweet chocolate chips

In a bowl with an electric mixer cream the butter, add the brown sugar, and beat the mixture until it is light and fluffy. Beat in the eggs, 1 at a time, beating well after each addition, and beat in the vanilla. In a small bowl stir together the flour, the baking soda, and the salt until the mixture is combined well and add it to the butter mixture gradually, beating. Beat the batter until it is just combined and stir in the coconut and the chocolate chips. Drop rounded tablespoons of the batter 2 inches apart onto lightly buttered baking sheets and bake the cookies in the middle of a preheated 375° F. oven for 12 to 15 minutes, or until they are golden. Transfer the cookies to a rack and let them cool. The cookies keep in an airtight container for 5 days. Makes about 40 cookies.

Chocolate Walnut Bars

For the crust
½ cup walnuts, toasted lightly and cooled
¾ cup all-purpose flour
⅓ cup sugar
¾ stick (6 tablespoons) cold unsalted butter,
    cut into pieces
For the topping
⅓ cup unsweetened cocoa powder
½ cup granulated sugar
2 tablespoons unsalted butter
1 teaspoon vanilla
2 large eggs

confectioners' sugar for dusting

Make the crust: In a food processor grind the walnuts with the flour and the sugar, add the butter, and blend the mixture, pulsing the motor, until it resembles coarse meal. Pat the mixture onto the bottom of a buttered 8-inch-square metal baking pan and bake the crust in a preheated 350° F. oven for 25 minutes.

Make the topping while the crust is baking: In a small bowl whisk together the cocoa and the granulated sugar. In a small saucepan bring ⅓ cup water to a boil with the butter, stirring until the butter is melted, add the cocoa mixture gradually, whisking, and whisk the mixture until the sugar is dissolved. Remove the pan from the heat, stir in the vanilla and a pinch of salt, and let the mixture cool for 5 minutes. Whisk in the eggs, whisk the mixture until it is smooth, and pour it over the crust.

Bake the confection in the middle of the 350° F. oven for 20 minutes, or until the topping is set, and let it cool in the pan on a rack. Cut the confection into 2½- by 1-inch bars and dust the bars decoratively with the confectioners' sugar. The bars keep in an airtight container, chilled, for 5 days. Makes 24 bars.

PHOTO ON PAGE 52

Ginger Preserve Cookies

5 tablespoons unsalted butter, softened
3 tablespoons superfine sugar

3 tablespoons ginger preserves (a type of jam available at specialty foods shops and some supermarkets; do not use preserved ginger)
1 cup all-purpose flour

In a bowl with an electric mixer cream the butter and the sugar until the mixture is light and fluffy. Beat in the ginger preserves and the flour and beat the mixture until it is just combined. Form the dough into a ball, flatten the ball, and chill the dough, wrapped in plastic wrap, for 1 hour. Roll the dough between pieces of plastic wrap into a 10- by 8-inch rectangle and remove the top piece of plastic. Press ridges into the dough with the tines of a fork and cut out about thirty-six 2-inch triangles. Arrange the cookies 1 inch apart on buttered baking sheets and bake them in the middle of a preheated 350° F. oven for 10 to 12 minutes, or until they are golden. Transfer the cookies to racks and let them cool. *The cookies may be made 3 days in advance and kept in airtight containers.* Makes about 36 cookies.

PHOTO ON PAGE 40

Pistachio Tuiles

2 tablespoons softened unsalted butter
¼ cup confectioners' sugar
¼ teaspoon almond extract
1 large egg white at room temperature
2 tablespoons all-purpose flour
¼ cup shelled natural pistachio nuts, blanched and oven-dried (procedure follows) and chopped

In a bowl cream the butter, add the sugar, and beat the mixture until it is light and fluffy. Add the almond extract, the egg white, and a pinch of salt and beat the mixture for 5 to 10 seconds, or until it is smooth but not frothy. Sift the flour over the mixture and fold it in with the pistachios. (The batter will be thin.) Spoon rounded teaspoons of the batter 3 inches apart onto buttered baking sheets and with a fork dipped in cold water spread them to form 2-inch rounds. Bake the cookies in batches in the middle of a preheated 375° F. oven for 5 to 8 minutes, or until the edges are golden brown. Transfer the cookies with a metal spatula to a rolling pin and curve them around the pin. (If the cookies become too firm to remove from the baking sheet, return them to the oven for a few seconds to soften.) Let the cookies cool on the rolling pin. *The*

cookies may be made 1 day in advance and kept in an airtight container. Makes about 12 cookies.

PHOTO ON PAGE 52

To Blanch and Oven-Dry Pistachio Nuts

In a heatproof bowl pour boiling water to cover over the desired amount of pistachio nuts, shelled, let the nuts stand for 10 minutes, and drain them. Turn the nuts out onto a kitchen towel and rub off the skins. Bake the nuts on a baking sheet in a preheated 300° F. oven for 10 to 15 minutes, or until they are dry.

Shortbread Cookies, Strawberries, and Cream

½ stick (¼ cup) unsalted butter, softened
¼ teaspoon salt
¼ cup firmly packed light brown sugar
½ cup all-purpose flour
½ pint strawberries, hulled
⅓ cup heavy cream

In a bowl cream the butter, add the salt and the brown sugar, and beat the mixture until it is light and fluffy. Beat in the flour gradually, form the dough into a ball, and on an ungreased baking sheet pat the ball into a round ¼ inch thick. Prick the round with a fork into 6 wedges, prick the edges decoratively, and bake the round in the middle of a preheated 300° F. oven for 25 minutes. Prick the outline of the wedges again with the fork, let the round cool slightly, and break it into the wedges. Halve or quarter the strawberries and divide them between dessert plates. In a small chilled bowl beat the cream until it just holds stiff peaks, divide it between the plates, and put 3 shortbread cookies on each plate. Serves 2.

Spiced Horseshoe Cookies

1¾ cups plus 1 tablespoon all-purpose flour
1½ teaspoons ground cardamom
2 teaspoons cinnamon
1½ sticks (¾ cup) unsalted butter, softened
¾ cup superfine sugar
1 teaspoon baking soda dissolved in
   1 tablespoon warm water
1 tablespoon unsulfured light molasses

Into a bowl sift together the flour, the cardamom, and the cinnamon. In a bowl with an electric mixer cream together the butter and the sugar until the mixture is light and fluffy, beat in the baking soda mixture and the molasses, and beat in the flour mixture until the mixture is just combined. Form level tablespoons of the dough into 3½-inch-long ropes and on buttered baking sheets form the ropes into horseshoe shapes 1½ inches apart, leaving a 1-inch space between the ends. Flatten the horseshoes ¼ inch thick and press designs into them with the tines of a fork. Bake the cookies in batches in the middle of a preheated 350° F. oven for 15 to 17 minutes, or until they are golden brown, transfer them to racks, and let them cool. *The cookies may be made 3 days in advance and kept in airtight containers.* Makes about 46 cookies.

PHOTO ON PAGE 40

PIES, TARTS, AND PASTRIES

Granny Smith Apple Pie with Honey Spice Whipped Cream

shortening pie dough (recipe follows)
¾ cup plus 2½ tablespoons sugar
3 tablespoons all-purpose flour
¾ teaspoon cinnamon
¼ teaspoon freshly grated nutmeg
¼ teaspoon ground ginger
¼ teaspoon salt
¾ teaspoon freshly grated lemon rind
2½ pounds (about 6) Granny Smith apples
1 teaspoon fresh lemon juice
3 tablespoons cold unsalted butter, cut
   into bits
1 tablespoon half-and-half or milk

honey spice whipped cream (recipe follows)
   as an accompaniment

Divide the dough into 2 pieces, one slightly larger than the other, and chill the larger piece, wrapped in wax paper. Roll out the smaller piece of dough ⅛ inch thick on a floured surface, fit it into a 9-inch (4-cup) pie plate, preferably ovenproof glass, and trim the edge, leaving a ½-inch overhang. Chill the pie shell while making the filling. In a large bowl stir together ¾ cup plus 2 tablespoons of the sugar, the flour, the cinnamon, the nutmeg, the ginger, the salt, and the rind. Peel, quarter, and core the apples, slice them thin crosswise, and add them to the sugar mixture, tossing them to coat them well. Mound the apple mixture in the shell, sprinkle it with the lemon juice, and dot it with the butter.

Roll out the larger piece of dough into a 13- to 14-inch round on a floured surface and drape it over the filling. Trim the top crust, leaving a 1-inch overhang, fold the overhang under the bottom crust, pressing the edge to seal it, and crimp the edge decoratively with the tines of a fork. Make slits in the top crust for steam vents, brush the crust with the half-and-half, and sprinkle it with the remaining ½ tablespoon sugar. Bake the pie in the lower third of a preheated 425° F. oven for 15 minutes, reduce the heat to 375° F., and bake the pie for 40 to 45 minutes more, or until the filling is bubbly and the crust is golden. Transfer the pie to a rack and let it cool. *The pie may be made 8 hours in advance and kept at room temperature.* Serve the pie warm or at room temperature with the honey spice whipped cream.

PHOTO ON PAGE 22

Shortening Pie Dough

2⅓ cups all-purpose flour
½ teaspoon salt
¾ cup cold vegetable shortening,
   cut into pieces

In a bowl stir together the flour and the salt, add the vegetable shortening, and blend the mixture until it resembles coarse meal. Add 4 tablespoons ice water, or enough to form the mixture into a soft but not sticky dough, tossing the mixture with a fork, and form the dough into a ball. Flatten the ball slightly, dust it lightly with flour, and chill it, wrapped in wax paper, for 1 hour. Makes enough dough for 1 double 9-inch crust or 2 single 9-inch crusts.

Honey Spice Whipped Cream

¾ cup well chilled heavy cream
1 tablespoon honey
¼ teaspoon cinnamon
¼ teaspoon ground ginger
⅛ teaspoon freshly grated nutmeg

In a chilled bowl beat the cream with the honey, the cinnamon, the ginger, and the nutmeg until it holds soft peaks and transfer it to a serving dish. Makes about 1½ cups.

PHOTO ON PAGE 22

Cherry Almond Pie

pâte brisée (page 248)
For the filling
5 cups (about 2 pounds) sour cherries
2 tablespoons quick-cooking tapioca
1 to 1½ teaspoons fresh lemon juice
½ teaspoon salt
1 cup sugar
¼ teaspoon almond extract
⅛ teaspoon ground cloves
For the almond paste lattice mixture
2 tablespoons unsalted butter, softened
7 ounces (about ⅔ cup) almond paste
½ teaspoon freshly grated lemon rind
2 large egg yolks
⅓ cup all-purpose flour

an egg wash, made by beating 1 large egg
    yolk with 1 teaspoon water

Roll out the dough ⅛ inch thick on a lightly floured surface and fit it into a 9-inch (1-quart) pie plate. Crimp the edge decoratively and chill the shell.

Make the filling: Working over a bowl, pit the cherries, combine them with the tapioca, the lemon juice, the salt, the sugar, the almond extract, and the cloves, and stir the mixture until it is combined well. Let the filling stand, stirring occasionally, for 15 minutes.

Make the almond paste lattice mixture: In a bowl with an electric mixer cream the butter, add the almond paste and the rind, and beat the mixture until it is combined well. Add the yolks, 1 at a time, beating well after each addition, beat in the flour, beating until the mixture is combined well, and transfer the mixture to a pastry bag fitted with a ¼-inch plain tip.

Spoon the filling into the shell, pressing down gently to level the top, and over it pipe the almond paste mixture, forming a lattice pattern of strips about 1 inch apart. Brush the edge of the shell with some of the egg wash and bake the pie in the lower third of a preheated 425° F. oven for 25 minutes. Reduce the heat to 350° F. and bake the pie for 15 to 20 minutes more, or until the crust and lattice are golden brown and the filling is bubbling. Let the pie cool on a rack.

JEANNE

Pâte Brisée

1¼ cups all-purpose flour
¾ stick (6 tablespoons) cold unsalted butter,
  cut into bits
2 tablespoons cold vegetable shortening
¼ teaspoon salt

In a large bowl blend the flour, the butter, the vegetable shortening, and the salt until the mixture resembles meal. Add 3 tablespoons ice water, toss the mixture until the water is incorporated, and form the dough into a ball. Knead the dough lightly with the heel of the hand against a smooth surface for a few seconds to distribute the fat evenly and re-form it into a ball. Dust the dough with flour and chill it, wrapped in wax paper, for 1 hour.

Chocolate Chip Bourbon Angel Pie

1 cup graham cracker crumbs
1½ cups chopped pecans, toasted lightly
  and cooled
1 cup plus 2 tablespoons semisweet
  chocolate chips
1½ teaspoons double-acting baking powder
5 large egg whites at room temperature
1 cup superfine sugar
1½ tablespoons bourbon

In a bowl toss together the graham cracker crumbs, the pecans, 1 cup of the chocolate chips, and the baking powder until the mixture is combined well. In a large bowl with an electric mixer beat the whites until they are foamy, beat in the sugar, a little at a time, and beat in 1 tablespoon of the bourbon. Beat the meringue until it holds stiff glossy peaks, sprinkle the crumb mixture over it, and fold the crumb mixture into the meringue gently but thoroughly. Spoon the meringue mixture into a buttered and floured 10-inch (6-cup) glass pie plate, bake it in the middle of a preheated 325° F. oven for 30 minutes for a soft meringue or for 50 minutes for a crisp meringue, and transfer it in the plate to a rack.

In a small heavy saucepan combine the remaining 2 tablespoons chocolate chips, the remaining ½ tablespoon bourbon, and 1 teaspoon water and heat the mixture over moderately low heat, whisking, until the chocolate is melted. Make a cone out of wax paper or parchment paper, leaving a hole as small as possible at the narrow end, transfer the chocolate mixture to the cone, and pipe it decoratively over the pie. Let the pie cool completely. *The pie may be made 6 hours in advance and kept at room temperature.*

Cherry Pecan Strudel

½ cup cherry preserves
2 tablespoons Cognac or other brandy,
  or to taste
1½ cups (about 6 ounces) pecans
½ cup firmly packed light brown sugar
½ teaspoon salt
5 cups (about 1⅔ pounds) dark sweet cherries,
  pitted
2 teaspoons freshly grated lemon rind
1½ tablespoons fresh lemon juice
6 sheets of *phyllo* (each approximately 17 by
  12 inches), stacked between 2 sheets of
  wax paper and covered with a dampened
  kitchen towel
1 stick (½ cup) unsalted butter, melted
⅓ cup fine dry bread crumbs
sifted confectioners' sugar for sprinkling over
  the strudel
vanilla ice cream or whipped cream as an
  accompaniment

In a small saucepan heat the preserves with the Cognac over moderately low heat, stirring, until the mixture is heated through and remove the pan from the heat. In a food processor grind fine the pecans with the brown sugar and the salt and in a large bowl stir together the cherries, 1⅓ cups of the pecan mixture, the rind, and the lemon juice. Arrange 1 sheet of the *phyllo* on a large kitchen towel with a long side facing you, brush it lightly with some of the butter, and sprinkle it with about 1 tablespoon of the remaining pecan mixture. Over the mixture layer the remaining *phyllo* with some of the remaining butter and pecan mixture in the same manner, brushing the top sheet with some of the butter. Spread the preserves mixture evenly over the *phyllo*, leaving a 1-inch border. In a bowl stir together the remaining ⅓ cup pecan mixture and the bread crumbs and sprinkle the mixture over the preserves mixture. Spoon the cherry mixture lengthwise across the bottom third of the *phyllo*, fold in the sides of the *phyllo*, and brush them with some of the remaining butter. Using the towel as a guide, roll up the strudel tightly lengthwise, enclosing the filling, transfer it carefully, seam side down, to a lightly buttered jelly-roll pan, and brush it with the remaining butter. Bake the strudel in the middle of a preheated 375° F. oven for 35 to 40 minutes, or until it is golden. (Some of the juices may run onto the pan.) Let the strudel cool in the pan on a rack for 15 minutes, sprinkle it with the confectioners' sugar, and serve it warm or at room temperature with the ice cream.

Mincemeat Pecan Strudels

½ cup bottled mincemeat
¼ cup finely chopped pecans
2 teaspoons freshly grated orange rind
four 16- by 12-inch sheets of *phyllo*, stacked
    between 2 sheets of wax paper and covered
    with a dampened kitchen towel
3 tablespoons unsalted butter, melted
    and cooled
vanilla ice cream as an accompaniment

In a small bowl stir together the mincemeat, the pecans, and the rind. Lay 1 sheet of the *phyllo*, a long side facing you, on a work surface and brush it lightly with some of the butter. Lay another sheet of the *phyllo* over the first sheet and brush it lightly with some of the remaining butter. With a sharp knife halve the sheets lengthwise, forming 2 strips, each approximately 16 by 6 inches. Put one fourth of the filling on an end of each strip, fold in the long sides, and roll up the strudels jelly-roll fashion. Make 2 more strudels in the same manner with the remaining *phyllo* and filling. Put the strudels, seam sides down, on a baking sheet, brush them with the remaining butter, and bake them in the lower third of a preheated 400° F. oven for 20 minutes, or until they are golden and crisp. Serve the strudels with the ice cream. Makes 4 individual strudels, serving 2.

Banana Pineapple Custard Tart

1 recipe *pâte brisée* (page 248)
raw rice for weighting the shell
⅓ cup sugar
2 large whole eggs
2 large egg yolks
3 tablespoons cornstarch
2 cups milk
½ cup well drained canned crushed pineapple
    packed in syrup, reserving the syrup
6 ripe bananas
1 cup apricot jam

Roll out the *pâte brisée* ⅛ inch thick on a lightly floured surface and fit it into a 9-inch tart pan with a removable fluted rim. Trim off the excess dough, leaving a ½-inch overhang, fold the overhang inward onto the sides of the shell, pressing it firmly against the rim of the pan, and chill the shell for 30 minutes. Line the shell with foil, fill the foil three fourths full with the rice, and bake the shell in the middle of a preheated 425° F. oven for 10 minutes. Remove the rice and foil carefully and bake the shell for 5 to 6 minutes more, or until it is golden. Let the shell cool for 1 minute and remove it from the pan carefully with a spatula. Transfer the shell to a rack, let it cool on the rack, and transfer it to a platter.

In a bowl whisk together the sugar, the whole eggs, the yolks, and the cornstarch until the mixture is combined well and add the milk, scalded, in a stream, stirring with the whisk. In a saucepan bring the custard to a boil over moderate heat, stirring with the whisk, and boil it, whisking, for 2 minutes. Strain the custard through a fine sieve into a bowl set in a larger bowl of ice and cold water. Stir the custard until it is cold, stir in the pineapple until the mixture is combined well, and chill the custard, its surface covered with plastic wrap.

Slice the bananas thin and arrange half of them in the shell, overlapping them. Spread the custard carefully and evenly over the bananas and arrange the remaining bananas over it, overlapping them. In a small saucepan heat the jam over moderate heat, stirring, until it is melted, strain it through a fine sieve into a small bowl, and thin it with some of the reserved pineapple syrup if necessary. Brush the bananas with the jam and chill the tart, covered loosely, for up to 1 hour.

Cranberry Walnut Tart

For the shell
1⅓ cups all-purpose flour
2 tablespoons sugar
¼ teaspoon salt
1 stick (½ cup) cold unsalted butter,
  cut into bits
1 large egg yolk, beaten with 1½ tablespoons
  ice water
raw rice for weighting the shell

For the filling
3 large eggs
⅔ cup firmly packed dark brown sugar
⅔ cup light corn syrup
½ stick (¼ cup) unsalted butter,
  melted and cooled
½ teaspoon salt
1 teaspoon vanilla
1¼ cups chopped cranberries
1 cup chopped walnuts

Make the shell: In a bowl stir together the flour, the sugar, and the salt, add the butter, and blend the mixture until it resembles coarse meal. Add the yolk mixture, toss the mixture until the liquid is incorporated, and form the dough into a ball. Dust the dough with flour and chill it, wrapped in plastic wrap, for 1 hour. Roll out the dough ⅛ inch thick on a floured surface, fit it into a 10- or 11-inch round tart pan with a removable fluted rim, and chill the shell for 30 minutes. Line the shell with foil, fill the foil with the rice, and bake the shell in the lower third of a preheated 425° F. oven for 15 minutes. Remove the foil and rice carefully and bake the shell for 5 to 10 minutes more, or until it is pale golden. Transfer the shell in the pan to a rack and let it cool completely.

Make the filling: In a bowl whisk together the eggs, the brown sugar, the syrup, the butter, the salt, and the vanilla until the mixture is smooth. Add the cranberries and the walnuts and combine the filling gently but thoroughly.

Pour the filling into the shell, bake the tart in the middle of a preheated 350° F. oven for 40 to 45 minutes, or until it is golden, and let it cool completely on a rack. *The cranberry walnut tart may be made 1 day in advance and kept, covered, at room temperature.* Remove the rim of the pan and slide the tart onto a serving plate.

Sour Cream Nectarine Tart

For the shell
1⅓ cups all-purpose flour
2 tablespoons sugar
½ teaspoon salt
¼ teaspoon cinnamon
1 stick (½ cup) cold unsalted butter,
  cut into bits

For the filling
5 cups peeled and thinly sliced ripe nectarines
  (about 2 pounds)
2 tablespoons fresh lemon juice
¾ cup sour cream
½ cup firmly packed light brown sugar
1 large egg
½ teaspoon salt
1 teaspoon vanilla
2 tablespoons all-purpose flour

For the topping
2 tablespoons unsalted butter, softened
2 tablespoons firmly packed light brown sugar
2 tablespoons all-purpose flour
½ teaspoon cinnamon
½ cup finely chopped walnuts, pecans, or
  almonds

whipped cream as an accompaniment
  if desired

Make the shell: In a bowl stir together the flour, the sugar, the salt, and the cinnamon, add the butter, and blend the mixture until it resembles meal. Tossing the mixture with a fork, add 1½ tablespoons ice water, or enough ice water to form the mixture into a soft dough. With well floured hands press the dough evenly onto the bottom and up the side of a 9-inch tart pan with a removable fluted rim and chill the shell for 30 minutes.

Make the filling: In a large bowl toss together the nectarines and the lemon juice. In a small bowl whisk together the sour cream and the brown sugar until the mixture is smooth and whisk in the egg, the salt, the vanilla, and the flour until the mixture is combined well. Pour the sour cream mixture over the nectarines and stir the filling until it is combined.

Make the topping: In a small bowl with a fork cream together the butter, the brown sugar, the flour, and the cinnamon, add the nuts, and stir the topping until it is combined well.

Transfer the filling to the shell, smoothing the top,

distribute the topping evenly over it, and bake the tart in the lower third of a preheated 425° F. oven for 25 minutes. Reduce the heat to 350° F. and bake the tart for 20 to 30 minutes more, or until the topping is golden and the filling is slightly puffed. Let the tart cool on a rack and serve it with the whipped cream.

Strawberry and Frangipane Tart

a double recipe *pâte brisée* (page 248)
raw rice for weighting the shell
3½ ounces (1 cup) blanched almonds
⅔ cup sugar
2 large eggs, beaten lightly
⅛ teaspoon almond extract
1½ pints strawberries, hulled and halved
   lengthwise
½ cup strawberry jelly

Roll the *pâte brisée* dough into a ⅛-inch-thick rectangle on a floured surface, fit it into a 14- by 4½-inch rectangular flan form set on a baking sheet, and fold over the edges, crimping them decoratively. Prick the bottom of the shell lightly with a fork and chill the shell for 30 minutes. Line the shell with wax paper, fill the paper with the rice, pressing the rice against the sides for support, and bake the shell in the lower third of a preheated 425° F. oven for 15 minutes. Remove the rice and wax paper carefully, bake the shell for 5 minutes more, or until it is pale golden, and let it cool in the flan form on the baking sheet.

In a food processor blend the almonds and the sugar until a powder is formed, add the eggs and the almond extract, and blend the mixture until it is combined well. Spoon the frangipane (it will be very thick) into the shell, spread it carefully over the bottom, and bake the shell in the lower third of a preheated 375° F. oven for 20 minutes, or until the frangipane is puffed and golden.

Let the shell cool completely in the flan form on the baking sheet on a rack, making sure the frangipane is also cooled completely, remove the flan form carefully, and transfer the shell to a rectangular platter. Arrange the strawberries decoratively over the frangipane, brush them with the jelly, melted and still slightly warm, and let the jelly glaze cool completely.

Walnut Ginger Tart

pâte brisée (page 248)
a 1-pound box of light brown sugar
½ cup loosely packed finely chopped peeled
   fresh gingerroot
4 large eggs, beaten lightly
2 tablespoons heavy cream
1 teaspoon vanilla
¼ teaspoon salt
1 stick (½ cup) unsalted butter, melted
1½ cups coarsely chopped walnuts
vanilla ice cream or whipped cream as
   an accompaniment

Roll out the dough ⅛ inch thick on a lightly floured surface and fit it into a 9-inch tart pan with a removable fluted rim. Trim the edge, leaving a ½-inch overhang, fold the overhang inward onto the side of the shell, pressing it firmly to extend the height of the rim by ¼ inch, and chill the shell for 1 hour. In a bowl combine well the brown sugar, the gingerroot, the eggs, the cream, the vanilla, and the salt, add the butter in a stream, whisking, and whisk the mixture until it is combined well. Sprinkle the walnuts over the bottom of the shell, pour the mixture into the shell, and bake the tart in the middle of a preheated 325° F. oven for 1 hour, or until the filling is puffed and just set. Let the tart cool completely in the pan on a rack and serve it with ice cream.

Plum Tarts

1 stick (½ cup) unsalted butter,
    softened
½ cup vegetable shortening
⅔ cup sugar plus additional for sprinkling
    the tarts
2 teaspoons vanilla
2 teaspoons freshly grated lemon rind
2 teaspoons fresh lemon juice
1 teaspoon salt
1 large whole egg
1 large egg yolk
2⅔ cups all-purpose flour
¾ cup currant jelly, melted and
    cooled slightly
8 firm-ripe red and/or purple plums (about
    1¾ pounds), halved, pitted, and each half
    sliced thin into rounds
1 cup well chilled heavy cream
raspberry brandy or *crème de cassis* to taste
    if desired

In a bowl with an electric mixer cream the butter and the shortening with ⅔ cup of the sugar, the vanilla, the rind, the lemon juice, and the salt until the mixture is light and fluffy, beat in the whole egg and the yolk, and beat the mixture until it is smooth. Add the flour, stir the mixture until it just forms a dough, and on plastic wrap pat the dough into a rectangle. Chill the dough, wrapped well, for 1 hour. Turn the dough onto a 17- by 14-inch baking sheet, discard the plastic wrap, and dust the dough with flour. Roll out the dough to cover the baking sheet, leaving a slight overhang on the long sides. (The dough will be like soft cookie dough.) Halve the dough lengthwise with a sharp knife, forming 2 rectangles, and brush each rectangle with ¼ cup of the jelly, leaving a 1-inch border on the long sides. Arrange the plums, overlapping them decoratively, on the jelly, fold the long sides of the dough with a spatula or pastry scraper up to the edge of the plums, and crimp the edges decoratively. Sprinkle the tarts with the additional sugar and bake them in a preheated 375° F. oven for 30 to 35 minutes, or until the crust is golden brown. Brush the plums with the remaining ¼ cup jelly and let the tarts cool. In a chilled large bowl beat the cream with the brandy until it just holds stiff peaks and serve it in a small serving bowl with the tarts.

PHOTO ON PAGE 61

CUSTARDS, MOUSSES, AND PUDDINGS

Crème Caramel with Sautéed Apples

⅓ cup plus ½ cup sugar plus additional for
    sprinkling the apples
3 large whole eggs
3 large egg yolks
3 tablespoons Calvados or applejack
2¼ cups milk
¾ cup heavy cream
1 red Delicious apple
1 yellow Delicious apple
1 Granny Smith apple
2 tablespoons unsalted butter

In a small heavy saucepan dissolve ⅓ cup of the sugar in 2 tablespoons water over moderate heat, stirring, bring the syrup to a boil, and boil it, undisturbed, until it begins to turn golden. Boil the syrup, swirling the pan, until it is a deep caramel and pour it immediately into a 4- to 5-cup ring mold. Swirl the mold to coat the side slightly, set the mold in a large baking pan, and let the caramel harden. In a large bowl whisk together well the whole eggs, the yolks, ½ cup of the remaining sugar, the Calvados, and a pinch of salt. In a saucepan scald the milk and the cream, add the mixture to the egg mixture in a stream, whisking, and strain the mixture through a fine sieve into the mold. Cover the mold with a piece of foil, transfer the baking pan with the mold to the middle of a preheated 325° F. oven, and add enough hot water to the pan to reach halfway up the side of the mold. Bake the *crème caramel* for 45 minutes, or until it is just set. Remove the mold from the pan, remove the foil, and let the *crème caramel* cool in the mold on a rack. Chill the *crème caramel* for 1 hour. *The crème caramel can be made 1 day in advance and kept covered and chilled.*

Quarter the apples, core them, and cut each quarter lengthwise into 4 slices. In a large heavy skillet (preferably non-stick) heat 2 teaspoons of the butter over moderately high heat until the foam subsides and in it cook some of the apple slices in one layer without crowding them for 2 minutes on each side, or until they are golden. Transfer the apples to a plate and sprinkle them with some of the additional sugar. Wipe out the skillet and sauté the remaining apples in the remaining butter in batches in the same manner, wiping out the skillet after each batch. *The apples may be made 4 hours in advance and kept at room temperature. Reheat the apples in a preheated 300° F. oven until they are warm before serving.*

Dip the *crème caramel* mold in hot water for 30 seconds and run a thin knife around the side and center of the mold. Invert a platter over the mold and invert the *crème caramel* onto it. Arrange some of the apples around the *crème caramel* and serve the remaining apples separately. Serves 4 to 6.

PHOTO ON PAGE 74

Oeufs à la Neige à l'Orange
(Poached Meringue Eggs with Orange Custard Sauce)

6 large eggs, separated, the whites at room
    temperature
⅓ cup granulated sugar
2 cups half-and-half or whole milk
four 3- by ¾-inch strips of orange rind,
    removed with a vegetable peeler
⅓ cup plus 1 tablespoon orange-flavored
    liqueur
¼ teaspoon cream of tartar
2 cups confectioners' sugar

In a heavy saucepan whisk together the yolks and the granulated sugar, add the half-and-half, scalded with the rind, in a slow stream, whisking, and cook the mixture over moderately low heat, stirring constantly with a wooden spoon, until it is thickened (175° F. on a candy thermometer), but do not let it boil. Remove the pan from the heat and stir in 1 tablespoon of the liqueur. Strain the custard sauce through a fine sieve into a metal bowl set in a bowl of ice and cold water, reserving the rind, let it cool, stirring, and chill it, covered, for 1 hour, or until it is cold. *The custard sauce may be made 2 days in advance and kept covered and chilled.*

In a bowl with an electric mixer beat the whites with the cream of tartar until they hold soft peaks, beat in the confectioners' sugar, a little at a time, and beat the meringue until it holds stiff, glossy peaks. In a 10-inch straight-sided skillet heat 2 inches of water until it reaches 175° F. on a candy thermometer. Dip an oval ice-cream scoop into hot water, scoop it into the meringue, and smooth the top, rounding it, with a moistened finger. Drop the meringue egg into the skillet of heated water, form 7 more eggs, dropping them in the heated water, and poach the meringue eggs for 2 min-

utes. Turn the meringue eggs with a slotted spoon, poach them for 2 minutes more, and transfer them with the slotted spoon to a triple thickness of paper towels to drain. Form and poach meringue eggs in batches with the remaining mixture in the same manner.

Rinse the reserved rind under cold water, pat it dry, and cut it into fine shreds. In a small saucepan combine the remaining ⅓ cup orange-flavored liqueur and the rind, bring the liqueur to a boil over moderately high heat, and simmer the rind, stirring occasionally, until the liqueur is nearly evaporated and the rind is candied (it will be nearly translucent).

Pour half the custard sauce into a footed compote, arrange the meringue eggs on the sauce, and top them with the candied rind. Serve the dessert with the remaining sauce. Serves 8.

PHOTO ON PAGE 31

Soft Orange Custards

2 large whole eggs
1 large egg yolk
¼ cup sugar
½ teaspoon grated orange rind
1½ teaspoons orange-flavored liqueur
⅔ cup heavy cream
⅔ cup milk

In a bowl whisk together the whole eggs, the egg yolk, the sugar, the rind, and the liqueur. In a 2-cup glass measuring cup combine the cream and the milk, microwave the mixture at high power (100%) for 1 minute and 30 seconds, and add it in a stream to the egg mixture, whisking. Divide the mixture among four ⅔-cup ceramic ramekins, arrange the ramekins 1 inch apart in the microwave oven, and microwave the custards at low power (20%), rotating them every 2 minutes, for 20 to 22 minutes, or until they are almost set on top. Let the custards cool on a rack, covered with a kitchen towel, for 5 minutes and chill them in a shallow dish of ice and cold water for 10 minutes. (The additional custards may be kept, covered and chilled, overnight.) Serves 2.

Cold Vanilla-Rum Zabaglione with Fruit

1 vanilla bean,
  split lengthwise
½ cup plus 2 tablespoons dark rum
1 envelope unflavored gelatin
6 large egg yolks
¼ cup plus 1 tablespoon sugar
1 cup heavy cream
1 cup raspberries
1 cup seedless green grapes,
  halved
1 cantaloupe, seeds discarded and the flesh
  scooped into balls with a melon-ball cutter
  (about 1½ cups)

In a small bowl let the vanilla bean soak in ½ cup of the rum for 20 minutes, scrape the seeds from the bean into the rum, and reserve the pod for another use (such as vanilla sugar) if desired. In a small saucepan combine the remaining 2 tablespoons rum with 2 tablespoons water, sprinkle the gelatin over the mixture, and let it soften while preparing the zabaglione. In a large heatproof bowl with an electric mixer beat the yolks, beat in the sugar and a pinch of salt, and beat the mixture until it is very thick and pale. Set the bowl over a saucepan of simmering water and beat the mixture for 1 minute. Add the vanilla-flavored rum in a slow stream, beating constantly, and beat the mixture at high speed for 7 to 10 minutes, or until it is very light and thickened and the beater leaves a pattern in its wake. Remove the bowl from the pan and beat the mixture for 1 minute more.

Heat the gelatin mixture over moderately low heat, stirring, until the gelatin is dissolved and beat it into the vanilla-rum mixture, beating until the mixture is combined well. In a chilled bowl with the beaters, cleaned, beat the cream until it barely holds stiff peaks and fold in the vanilla-rum mixture gently but thoroughly. Pour the zabaglione into a 1-quart decorative mold, rinsed in cold water but not dried, and chill it, covered, for at least 3 hours or overnight. Dip the mold into a larger bowl of warm water for 20 seconds and invert the zabaglione carefully onto a chilled serving plate. In a bowl toss together the raspberries, the grapes, and the cantaloupe and spoon the fruit in the center and decoratively around the edge of the zabaglione. Serves 6.

PHOTO ON PAGE 62

Lemon Gin Mousse

2 large eggs, separated, the whites
  at room temperature
3 tablespoons sugar
2 tablespoons fresh lemon juice
2 teaspoons freshly grated lemon rind
1 tablespoon gin
⅓ cup well chilled heavy cream

In a bowl with an electric mixer beat the yolks and 2 tablespoons of the sugar for 5 minutes, or until the mixture is very thick and pale, beat in the lemon juice, the rind, and the gin, and beat the mixture for 3 minutes. In another bowl with clean beaters beat the whites with a pinch of salt until they hold soft peaks, beat in the remaining 1 tablespoon sugar, and beat the whites until they just hold stiff peaks. Add the whites to the yolk mixture. In the egg-white bowl beat the cream until it just holds stiff peaks. Fold the whites into the yolk mixture and fold in the whipped cream gently but thoroughly. Spoon the mousse into 2 chilled stemmed glasses. *The mousse may be made 45 minutes in advance and kept chilled.* (The mousse will separate as it stands.) Serves 2.

Mango Lime Mousse with Raspberry Sauce

For the mousse
1 envelope unflavored gelatin
¼ cup fresh lime juice
2 mangoes (about 3½ pounds),
  peeled and pitted
¼ cup sugar
½ cup heavy cream
For the sauce
2 cups red raspberries
2 tablespoons fresh lime juice
¼ cup sugar

1 cup red raspberries for garnish
1 cup golden raspberries for garnish

Make the mousse: In a small saucepan sprinkle the gelatin over the lime juice, let it soften for 5 minutes, and heat the mixture over moderately low heat, stirring, until the gelatin is dissolved. In a food processor purée the mangoes with the sugar and the cream, add the gelatin mixture, and blend the mixture well. Pour the mousse into an 8-inch round cake pan that has been rinsed in cold water but not dried and chill it, covered, for 4 to 6 hours, or until it is set.

Make the sauce: In a blender or food processor purée the raspberries with the lime juice and the sugar until the sauce is smooth and force the sauce through a fine sieve into a serving bowl.

Run a thin knife around the edge of the mousse, dip the pan into a larger pan of warm water for 15 seconds, and invert the mousse onto a chilled serving plate. Garnish the mousse with the raspberries and serve it, cut into wedges, with the sauce. Serves 6.

PHOTO ON PAGE 49

Bittersweet Chocolate and White Chocolate Pecan Mousse Swirl

For the bittersweet chocolate mixture
12 ounces fine-quality bittersweet chocolate,
  broken into pieces
¾ cup heavy cream
For the white chocolate pecan mixture
8 ounces fine-quality white chocolate, broken
  into pieces
½ cup heavy cream
1 teaspoon unflavored gelatin
⅔ cup pecans, chopped fine and toasted
  lightly

2¾ cups well chilled heavy cream
¼ cup sugar
3 ounces fine-quality white chocolate at room
  temperature (about 72° F.), shaved with a
  vegetable peeler into curls and chilled,
  covered loosely, for garnish

Make the bittersweet chocolate mixture: In a metal bowl set over barely simmering water melt the chocolate with the cream and ¼ cup water, stirring occasionally, until the mixture is smooth, remove the bowl from over the pan of hot water, and let the chocolate mixture cool to room temperature.

Make the white chocolate pecan mixture: In a large metal bowl set over barely simmering water melt the chocolate with the cream, stirring occasionally, until the mixture is smooth and remove the pan from the heat, keeping the bowl set over the hot water. In a small bowl sprinkle the gelatin over 2 tablespoons cold water, let it soften for 5 minutes, and stir the mixture into the chocolate mixture, stirring until the gelatin is dissolved. Re-move the bowl from over the pan of hot water, stir in the pecans, and let the white chocolate pecan mixture cool to room temperature.

While the white chocolate pecan mixture is cooling, in a chilled large bowl with an electric mixer beat 1¾ cups of the cream until it begins to thicken, beat in the sugar, and beat the cream until it holds soft peaks. Stir one fourth of the whipped cream into the cooled bittersweet chocolate mixture and fold in the remaining whipped cream gently but thoroughly. In a chilled large bowl with the electric mixer beat the remaining 1 cup cream until it holds soft peaks, stir one fourth of the whipped cream into the cooled white chocolate pecan mixture, and fold in the remaining whipped cream gently but thoroughly.

Spoon the mousses in layers into 12 goblets, beginning and ending with the bittersweet chocolate mousse. Chill the mousses, covered loosely, for at least 2 hours or overnight and garnish them with the white chocolate curls. Serves 12.

PHOTO ON PAGE 10

Strawberry Meringue Mousse

two 3½-inch rounds of pound cake, each
  about ½ inch thick
1 cup finely chopped strawberries
3 large egg whites
a pinch of cream of tartar
⅓ cup sugar

Fit the pound-cake rounds into the bottoms of two 1-cup flameproof ramekins. In a food processor purée ½ cup of the strawberries and in a small bowl combine the purée with the remaining ½ cup strawberries. In a bowl beat the whites with the cream of tartar and a pinch of salt until the mixture is foamy, add the sugar, a little at a time, beating, and beat the meringue until it just holds stiff peaks. Fold one third of the meringue into the strawberry mixture thoroughly and divide the mixture between the ramekins. Divide the remaining meringue between the ramekins, covering the strawberry mixture completely, and broil the mousses under a preheated broiler about 3 inches from the heat for 1 to 2 minutes, or until the meringue is golden. Serves 2.

Spiced Apple Pudding

2 cups apple juice
1 tablespoon cornstarch
½ cup milk
1 whole large egg
1 large egg yolk
1 tablespoon plus 1½ teaspoons sugar
⅛ teaspoon allspice
½ cup heavy cream
¼ teaspoon cinnamon

In a saucepan bring the juice to a boil and boil it until it is reduced to about 3 tablespoons. In a bowl dissolve the cornstarch in 2 tablespoons of the milk, add the whole egg, the yolk, 1 tablespoon of the sugar, the allspice, and a pinch of salt, and whisk the mixture until it is combined well. In another saucepan scald the cream and the remaining milk, add the mixture to the egg mixture in a stream, whisking, and whisk in the reduced apple juice. Bring the mixture to a boil over moderate heat, whisking constantly, and boil it, whisking, for 3 minutes. Transfer the pudding to a metal bowl set in a bowl of ice and cold water, stir it until it is thickened and cold, and divide it between 2 custard cups. In another bowl stir together the remaining 1½ teaspoons sugar and the cinnamon and sprinkle the mixture over the pudding. Serves 2.

Prune Batter Pudding

¾ cup (about 6 ounces) pitted prunes, chopped coarse
⅓ cup Armagnac or other brandy
½ cup all-purpose flour
1 tablespoon granulated sugar
3 large eggs, beaten lightly
½ cup milk
½ teaspoon vanilla
3 tablespoons unsalted butter, cut into pieces
confectioners' sugar for sifting over the pudding
crème fraîche (available at specialty foods shops and some supermarkets) or vanilla ice cream as an accompaniment

In a small bowl let the prunes macerate in the Armagnac, covered, for at least 20 minutes and up to 2 hours. Into a bowl sift together the flour, the granulated sugar, and a pinch of salt, add the eggs, and whisk the mixture

until it is smooth. Add the milk and the vanilla, whisk the batter until it is combined well, and stir in the prune mixture. In a 12-inch straight-sided heavy skillet (or a 13- by 9-inch baking dish) heat the butter in the middle of a preheated 425° F. oven until it is sizzling but do not let it brown. Pour the batter into the skillet, distributing the prunes evenly, and bake the pudding in the 425° F. oven for 15 to 20 minutes, or until it is puffed and golden. Sift the confectioners' sugar over the hot pudding and serve the pudding with the *crème fraîche*. Serves 6.

Vanilla Pudding with Summer Fruit

¼ cup sugar
2 tablespoons cornstarch
1⅓ cups milk
1 large egg yolk, beaten lightly
1 tablespoon unsalted butter
¾ teaspoon vanilla
⅛ teaspoon almond extract
1 cup blueberries, picked over, or 1 nectarine, halved, pitted, and sliced thin
whipped cream for garnish if desired

In a heavy saucepan whisk together the sugar, the cornstarch, and a pinch of salt. Whisk in the milk gradually, add the yolk, whisking, and whisk the mixture until it is combined well. Bring the mixture to a boil over moderate heat, whisking, and boil it, whisking, for 1 minute. Remove the pan from the heat and stir in the butter, the vanilla, and the almond extract. Divide the blueberries and the pudding in layers between 2 wineglasses, beginning and ending with the fruit. Chill the desserts in the refrigerator for 30 minutes for a slightly warm dessert or in the freezer for 15 minutes for a cold dessert. Garnish the desserts with the whipped cream. Serves 2.

Cold Eggedosis Soufflés with Lingonberries
(Cold Norwegian Egg Sauce Soufflés)

4 teaspoons unflavored gelatin
For the eggedosis
12 large egg yolks
⅔ cup sugar

6 large egg whites at room temperature
5 tablespoons sugar
3 tablespoons dark rum

1½ cups plus ⅓ cup well chilled heavy cream
3½ cups (about three 10-ounce jars) wild
　　lingonberries in sugar, reserving ¼ cup of
　　the lingonberries for garnish

In a very small saucepan sprinkle the gelatin over ¼ cup cold water, let it soften for 5 minutes, and heat the mixture over moderate heat, stirring, until the gelatin is dissolved. Remove the pan from the heat.

Make the *eggedosis*: In the large bowl of an electric mixer beat together the yolks, add the sugar, a little at a time, beating, and beat the *eggedosis* until it is thick and pale and the sugar is dissolved.

While the yolks are being beaten, in a large bowl with a hand-held mixer beat the whites until they hold soft peaks, beat in 3 tablespoons of the sugar, a little at a time, and beat the whites until they just hold stiff peaks. Beat in the rum and the gelatin mixture until the mixture is just combined. In another bowl beat 1½ cups of the cream until it holds soft peaks, beat in the remaining 2 tablespoons sugar, and beat the cream until it just holds stiff peaks. Stir one fourth of the whites into the *eggedosis*, fold in the remaining whites gently but thoroughly, and fold in the whipped cream gently but thoroughly. Spoon the *eggedosis* mixture and 3¼ cups of the lingonberries in alternating layers into twelve 1-cup glasses and chill the soufflés for at least 6 hours or overnight. (Alternatively the *eggedosis* mixture and the lingonberries can be layered in a 3-quart serving bowl.) In a bowl beat the remaining ⅓ cup cream until it just holds stiff peaks and with a pastry bag fitted with a decorative tip pipe the whipped cream into rosettes onto the soufflés. Pat the reserved ¼ cup berries with paper towels and garnish the soufflés with them. Serves 12.

PHOTO ON PAGE 40

FROZEN DESSERTS

Green Grape Ice

8 cups (about 3 pounds) green grapes,
　　preferably seedless
⅔ cup superfine sugar
¼ cup plus 2 tablespoons fresh lemon juice
almond thins (recipe follows) as an
　　accompaniment

Force the grapes through a food mill fitted with the medium disk into a bowl and measure the juice. In a bowl combine 3⅓ cups of the juice, reserving any remaining juice for another use if desired, with the sugar, stirring until the sugar is dissolved, and stir in the lemon juice. Set the bowl in a larger bowl of ice and cold water and stir the mixture until it is cold. Freeze the mixture in an ice-cream freezer according to the manufacturer's instructions until it is frozen but not firm. Remove the dasher and freeze the grape ice, covered, until it is firm. *The grape ice may be made up to 2 days in advance and kept covered tightly and frozen.* Serve the grape ice with the almond thins. Makes about 1½ pints.

Almond Thins

½ cup sugar
3½ tablespoons unsalted butter
2½ tablespoons honey
2½ tablespoons heavy cream
⅔ cup sliced blanched almonds

In a heavy saucepan combine the sugar, the butter, the honey, and the cream, bring the mixture to a boil over moderate heat, stirring, and boil it, stirring constantly, for 5 minutes. Stir in the almonds and let the mixture cool for 5 minutes. (The mixture will be very thin.) Spoon heaping ½ teaspoons of the mixture 3 inches apart on baking sheets lined with parchment paper and bake the cookies in the middle of a preheated 400° F. oven for 8 minutes, or until they are golden brown and bubbly. (The cookies will look runny and not done at this point but will continue to cook as they cool.) Set the baking sheets on racks, let the cookies cool completely, and peel off the parchment paper gently. Makes about 40 cookies.

Chocolate Cherry Ice Cream

6 cups (about 2 pounds) dark sweet cherries,
   pitted
¾ cup sugar
¼ cup fresh lemon juice
2 tablespoons kirsch
2 cups heavy cream
1 cup milk
6 large egg yolks
3 tablespoons unsweetened cocoa powder
1 teaspoon vanilla
4 ounces fine-quality bittersweet or semisweet
   chocolate, chopped

In a saucepan combine 3 cups of the cherries, ¼ cup of the sugar, and the lemon juice, bring the mixture to a boil, and simmer it, covered, for 5 minutes. Simmer the mixture, uncovered, stirring occasionally, for 10 to 15 minutes, or until most of the liquid has evaporated and the mixture is very thick, and in a food processor purée it with the kirsch. In a heavy saucepan combine the cream and the milk and bring the mixture just to a boil. In a bowl whisk together the yolks, the remaining ½ cup sugar, the cocoa powder, sifted, and a pinch of salt until the mixture is combined well, add the cream mixture in a stream, whisking, and transfer the mixture to the heavy pan. Cook the mixture over moderately low heat, stirring constantly with a wooden spoon, until it coats the spoon (175° F. on a candy thermometer), strain the custard through a fine sieve into a metal bowl, and whisk in the cherry purée and the vanilla. Set the metal bowl in a larger bowl of ice and cold water and let the cherry custard cool completely, stirring occasionally. Freeze the cherry custard in an ice-cream freezer according to the manufacturer's instructions until the ice cream is almost firm, add the remaining 3 cups cherries, chopped coarse, and the chocolate, and freeze the ice cream until it is firm. Makes about 2 quarts.

Cinnamon Ice Cream

2 cups heavy cream
2 cups milk
four 3- to 4-inch cinnamon sticks, halved
8 large egg yolks
⅔ cup sugar
¾ teaspoon vanilla
1½ teaspoons ground cinnamon

In a large saucepan combine the cream, the milk, and the cinnamon sticks, bring the mixture just to a boil, and remove the pan from the heat. Let the mixture stand, covered, for 1 hour. Return the pan to the heat and bring the mixture just to a boil. In a large bowl whisk together the yolks and the sugar, add the cream mixture in a stream, whisking, and transfer the custard to the pan. Cook the custard over moderately low heat, stirring constantly with a wooden spoon, until it coats the spoon (175° F. on a candy thermometer) and strain it through a fine sieve into a bowl. Stir in the vanilla, let the custard cool, and chill it, covered, for at least 6 hours or overnight. Stir in the ground cinnamon and freeze the custard in an ice-cream freezer according to the manufacturer's instructions. Makes about 1 quart.

Mocha Chip Ice Cream

1 cup (6 ounces) miniature semisweet
   chocolate chips
3 tablespoons instant espresso powder,
   dissolved in 3 tablespoons boiling water
2 large eggs
½ cup sugar
1 teaspoon vanilla
1 cup milk
1 cup heavy cream

In a bowl set over barely simmering water melt ½ cup of the chocolate chips with the espresso mixture, stirring occasionally, remove the bowl from the heat, and let the mixture cool. In a large bowl with an electric mixer beat the eggs with the sugar and a pinch of salt until the mixture is very thick and pale, beat in the vanilla and the chocolate mixture, and whisk in the milk and the cream until the mixture is combined well. Freeze the mixture in an ice-cream freezer according to the manufacturer's instructions until the ice cream is almost firm, stir in the remaining ½ cup chocolate chips, and freeze the ice cream until it is firm. Makes about 1 quart.

Coconut Parfaits

1½ cups milk
½ cup heavy cream
2 large eggs, beaten lightly
1 cup canned cream of coconut

3 tablespoons coconut-flavored rum if desired
1 cup sweetened flaked coconut, toasted
    lightly

In a heavy saucepan scald the milk with the cream and in a bowl add the mixture in a slow stream to the eggs, whisking. Transfer the mixture to the pan and cook it over moderately low heat, stirring constantly with a wooden spoon, until it is thickened (175° F. on a candy thermometer), but do not let it boil. Remove the pan from the heat, strain the custard through a fine sieve into a metal bowl set in a larger bowl of ice and cold water, and stir in the cream of coconut and the coconut-flavored rum. Let the custard cool, stirring occasionally, until it is cold and freeze it in an ice-cream freezer according to the manufacturer's instructions. Transfer the ice cream to a freezer container and freeze it until it is firm. *The ice cream may be made 1 week in advance and kept frozen.* Scoop the ice cream with a small scoop into 4 parfait glasses, sprinkling each scoop with some of the toasted coconut. Serves 4.

Blood Orange Sorbet

2 ounces sugar cubes (about thirty ½-inch
    cubes)
2¼ pounds blood oranges
1 tablespoon fresh lemon juice
For the rind garnish
strips of blood orange rind, removed with a
    channel knife
1 large egg white, beaten lightly
sugar for coating the rind
fresh mint sprigs for garnish if desired

Rub the sugar cubes over the surface of all but 2 of the oranges until each cube is slightly orange colored and using the fine side of a grater, grate the rind from the remaining 2 oranges, being careful not to grate the pith. Squeeze enough of the oranges to yield 2 cups juice. In a saucepan combine 1 cup of the juice and the sugar cubes and heat the mixture over moderately low heat, stirring, until the sugar is just dissolved. Transfer the mixture to a bowl, stir in the remaining 1 cup orange juice, the lemon juice, and the grated rind, and chill the mixture, covered loosely, until it is cold. Freeze the mixture in an ice-cream freezer according to the manufacturer's instructions.

Make the rind garnish while the mixture is freezing: Roll up the rind tightly into spirals and bake it on a baking sheet in a preheated 400° F. oven for 5 minutes. Brush the spirals lightly with the egg white, dip them lightly in the sugar, and bake them for 5 minutes in the 400° F. oven. Let the spirals cool and form them into decorative shapes.

With a small ice-cream scoop, scoop the *sorbet* into bowls and garnish it with the rind and the mint. Makes about 2 cups.

Nectarine Sorbet with Strawberry Nectarine Sauce

¾ cup sugar
2½ pounds ripe nectarines, pitted and
    chopped, plus nectarine slices for garnish
¼ cup fresh lemon juice, or to taste
1 to 2 tablespoons dark rum, or to taste
strawberry nectarine sauce (page 260)
    as an accompaniment
hulled and halved strawberries for garnish
mint sprigs for garnish

In a heavy saucepan combine the sugar and ⅔ cup water, bring the mixture to a boil, stirring until the sugar is dissolved, and boil it for 2 minutes. Remove the syrup from the heat and let it cool completely. In a food processor or blender purée the chopped nectarines with the lemon juice until the mixture is smooth, force the purée through a fine sieve set over a bowl, pressing hard on the solids (there should be about 3 cups purée), and stir in the syrup and the rum. Freeze the mixture in an ice-cream freezer according to the manufacturer's instructions, pack the *sorbet* into airtight containers, and freeze it until it is firm. (Makes about 1 quart.)

On each of 6 dessert plates pour some of the sauce, arrange 2 scoops of the *sorbet* on it, and garnish the plates with the nectarine slices, the strawberries, and the mint. Serves 6.

PHOTO ON FRONTISPIECE

Strawberry Nectarine Sauce

1 pint strawberries, hulled and chopped
1 pound ripe nectarines, pitted and chopped
2 tablespoons fresh lemon juice plus
    additional to taste
2 to 3 tablespoons superfine sugar, or to taste

In a food processor or blender purée the strawberries and the nectarines with 2 tablespoons of the lemon juice until the mixture is smooth, force the purée through a fine sieve set over a bowl, pressing hard on the solids, and stir in the sugar and the additional lemon juice. *The sauce may be made 1 day in advance and kept covered and chilled.* Makes about 2½ cups.

PHOTO ON FRONTISPIECE

Rosé Sorbet

2½ cups medium-dry rosé wine
1 cup sugar
2 tablespoons fresh lemon juice, or to taste
4 mint sprigs for garnish if desired

In a saucepan bring the wine to a boil, simmer it for 5 minutes, and pour it into a metal bowl set in a larger bowl of ice and cold water. In the pan combine the sugar and 1 cup water, bring the mixture to a boil, stirring until the sugar is dissolved, and stir the syrup into the wine. Let the mixture stand, stirring occasionally, until it is cold, stir in the lemon juice, and freeze the mixture in an ice-cream freezer according to the manufacturer's instructions. Transfer the *sorbet* to a freezer container and freeze it until it is firm. *The* sorbet *may be made 1 week in advance and kept frozen.* Scoop the *sorbet* with a small scoop into 4 parfait glasses and garnish each serving with a mint sprig. Serves 4.

Frozen Walnut Rum Soufflé with Cranberry Sauce
For the soufflé
4 large egg whites at room temperature
½ cup sugar
1 cup well chilled heavy cream
2 to 4 tablespoons dark rum, or to taste
1½ cups walnuts, toasted lightly, cooled, and
    chopped coarse
For the sauce
2 cups fresh or frozen cranberries,
    picked over
1 cup sugar

Make the soufflé: Line an oiled metal loaf pan, 9 by 5 by 3 inches, with plastic wrap. In a large metal bowl set over a saucepan of simmering water stir together the egg whites and the sugar until the sugar is dissolved, remove the bowl from the pan, and with a mixer beat the whites until they just hold stiff peaks. In another bowl with the mixer beat the cream until it holds soft peaks, beat in the rum, and beat the cream until it just holds stiff peaks. Add the walnuts and the cream mixture to the whites, fold the mixture together gently but thoroughly, and spread it in the lined pan. Freeze the soufflé, covered with plastic wrap, for at least 6 hours. *The soufflé can be made 5 days in advance and kept covered and frozen.*

Make the sauce: In a saucepan combine the cranberries, the sugar, and 1 cup water, bring the mixture to a boil, stirring until the sugar is dissolved, and simmer it, stirring occasionally, for 10 to 15 minutes, or until it is thickened slightly. In a blender purée the mixture, force the purée through a fine sieve into a small bowl, and if desired thin the sauce with additional water. *The sauce can be made 5 days in advance and kept covered and chilled.*

Invert the soufflé onto a work surface and remove the plastic wrap carefully. Slice the soufflé and serve it with the sauce.

FRUIT FINALES

Broiled Ambrosia with Toasted Coconut

1 cup sweetened flaked coconut
2 grapefruits, rind and pith cut away with a
    serrated knife and the fruit cut crosswise
    into ⅓-inch-thick slices
3 navel oranges, rind and pith cut away with a
    serrated knife and the fruit cut crosswise
    into ⅓-inch-thick slices
3 tablespoons sugar, or to taste

Spread the coconut in a jelly-roll pan, bake it in the middle of a preheated 350° F. oven, stirring occasionally, for 10 to 12 minutes, or until it is golden, and transfer it to a bowl. Arrange the grapefruit slices and the orange slices in alternating rows, overlapping them, on a flameproof platter or shallow gratin dish, sprinkle the grapefruit with 2 tablespoons of the sugar, and sprinkle the orange with the remaining 1 tablespoon sugar. Broil the fruit under a preheated broiler about 2 inches from the heat for 3 to 5 minutes, or until it is hot and caramelized lightly in spots. Sprinkle the toasted coconut over the fruit. Serves 6.

Apple and Apricot Crisp

⅓ cup finely chopped dried apricots
2 tablespoons brandy
¼ cup all-purpose flour
3 tablespoons firmly packed dark brown sugar
⅛ teaspoon salt
3 tablespoons cold unsalted butter, cut into
  bits
⅓ cup old-fashioned rolled oats
2 tablespoons sliced almonds
2 Golden Delicious apples, peeled, quartered,
  cored, and sliced thin crosswise

In a small bowl let the apricots soak in the brandy for 5 minutes. In a bowl blend the flour, the brown sugar, the salt, and the butter until the mixture resembles coarse meal, add the oats and the almonds, and toss the mixture until it is combined well. In a 9-inch (4-cup) glass pie plate toss together the apples and the apricot and brandy mixture, sprinkle the oat mixture over the top, and bake the crisp in a preheated 400° F. oven for 25 minutes, or until the apples are tender and the topping is browned lightly. Serves 2 generously.

Apple, Walnut, and Coconut Crisp

4 Granny Smith apples
¼ cup fresh lemon juice
⅓ cup all-purpose flour
½ cup quick-cooking rolled oats
⅓ cup finely chopped walnuts
⅓ cup sweetened flaked coconut
⅓ cup firmly packed light brown sugar

1 teaspoon cinnamon
¼ teaspoon ground allspice
¼ teaspoon salt
½ teaspoon vanilla
⅓ cup (5⅓ tablespoons) cold unsalted butter,
  cut into bits

In a large bowl toss the apples, cored, peeled, and cut into ⅓-inch slices, with the lemon juice. Layer the apples, drained, in a well buttered 9-inch-square baking pan. In another large bowl combine well the flour, the oats, the walnuts, the coconut, the brown sugar, the cinnamon, the allspice, the salt, and the vanilla, add the butter, and blend the mixture with a fork until it resembles coarse meal. Sprinkle the mixture over the apples and bake the crisp in the middle of a preheated 350° F. oven for 35 to 40 minutes, or until the topping is browned and the apples are tender. Serves 6.

Baked Apples in White Wine

½ cup dry white wine
¼ cup apple cider or apple juice
2 tablespoons sugar
⅓ cup golden raisins
1 tablespoon unsalted butter
⅛ teaspoon cinnamon
4 Golden Delicious apples

In a saucepan combine well the wine, the cider, the sugar, the raisins, the butter, and the cinnamon, bring the mixture to a boil, stirring occasionally, and simmer it for 5 minutes. Arrange the apples, cored and the top third peeled, in a baking dish, pour the warm wine mixture over them, filling the cavities of the apples with the raisins, and bake the apples in the middle of a preheated 350° F. oven, basting them with the wine mixture occasionally, for 1 hour and 20 minutes, or until they are tender. Transfer the apples to a serving dish and spoon the cooking liquid over them. Serves 4.

Apricot Citrus Cranberry Compote

⅔ cup sugar
½ cup picked-over cranberries
6 ounces dried apricots
1 grapefruit
2 navel oranges

In a small saucepan combine ⅓ cup of the sugar and ⅓ cup water, bring the mixture to a boil, stirring until the sugar is dissolved, and add the cranberries. Simmer the cranberries for 5 minutes, or until they have barely popped. Transfer the mixture to a small bowl, let it cool, and chill it, covered. In the saucepan combine the remaining ⅓ cup sugar and ⅓ cup water, bring the mixture to a boil, stirring until the sugar is dissolved, and add the apricots. Simmer the apricots, covered, for 5 minutes, or until they are tender. Transfer the mixture to another small bowl, let it cool, and chill it, covered. Working over a bowl, cut away the rinds and the piths from the grapefruit and the oranges with a serrated knife, cut the fruit into sections, and chill it, covered. *The fruit may be prepared up to this point 2 days in advance and kept covered and chilled.* Stir the cranberries and the apricots with their syrups into the citrus mixture and divide the mixture among individual coupes. Serves 6.

PHOTO ON PAGE 80

Bananas Foster with Orange and Raisins

½ stick (¼ cup) unsalted butter, cut into pieces
¼ cup firmly packed dark brown sugar
1 teaspoon cinnamon
3 firm-ripe bananas
1 navel orange, rind and pith cut away with a
    serrated knife and the fruit cut into ½-inch-
    thick pieces (about 1 cup)
¼ cup raisins
⅓ cup banana-flavored liqueur
¼ cup light rum
vanilla ice cream as an accompaniment

In a large skillet melt the butter over moderate heat, add the brown sugar and the cinnamon, and whisk the mixture until it is combined well. Add the bananas, cut diagonally into 1-inch pieces, cook them, turning them carefully, for 1 to 2 minutes, or until they begin to soften, and stir in gently the orange, the raisins, and the liqueur. Cook the mixture, stirring gently, for 1 minute, add the rum, heated, and ignite it, shaking the skillet gently until the flames go out. Serve the banana sauce over the ice cream. Serves 6.

Sopaipillas de Banana
(Puffed Banana Fritters)

¼ cup superfine sugar
1½ teaspoons ground cardamom
2 cups all-purpose flour
2 teaspoons double-acting baking powder
1 teaspoon salt
2 tablespoons vegetable shortening
1 cup mashed ripe banana (about 3 bananas)
vegetable oil for deep-frying

In a bowl combine well the sugar and the cardamom. Into another bowl sift together the flour, the baking powder, and the salt, add the shortening, and blend the mixture until it resembles coarse meal. Stir in the banana and 6 tablespoons water, or enough to form the mixture into a soft but not sticky dough, and knead the dough on a lightly floured surface until it is smooth. Roll the dough out 1/16 inch thick on a floured surface, cut it into 3-inch squares, and cover the squares with a dampened kitchen towel. In a deep fryer heat 3 inches of the oil to 375° F. and in it fry the squares in batches, turning them once, for 50 seconds to 1 minute, or until they are puffed and golden, transferring them with a slotted spoon as they are fried to paper towels to drain. Sprinkle the *sopaipillas* with the cardamom sugar and keep them warm in a preheated 250° F. oven. Makes about 30 fritters.

Banana Soufflés with Rum Chocolate Sauce
For the soufflés
⅓ cup mashed ripe banana
    (1 medium banana)
2 teaspoons fresh lemon juice
2 tablespoons firmly packed light brown sugar
2 large eggs, separated, the whites at room
    temperature
¼ cup finely chopped pecans if desired
a pinch of cream of tartar
1 tablespoon granulated sugar plus additional
    for sprinkling the dishes
For the sauce
2 ounces bittersweet or semisweet
    chocolate, chopped

3 tablespoons heavy cream
1 tablespoon dark rum, or to taste

Make the soufflés: In a bowl stir together the banana, the lemon juice, the brown sugar, and a pinch of salt until the sugar is dissolved, add the yolks and the pecans, and stir the mixture until it is combined well. In a bowl with an electric mixer beat the whites with a pinch of salt until they are foamy, add the cream of tartar, and beat the whites until they hold soft peaks. Add 1 tablespoon of the granulated sugar, beating, and beat the whites until they barely hold stiff peaks. Stir one third of the whites into the banana mixture and fold in the remaining whites gently but thoroughly. Sprinkle 2 buttered 1-cup soufflé dishes with the additional granulated sugar, divide the mixture between them, and bake the soufflés on a baking sheet in the middle of a preheated 375° F. oven for 18 to 20 minutes, or until they are puffed and golden.

Make the sauce while the soufflés are baking: In a metal bowl set over barely simmering water melt the chocolate with the cream, whisk the mixture until it is smooth, and whisk in the rum.

With a spoon break open the tops of the soufflés and ladle the sauce into them. Serves 2.

Nectarine Cobbler

8 cups sliced ripe nectarines (about 3 pounds)
3 tablespoons fresh lemon juice
½ cup granulated sugar
1½ tablespoons cornstarch
1½ cups all-purpose flour
2¼ teaspoons double-acting baking powder
½ teaspoon salt
¼ cup plus 1 tablespoon firmly packed light
    brown sugar
5 tablespoons cold unsalted butter,
    cut into bits
½ cup plus 1 tablespoon heavy cream
vanilla ice cream or whipped cream
    as an accompaniment

In a large bowl toss together the nectarines, the lemon juice, the granulated sugar, and the cornstarch, sifted, and transfer the mixture to a buttered 9-inch-square baking pan. Into another large bowl sift together the flour, the baking powder, the salt, and ¼ cup of the brown sugar, add the butter, and blend the mixture

until it resembles meal. Add ½ cup of the cream gradually, stirring with a fork until the cream is incorporated and the dough forms a ball, turn the dough out onto a lightly floured surface, and pat it into a 9-inch square about ½ inch thick. Transfer the dough carefully to the baking pan, covering the nectarine mixture completely, brush it with the remaining 1 tablespoon cream, and sprinkle it evenly with the remaining 1 tablespoon brown sugar, forced through a sieve. Bake the cobbler in the middle of a preheated 425° F. oven for 35 to 40 minutes, or until it is golden and bubbling around the edges, and serve it with the ice cream. Serves 6 to 8.

Gingered Nectarine Melba

4 firm-ripe nectarines (about 1½ pounds),
    halved, pitted, and peeled
½ cup dry white wine
1 cup sugar
3 tablespoons fresh lemon juice
a 1-ounce piece fresh gingerroot (about
    1- by 1-inch), sliced thin
2 cups fresh raspberries
1 tablespoon fresh lemon juice, or to taste
1 tablespoon framboise or raspberry brandy,
    or to taste
vanilla ice cream as an accompaniment

In a heavy kettle or skillet large enough to hold the nectarine halves in one layer combine the wine, the sugar, the lemon juice, and ¾ cup water, bring the mixture to a boil, stirring until the sugar is dissolved, and add the gingerroot. Boil the mixture for 2 minutes, add the nectarine halves, cut sides down, and simmer them, turning them once, for 10 to 15 minutes, or until they are tender but not mushy. Transfer the nectarines with a slotted spoon to a heatproof dish, pour the syrup over them, discarding the gingerroot, and let the mixture cool. Chill the mixture, covered, for at least 1 hour or overnight.

In a blender or food processor purée the raspberries, the lemon juice, the framboise, and ½ cup of the poaching syrup and force the mixture through a fine sieve set over a bowl, pressing hard on the solids. In each of 4 bowls arrange 2 nectarine halves, drained, and a scoop of vanilla ice cream and top each serving with some of the raspberry sauce. Serves 4.

Orange and Kiwifruit Gratin with Madeira Sabayon

For the sabayon
4 large egg yolks
¼ cup sugar
½ cup Sercial Madeira

1 navel orange, rind and pith cut away and the
  flesh cut into sections
1 kiwifruit, peeled and sliced crosswise
2 tablespoons sliced almonds

Make the sabayon: In a metal bowl with an electric mixer beat the yolks with the sugar until the mixture is light and lemon-colored, set the bowl over a pan of simmering water, and beat in the Madeira gradually. Beat the mixture at high speed for 5 to 8 minutes, or until it is very light in volume and the beaters leave a pattern in their wake. (The sabayon should be hot to the touch.)

Cover the bottom of a buttered 11-inch oval gratin dish (or 1½-quart shallow baking dish) with one third of the sabayon and arrange the fruit on it. Spread the remaining sabayon over the fruit and sprinkle the top with the almonds. Broil the gratin under a preheated broiler about 2 inches from the heat for 30 seconds to 1 minute, or until the sabayon is golden. Serve the gratin immediately. Serves 4.

Gingered Pear Crisp

⅓ cup all-purpose flour
1½ teaspoons finely grated peeled fresh
  gingerroot
¼ cup firmly packed brown sugar
2 tablespoons softened unsalted butter
¼ cup finely chopped pecans
2 firm-ripe pears
  (preferably Bosc)

In a small bowl combine well the flour, the gingerroot, and the brown sugar, add the butter, and blend the mixture until it is pebbly. Add the pecans and toss the mixture gently. Peel, quarter, and core the pears and cut them crosswise into ¼-inch slices. In a buttered 8-inch-square pan spread the pear slices evenly, sprinkle them with the pecan mixture, and bake the crisp in the upper third of a preheated 400° F. oven for 30 minutes. Serve the crisp warm. Serves 2.

CONFECTIONS

Maple Almond Brittle

1½ cups maple syrup
¼ cup light corn syrup
½ teaspoon salt
1½ cups sugar
2 cups sliced unblanched almonds, toasted
  lightly

In a heavy saucepan combine the maple syrup, the corn syrup, the salt, and the sugar, bring the mixture to a boil over moderate heat, stirring and washing down any sugar crystals clinging to the side with a brush dipped in cold water, and boil the mixture, undisturbed, until it registers 300° F. on a candy thermometer. Stir in the almonds quickly and pour the mixture onto an oiled marble slab or a baking sheet lined with foil. Spread the mixture as thin as possible with a metal spatula and let it cool. Break the almond brittle into serving pieces. Makes about 1½ pounds.

PHOTO ON PAGE 78

Chocolate Apricot Cashew Clusters

2 cups (12 ounces) semisweet chocolate chips
1 cup (about 6 ounces) chopped dried apricots
1 cup (about 6 ounces) chopped salted
  cashew nuts

In a bowl set over barely simmering water melt the chocolate chips, stirring occasionally, remove the bowl from the heat, and add the apricots and the cashews, stirring until the mixture is combined well. Drop the mixture by rounded teaspoons into 36 paper or foil candy cups, each measuring 1 inch in diameter by ¾ inch deep, and chill the clusters for 20 to 30 minutes, or until they are hardened. (Alternatively the mixture can be dropped by rounded teaspoons onto a baking sheet lined with wax paper and chilled.) The clusters may be stored, covered and chilled, for 1 week. Makes 36 confections.

Frozen Chocolate-Covered Banana Peanut Clusters

½ cup chunky peanut butter
¼ cup coffee-flavored liqueur
2 large ripe bananas, chopped
3 cups semisweet chocolate chips

In a bowl combine well the peanut butter, the liqueur, and 6 tablespoons water and stir in the bananas until the mixture is combined well. Drop the banana mixture by rounded tablespoons onto a baking sheet lined with wax paper and freeze the clusters for at least 6 hours or overnight. In a bowl set over barely simmering water melt the chocolate chips, stirring, until the chocolate is smooth and remove the bowl from over the water. Dip each cluster into the chocolate and transfer it with a fork, letting the excess drip off, to the baking sheet. Freeze the clusters, covered, for 30 minutes to 1 hour, or until the chocolate is set. Makes about 16 clusters.

Bittersweet Champagne Truffles

1 split (6.3 ounces) of Champagne
12 ounces fine-quality bittersweet chocolate, chopped
3 large egg yolks
¼ cup heavy cream
1 stick (½ cup) unsalted butter, cut into bits and softened
½ cup sifted unsweetened cocoa powder for coating the truffles

In a small saucepan cook the Champagne over high heat for 10 minutes, or until it is reduced to about ⅓ cup, and reserve it, chilled. In the top of a double boiler or in a metal bowl set over barely simmering water melt the chocolate, stirring, until it is smooth and remove the pan from the heat. In a heavy saucepan whisk together the yolks and the cream and cook the mixture over low heat, stirring constantly with a wooden spoon, for 3 minutes, or until it is thickened slightly. Do not let it boil. Remove the pan from the heat and add the chocolate, stirring. Beat in the butter, bit by bit, and beat the mixture until it is thick and smooth. Stir in the reserved Champagne, transfer the truffle mixture to a bowl, and chill it, covered, for 4 hours, or until it is firm. Form the mixture by heaping teaspoons into balls and roll the balls in the cocoa powder. Chill the truffles on a baking sheet lined with wax paper for 1 hour, or until they are firm. The truffles keep in an airtight container, chilled, for 3 days. Makes about 40 truffles.

Chocolate Peanut Butter Truffles

2 cups (12 ounces) semisweet chocolate chips
½ cup heavy cream
2 tablespoons unsalted butter, cut into bits
¾ cup chunky peanut butter
2 teaspoons vanilla
about ½ cup finely chopped salted peanuts for coating the truffles

In a large saucepan combine the chocolate chips, the cream, the butter, and the peanut butter and heat the mixture over moderate heat, stirring, until the chocolate is melted completely. Remove the pan from the heat and stir in the vanilla and a pinch of salt. Transfer the mixture to a bowl and chill it, covered, for 4 hours, or until it is firm. Form the mixture by heaping teaspoons into balls and roll the balls lightly in the peanuts. Chill the truffles on a baking sheet lined with wax paper for 1 hour, or until they are firm. The truffles keep in an airtight container, chilled, for 2 weeks. Makes about 40 truffles.

Chocolate Raspberry Truffles

½ cup heavy cream
12 ounces semisweet chocolate, chopped fine
½ stick (¼ cup) unsalted butter, cut into bits and softened
½ cup seedless red raspberry jam
2 tablespoons Chambord (black raspberry liqueur), or to taste
½ cup sifted unsweetened cocoa powder for coating the truffles

In a saucepan bring the cream just to a boil over moderate heat and remove the pan from the heat. Add the chocolate, stirring, and stir the mixture until the chocolate is melted completely and the mixture is smooth. Let the mixture cool slightly, add the butter, bit by bit, stirring, and stir the mixture until it is smooth. Stir in the jam, the Chambord, and a pinch of salt, transfer the mixture to a bowl, and chill it, covered, for 4 hours, or until it is firm. Form the mixture by heaping teaspoons into balls and roll the balls in the cocoa powder. Chill the truffles on a baking sheet lined with wax paper for 1 hour, or until they are firm. The truffles keep in an airtight container, chilled, for 2 weeks. Makes about 40 truffles.

Milk Chocolate Kahlúa Truffles

12 ounces fine-quality milk chocolate, chopped
½ cup heavy cream
½ stick (¼ cup) unsalted butter, cut into bits
　and softened
1 tablespoon instant espresso powder
2 tablespoons Kahlúa
about ½ cup sifted unsweetened cocoa powder
　for coating the truffles
about 18 small chocolate coffee beans
　(available at specialty foods shops), halved,
　for garnish if desired

In a large saucepan combine the chocolate, the cream, the butter, the espresso powder, and the Kahlúa and heat the mixture over moderately low heat, stirring, until it is smooth. Transfer the mixture to a bowl and chill it, covered, for 4 hours, or until it is firm. Form the mixture by heaping teaspoons into balls and roll the balls in the cocoa powder. Press a coffee bean half onto each truffle and chill the truffles on a baking sheet lined with wax paper for 1 hour, or until they are firm. The truffles keep in an airtight container, chilled, for 2 weeks. Makes about 35 truffles.

Toasted Coconut Chocolate Rum Truffles

two 3½-ounce cans (about 2⅔ cups loosely
　packed) sweetened flaked coconut
2 cups (12 ounces) semisweet chocolate chips
½ stick (¼ cup) unsalted butter,
　cut into bits
½ cup heavy cream
¼ cup dark rum,
　or to taste

In a jelly-roll pan toast the coconut in one layer in a preheated 375° F. oven, stirring frequently, for 15 minutes, or until it is golden, let it cool, and crumble it. In a large saucepan combine the chocolate chips, the butter, the cream, the rum, 1 cup of the toasted coconut, and a pinch of salt and heat the mixture over moderately low heat, stirring, until the chocolate is melted completely. Transfer the mixture to a bowl and chill it, covered, for 4 hours, or until it is firm. Form the mixture by heaping teaspoons into balls and roll the balls lightly in the remaining coconut. Chill the truffles on a baking sheet lined with wax paper for 1 hour, or until they are firm. The truffles keep in an airtight container, chilled, for 2 weeks. Makes about 40 truffles.

BEVERAGES

ALCOHOLIC BEVERAGES

Amaretto Coffee

½ cup (4 ponies) Amaretto
¼ cup (2 ponies) brandy
4 teaspoons sugar, or to taste
3 cups freshly brewed strong coffee
lightly sweetened whipped cream to taste
lightly toasted sliced almonds for garnish

In each of four 8-ounce mugs combine 2 tablespoons (1 pony) of the Amaretto, 1 tablespoon of the brandy, and 1 teaspoon of the sugar, divide the coffee, heated if necessary, among the mugs, and stir the drinks until the sugar is dissolved. Top each drink with a dollop of the whipped cream and sprinkle the whipped cream with the almonds. Makes 4 drinks.

Orange Belgian Coffee

1 large egg white at room temperature
3 tablespoons sugar
⅛ teaspoon cinnamon plus additional
  for garnish
½ cup well chilled heavy cream
¼ teaspoon vanilla
3 cups freshly brewed strong coffee
½ cup (4 ponies) orange-flavored liqueur

In a bowl with an electric mixer beat the egg white with a pinch of salt until it holds soft peaks, add the sugar and ⅛ teaspoon of the cinnamon, beating, and beat the mixture until it just holds stiff peaks. In a chilled bowl with the electric mixer beat the cream with the vanilla until it just holds stiff peaks, fold the egg white

mixture into the cream, and divide the mixture among four 8-ounce mugs. In a pitcher stir together the coffee, heated if necessary, and the liqueur, divide the mixture among the mugs, and sprinkle each drink with some of the additional cinnamon. Makes 4 drinks.

Dutch Coffee

½ cup (4 ponies) crème de cacao
¼ cup (2 ponies) crème de menthe
3 cups freshly brewed strong coffee
lightly sweetened whipped cream to taste
grated semisweet chocolate for garnish

In each of four 8-ounce mugs combine 2 tablespoons (1 pony) of the crème de cacao and 1 tablespoon of the crème de menthe, divide the coffee, heated if necessary, among the mugs, and stir the drinks until they are combined well. Top each drink with a dollop of the whipped cream and sprinkle the whipped cream with the chocolate. Makes 4 drinks.

Irish Coffee

¾ cup (4 jiggers) Irish whiskey
2 tablespoons sugar, or to taste
3 cups freshly brewed strong coffee
lightly sweetened whipped cream to taste

In each of four 8-ounce mugs combine 3 tablespoons (1 jigger) of the whiskey and 1½ teaspoons of the sugar, divide the coffee, heated if necessary, among the mugs, and stir the drinks until the sugar is dissolved. Top each drink with a dollop of the whipped cream. Makes 4 drinks.

Mexican Coffee

¾ cup (4 jiggers) coffee-flavored liqueur
4 teaspoons firmly packed dark brown
  sugar, or to taste
3 cups freshly brewed strong coffee
lightly sweetened whipped cream to taste
cinnamon for garnish

In each of four 8-ounce mugs combine 3 tablespoons (1 jigger) of the liqueur and 1 teaspoon of the brown sugar, divide the coffee, heated if necessary, among the mugs, and stir the drinks until the sugar is dissolved. Top each drink with a dollop of the whipped cream and sprinkle the whipped cream with the cinnamon. Makes 4 drinks.

Spiced Rum Coffee

8 cloves
four 2-inch strips of orange rind, removed
  with a vegetable peeler
2 tablespoons sugar, or to taste
¾ cup (4 jiggers) dark rum
3 cups freshly brewed strong coffee
lightly sweetened whipped cream to taste
freshly grated nutmeg for garnish

In each of four 8-ounce mugs combine 2 of the cloves, 1 strip of the rind, 1½ teaspoons of the sugar, and 3 tablespoons (1 jigger) of the rum and let the mixture stand for 5 minutes. Divide the coffee, heated if necessary, among the mugs and stir the drinks until the sugar is dissolved. Top each drink with a dollop of the whipped cream and sprinkle the whipped cream with the nutmeg. Makes 4 drinks.

Brandied Viennese Coffee

4 ounces semisweet chocolate, chopped, plus
  additional, grated, for garnish
¼ cup heavy cream
3 cups freshly brewed strong coffee
½ cup (4 ponies) brandy
lightly sweetened whipped cream to taste

In the top of a double boiler set over simmering water melt the chopped chocolate with the cream, stirring, and stir the mixture until it is smooth. Add the coffee, heated if necessary, and the brandy in a stream, stirring, and stir the mixture until it is combined well. Divide the coffee among four 8-ounce mugs, top each drink with a dollop of the whipped cream, and sprinkle the whipped cream with the grated chocolate. Makes 4 drinks.

Blood Orange Cordial

3 to 4 blood oranges
⅓ cup sugar
2 cups Cognac or other brandy
a 3-inch cinnamon stick, broken into pieces

With a vegetable peeler remove the rind in strips from 2 of the oranges and reserve it. Squeeze enough of the oranges to yield 1 cup juice. In a saucepan combine the juice and the sugar and simmer the mixture, stirring, until the sugar is dissolved. Let the mixture cool, stir in the Cognac, the reserved rind, and the cinnamon stick, and transfer the mixture to a jar. Seal the jar tightly with the lid and store the cordial in a cool dry place, shaking it occasionally, for 1 month. Strain the cordial through a fine sieve into a bottle and let it stand, covered, for an additional month before serving. Makes about 2 cups.

Traditional Daiquiri

2 ounces (2 ponies) light rum
2 tablespoons fresh lime juice
1 teaspoon superfine sugar
1 lime wedge for garnish

In a blender blend the rum, the lime juice, the sugar, and 1 cup ice cubes until the drink is smooth, pour the drink into a chilled cocktail glass, and garnish it with the lime wedge. Makes 1 drink.

Lemon Vodka Gimlet

1½ ounces (1 jigger) lemon-flavored vodka
3 tablespoons fresh lime juice
1 tablespoon Rose's lime juice
a twist of lime rind for garnish

In an Old Fashioned glass stir together the vodka, the fresh lime juice, and the Rose's lime juice, fill the glass with ice cubes, and garnish the drink with the rind. Makes 1 drink.

Ruby Red Margarita
(Tequila and Pink Grapefruit Cocktail)

1 lime wedge
coarse salt for coating the rim of the glass
1½ ounces (1 jigger) tequila
3 tablespoons fresh pink grapefruit juice
  (preferably ruby red)
1 ounce (1 pony) orange-flavored liqueur
½ teaspoon superfine sugar if desired
1 quarter of a slice of ruby red grapefruit
  for garnish

Rub the rim of a cocktail glass with the lime wedge, dip it in the salt, coating it lightly, and chill the glass. In a blender blend the tequila, the grapefruit juice, the liqueur, the sugar, and 1 cup ice cubes for 30 seconds, pour the drink into the glass, and garnish it with the grapefruit slice. Makes 1 drink.

Mexicali Maria
(Spicy Bloody Mary with Cumin)

1½ ounces (1 jigger) vodka or tequila
¾ cup chilled tomato-vegetable juice
2 teaspoons fresh lime juice, or to taste
½ teaspoon Worcestershire sauce, or to taste
¼ teaspoon ground cumin, or to taste
¼ teaspoon pickled *jalapeño* pepper juice
  if desired
Tabasco to taste

In a tall glass, half filled with ice cubes if desired, combine the vodka, the tomato-vegetable juice, the lime juice, the Worcestershire sauce, the cumin, the *jalapeño* pepper juice, and the Tabasco and stir the drink well. Makes 1 drink.

Summer Breezes
(Wine, Rum, and Triple Sec Punch)

a 1-liter bottle dry white wine, chilled
½ cup dark rum
½ cup triple sec
1 orange, sliced
1 lemon, sliced
1 cup strawberries, hulled
2 cups chilled seltzer or club soda
fresh mint sprigs for garnish if desired

In a large pitcher or punch bowl combine the wine, the rum, the triple sec, the orange, the lemon, and the strawberries. *The punch may be prepared up to this point 6 hours in advance and kept covered and chilled.* Stir in the seltzer, pour or ladle the punch into glasses over ice, and garnish each serving with a mint sprig. Makes about 9 cups.

PHOTO ON PAGE 56

Tequila Sunrise

1½ ounces (1 jigger) tequila
½ cup chilled fresh orange juice
1 tablespoon fresh lime juice, or to taste
1 teaspoon grenadine, or to taste
½ a lime slice for garnish

In an 8-ounce stemmed glass, half filled with ice cubes, combine the tequila, the orange juice, and the lime juice and stir the drink. Add the grenadine, let it sink to the bottom, and garnish the drink with the lime slice. Makes 1 drink.

PHOTO ON PAGE 14

NONALCOHOLIC BEVERAGES

Cranberry Tangerine Juice

3 cups tangerine juice
1 cup cranberry juice

In a pitcher stir together the juices and chill the mixture, covered, for at least 1 hour or overnight. Makes 4 cups, serving 6.

PHOTO ON PAGE 81

Minted Citrus Juice

4½ cups fresh pink grapefruit juice
2 cups fresh orange juice
6 tablespoons fresh lemon juice
1 cup loosely packed fresh mint leaves

In a pitcher stir together the grapefruit juice, the orange juice, and the lemon juice. In a blender blend together 1½ cups of the juice mixture and the mint leaves, stir the mixture into the remaining juice mixture, and chill the juice, covered, stirring occasionally, for at least 3 hours or overnight. Pour the juice through a fine sieve set over another pitcher. Makes about 6 cups.

269

PART THREE

A GOURMET ADDENDUM

ELEGANT, EASY
VEGETABLE COMBINATIONS

 ach year the annual Addendum to *The Best of Gourmet* has expanded its scope in an attempt to address the needs of contemporary cooks. Last year, using basic procedures as a springboard, we presented newly developed recipes that were lower in fat, higher in protein, and higher in energy-providing complex carbohydrates or starches.

Intelligent eating is healthy eating, and we hoped that our focus on nutrition would be a welcome supplement to the best of the creative, mouth-watering reci-

pes that appear monthly in *Gourmet* magazine. In an effort to answer the continuing call for light, healthy, and, hopefully, not too time-consuming recipes, we once again present a natural progression from addenda past. Basic recipes and procedures can be found within A Recipe Compendium. The 1989 Addendum is a celebration of humble-yet-newly-respected vegetables, the most bounteous and healthy of nature's gifts.

Garden fresh sugar snap peas, broccoli, tomatoes, the latest chorus line of lettuces, *radicchio, arugula*, endive, escarole, aromatic peppers, and subtly sweet parsnips should be the stars of many of our meals, doctors and nutritionists tell us. The quest for lighter-but-flavorful variations on the cholesterol-rich menus of our innocent childhoods has led cooks everywhere to the farmers' market, the greengrocer, the country fruit and vegetable stand. Happily, the kaleidoscope of leaves, greens, bulbs, and beans before us is not only becoming more reliably available on a year-round basis, but is also increasing in its exotic variety. To meet the demands of our new curiosity and healthy sensibility, we find Napa cabbage in Illinois, okra in California, and *daikon* in Pennsylvania. Of utmost importance, of course, is picking the freshest of vegetables and taking advantage of seasonal favorites when they are in overwhelming abundance.

For our salute to farm-fresh produce we have put together eight menus of vegetable combinations, both classic and inventive. All of the menus can be prepared within an hour, and all have been designed to be lighter in fat content, but rich in flavor and texture. Butter and cream have been included judiciously. When cheese has been called for, a Cheddar or Monterey Jack, for instance, it can generally be purchased in low-fat, low-salt varieties, if preferable.

Seasonal availability must clearly be considered, therefore, look to the vegetable and fruit suggestions here as guidelines. Let the day's market and personal preference take precedence when choosing the ingredients for the menus. Vegetables of similar textures can be substituted for one another with just a slight adjustment in measurements and cooking times. For instance, chives can easily replace the scallions in the scallion brown rice with pine nuts. *Daikon* would make a witty addition in the dilled coleslaw with yogurt dressing.

While all of the menus consist of three recipes, each menu is distinctive in its pacing and theme. Some menus have a traditional first course, entrée, and dessert sequence, such as minted avocado, Bibb, and orange salad followed by chili cheese enchiladas and melon with Port. Others include an additional vegetable dish, bread or soup and leave the dessert up to the individual cook. The menu featuring roasted chicken and vegetables with fennel-scented tomato sauce is an example of an ingenious menu that leaves the enhancement of a complementary dessert up to the host or hostess and is particularly well-suited to entertaining.

No, these are not strictly vegetarian menus. "Everything in moderation," we have all been told—even

a bit of red meat now and then. So, while our emphasis this year is on the fruits of the land, we also have included a sparing amount of fruits from the sea, poultry, and pork.

The most appealing aspect of this year's Addendum, we feel, is not only that the recipes have been developed with an awareness of both the components of sensible, healthy eating and the everyday constrictions of time, but that their simplicity leaves much room for creativity. Recipes that presently feature vegetables sans protein can certainly, if preferred, accommodate the addition of meat. Prosciutto or ham, for example, can easily be added to the spinach, dried mushroom, and Fontina pizzas. In turn, recipes that now include pork or poultry can be adapted to be just as satisfying without the added meat. In the spicy Chinese specialty stir-fried vegetables with ground pork and *shiitake* mushrooms the ground pork is, obviously, not a necessity.

The recipes can readily be used for both family meals as well as entertaining. *Linguine* with sun-dried tomatoes and seasonal vegetables, for instance, can be served at room temperature or even cold, by refreshing the hot, drained pasta and vegetables with cold water, tossing the mixture with three tablespoons of olive oil, then combining the pasta with the sauce just before serving. Presented at room temperature, the *linguine* is a nice possibility for a luncheon or evening buffet. Additionally, the *linguine* recipe encourages cooks to incorporate their own inspirations as well as the very best of the garden's daily miracles.

The desserts here also leave room for individual preference. Nectarines could certainly make a new interpretation of brandied peaches with sour cream and *Amaretti*, but Bing cherries, pitted and stemmed, would also be an interesting substitute. Frozen or plain yogurt, ice milk, or sherbet are all light alternatives in desserts made with sour cream, *mascarpone*, or ice cream.

As we approach the turn of the century, we continue to become increasingly sophisticated and cosmopolitan in our knowledge of the excitement of international herbs, spices, and ingredients and the latest wonders of time-efficient food preparation. We also, however, continue to learn that the vitamins, minerals, and essential fiber in vegetables are vital to a more healthy existence. We hope that the 1989 Addendum will serve as a pleasing supplement of master plans for nutritious-but-also-delicious dining.

*Linguine with Sun-Dried Tomatoes
and Seasonal Vegetables*

Bruschetta

Orange-Flavored Strawberries with Mascarpone

Linguine with sun-dried tomatoes and seasonal vegetables offers an opportunity to substitute personal vegetable preferences as well as home-grown favorites that you may currently have in abundance. Fresh green beans, for instance, can easily take the place of the sugar snap peas. Broccoli rabe is a more exotic alternative to the broccoli flowerets. Softened cream cheese, sour cream, or yogurt are possible alternatives to the *mascarpone* garnish in the light-but-multiflavored dessert. While this menu can readily be completed within an hour, it is advisable to begin by bringing the pasta water to a rolling boil, simultaneously mascerating the strawberries, so they have time to develop in flavor.

Linguine with Sun-Dried Tomatoes and Seasonal Vegetables

For the sauce
1 cup firmly packed basil leaves
1 cup sun-dried tomatoes packed in oil,
    drained*
1 to 2 garlic cloves, chopped
1 to 2 tablespoons fresh lemon juice,
    or to taste
1 tablespoon red-wine vinegar
½ teaspoon red pepper flakes
¼ cup freshly grated Pecorino Romano or
    Parmesan
⅓ to ½ cup extra-virgin olive oil*

12 ounces dried *linguine* or spaghetti
½ cup fresh or frozen peas
2 cups broccoli flowerets (about 5 to 6 ounces)
2 cups sugar snap peas or snow peas, trimmed and
    strings discarded
12 thin asparagus spears, trimmed and cut into
    3-inch lengths
2 small zucchini or summer squash, trimmed and
    cut into ½-inch pieces
½ cup freshly grated Pecorino Romano or
    Parmesan

*available at specialty foods shops and some
    supermarkets

Make the sauce: In a food processor or blender purée the basil, the tomatoes, the garlic, the lemon juice, the vinegar, the red pepper flakes, the cheese, and salt to taste. With the motor running, add the oil in a stream and blend the sauce until it is combined well.

In a kettle of boiling salted water cook the *linguine* for 7 to 8 minutes, or until it is softened but not yet *al dente*. Add the fresh peas and cook them over moderately high heat, stirring, for 1 minute. Add the broccoli and the sugar snap peas and cook them, stirring, for 1 minute. Add the asparagus, the zucchini, and the frozen peas, if using, and cook the mixture, stirring, until the pasta is *al dente* (about 2 minutes). Add the snow peas, if using, and bring the mixture to a boil, stirring. Drain the mixture well and transfer it to a large bowl. Pour the sauce over the pasta and the vegetables and toss the mixture until it is combined well. Serve the pasta and the vegetables with the cheese. Serves 4.

Bruschetta (Garlic Bread)

1 large garlic clove, crushed with the side of a large
    knife or cleaver
½ teaspoon salt
½ cup olive oil
a 10-inch loaf Italian bread, cut into ½-inch-thick
    slices

Using a heavy knife, mince and mash the garlic with the salt to form a paste and in a bowl combine it well with the olive oil. Brush one side of each slice of bread with the garlic mixture, arrange the slices on a baking sheet, and broil them under a preheated broiler about 6 inches from the heat for 3 minutes, or until the edges are golden brown. Serves 4.

Orange-Flavored Strawberries with Mascarpone

1½ pints strawberries,
    hulled and halved lengthwise,
    if large
¼ cup fresh orange juice
2 tablespoons orange-flavored liqueur
    if desired
1 to 2 tablespoons granulated sugar
1½ teaspoons freshly grated orange rind
1 teaspoon balsamic vinegar (available at specialty
    foods shops and some supermarkets)
6 ounces *mascarpone* (available at most cheese
    shops and specialty foods shops)
2 tablespoons confectioners' sugar
    if desired
2 tablespoons heavy cream
½ teaspoon vanilla

In a large bowl combine the strawberries with the orange juice, the orange liqueur, the granulated sugar, the rind, and the vinegar, stir the mixture to dissolve the sugar, and chill it, covered, for 30 minutes. In a small bowl whisk together the *mascarpone*, the confectioners' sugar, the heavy cream, and the vanilla until the mixture is smooth and chill the mixture, covered. Divide the strawberry mixture among 4 dessert dishes and garnish each serving with a dollop of the *mascarpone* mixture. Serves 4.

*Stir-Fried Vegetables with Ground Pork
and Shiitake Mushrooms*

Sweet-and-Sour Sesame Cabbage Salad

Scallion Brown Rice with Pine Nuts

———————————————

The delicate-yet-dramatic culinary aesthetic of far-off China continues to appeal and intrigue. Here we present a combination of home-cooked dishes that should satisfy aficionados of Far Eastern fare, but that also leaves room for variation. We leave the choice of using regular or low-salt soy sauce up to the individual cook. There is not always a marked difference in taste, and lighter varieties of soy sauce are ideal for those who are watching their sodium intake. It is important to begin this menu by preparing the brown rice, as it takes a full 45 minutes to cook. Steamed white rice can be substituted, if time is of the essence, and the stir-fried vegetables are equally good without the pork.

———————————————

274

Stir-Fried Vegetables with Ground Pork and Shiitake Mushrooms

1 ounce dried *shiitake* mushrooms*
For the sauce
2 tablespoons cornstarch
1½ cups vegetable stock (page 287), chicken stock
  (page 123), or canned chicken broth
3 tablespoons soy sauce
3 tablespoons rice wine* or Scotch
2 tablespoons rice vinegar*
2 tablespoons oyster sauce*
2 teaspoons bean paste* if desired
½ teaspoon sugar
¼ teaspoon salt, or to taste

2 tablespoons peanut or vegetable oil
⅓ cup minced scallion
2 tablespoons minced garlic
2 tablespoons minced and peeled fresh gingerroot
6 ounces lean ground pork
1 red bell pepper, cut into 1-inch pieces
1 cup sliced celery
2½ cups small broccoli flowerets or 1 pound
  broccoli rabe, trimmed and cut into 2-inch pieces
an 8-ounce can sliced bamboo shoots, rinsed and
  drained
1 tablespoon Oriental sesame oil*

*available at Oriental markets and some
  specialty foods shops and supermarkets

In a small bowl let the *shiitake* mushrooms soak in very hot water to cover for 15 minutes, or until they are soft and spongy, and drain them. Cut off and discard the stems and slice the mushrooms.

Make the sauce: In a small bowl dissolve the cornstarch in the stock and stir in the soy sauce, the rice wine, the rice vinegar, the oyster sauce, the bean paste, the sugar, and the salt.

In a heated wok or large skillet heat the oil over moderately high heat until it is hot but not smoking. Add the scallion, the garlic, and the gingerroot and stir-fry the mixture for 10 seconds, or until it is fragrant. Add the pork and stir-fry the mixture for 30 to 45 seconds, or until the pork is no longer pink. Add the bell pepper, the celery, and the *shiitake* mushrooms and stir-fry the mixture for 1 minute. Add the broccoli and the bamboo shoots and stir-fry the mixture for 1 minute.

Stir the sauce, add it to the wok, stirring, and bring it to a boil, stirring. Simmer the mixture, covered, for 3 to 4 minutes, or until the vegetables are just tender. Drizzle the mixture with the sesame oil, toss it, and divide it among 4 heated plates. Serves 4.

Sweet-and-Sour Sesame Cabbage Salad

4 tablespoons rice* or cider vinegar
1 to 1½ tablespoons sugar
2 tablespoons vegetable oil
1 tablespoon Oriental sesame oil*
½ teaspoon salt, or to taste
¾ to 1 pound Napa cabbage (celery cabbage),
  sliced thin
¼ cup minced fresh coriander
1 small green hot chili pepper, if desired, seeded
  and minced (wear rubber gloves)
toasted sesame seeds for garnish

*available at Oriental markets and some
  specialty foods shops and supermarkets

In a saucepan combine the vinegar, the sugar, the vegetable oil, the sesame oil, and the salt and cook the mixture over moderate heat, stirring, until the sugar is dissolved. In a bowl toss the cabbage with the dressing and stir in the coriander and the chili pepper. Chill the salad, covered, for at least 30 minutes and sprinkle it with the sesame seeds. Serves 4.

*Scallion Brown Rice
with Pine Nuts*

3 cups chicken stock (page 123),
  vegetable stock (page 287),
  or canned chicken broth
½ teaspoon salt,
  or to taste
2 tablespoons unsalted butter
1½ cups long-grain brown rice
½ cup pine nuts, lightly toasted
⅓ cup minced scallion

In a saucepan combine the chicken stock with the salt and 1 tablespoon of the butter, bring the liquid to a boil, and sprinkle in the rice, stirring. Simmer the rice, covered, for 40 to 45 minutes, or until it is tender. Stir in the pine nuts, the scallion, and the remaining 1 tablespoon butter and combine the mixture. Serves 4.

Cannellini and Fennel Salad

Spinach, Dried Mushroom, and Fontina Pizzas

Brandied Peaches with Sour Cream and Amaretti

No matter how nutritionally sound they are, vegetables can hardly claim universal appeal. Inevitably, someone at a given gathering admits an aversion to hallowed, healthy greens. This menu should speak to those of us who prefer our vegetables in disguise. The cannellini and fennel salad leaves plenty of room for individual interpretation. Celery can be substituted for the fennel, which has a very distinctive licorice taste. Dill, parsley, or even chives, measured to taste, can readily replace the basil leaves. The pizza here is remarkably high in vitamins, low in salt and fat content. *Porcini*, *cèpes*, or morels offer distinctive possibilities for variety and, if preferred, ham or prosciutto can easily be added.

Cannellini and Fennel Salad

a 1-pound 3-ounce can cannellini beans, rinsed and
  drained
2 large whole scallions, sliced thin
2 tablespoons minced fresh basil leaves
romaine lettuce leaves, rinsed and patted dry, for
  lining the platter
2 tomatoes, cut into wedges
1 fennel bulb, trimmed and sliced thin
2 tablespoons fresh lemon juice
1 tablespoon white-wine vinegar
¼ cup extra-virgin olive oil (available at specialty
  foods shops and some supermarkets)

In a bowl stir together the beans, the scallions,
and the basil. On a platter arrange the lettuce leaves,
the bean mixture, the tomatoes, and the fennel and
chill the salad, covered, for 15 minutes. In a small
bowl combine the lemon juice, the vinegar, and salt
and pepper to taste, add the oil in a stream, whisking,
and whisk the dressing until it is emulsified. Before
serving, spoon the dressing over the salad. Serves 4.

Spinach, Dried Mushroom, and Fontina Pizzas

½ ounce dried mushrooms
1 onion, minced
3 tablespoons olive oil
6 ounces fresh mushrooms, sliced thin
¼ teaspoon dried sage, crumbled
¼ teaspoon dried thyme, crumbled
¼ teaspoon red pepper flakes
2 garlic cloves, minced
⅓ cup dry white wine
2 teaspoons tomato paste
1 cup coarsely chopped well-washed spinach
  leaves, *arugula* leaves, or fresh basil, or a
  combination of all three
four 7-inch *pita* loaves, left whole and lightly
  pricked with a fork on flattest side
8 ounces Fontina or mozzarella, diced
2 tablespoons freshly grated Parmesan

In a bowl let the dried mushrooms soak in very
hot water to cover for 15 minutes, or until they are soft
and spongy. Drain the mushrooms, reserving 1 cup of
the soaking liquid, discard the tough stems, and chop
the mushrooms. Strain the reserved liquid through a
fine sieve into a small bowl.

In a skillet cook the onion in 2 tablespoons of the
oil over moderate heat, stirring occasionally, until it is
golden. Add the fresh mushrooms, the sage, the
thyme, the red pepper flakes, and salt and pepper to
taste and cook the mixture, stirring occasionally, for
3 to 4 minutes, or until almost all the liquid the mushrooms give off has evaporated. Add the dried mushrooms and the garlic and cook the mixture, stirring, for
1 minute. Add the wine and boil it until it is reduced by
half. Add the reserved mushroom liquid and the tomato paste and simmer the mixture until the liquid is
thickened and reduced to about 3 tablespoons. Add the
spinach and salt and pepper to taste and cook the mixture, stirring, until the spinach is just wilted.

Top each *pita* loaf with some of the mixture,
sprinkle each *pita* with some of the Fontina, the Parmesan, and the remaining 1 tablespoon oil, and arrange the loaves on a baking sheet. Bake the pizzas in a
preheated 450° F. oven for 5 to 6 minutes, or until the
cheese is melted and the topping is heated through.
If desired, put the pizzas under a preheated broiler
about 4 inches from the heat until the cheese is lightly
golden. Serves 4.

Brandied Peaches
with Sour Cream and Amaretti

¼ cup sugar
2 tablespoons unsalted butter
3 tablespoons brandy
2 tablespoons fresh lemon juice
¼ teaspoon vanilla
4 large firm-ripe peaches, peeled, pitted, and sliced
¼ cup sour cream
4 *amaretti* (available at specialty foods shops and
  some supermarkets) or almond macaroon
  cookies, crumbled

In a saucepan combine the sugar, the butter, the
brandy, the lemon juice, the vanilla, and ¼ cup water,
bring the mixture to a boil, stirring, and simmer it until
the sugar is dissolved. Add the peaches and simmer
them, covered, for 5 to 7 minutes, or until they are just
tender. Let the peaches cool. (The peaches may be
served warm or at room temperature.)

Divide the peaches and the poaching liquid
among 4 dessert dishes and garnish each serving with
sour cream and *amaretti*. The peaches may also be
served with ice cream or frozen yogurt. Serves 4.

Green Bean, Tomato, and Black Olive Salad

Spaghetti Frittata with Sautéed Ham,
Peppers, Onions, and Tomatoes

Raspberry Parfaits

Leftover pasta leaves many a clever cook in a quandary. The frittata recipe here, however, not only offers an innovative solution, but also, because it can be served at room temperature and even cold, serves as an unexpected picnic offering. The timing for this menu has been plotted on the assumption that you already have some cooked pasta on hand. Preparing the raspberry sauce first and chilling it will give the sauce time to develop a richer flavor. And, eliminating the ham in the frittata recipe is a simple way to reduce the fat and salt content of this menu, without dramatically sacrificing the pleasant variation of tastes.

Green Bean, Tomato, and Black Olive Salad

1 pound green beans or a combination of green
  beans and wax beans, trimmed
2 tomatoes, sliced
1 small red onion, minced
24 oil-cured niçoise or Kalamata olives
12 large basil leaves, rinsed, patted dry, and cut
  into shreds
2 tablespoons Sherry vinegar* or red-wine vinegar
6 tablespoons extra-virgin olive oil*

*available at specialty foods shops and some
  supermarkets

In a large saucepan of boiling salted water cook the green beans for 6 to 7 minutes, or until they are crisp-tender, drain them, and refresh them under running cold water. Arrange the green beans, patted dry, on a platter with the tomatoes, the onion, and the olives, sprinkle the vegetables with the basil, and chill the salad, covered, for 15 minutes. In a small bowl whisk together the vinegar with salt and pepper to taste, add the olive oil in a stream, whisking until the dressing is emulsified, and spoon the dressing over the salad. Serves 4.

*Spaghetti Frittata with Sautéed Ham,
Peppers, Onions, and Tomatoes*

¼ pound finely diced smoked ham or prosciutto
1 onion, sliced
1 small green bell pepper, sliced
5 tablespoons olive oil
a 1-pound can plum tomatoes, drained and chopped
1 tablespoon tomato paste
2 large garlic cloves, minced
½ teaspoon dried thyme, crumbled
½ teaspoon dried basil, crumbled
¼ teaspoon dried orégano, crumbled
4 large eggs
4 tablespoons freshly grated Parmesan
½ teaspoon salt, or to taste
¼ teaspoon freshly ground pepper, or to taste
3 cups already-cooked spaghetti, *linguine,*
  or *capellini*, drained and tossed with
  1 tablespoon olive oil (This is ½ pound dry pasta
  cooked *al dente.*)
4 ounces mozzarella, grated or diced
3 tablespoons minced fresh basil leaves

In a skillet cook the ham, the onion, and the bell pepper in 2 tablespoons of the oil over moderately high heat, stirring, until the vegetables are softened. Add the tomatoes, the tomato paste, the garlic, the thyme, the dried basil, the orégano, and salt and pepper to taste and simmer the mixture, stirring occasionally, until it is thickened and almost all the liquid has evaporated. Cover the mixture and keep it warm.

In a bowl whisk together the eggs, 2 tablespoons of the Parmesan, the salt, and the pepper until the mixture is combined well.

In a 10-inch non-stick skillet heat 2 tablespoons of the remaining oil over moderate heat until it is hot but not smoking, add the cooked pasta, and toss it for 1 minute. Flatten the pasta into an even layer, pour in the egg mixture, and cook the frittata over low heat, covered, for 8 to 10 minutes, or until the bottom is golden. Spoon the onion and pepper mixture over the pasta, smoothing the top, sprinkle the top with the mozzarella, the remaining Parmesan, the minced basil leaves, and the remaining 1 tablespoon of oil, and put the frittata under a preheated broiler 6 inches from the heat for 4 to 5 minutes, or until the cheese has melted and the top is lightly golden. Serve the frittata warm, at room temperature, or chilled. Serves 4.

Raspberry Parfaits

a 10-ounce package frozen raspberries in syrup,
  thawed, reserving the juice
1 to 2 tablespoons *framboise* (raspberry brandy) or
  Chambord if desired
2 teaspoons fresh lemon juice, or to taste
sugar to taste
1 pint vanilla ice cream, softened, or raspberry or
  lemon sherbet
1 pint fresh raspberries
chopped pistachios for garnish if desired

In a food processor or blender purée the frozen raspberries with the reserved juice, the *framboise*, and the lemon juice, add the sugar, and strain the sauce through a fine sieve into a bowl. Chill the sauce, covered, until ready to use.

To assemble the parfaits, spoon some of the sauce into each of 4 parfait glasses, top it with ice cream or sherbet and some of the fresh berries, and continue to layer the parfaits in the same manner, ending with fresh berries. Garnish each parfait with some of the pistachios. Serves 4.

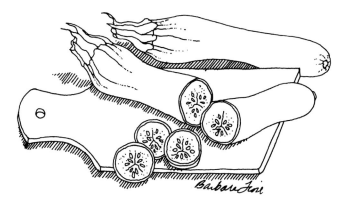

Mozzarella, Arugula, and Radicchio Salad

*Roasted Chicken and Vegetables with
Fennel-Scented Tomato Sauce*

Polenta with Parmesan

A full 60 minutes will be needed to prepare this menu. Cooking the fennel-scented tomato sauce first will leave you a more relaxed 40 minutes to assemble the salad, roasted chicken and vegetables, and the polenta. Curly endive would make a tart-but-interesting variation in the mozzarella salad, if *radicchio* or *arugula* is not available. If you have recently had a surfeit of chicken, simply eliminate it, and add some green bell peppers and a few leeks to the roasted vegetable medley. Should you wish to serve the roasted vegetables at room temperature or as a cold salad, in the sauce's stead, a mustard or tarragon vinaigrette or a light *aïoli* (garlic mayonnaise) would be complementary. Lots of room for creativity here!

Mozzarella, Arugula, and Radicchio Salad

1 head of *radicchio*, torn into bite-size pieces
1 bunch of *arugula*, stems discarded, washed well,
    and spun dry
6 tablespoons extra-virgin olive oil*
2 tablespoons balsamic* or red-wine vinegar
¾ pound fresh unsalted mozzarella, cut into
    ¼-inch-thick slices
freshly ground black pepper

*available at specialty foods shops and some
    supermarkets

In a bowl toss together the *radicchio* and the
arugula with 3 tablespoons of the oil until the lettuces
are coated well. Add the vinegar and salt and pepper to
taste and toss the salad until it is combined well. Divide the salad among 4 salad plates, arrange the sliced
mozzarella over each, and drizzle the remaining oil
over the mozzarella. Season each salad generously
with the ground pepper. Serves 4.

Roasted Chicken and Vegetables with Fennel-Scented Tomato Sauce

For the sauce
1 onion, minced
1 small fennel bulb, trimmed and chopped, or
    1 large rib of celery, chopped
2 tablespoons olive oil
2 garlic cloves, minced
a 28-ounce can crushed tomatoes in purée
1 teaspoon fennel seeds, crushed
¼ teaspoon dried thyme, crumbled
½ teaspoon dried basil, crumbled
1 cup vegetable stock (page 287), chicken stock
    (page 123), or canned chicken broth

2 whole chicken breasts, halved
a ½-pound eggplant, trimmed and cut into quarters
2 small zucchini, trimmed and halved lengthwise
1 red bell pepper, cut into squares
¼ to ⅓ cup olive oil
¾ teaspoon dried thyme, crumbled

Make the sauce: In a saucepan cook the onion and
the fennel in the oil over moderate heat, stirring occasionally, until the vegetables are softened. Add the
garlic and cook the mixture, stirring, for 1 minute.
Add the tomatoes, including the purée, the fennel
seeds, the thyme, the basil, the stock, and salt and
pepper to taste and simmer the sauce, stirring occasionally, for 20 minutes.

Arrange the chicken, the eggplant, the zucchini,
and the bell pepper in a single layer in a large baking
pan, brush the vegetables and chicken with the oil, and
season the mixture with the thyme and salt and pepper
to taste. Roast the vegetables and chicken in a preheated 500° F. oven for 10 to 15 minutes, turning the
vegetables and chicken once, or until the chicken is
firm but still springy to the touch and the vegetables
are tender. Divide the chicken and the vegetables
among 4 plates, spoon some of the sauce over each,
and serve the remaining sauce separately. Serves 4.

Polenta with Parmesan

1½ teaspoons salt
1½ cups yellow cornmeal (not stone-ground)
3 tablespoons unsalted butter, or to taste, cut into
    pieces
½ cup freshly grated Parmesan

In a heavy saucepan bring 5 cups water to a boil,
add the salt and the cornmeal carefully in a very slow
stream, whisking constantly, and cook the polenta
over moderately low heat, stirring, for 15 to 20 minutes, or until it is smooth and thick. Stir in the butter
and pepper to taste and just before serving, stir in the
cheese. Serves 4.

Minted Avocado, Bibb, and Orange Salad

Chili Cheese Enchiladas

Melon with Port

With the continuing popularity of ''south of the border'' cuisine, the Mexican fiesta endures as a favorite entertaining theme. This menu offers Mexican flair with a light combination of ingredients. Because each tortilla must first be softened in the sauce, filled, and rolled, this menu will take a full hour. In order to avoid producing soggy enchiladas, the casserole should go into the oven immediately after being topped with the sauce and should also be served as soon as the enchiladas have been fully heated. You can vary the spiciness of this dish by using either mild or hot green chilies.

Minted Avocado, Bibb, and Orange Salad

¼ cup fresh orange juice
2 tablespoons red-wine or balsamic vinegar*
1 teaspoon Dijon-style mustard, or to taste
1 teaspoon freshly grated orange rind
6 tablespoons extra-virgin olive oil*
3 tablespoons minced fresh mint leaves
3 heads of Bibb lettuce, rinsed, torn into bite-size
    pieces, and spun dry
1 avocado (preferably California), peeled, pitted,
    and cubed
2 whole scallions, sliced thin
1 large navel orange, peel and pith cut away with a
    serrated knife, the fruit cut into sections

*available at specialty foods shops and some
    supermarkets

In a small bowl whisk together the orange juice,
the vinegar, the mustard, the orange rind, and salt and
pepper to taste. Add the oil in a stream, whisking, and
whisk the dressing until it is emulsified. Stir in the
mint. In a salad bowl toss the lettuce, the avocado, the
scallions, and the orange with the dressing. Serves 4.

Chili Cheese Enchiladas

For the sauce
1 onion, chopped
3 tablespoons vegetable oil
3 garlic cloves, minced
3 tablespoons chili powder, or to taste
1 teaspoon ground cumin, or to taste
a 28-ounce can crushed tomatoes in purée
1½ cups vegetable stock (page 287), chicken stock
    (page 123), or canned chicken broth
½ teaspoon dried orégano, crumbled
¼ teaspoon cinnamon
⅛ teaspoon cloves
⅓ cup minced fresh coriander

8 corn tortillas
12 ounces sharp Cheddar or jack cheese, grated

1 small red onion, minced
a 4-ounce can chopped mild or hot green chilies,
    drained
½ cup chopped pitted black olives
minced coriander for garnish

Make the sauce: In a saucepan cook the onion in
the oil over moderately low heat, stirring occasionally,
until it is softened, add the garlic, and cook the mixture, stirring, for 1 minute. Add the chili powder and
the cumin and cook the mixture over low heat, stirring,
for 2 minutes. Add the tomatoes, the vegetable stock,
the orégano, the cinnamon, the cloves, and salt to
taste and simmer the sauce, stirring occasionally, for
15 minutes. Stir in the coriander.

Dip each tortilla into the sauce to soften it, lay the
tortilla open on a flat surface, and sprinkle the lower
third of it with some of the cheese (reserving 1 cup for
the topping) onion, chilies, and black olives. Roll up
the tortilla and arrange it seam side down in a lightly
oiled baking dish. Soften, fill, and roll up the remaining tortillas in the same manner.

Ladle all but 1½ cups of the sauce over the tortillas, top them with the remaining cheese, and bake the
enchiladas in a preheated 350° F. oven for 20 minutes,
or until they are heated through and the sauce is bubbling. Garnish the dish with the remaining coriander
and serve the remaining sauce separately. Serves 4.

Melon with Port

2 pounds sliced honeydew melon, rind removed
2 tablespoons fresh lemon juice
2 teaspoons sugar if desired
¼ to ⅓ cup Ruby Port

In a shallow bowl arrange the melon slices and
sprinkle them with the lemon juice and sugar to taste.
Add the Port. Macerate the melon, covered and
chilled, turning it occasionally. Serve the melon on
chilled plates with the sauce spooned over the top.
Serves 4.

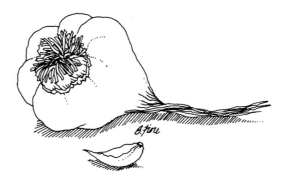

Barbecued Chicken

Cheddar Corn Muffins

Dilled Coleslaw with Yogurt Dressing

The flavor that comes from cooking over glowing coals or mesquite cannot be beat. Barbecue is a favorite in any season. Because this barbecued chicken recipe can either be broiled or grilled, you can indulge in this typically summertime entrée during frosty winter days as well as during the sultry dog days of July and August. Simply by changing the oven temperature to 400° F. and the cooking time to 20 to 25 minutes, you can create Cheddar corn bread rather than Cheddar corn muffins. We hope the menu here provides a convenient outline for a casual meal of fond, familiar favorites, a repast that celebrates the easy comfort foods of summers past.

Barbecued Chicken

4 tablespoons olive oil
2 garlic cloves, minced
½ teaspoon dried rosemary, crumbled
½ teaspoon dried thyme, crumbled
a 3- to 3½-pound chicken, split in half, backbone
    removed
For the barbecue sauce
¼ cup ketchup
¼ cup chili sauce
¼ cup cider vinegar
1 to 2 tablespoons brown sugar
1 tablespoon Worcestershire sauce
1 tablespoon Dijon-style mustard
1 teaspoon ground cumin
½ teaspoon cayenne, or to taste
Tabasco to taste

In a bowl combine the oil, the garlic, the rosemary, the thyme, and salt and pepper to taste and brush the chicken with the mixture. Broil the chicken, skin side down, under a preheated broiler about 6 inches from the heat for 15 minutes. Turn the chicken, brush it with the pan juices, and continue to broil it for 5 minutes, or until it is golden brown. Reduce the oven temperature to 450° F. and cook the chicken for 10 minutes more, covering it with a piece of aluminum foil if it begins to brown too much.

Make the barbecue sauce: In a bowl combine the ketchup, the chili sauce, the cider vinegar, the brown sugar, the Worcestershire sauce, the mustard, the cumin, the cayenne, the Tabasco, and salt to taste.

Brush the chicken with the sauce and continue to cook it for 10 minutes more, or until the juices run clear when a thigh is pricked with a skewer. Serves 4.

(The chicken may also be grilled. Arrange the chicken, skin side up, over glowing coals about 6 to 8 inches from the heat and grill it, turning it often, for 30 minutes. Brush the chicken with the barbecue sauce and continue to grill it, turning once and basting it frequently with the sauce, for 10 to 15 minutes more, or until it is cooked.)

Cheddar Corn Muffins

1 cup yellow cornmeal (preferably stone-ground)
1 cup all-purpose flour
1 tablespoon double-acting baking powder
½ teaspoon salt, or to taste
1 cup milk
2 large eggs, beaten lightly
½ stick (¼ cup) unsalted butter, melted
1 cup grated sharp Cheddar
1 to 2 bottled pickled *jalapeño* peppers, drained,
    seeded, and chopped, if desired (wear rubber
    gloves)

Into a bowl sift together the cornmeal, the flour, the baking powder, and the salt. In another bowl combine the milk, the eggs, and the butter, add the mixture to the dry ingredients, and fold in the Cheddar and the *jalapeño* pepper. Stir the batter until it is just combined, divide it among well-buttered ⅓-cup muffin tins, filling the tins ⅔ full, and bake the muffins in a preheated 425° F. oven for 15 to 20 minutes, or until the muffins are golden and a tester comes out clean. Makes 12.

Dilled Coleslaw with Yogurt Dressing

an 8-ounce container plain yogurt
⅓ cup sour cream
1 to 2 tablespoons cider vinegar
2 teaspoons Dijon-style mustard
½ to 1 teaspoon sugar
1 teaspoon caraway seeds
a 1½-pound head of green cabbage, cored and
    shredded
1 small onion, grated, if desired
2 tablespoons snipped fresh dill

In a large bowl whisk together the yogurt, the sour cream, the vinegar, the mustard, the sugar, the caraway seeds, and salt to taste until the dressing is combined well. Add the cabbage, the onion, and the dill and toss the salad with the dressing. Chill the coleslaw, covered, for 30 minutes. Serves 4.

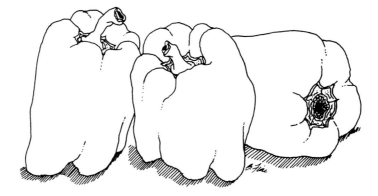

Scallops Creole

Lemon-Parsley Rice Pilaf

Steamed Okra

Peppery Creole combinations have traditionally been American cuisine's answer to cries for hot and spicy dishes of consequence. This filling scallops Creole recipe balances nicely with the light lemony rice pilaf and the Creole favorite, okra. Numerous seasonal vegetables, however, would also make an appealing, less-spirited complement to the piquant Creole flavors. Garden-fresh zucchini, peas, summer squash, or crisp steamed green beans are all possible, and perhaps more widely available, alternatives to okra. The elegant-but-easy nature of the menu here makes it particularly attractive for entertaining. Dessert might be a refreshing mélange of sweet, colorful sherbet or *sorbet* and berries.

Scallops Creole

2 cups minced onion
1 cup minced celery
2 tablespoons unsalted butter
1½ cups chopped green bell pepper
2 teaspoons minced garlic
½ teaspoon dried thyme, crumbled
½ teaspoon dried basil, crumbled
½ teaspoon cayenne
½ teaspoon black pepper
1 bay leaf
2 cups peeled, seeded, and chopped tomatoes
1 cup canned tomato sauce
½ cup dry white wine
½ teaspoon sugar
Tabasco to taste
1¼ pounds sea scallops, halved, if large

In a saucepan cook the onion and the celery in the butter over moderate heat, stirring occasionally, until the onion is golden. Add the green pepper and cook the mixture, stirring, until the pepper is softened. Add the garlic, the thyme, the basil, the cayenne, the pepper, and the bay leaf and cook the mixture, stirring, for 1 minute. Add the tomatoes, the tomato sauce, the wine, the sugar, and the Tabasco and salt to taste and simmer the mixture, stirring occasionally, for 20 minutes. Add the scallops and cook them over moderate heat, stirring, until they are opaque and are just firm to the touch. Serves 4.

Lemon-Parsley Rice Pilaf

1 cup minced onion
2 tablespoons unsalted butter
2 cups long-grain rice
2 ¾ cups chicken stock (page 123) or canned chicken broth
2 tablespoons fresh lemon juice
2 strips of lemon peel
¼ cup minced fresh parsley leaves

In an ovenproof saucepan cook the onion in the butter over moderately low heat, stirring, until it is softened. Add the rice, stir to coat it with the butter, and add the stock, the lemon juice, the lemon peel, and salt and pepper to taste. Bring the liquid to a boil and bake the pilaf, covered with a buttered round of wax paper and the lid, in a preheated 350° F. oven for 20 minutes. Let the rice stand for 5 minutes, discard the lemon peel, and stir in the parsley. Serves 4.

Steamed Okra

1 pound okra, trimmed, leaving the stem ends intact
2 tablespoons unsalted butter, softened
1 tablespoon white-wine vinegar if desired

In a steamer set over boiling water steam the okra, covered, for 10 to 12 minutes, or until it is tender. Transfer the okra to a bowl and toss it with the butter, the vinegar, and salt and pepper to taste. Serves 4.

Homemade vegetable stock is a preferred ingredient in a number of the preceding recipes and should ideally be on hand. It will not be possible to both make the stock and create one of the preceding menus within an hour. If necessary, chicken stock or canned chicken broth can be used as an alternative to homemade vegetable stock.

Vegetable Stock

1 large onion, chopped
2 carrots, sliced
2 large ribs of celery, including the leaves, sliced
4 large garlic cloves, sliced
2 tablespoons unsalted butter
2 cups chopped tomatoes
1 cup sliced fresh mushrooms
1 large potato, unpeeled and cut into cubes
1 ounce dried mushrooms
½ cup chopped fresh parsley leaves
2 bay leaves
½ teaspoon dried thyme, crumbled
½ teaspoon dried basil, crumbled
12 black peppercorns

In a large saucepan cook the onion, the carrots, the celery, and the garlic in the butter, stirring occasionally, over moderate heat until the onion is golden. Add the tomatoes, the fresh mushrooms, the potato, the dried mushrooms, the parsley, the bay leaves, the thyme, the basil, the peppercorns, and 10 cups cold water, bring the liquid to a boil, and simmer the stock, partially covered, for 1 hour. Strain the stock into a bowl, let it cool, and chill it, covered, for up to 3 days. The stock may also be frozen. Makes about 8 cups.

GUIDES TO THE TEXT

GENERAL INDEX

(M) indicates a microwave recipe

INDEX OF 45-MINUTE RECIPES

*Starred entries can be prepared in 45 minutes or less
but require additional unattended time
(M) indicates a microwave recipe

INDEX OF RECIPE TITLES

Page numbers in *italics* indicate color photographs
(M) indicates a microwave recipe

TABLE SETTING ACKNOWLEDGMENTS

To avoid duplication below of table setting information within the same menu, the editors have listed all such credits for silverware, plates, linen, and the like in its most complete form under "Table Setting."

Any items in the photographs not credited are privately owned.

Front Jacket: Lemon- and garlic-marinated shrimp with green beans and endive on an "Atlantis" Swid-Powell porcelain dinner plate from Bloomingdale's, 1000 Third Avenue, New York City.

Back Jacket: Ginger pound cake on a St. Louis glass plate, circa 1840, from James II Galleries, Ltd., 15 East 57th Street, New York City.

The Menu Collection

Table Setting (page 8): Spode "Wild Flower Series" hand-painted bone china dinner plates—Royal Worcester Spode, Inc., 41 Madison Avenue, New York City. "Quirinale" handmade sterling flatware; handmade sterling salt-cellars—Buccellati, Inc., 46 East 57th Street, New York City. "Paris" crystal water goblets and wineglasses—Baccarat, Inc., 55 East 57th Street, New York City. English silver candlestick, circa 1870 (one of a pair)—James II Galleries, Ltd., 15 East 57th Street, New York City. English mahogany chair, circa 1795 (one of a set of twelve)—Stair & Company, Inc., 942 Madison Avenue, New York City.

Rose Bowl Open House

Bittersweet Chocolate and White Chocolate Pecan Mousse Swirl (page 10): "Montaigne Optic" crystal compotes—Baccarat, Inc., 55 East 57th Street, New York City. English brass footed salver, circa 1770—James II Galleries, Ltd., 15 East 57th Street, New York City.
Buffet Setting (page 11): Swid Powell "Stripes Black and White" porcelain buffet plates—Bloomingdale's, 1000 Third Avenue, New York City. Capricorne Collection "Oasis" stainless flat-ware by Christofle—Pavillon Christofle, 680 Madison Avenue, New York City. Wine goblets—Conran's, 160 East 54th Street, New York City. Hand-painted linen napkins by Leslie Ponte—Frank McIntosh at Henri Bendel, 10 West 57th Street, New York City. Scottish horn and sterling beakers, circa 1874; English brass tankard, circa 1830; English brass wine cooler, circa 1835—Bob Pryor Antiques, 1023 Lexington Avenue, New York City. Nineteenth-century French mahogany sideboard with marble top—J. Garvin Mecking Antiques, 72 East 11th Street, New York City. English leather Chesterfield club chair (special order); English photographs, circa 1900—Howard Kaplan Antiques, 827 Broadway, New York City.
Oysters with Pickled Carrot and Daikon, Venison Stew with Root Vegetables, Buttered Spätzle with Scallions, Red Cabbage and Celery Slaw, Chewy Rye Caraway Breadsticks (pages 12 and 13): Nineteenth-century Palissy-style oyster server—J. Garvin Mecking Antiques, 72 East 11th Street, New York City. Copper serving dish, circa 1840—Bob Pryor Antiques, 1023 Lexington Avenue, New York City. Wood salad bowl—The Pottery Barn, 117 East 59th Street, New York City.

New Year's Day Brunch

Tequila Sunrises (page 14): Wineglasses—Conran's, 160 East 54th Street, New York City.

Two Birthday Parties

Frozen Hazelnut Praline Meringue Cake (page 16): Frosted glass plate designed by Judy Smilow—The Museum Store, The Museum of Modern Art, 11 West 53rd Street, New York City.

For the Adults' Party (page 17): "Wiener" porcelain dinner plates—Bernardaud, 41 Madison Avenue, New York City. French acrylic and stainless steel flatware; hand-painted cotton place mats and napkins by Leslie Pontz; French handwrought iron candelabra—Frank McIntosh at Henri Bendel, 10 West 57th Street, New York City. Hand-etched goblets designed by Christine Van Der Hurd; anodized aluminum and glass dining table and console designed by Derek Richards—Rogers-Tropea, Inc., 1357 Third Avenue, New York City. Italian silver-plate salt and pepper shakers—Avventura, 463 Amsterdam Avenue, New York City. Silvestri glass and oxidized copper candlesticks; glass bowl and oxidized copper stand—Garden Path, 560 Lexington Avenue, New York City. French Art Decostyle polished-steel chairs with brass trim—Newel Art Galleries, Inc., 425 East 53rd Street, New York City.
Filets Mignons with Orange Béarnaise Sauce, Roasted Green Beans, Roasted Scallions, Fried Potato Thins (page 18): Swid Powell silver-plate tray by Richard Meier—D. F. Sanders & Co., 386 West Broadway, New York City. Glass serving plate—Mayhew, 507 Park Avenue, New York City. Glass sauce bowl—Hoya Crystal Gallery, 450 Park Avenue, New York City.
For the Children's Party (page 19): Pillivuyt porcelain plates—Barneys New York, Seventh Avenue and 17th Street, New York City. Plastic-handled child's flatware by David Mellor—Simon Pearce, 385 Bleecker Street, New York City. Painted wood chairs—Penny Whistle Toys, 1283 Madison Avenue, New York City. Cotton rug—Conran's, 160 East 54th Street, New York City.

319

Meatless Lasagne Dinners

Shrimp, Scallop, and Monkfish Lasagne, Watercress and Bibb Salad with Parsley Dressing (page 20): Reproduction eighteenth-century French "Revolution" faience dinner plates—Faïence, 120 Washington Street, South Norwalk, Connecticut. Mariposa glass salad bowl—Mayhew, 507 Park Avenue, New York City.

A Spring Skiing Weekend

Granny Smith Apple Pie with Honey Spice Whipped Cream (page 22): Hand-painted earthenware dessert plates by Barbara Eigen—Eigen Arts, 579 Broadway, New York City.
Table Setting (page 23): Spongeware dinner plates and pitchers by Barbara Eigen—Eigen Arts, 579 Broadway, New York City. Acrylic and stainless steel flatware; wineglasses; cotton napkins—Wolfman • Gold & Good Company, 484 Broome Street, New York City. "Marqueroy Plaid" cotton, rayon, and linen fabric (available through decorator)—Cowtan & Tout, 979 Third Avenue, New York City. Hickory benches—Newel Art Galleries, Inc., 425 East 53rd Street, New York City. Nineteenth-century English wood and brass bottle—Bob Pryor Antiques, 1023 Lexington Avenue, New York City.
Orange Pecan Waffles with Orange Maple Syrup, Breakfast Sausage Links (page 24): "Bunny" hand-painted earthenware plates, cups, saucers, and platter by The Pottery Shed—Mayhew, 507 Park Avenue, New York City.

An Irish Sunday Dinner

Lemon-Baked Chicken Breasts, Creamed Leeks, Irish Whiskey Carrots (page 27): Handmade reproduction nineteenth-century side chair with rush seat—Howard Kaplan Antiques, 827 Broadway, New York City. "Star" crystal wineglasses by Simon Pearce—Simon Pearce, 385 Bleecker Street, New York City. "Irish Molly" cotton fabric (available through decorator)—Brunschwig & Fils, Inc., 979 Third Avenue, New York City. "Madagascar" cotton and polyester fabric (available through decorator)—China Seas, 979 Third Avenue, New York City. Flowers—Mädderlake, 25 East 73rd Street, New York City.

Easter Luncheon

Table Setting (page 29): Reproduction seventeenth-century Richard Ginori "Rapallo" porcelain dinner plates; Limoges service plates—Mayhew, 507 Park Avenue, New York City. "Malmaison" silver-plate flatware; silver-plate salt and pepper shakers—Pavillon Christofle, 680 Madison Avenue, New York City. Lalique "Treves" crystal water goblets and wineglasses and "Nogent" crystal coupes—Jacques Jugeat, Inc., 225 Fifth Avenue, New York City. "Doriana" cotton damask napkins—Frette, 799 Madison Avenue, New York City. "Cecily's Ribbons" cotton fabric (available through decorator)—Brunschwig & Fils, Inc., 979 Third Avenue, New York City. Painted Regency chairs with leather seats (from a set of 8), circa 1820—Trevor Potts Antiques, 1011 Lexington Avenue, New York City. One of a pair of English Bott pearl ware bulb pots, circa 1810; one of a pair of Wedgwood soup tureens and stands, circa 1800; two of a set of ten English Wilson pearl ware botanical dinner plates, circa 1810—Bardith Ltd., 901 Madison Avenue, New York City. Ninteenth-century English silver-resist and pink lustre pitchers (from a collection)—Ages Past Antiques, 1030 Lexington Avenue, New York City. Flower arrangements—Mädderlake, 25 East 73rd Street, New York City.
Roast Saddle of Lamb Persillé; Tomatoes Stuffed with White Bean, Parsley, and Garlic Purée; Green Bean and Yellow Bell Pepper Mélange (page 30): "Perles" silver-plate tray—Pavillon Christofle, 680 Madison Avenue, New York City. Kirk Stieff "Kirk King" sterling carving set—The Kirk Stieff Company, 800 Wyman Park Drive, Baltimore, Maryland. Reproduction seventeenth-century Richard Ginori "Rapallo" porcelain vegetable dish—Mayhew, 507 Park Avenue, New York City.
Oeufs à la Neige à l'Orange (page 31): Colony crystal compote—Mayhew, 507 Park Avenue, New York City. Flower arrangements—Mädderlake, 25 East 73rd Street, New York City.

April Fool's Cocktail Pary

Cheddar "Carrots" and "Parsnips," Caviar "Raspberries" and "Blackberries" (page 32): Handmade earthenware plate by Ann Schliesel-Harris—Rogers-Tropea, Inc., 1357 Third Avenue, New York City. "Harcourt" Old Fashioned glasses—Baccarat, Inc., 55 East 57th Street, New York City.
Black Olive and Roasted Red Pepper "Backgammon Board," Ham and Mustard Mayonnaise Sandwich "Playing Cards," Pumpernickel Cheese "Dominoes" (page 33): Viking glass platter; iittala "Kolibri" wineglasses—Mayhew, 507 Park Avenue, New York City. Handmade earthenware plate by Ann Schliesel-Harris; handmade acrylic and painted wood tray by Godley-Schwan—Rogers-Tropea, Inc., 1357 Third Avenue, New York City. *Faux-marbre* and *faux-bois* table by Edward Schaefer—Edward Schaefer, New York City. (212) 627-2137 (by appointment only).

A Charleston Luncheon

Table Setting (pages 34 and 35): "Cornelia" ironstone dinner plates by Mottahedeh for Historic Charleston Reproductions—Cardel Ltd., 621 Madison Avenue, New York City. Gorham "Old Versailles" sterling flatware (made to order)—Gorham, P.O. Box 6150, Providence, Rhode Island 02940. Embroidered linen and lace napkins—Françoise Nunnallé Fine Arts, 105 West 55th Street, New York City (by appointment only). English silver-plate cruet set, circa 1870—James II Galleries, Ltd., 15 East 57th Street, New York City. Flowers—Flower Market & Flowers Unique, Yvonne Bishop Associates, 281 Meeting Street, Charleston, South Carolina 29401.
Shrimp Creole, Rice Ring, Glazed Smithfield Ham (page 36): English Sheffield plate footed waiter, circa 1785; silver-plate platter—F. Gorevic & Son, Inc., 635 Madison Avenue, New York City.
Juliette Staats's Pecan Roll, Caramel Sauce (page 37): English silver-plate salver, circa 1875; cut-glass bowl with sterling rim, Birmingham, 1913—James II Galleries, Ltd., 15 East 57th Street, New York City.

A Spring Dinner

Stuffed Artichoke Leaves (page 38): Ceramic plate (from a fifty-seven piece set designed by Marcel Goupy, 1937)—Delorenzo, 958 Madison Avenue, New York City.

Cheese and Chive Ravioli with Tomato Red Pepper Sauce, Tossed Green Salad with Dill Dressing (page 39): Handmade earthenware dinner plate by Dan Bleier—Creative Resources, Inc., 24 West 57th Street, New York City.

A Smorgasbord

Dessert (page 40): iittala "Tapio" glasses; Georg Jensen "Pyramid" silver-plate dessert spoons—Royal Copenhagen Porcelain/Georg Jensen Silversmiths, 683 Madison Avenue, New York City. West Virginia Glass platter—Mayhew, 507 Park Avenue, New York City.

Buffet Setting (page 41): Taitu Uno "Sky" porcelain buffet plates—Mayhew, 507 Park Avenue, New York City. Georg Jensen "Pyramid" silver-plate flatware; Orrefors "Victoria" aquavit glasses; iittala "Aarne" schnapps glass—Royal Copenhagen Porcelain/Georg Jensen Silversmiths, 683 Madison Avenue, New York City. Swedish pine corner cabinet, sofa, and rib-back chair, circa 1850, all hand-painted and hand-decorated in Sweden; wire iron stands, circa 1820—Swedish Cottage, 1281 Madison Avenue, New York City. Hand-dyed and hand-woven wool rug and hand-woven wool pillows—Elizabeth Eakins, Inc., 1053 Lexington Avenue, New York City. Lemon-scented geranium topiaries—Robert Homma, Inc., 27 East 61st Street, New York City.

Smorgasbord (pages 42 and 43): Nissan cast-iron casserole and beechwood stand (wood handles not shown); Aalton "Kukka" glass bowls; Orrefors "Victoria" aquavit glasses; iittala "Aarne" pilsner glasses—Royal Copenhagen Porcelain/Georg Jensen Silversmiths, 683 Madison Avenue, New York City. Rosenthal "Fjord" glass cheese platter; West Virginia Glass square tray—Mayhew, 507 Park Avenue, New York City. Pine gateleg table, circa 1800, hand-painted and hand-decorated in Sweden—Swedish Cottage, 1281 Madison Avenue, New York City.

Bachelor Dinner

Coffee Almond Ice-Cream Cake with Dark Chocolate Sauce (page 44): Swid Powell "Montreal" porcelain salad plate by George Sowden—Blooming-

dale's, 1000 Third Avenue, New York City.

Rosemary Lamb Kebabs, Shredded Potato Pancakes, Mixed Greens and Fennel with Balsamic Vinaigrette (page 45): Swid Powell "Montreal" porcelain dinner plates by George Sowden—Bloomingdale's, 1000 Third Avenue, New York City. Christofle "Commodore" sterling flatware—Pavillon Christofle, 680 Madison Avenue, New York City. Scandinavian crystal wineglasses and salad bowl; Italian linen napkins; lacquered bamboo place mats; glass pitcher—Frank McIntosh at Henri Bendel, 10 West 57th Street, New York City.

A Country Luncheon

Lemon and Herb Marinated Cornish Hens, Vegetable Pasta Salad with Red Pepper Dressing, Garden Tomatoes (page 48): Angela Cummings "Blue Fishnet" porcelain dinner and salad plates for Arita—Bergdorf Goodman, 754 Fifth Avenue, New York City. Ricci "Morandi" silver-plate flatware—Mayhew, 507 Park Avenue, New York City. Wineglasses—The Pottery Barn, 117 East 59th Street, New York City. China Seas "Tropicana Yellow" cotton fabric (available through designers and architects)—China Seas, Inc., 21 East 4th Street, New York City. Royal blue cotton napkins—Conran's, 160 East 54th Street, New York City.

Mango Lime Mousse with Raspberry Sauce (page 49): Taitu porcelain plate—Mayhew, 507 Park Avenue, New York City.

Fourth of July Dinner

Peach Almond Torte (page 50): Ceramic plate—Frank McIntosh at Henri Bendel, 10 West 57th Street, New York City.

Grilled Salmon with Mustard Mint Sauce, Wild Rice Pilaf with Scallions, Fireworks Salad (page 51): Deruta "Grappa" earthenware dinner plates—Wolfman • Gold & Good Company, 484 Broome Street, New York City. Stainless steel flatware, Scandinavian hand-blown wineglasses, cotton napkins, glass salad bowl, Scandinavian composition granite and chrome candlesticks—Frank McIntosh at Henri Bendel, 10 West 57th Street, New

York City. Wine carafe—Conran's, 160 East 54th Street, New York City.

Luncheons on the Veranda

Pistachio Tuiles, Chocolate Walnut Bars (page 52): Giraud Limoges cake plates—Mayhew, 507 Park Avenue, New York City. Porcelain demitasse cups and saucers designed by Andrée Putman; anodized aluminum demitasse spoons designed by David Tisdale; Alessi stainless steel and copper espresso maker designed by Aldo Rossi—Sointu, The Design Store, 20 East 69th Street, New York City. Wire tray table—Pierre Deux, 870 Madison Avenue, New York City.

Table Setting (page 53): "Fold Here" Italian faience dinner plates designed by Paul Steinberg for Deruta; black-matted stainless steel flatware designed by Patino/Wolf—Barneys New York, Seventh Avenue and Seventeenth Street, New York City. "Asimmetrica" wineglasses designed by Carlo Moretti—Avventura, 463 Amsterdam Avenue, New York City. Handmade pewter salt and pepper shakers designed by Jon Michael Route—Rogers-Tropea, Inc., 1357 Third Avenue, New York City. Hand-painted linen napkins by Leslie Pontz—Bergdorf Goodman, 754 Fifth Avenue, New York City. Wine carafes—Bridge Kitchenware Corporation, 214 East 52nd Street, New York City. "Mountain" plaster bud vase designed by Patino/Wolf—Lazy Susan, 1049 Third Avenue, New York City. "Young Tree" carved wood table base and glass top (available through decorator)—Circa David Barrett, Ltd., 232 East 59th Street, New York City. Brown Jordan "Florentine" wrought-iron chairs with polyester cushions—Roberts Fine Furniture, 75 Greenwich Avenue, Greenwich, Connecticut 06830. Plants—Sam Bridge Nurseries, 437 North Street, Greenwich, Connecticut 06830.

Mushroom Salad with Radish and Chives, Thai-Style Steak and Green Bean Salad with Spicy Mint Dressing, Vegetables à la Grecque, Tricolor Scallop Terrine with Basil, Corn, and Red Pepper (pages 54 and 55): Italian faience salad plates designed by Paul Steinberg for Deruta—Barneys New York, Seventh Avenue and Seventeenth Street, New York City.

A Cocktail Party Alfresco

Marinated Shrimp with Yellow Bell Pepper and Red Onion, Garlic Toast Rounds, Summer Breezes (page 56): "Silver Wave" crystal serving dish with handle—Hoya Crystal, 450 Park Avenue, New York City. Italian "Liscio" crystal serving tray by Colle; "Tapio" wineglasses by iittala—Mayhew, 507 Park Avenue, New York City. Cotton cocktail napkins—Frank McIntosh at Henri Bendel, 10 West 57th Street, New York City.

Carrot and Herbed Goat Cheese Spirals; Cucumber and Liptauer Spirals; Crab-Salad-Stuffed Cherry Tomatoes; Anchovy Lemon Dip with Vegetables; Prosciutto, Pear, and Chive Cornets with Ginger Cream (page 57): "Pantheon" crystal platter and bowl by Riedel; "New York" crystal pitcher and pilsner glasses by iittala—Mayhew, 507 Park Avenue, New York City. Frosted-glass plate designed by Judy Smilow—The Museum Store, The Museum of Modern Art, 11 West 53rd Street, New York City. English wicker cart, circa 1900; French iron folding table and iron and brass chairs, circa 1900—Howard Kaplan Antiques, 827 Broadway, New York City.

A Mediterranean Dinner

Table Setting (page 59): Quimper "Fleuri Royal" faience dinner plates; "Rummer" wineglasses; French hand-painted chairs with rush seats, circa 1890—Pierre Deux, 870 Madison Avenue, New York City. Cassetti "Piccadilly" silver-plate flatware; linen napkins by Castellini for Frank McIntosh; glass pitcher by Simon Pearce—Henri Bendel, Frank McIntosh Shop, 10 West 57th Street, New York City. Nineteenth-century French oak table—Pierre Deux, 367 Bleecker Street, New York City. Flowers—Mädderlake, 25 East 73rd Street, New York City. Plants—Strakes Flowers, 1140 Lexington Avenue, New York City. "Small Ocean" painted backdrop—Oliphant Studios, 38 Cooper Square, New York City. Nineteenth-century French drying rack—Howard Kaplan Antiques, 827 Broadway, New York City.

Herb-Marinated Butterflied Leg of Lamb, Roasted Quartered Potatoes with Garlic, Provençal Vegetable Gratin, Curly Chicory and Red-Leaf Lettuce Salad (page 60): French oven-proof dish—Bridge Kitchenware Corporation, 214 East 52nd Street, New York City.

Plum Tarts (page 61): Nineteenth-century walnut cutting board—Gail Lettick's Pantry & Hearth Antiques, 121 East 35th Street (by appointment, (212) 532-0535). Deruta "Griglia" ceramic plates—Mayhew, 507 Park Avenue, New York City.

Brunch for Six

Cold Vanilla-Rum Zabaglione with Fruit (page 62): Glass plate—Henri Bendel, Frank McIntosh Shop, 10 West 57th Street, New York City.

Lemon Walnut Scones; Potato and Leek Frittata; Cherry Tomato, Bacon, and Basil Salad; Coffee (page 63): "Bennington Black" spatterware dinner plates—D. F. Sanders & Co., 386 West Broadway, New York City. Earthenware mugs (from a set of six), circa 1880—Gail Lettick's Pantry & Hearth, 121 East 35th Street, New York City (by appointment only).

Cocktails In the City

Spinach, Feta, and Phyllo Purses (page 65): Sterling tray, London, 1910—James Robinson, 15 East 57th Street, New York City. Martini glass and "Brummel" wineglasses—Baccarat, Inc., 55 East 57th Street, New York City. Hand-painted linen cocktail napkins by Liz Wain—Barneys New York, Seventh Avenue at 17th Street, New York City. English papier-mâché tray, circa 1810, and stand; English cut-glass jars, circa 1860 (lids not shown); English Ridgway porcelain bowl, circa 1820; Leeds creamware covered pot, circa 1770—Bardith Ltd., 901 Madison Avenue, New York City. Flowers—Mädderlake, 25 East 73rd Street, New York City.

Sweet Potato, Crème Fraîche, and Caviar Bites; Hummus; Toasted Pita Thins (page 66): French porcelain leaf dish, circa 1810—Bardith Ltd., 901 Madison Avenue, New York City. English soft-paste porcelain leaf dish, circa 1870; Irish cut-glass compote, circa 1840 (one of a pair); English glass rummer, circa 1810 (from a set of 7)—The Collector's Gallery at Kentshire, 37 East 12th Street, New York City. English silver-plate tankard, circa 1875—James II Galleries, Ltd., 15 East 57th Street, New York City. Flowers—Mädderlake, 25 East 73rd Street, New York City.

Shrimp and Jalapeño Brochettes, Stilton Walnut Tart (page 67): "Gold Corail" Limoges platters—Mayhew, 507 Park Avenue, New York City.

Columbus Day Dinner

Pizza di Noci e Cioccolata (page 68): "Venetian" china salad plates designed by The David Linley Company for Mappin & Webb Ltd.—Mappin & Webb Ltd., 170 Regent Street, London W.1, England.

Vitello alla Genovese, Fagiolini alla Genovese (page 69): "Venetian" china dinner plates designed by The David Linley Company for Mappin & Webb Ltd.—Mappin & Webb Ltd., 170 Regent Street, London W.1, England. "Savoy" hand-forged sterling flatware—Buccellati, Inc., 46 East 57th Street, New York City. "Tritondo" wineglasses designed by Carlo Moretti—Avventura, 463 Amsterdam Avenue, New York City. Silver-plate salt and pepper shakers designed by Robert and Trix Haussmann for Swid Powell—Bloomingdale's, 1000 Third Avenue, New York City. "Ramage" cotton jacquard napkins (not shown) and tablecloth—Frette, 799 Madison Avenue, New York City. English rosewood, *faux* rosewood, and cane chairs, circa 1810 (from a set of 6)—Kentshire Gallery, 37 East 12th Street, New York City. "Bay of Naples" framed gouache, circa 1850 (from a collection)—J. Garvin Mecking Antiques, 72 East 11th Street, New York City. "Marcelline Moire" fabric as wall covering (available through decorator)—Brunschwig & Fils, Inc., 979 Third Avenue, New York City.

A Country Thanksgiving

Table Setting (page 71): English Staffordshire transferware dinner plates, circa 1830—Ages Past Antiques, 1030 Lexington Avenue, New York City. Old Newbury Crafters "Classic English" hand-forged sterling flatware—Cardel Ltd., 621 Madison Avenue, New York City. "Hawks Cloth" cotton and linen fabric (available through decorator)—Hinson & Company, 979 Third Avenue, New York City. Cotton tea towels/place mats; "Marriage Box" hand-painted wood box; nineteenth-century quilt top—Sweet Nellie, 1262 Madison Avenue, New York City. Nineteenth-century English candlesticks—Bob Pryor Antiques, 1023 Lexington Avenue, New York City.

Roast Turkey with Chestnut and Apple Corn Bread Stuffing and Brandied Giblet Gravy, Sweet Potato Cloverleaf Rolls, Jellied Orange Cranberry Sauce, Glazed Carrots and Parsnips (pages 72 and 73): English ironstone platter, circa 1820 (the smaller of a set of 2)—J. Garvin Mecking Antiques, 72 East 11th Street, New York City. English silver-plate hot-water dish, circa 1890—Bob Pryor Antiques, 1023 Lexington Avenue, New York City. Nineteenth-century English Staffordshire transferware serving dishes—Ages Past Antiques, 1030 Lexington Avenue, New York City. Old Newbury Crafters "Classic English" hand-forged sterling serving pieces—Cardel Ltd., 621 Madison Avenue, New York City. English silver-plate pitcher, circa 1865—S. Wyler, Inc., 713 Madison Avenue, New York City. Nineteenth-century English oak table (available through decorator)—Yale R. Burge Antiques, Inc., 305 East 63rd Street, New York City.

A Small Formal Thanksgiving

Crème Caramel with Sautéed Apples (page 74): Bernardaud "Famille Verte" porcelain plate—Mayhew, 507 Park Avenue, New York City.

Thanksgiving Dinner (page 75): Sterling tray by Reed & Barton; sterling servers, London, 1840-1850; sterling sauceboat by Gorham; sterling sauce ladle, London, 1800; nineteenth-century English silver-plate soufflé dish with liner; sterling entrée dish and cover by Thomas Heming, London, 1765; silver-plate entrée dish (cover not shown)—F. Gorevic & Son, Inc., 635 Madison Avenue, New York City. Nineteenth-century Dutch elm silver table; hand-colored copper plate engravings by Johann Weinmann, 1735-1745 (table and engravings available through decorator)—Yale R. Burge, 305 East 63rd Street, New York City.

A Formal Christmas Dinner

Table Setting (page 77): Mason's ironstone dinner service for 12, circa 1826—James II Galleries, Ltd., 15 East 57th Street, New York City. English silver-plate "Fancy Victorian" flatware by John Round & Son, circa 1875—S. Wyler, Inc., 941 Lexington Avenue, New York City. Lalique "Bourgueil" crystal red-wine and water glasses—Barneys New York, Seventh Avenue and 17th Street, New York City. English nineteenth-century glass Champagne flutes—Bardith Ltd., 901 Madison Avenue, New York City. English sterling salt cellars by Omar Ramsden, circa 1930—Bulgari, 2 East 61st Street, New York City. Two pairs of sterling candlesticks, one by William Gould, London, 1751; the other by Thomas Jeannes, London, 1750—James Robinson, 15 East 57th Street, New York City. Cotton damask napkins, circa 1930—Françoise Nunnallé Fine Arts, 105 East 55th Street (by appointment only), New York City. English eighteenth-century Chippendale Gothic mahogany chairs with armorial needlepoint seats—Florian Papp Inc., 962 Madison Avenue, New York City. *(In niche)* English nineteenth-century overlaid glass vase (one of a pair)—James II Galleries, Ltd., 15 East 57th Street, New York City.

Pineapple Orange Meringue Torte, Maple Almond Brittle (page 78): English Ashworth ironstone cake stand, circa 1830; English engraved glass dessert plates, circa 1870; Victorian glass candy dish, circa 1880—James II Galleries, Ltd., 15 East 57th Street, New York City. Portuguese eighteenth-century rosewood stool with needlepoint seat—Florian Papp Inc., 962 Madison Avenue, New York City.

Roast Prime Ribs of Beef with Herbed Crust, Cauliflower and Broccoli Timbales, Potato Caraway Croquettes (page 79): Mason's ironstone platter, circa 1826—James II Galleries, Ltd., 15 East 57th Street, New York City. English silver-plate basket, circa 1880; "Videau" English silver-plate platter—S. Wyler, Inc., 941 Lexington Avenue, New York City. English eighteenth-century mahogany pedestal table—Florian Papp Inc., 962 Madison Avenue, New York City.

Christmas Breakfast

Apricot Citrus Cranberry Compote (page 80): Glass coupes—Baccarat, Inc., 55 East 57th Street, New York City.

Cheddar Bread Pudding, Bacon Spirals, Cranberry Tangerine Juice, Chocolate Pecan Gems (page 81): Wedgwood "Strawberry & Vine" bone china plates, cups, and saucers—Bloomingdale's, 1000 Third Avenue, New York City. "Bellflower" American nineteenth-century reproduction 1-quart glass pitcher; English eighteenth-century reproduction ceramic basket—Metropolitan Museum of Art Gift Shop, Fifth Avenue at 82nd Street, New York City. "Betsy Brown Blanket Red" cotton fabric curtains; "Quilt Star" cotton fabric cloth (available through decorator)—Hinson & Company, 979 Third Avenue, New York City.

A Recipe Compendium

Vegetables Primavera with Polenta (page 82): Moustiers faïence dinner plate, hand-blown wineglass, and Siècle flatware from Barneys New York, Seventh Avenue and Seventeenth Street, New York City.

If you are not already a subscriber to *Gourmet* Magazine and would be interested in subscribing, please call *Gourmet's* toll-free number, 1-800-525-0643.